JUDGES AT WORK

LORD DE VILLIERS
The first Chief Justice of South Africa 1910–14

JUDGES AT WORK

The Role and Attitudes of the South African Appellate Judiciary, 1910–50

by

HUGH CORDER
BCom LLB (Cape Town), LLB (Cantab), DPhil (Oxon)
Advocate of the Supreme Court of South Africa
Senior Lecturer in Public Law, University of Stellenbosch

Juta & Co, Ltd
CAPE TOWN WETTON JOHANNESBURG

First Published 1984

PO Box 123, Kenwyn 7790

ISBN 0 7021 1435 9

SET, PRINTED AND BOUND IN THE REPUBLIC OF SOUTH AFRICA
BY THE RUSTICA PRESS (PTY) LTD, WYNBERG, CAPE

D598

To my parents

PREFACE

This book is based largely upon the research undertaken for a thesis at the University of Oxford in the years 1979 to 1982. It is written from the viewpoint of a lawyer, but one who is concerned with the wider meaning and application of the concept "Law". It is hoped, therefore, that this work will be relevant to a larger group of persons—those interested in the government of society and the wielding of judicial power, such as it is.

More particularly, this study is an attempt to stimulate discussion about the part played by law and the judiciary in South Africa, both in the past, at present, and in an uncertain future. There are two aspects of what follows which, I feel, need further explanation. First, there is, by design, a minimum of theoretical discussion. This is because the text is an attempt to present facts about judicial behaviour, rather than to prove a particular theory. It will be evident that my approach was influenced by realism and liberalism. What is more important, however, are the theoretical conclusions to which my findings have led me, and which appear in the "Postscript".

Secondly, readers familiar with the topic may be surprised to find a group of cases, dealing largely with executive and legislative power (eg *Sachs v Minister of Justice* 1934 AD 11), absent from this book. It is important to note that they were seriously considered, but were left out, *not* because they tended to disturb the conclusions actually reached (indeed, the very opposite), but because they were felt not to fit in with the structure and theme of the book as a whole. I hope to publish my findings in that area separately in the future.

My interest in this subject arose partly as a reaction to the lack of debate on the social role of the South African judiciary. As will be seen, much of my thought has been influenced by the writing of those critical of judicial performance, and in this respect Professor John Dugard of the University of the Witwatersrand provided early encouragement. In Oxford, I benefited from the wide-ranging knowledge of those scholars working on southern Africa, not least the political economists and historians centred on Queen Elizabeth House. Dr J M Finnis of University College helped me find my feet in the first eighteen months, and Dr J W Harris of Keble College retained a benevolent interest throughout. The staff of the Bodleian Law Library were unfailingly helpful, and often provided a refreshing link with the outside world.

Many friends sustained me and discussed the issues dealt with in this book. Among them, I am particularly grateful to Sandy Fredman, Bryan Hillis, Paul Kumleben, Shelagh Scarth and Stephen

Watson. Edwin Cameron spent much time and effort in reading and criticizing an early draft, an invaluable contribution which I greatly appreciate. Shushy Hugo-Hamman waded patiently and efficiently through a sometimes unorganized manuscript, and converted it into a presentable typescript. My family was a constant source of inspiration and understanding. Above all, Professor A M Honoré of All Souls College, Oxford, kindly and constructively supervised my work from early 1981 onwards. Without his support and criticism I would have made little progress.

Since my return to South Africa, I have had the good fortune to teach a course on the "Judicial Process" to small groups of final-year law students at the Universities of Cape Town and Stellenbosch, as well as to have extensive discussions with a colleague and friend, Dennis Davis. This experience has been of great benefit to me, and the "Postscript" below crystallized during these sessions.

My great thanks go to all these people. Naturally, the remaining shortcomings are my responsibility.

My thanks, too, are due to Richard Cooke of Juta's for allowing this project to proceed and to The Rustica Press for bringing it to fruition.

I should also like to express my appreciation to the Cape Archives, for permission to reproduce the photograph of some of the early Appeal Court personalities taken in Amsterdam; and The South African Library, for their help in locating photographs.

H M Corder
Stellenbosch
February, 1984

CONTENTS

LIST OF ILLUSTRATIONS

TABLE OF CASES

BIBLIOGRAPHY

The following works were used in the preparation of this book.

I. Published

A. *Books*

Abel-Smith, B & Stevens, R *Lawyers and the Courts* (London: Heinemann, 1967)
——— *In Search of Justice* (London: Allen Lane, 1968)
Annual Survey of Race Relations in South Africa (Johannesburg: South African Institute of Race Relations, 1977 and 1978)
Blackwell, Leslie *Are Judges Human?* (London: Bailey Bros & Swinfen, 1962)
Blom-Cooper, L & Drewry, G *Final Appeal* (Oxford: The Clarendon Press, 1972)
Brookes, E *et al Coming of Age* (Cape Town: Maskew Miller, 1930)
Broome, F N *Not the Whole Truth* (Pietermaritzburg: University of Natal Press, 1962)
Bundy, Colin *The Rise and Fall of the South African Peasantry* (London: Heinemann, 1979)
Cardozo, B N *The Nature of the Judicial Process* (New Haven: Yale University Press, 1921)
——— *The Growth of Law* (New Haven: Yale University Press, 1924)
Carlson, Joel *No Neutral Ground* (London: Davis-Poynter, 1973)
Centlivres, A vdS *Blundering into University Apartheid* (Cape Town: University Academic Freedom Committee, 1959)
Comaroff, J L *Judges of the Appellate Division and Transvaal Bench from 1943 to 1970* (Johannesburg: University of the Witwatersrand, 1972)
Cowen, D V *Parliamentary Sovereignty and the Entrenched Sections of the South Africa Act* (Cape Town: Juta's, 1951)
De Crespigny, A & Schrire, R *The Government and Politics of South Africa* (Cape Town: Juta's, 1978)
Department of Justice, South Africa *Annual Reports and Statistics, 1912–1950*
Dugard, C J R *Human Rights and the South African Legal Order* (Princeton: Princeton University Press, 1978)
Dworkin, R M *Taking Rights Seriously* (London: Duckworth, 1978)
Fagan, H A *Our Responsibility* (Stellenbosch: Die Universiteitsuitgewers, 1960)
——— *Co-existence in South Africa* (Cape Town: Juta's, 1963)
Feetham, Richard *The Rule of Law—our Ancient Right* (1952); *The High Court of Parliament Act and the Rule of Law* (1953); *Political Apartheid and the Entrenched Clauses of the South Africa Act* (not dated); *The "Suspended" Bill* (not dated); *Then (1931) and Now (1955)* (1955); *Guarantees and National Unity* (1956). All published by Defenders of the Constitution.
Freislich, R *The Last Tribal War* (Cape Town: C Struik, 1964)
Griffith, J A G *The Politics of the Judiciary* (London: Fontana, 1977)
Hahlo, H R & Kahn, Ellison *South Africa: The Development of its Laws and Constitution* (Cape Town: Juta's, 1960)
——— *The South African Legal System and its Background* (Cape Town: Juta's, 1968)
Hand, Learned *The Bill of Rights* (Cambridge, Massachusetts: Harvard University Press, 1958)
Hosten, W G; Edwards, A B; Nathan, C; & Bosman, F *Introduction to South African Law and Legal Theory* (Durban: Butterworths, 1977)
International Commission of Jurists *South Africa and the Rule of Law* (Geneva, 1960)
——— *Erosion of the Rule of Law in South Africa* (Geneva, 1968)
Jackson, John D *Justice in South Africa* (London: Secker and Warburg, 1980)
Keeton, G W (Gen Ed) *The British Commonwealth: The Development of its Laws and Constitutions* vol 5 (London: Stevens, 1960)
Kotzé, J G *Biographical Memoirs and Reminiscences* (Cape Town: Maskew Miller, 1934)
——— *Memoirs and Reminiscences* vol 2 (Prepared and introduced by B A Tindall) (Cape Town: Maskew Miller, not dated)

Law Students' Council, University of the Witwatersrand *Mutatis Mutandis* (Johannesburg, 1978)

Levy, B H *Cardozo and Frontiers of Legal Thinking* (Revised Edition) (Cleveland and London: The Press of Case Western Reserve University, 1969)

Mandela, Nelson *The Struggle is my Life* (London: International Defence and Aid Fund for Southern Africa, 1978)

Marks, S *Reluctant Rebellion* (Oxford: Clarendon Press, 1970)

Mathews, A S *Law, Order, and Liberty in South Africa* (Cape Town: Juta's, 1971)

May, H J *The South African Constitution* (Third Edition) (Cape Town: Juta's, 1955)

McWhinney, E *Judicial Review* (Fourth Edition of *Judicial Review in the English-Speaking World*) (Toronto: University Press, 1969)

Minutes of Proceedings of the South African National Convention (Cape Town: Cape Times, 1911)

Moodie, T Dunbar *The Rise of Afrikanerdom* (Berkley—Los Angeles—London: University of California Press, 1975)

Pachai, B *The International Aspects of the South African Indian Question, 1860–1971* (Cape Town: C Struik, 1971)

Papers Relating to a Federation of the South African Colonies (London, 1907)

Preller, J F (ed) *Die Konvensie-Dagboek van F S Malan 1908–1909* (Cape Town: Van Riebeeck Society, 1951)

Roberts, A A *A South African Legal Bibliography* (Pretoria: The Author, 1942)

Rose Innes, James *Autobiography* (Edited by B A Tindall) (Cape Town—London—New York: Oxford University Press, 1949)

Roux, Edward *Time Longer than Rope* (Madison: University of Wisconsin Press, 1964)

Sachs, Albie *Justice in South Africa* (London: Chatto–Heinemann, 1973)

Sampson, Victor *My Reminiscences* (London: Longmans, Green, 1926)

Schoeman B M *Van Malan tot Verwoerd* (Cape Town and Pretoria: Human and Rousseau, 1973)

Schreiner, O D *The Nettle* (Johannesburg: South African Institute of Race Relations, 1964)

——— *The Contribution of English Law to South African Law; and The Rule of Law in South Africa* (London: Stevens, 1967)

Shetreet, S *Judges on Trial* (Amsterdam—New York—Oxford: North-Holland, 1976)

South Africa and the Rule of Law (Department of Foreign Affairs, Republic of South Africa, 1968)

South African Outlook (Cape Town: January, 1981)

Spro-Cas Legal Commission *Law, Justice and Society* (Johannesburg: Spro-Cas, 1972)

Stevens, R *Law and Politics* (London: Weidenfeld and Nicolson, 1979)

Summers, R S (ed) *Essays in Legal Philosophy* (Oxford: Basil Blackwell, 1970)

The Conference (Cape Town: William Foster, 1875)

Thompson, L M *The Unification of South Africa 1902–1910* (Oxford: At the Clarendon Press, 1960)

Thompson, L M & Butler J (eds) *Change in Contemporary South Africa* (Berkley and Los Angeles: University of California Press, 1975)

Twining, William *Karl Llewellyn and the Realist Movement* (London: Weidenfeld and Nicolson, 1973)

Van den Heever, C M *Generaal J B M Hertzog* (Johannesburg: AP Boekhandel, 1944)

Van den Heever, F P *Breach of Promise and Seduction in South African Law* (Cape Town: Juta's, 1954)

Van der Merwe, H W *et al White South African Elites* (Cape Town: Juta's, 1974)

Van der Vyver, J D *Seven Lectures on Human Rights* (Cape Town: Juta's, 1976)

Van Reenen, T H *Land—Its Ownership and Occupation in South Africa* (Cape Town: Juta's, 1962)

VerLoren van Themaat, J P *Staatsreg* (Second Edition by M Wiechers) (Durban: Butterworths, 1967)

Walker, E A *A History of Southern Africa* (Third Edition) (London: Longmans, Green, 1957)

——— *Lord de Villiers and his Times* (London: Constable, 1925)

Walton, Edgar H *The Inner History of the National Convention* (Cape Town and Pretoria: Maskew Miller, 1912)

Wedderburn, K W *The Worker and the Law* (London: Penguin, 1965)

Wilson, M & Thompson, L M (eds) *Oxford History of South Africa. Volume II (1870–1966)* (Oxford: At the Clarendon Press, 1971)

B. *Articles*

(It is likely that most of the "Anonymous" entries below were contributed by the editors of the journals in which they appeared. Where appropriate, the subject of the article, rather than its title, has been listed.)

Anonymous "Sir Henry de Villiers" (1901) 18 *SALJ* 1
—— "Sir James Rose Innes" (1902) 19 *SALJ* 1
—— "The Hon J G Kotzé" (1903) 20 *SALJ* 101
—— "William Henry Solomon" (1904) 21 *SALJ* 189
—— "J W Wessels" (1905) 22 *SALJ* 241
—— "C G Maasdorp" (1907) 24 *SALJ* 129
—— "The Hon Jacob de Villiers" (1907) 24 *SALJ* 237
—— "Coming Judicial Changes" (1910) I *Union Law Review* 171
—— "The New Judicial Appointments" (1910) I *Union Law Review* 274
—— "Native Practitioners" (1910) I *Union Law Review* 465
—— "The 'Black Peril' Question" (1911) II *Union Law Review* 3
—— "F W Beyers" (1911) II *Union Law Review* 342
—— "Note" (1912) 29 *SALJ* 223
—— "The Training of Judges" (1913) 30 *SALJ* 324
—— "Case-note" (1913) 30 *SALJ* 462
—— "The High Court of Parliament" (1914) 31 *SALJ* 165
—— "N J de Wet" (1914) 31 *SALJ* 369
—— "The Hon Sir Henry Hubert Juta" (1915) 32 *SALJ* 1
—— "Women and the Legal Profession" (1917) 34 *SALJ* 342
—— "The Judiciary and Legislation" (1918) 35 *SALJ* 54
—— "Women and the Legal Profession" (1919) 36 *SALJ* 173
—— "J E R de Villiers" (1920) 37 *SALJ* 1
—— "James Stratford" (1921) 38 *SALJ* 248
—— "Women as Practitioners" (1922) 39 *SALJ* 39
—— "E F Watermeyer" (1923) 40 *SALJ* 99
—— "B A Tindall" (1923) 40 *SALJ* 245
—— "F W Beyers" (1924) 41 *SALJ* 417
—— "John Stephen Curlewis" (1925) 42 *SALJ* 121
—— "L Greenberg" (1926) 43 *SALJ* 1
—— "R Feetham" (1928) 45 *SALJ* 179
—— "T J de V Roos" (1930) 47 *SALJ* 169
—— "A vdS Centlivres" (1935) 52 *SALJ* 409
—— "Sir John Wessels" (1937) 54 *SALJ* 451
—— "O D Schreiner" (1938) 55 *SALJ* 1
—— "*Crimen Laesae Majestatis*" (1938) 55 *SALJ* 14
—— "O H Hoexter" (1940) 57 *SALJ* 241
—— "John Stephen Curlewis" (1940) 57 *SALJ* 361
—— "H A Fagan" (1943) 60 *SALJ* 1
—— "N J de Wet" (1943) 60 *SALJ* 275
—— "James Stratford" (1944) 61 *SALJ* 258
—— "F P van den Heever" (1949) 66 *SALJ* 135
—— "E F Watermeyer (1950) 67 *SALJ* 332
—— "James Stratford" (1952) 69 *SALJ* 1
—— "L Greenberg" (1955) 72 *SALJ* 1
—— "F P van den Heever" (1956) 73 *SALJ* 117
—— "A vdS Centlivres" (1957) 74 *SALJ* 1
—— "H A Fagan" (1957) 74 *SALJ* 6
—— "E F Watermeyer" (1958) 75 *SALJ* 233
—— "H A Fagan" (1959) 76 *SALJ* 117
—— "N J de Wet" (1960) 77 *SALJ* 133
—— "O D Schreiner" (1961) 78 *SALJ* 10
—— "B A Tindall (1963) 80 *SALJ* 164
—— "O H Hoexter" (1963) 80 *SALJ* 165
—— "H A Fagan" (1964) 81 *SALJ* 127
—— "L Greenberg" (1964) 81 *SALJ* 405
—— "R Feetham" (1966) 83 *SALJ* 1
—— "A vdS Centlivres" (1966) 83 *SALJ* 387
—— "A vdS Centlivres" (1967) 84 *SALJ* 87

Aquilius "Immorality and Illegality in Contract" (1942) 59 *SALJ* 16 and 333
Bamford, B R "Aspects of Judicial Independence" (1956) 73 *SALJ* 380
Behrmann, L B "*Jajbhay v Cassim*" (1946) 63 *SALJ* 40
Beinart, B "Parliament and the Courts" 1954 Butterworths South African Law Review 134
——— "The Rule of Law" 1962 *Acta Juridica* 99
Blackwell, Leslie "Fifty Years at the Bar" (1959) 76 *SALJ* 77
——— "The Judge's Function" (1961) 78 *SALJ* 80.
Cameron, E "Mute Concurrence in the Appellate Division: is silence golden?" (1979) 42 *THR-HR* 419
Caney, L R & Bizzell, H V L "Some Observations upon Sections 35 and 64 of the Industrial Conciliation Act, 1937" (1951) 68 *SALJ* 30
Carey Miller, D "South African Judges as Natural Lawyers—a Roman-Dutch Basis?" (1973) 90 *SALJ* 86
Centlivres, A vdS "Report of the US Commission on Civil Rights" 1962 *Acta Juridica* 1
Claassen, C J "Retain the Bar and the Side-Bar" (1970) 87 *SALJ* 25
Coertze, L I "Vonnisbespreking" (1937) 1 *THR-HR* 114
Coote, Brian "Another Look at *Bowmakers v Barnet Instruments*" (1972) 35 *Modern Law Review* 38
Davenport, T R H "Civil Rights in South Africa, 1910–1960" 1960 *Acta Juridica* 11
Davis, R P B "Women as Advocates and Attorneys" (1914) 31 *SALJ* 383
Dean, W H B "Whither the Constitution?" (1976) 39 *THR-HR* 266
Denning, A T "The Independence and Impartiality of the Judges" (1954) 71 *SALJ* 345
De Villiers, Melius "Fair Comment in Defamation Cases" (1917) 34 *SALJ* 202
——— "Women and the Legal Profession" (1918) 35 *SALJ* 289
——— "The Court and the Constitution" (1919) 36 *SALJ* 365
De Vos, W "Vrye Regsvinding?" (1967) 30 *THR-HR* 362
Dugard C J R "The Courts and section 6 of the Terrorism Act" (1970) 87 *SALJ* 289
——— "The Judicial Process, Positivism and Civil Liberty" (1971) 88 *SALJ* 181
——— "Judges, Academics and Unjust Laws: The Van Niekerk Contempt Case" (1972) 89 *SALJ* 271
——— "Human Rights in South Africa—retrospect and prospect" 1979 *Acta Juridica* 263
E R R "The Jurisdiction of the Appellate Division" (1915) 32 *SALJ* 20
Findlay, George "The Source of Law" (1948) 65 *SALJ* 497
Frankfurter, F "Twenty Years of Mr. Justice Holmes' Constitutional Opinions" (1922–3) 36 *Harvard Law Review* 909
Friedmann, W "Judges, Politics and the Law" (1951) 29 *Canadian Bar Review* 811
Fuller, Lon L "Reason and Fiat in Case Law" (1945–6) 59 *Harvard Law Review* 376
Gauntlett, Jeremy "Aspects of the Value Problem in Judicial Positivism" (1969) 2 *Responsa Meridiana* 204
Gonin, H L "*Perduellio*" (1951) 14 *THR-HR* 1
Grossman, J B "Social Backgrounds and Judicial Decision-Making" (1966) 79 *Harvard Law Review* 1551
H J F "Some Impressions of the Court of Appeal" (1911) II *Union Law Review* 324
Haasbroek, D J P "Die Federasiebeweging in Suid-Afrika" (1968) 13 *Historia* 6
Hahlo, H R & Maisels, I A "The Rule of Law in South Africa" (1966) 52 *Virginia Law Review* 1
Kahn, Ellison "Recent Legislation" (1950) 67 *SALJ* 283
——— "The Definition of Racial Groups" (1951) 68 *SALJ* 108
——— "The Judicial Oath" (1954) 71 *SALJ* 22
——— "Book Review" (1958) 75 *SALJ* 112
——— "The History of the Administration of Justice in the South African Republic" (1958) 75 *SALJ* 397
——— "Appointment of Magistrates as Judges" (1971) 88 *SALJ* 512
——— "Oliver Deneys Schreiner — The Man and his Judicial World" (1980) 97 *SALJ* 566
Kahn-Freund, O "Trade Unions, the Law and Society" (1970) 33 *Modern Law Review* 241
Kentridge, S "The Pathology of a Legal System: Criminal Justice in South Africa" (1980) 128 *University of Pennsylvania Law Review* 603
Lee, R W "Law and Legislation in the Union of South Africa" (1923) 40 *SALJ* 442
——— "Roman-Dutch Law in South Africa" (1924) 41 *SALJ* 297
——— "Extracts from Letters written by Sir John Kotzé" (1950) 67 *SALJ* 174 and 265

Le May, G H L "Parliament, the Constitution, and the 'Doctrine of the Mandate'" (1957) 74 *SALJ* 33
Lourie, Arthur "Administrative Law in South Africa" (1927) 44 *SALJ* 10
Maister, P "Judicial Attitudes to Race in South Africa" (1969) 2 *Responsa Meridiana* 1
Mathews, A S & Albino, R C "The Permanence of the Temporary—An Examination of the 90- and 180-day Detention Laws" (1966) 83 *SALJ* 16
Mathews, A S & Van Niekerk, B v D "Eulogising the A-G—a qualified dissent" (1972) 89 *SALJ* 292
McWhinney, E "Court versus Legislature in the Union of South Africa: The Assertion of a Right of Judicial Review" (1953) 31 *Canadian Bar Review* 52
——— "The Supreme Court and the Bill of Rights—The Lessons of Comparative Jurisprudence" (1959) 37 *Canadian Bar Review* 16
Millner, M A "Apartheid and the South African Courts" (1961) 14 *Current Legal Problems* 280
——— "Eclipse of a Judiciary: The South African Position" (1962) 11 *International and Comparative Law Quarterly* 886
Milton, J R L "A Cloistered Virtue?" (1970) 87 *SALJ* 424
Mulligan, G A "Judicial Criticism of Legislation" (1953) 70 *SALJ* 35
Ogilvie Thompson, N "Centenary Celebrations of the Northern Cape Division" (1972) 89 *SALJ* 23
Pollak, Walter "The Legislative Competence of the Union Parliament" (1931) 48 *SALJ* 269
Radcliffe, C J "Law and Order" (1964) 61 *Law Society's Gazette* 820
Rumpff, F L H "Centenary of the OFS Supreme Court" (1974) 91 *SALJ* 529
Rumpff, Irene "Lord de Villiers" (1965) VI *Codicillus* 39
Rissik, P U "The Legislative Authority of the Union Parliament" (1921) 38 *SALJ* 132
Schaeffer, M "Some further considerations on Sections 35 and 64, Industrial Conciliation Act" (1951) 68 *SALJ* 314
Schmidhauser, J R "Stare Decisis, Dissent, and the Background of the Justices of the Supreme Court of the United States" (1962) 14 *University of Toronto Law Journal* 194
Scrutton, Lord Justice "The Work of the Commercial Courts" (1923) 1 *Cambridge Law Journal* 6
Seidman, R B "The Judicial Process Reconsidered in the light of Role-Theory" (1969) 32 *Modern Law Review* 516
Snyman, C R "Sedition Revived" (1980) 97 *SALJ* 14
Stevens, R B "The Role of a final Appeal Court in a democracy: The House of Lords Today" (1965) 28 *Modern Law Review* 509
Steyn, L C "Oor die taak van Regbank en Regsfakulteit" (1967) 30 *THR-HR* 101
Suzman, A "The Inarticulate Major Premise" (1971) 88 *SALJ* 246
Swanepoel, H L "Vonnisbespreking" (1950) 13 *THR-HR* 106
"T" "President Roosevelt and the Supreme Court" (1942) 59 *SALJ* 103
Thompson, L M "Constitutionalism in the South African Republics" 1954 *Butterworths South African Law Review* 49
Van Niekerk, B v D ". . . Hanged by the Neck until you are dead" (1969) 86 *SALJ* 457; and (1970) 87 *SALJ* 60
——— "The Warning Voice from Heidelberg—The Life and Thought of Gustav Radbruch" (1973) 90 *SALJ* 234
——— "Social Engineering in the German Constitutional Court—Some Reflections on a recent judgment" (1975) 92 *SALJ* 298
——— "The Uncloistering of the Virtue. Freedom of Speech and the Administration of Justice—a comparative overview" (1978) 95 *SALJ* 362 and 534
——— "Book Review" (1978) 95 *SALJ* 589
——— "To Pretoria, Washington, and Stockholm . . . With Love" (1980) 97 *SALJ* 389
VerLoren van Themaat H "Die Soewereiniteit van die Unie-Parlement" (1954) 71 *SALJ* 60
VerLoren van Themaat, J P "Vonnisbespreking" (1957) 20 *THR-HR* 225
Wade, H W R "The Senate Act Case and the Entrenched Sections of the South Africa Act" (1957) 74 *SALJ* 160
Wallance, G "Racism and the Death Penalty" (1978) XIX *Race and Class* 404
Wechsler, H "Towards Neutral Principles of Constitutional Law" (1959–60) 73 (1) *Harvard Law Review* 1
Wessels, Sir John "The Future of Roman-Dutch Law in South Africa" (1920) 37 *SALJ* 265
——— "Codification" (1928) 45 *SALJ* 5
Wille, G "A Comparison of English and South African Law" (1942) 59 *SALJ* 124

II. Unpublished

Beinart, B (ed) Material collected for the Second Edition of Roberts *SA Legal Bibliography* Faculty of Law, University of Cape Town

Kuper, M *The Supreme Court and Race Relations in South Africa*, dissertation submitted for BA (Honours) degree, Department of African Government, University of the Witwatersrand, 1965

Rose Innes, James *Archive* (particularly letters received) Cape Town, South African Public Library

Trapido, Stanley *White Conflict and Non-White Participation in the Politics of the Cape of Good Hope 1853–1910* University of London, PhD thesis, 1970

SUMMARY OF SOUTH AFRICAN HISTORY 1910–50

Although some detail of particular phases or events in South African history is provided at the beginning of each of the chapters of this book, it is perhaps necessary to provide a skeletal survey of overall trends for the benefit of those unfamiliar with them. Further details can be found in most South African history books, although two contemporary histories might be particularly useful: Roux's *Time Longer than Rope*, and Walker's *A History of Southern Africa*. Each gives a flavour of those times, but from different perspectives.

The Union of South Africa of 1910 attempted to consolidate white power in the subcontinent by bringing together the former Boer republics and the predominantly British colonies. Some kind of unity was essential for the continued economic exploitation of the mineral wealth of the country, as well as finally to tackle the 'native question' in an organized manner so as to remove any threat of rebellion and to provide the necessary labour force for the mines and nascent industries.

The South African Party, a coalition of ex-Boer leaders and some Cape politicians, ruled the new state for the first fourteen years, with Generals Botha and Smuts as Prime Ministers. Two events in white politics dominated these years: both were founded in tensions between English- and Afrikaans-speakers. First, there was the rebellion against South Africa's entry into the war and the South-West African campaign at the outbreak of the First World War (see Ch IV). Secondly, there was constant disturbance on the labour front, especially among white workers on the Witwatersrand. Most of these people were immigrants from Britain and Europe, or Afrikaners who had lost their farms in the aftermath of the Anglo-Boer War, and they feared replacement by cheap black labour. Major eruptions occurred in 1913–14, and in the Rand Revolt of 1922 (see Ch V): all were crushed by force.

Black resistance at this time was channelled, on one level, through the "diplomatic" representations of the Native National Congress (founded in 1912, later the African National Congress), and on another in open acts of defiance, such as the Bondelswarts resistance (see Ch IV) and the massacre of religious zealots (the "Israelites") at Bulhoek, Eastern Cape. Indian South Africans participated in Gandhi's passive resistance campaigns in the Transvaal and Natal (Ch VII).

In the 1924 general election, the "Pact" Government, formed by the National (mainly Afrikaner) and Labour (mainly English) Parties, came to power. Industrial legislation, which entrenched white dominance, brought relative labour peace, but the nine-year period of office was characterized by economic depression and drought. On the Parliamentary front, white women were enfranchised in 1930, and the passage of the Statute of Westminster in 1931 made South Africa more or less a sovereign independent state.

In 1933, the Prime Minister, General Hertzog, took most of his National Party into the United Party, formed with the rump of the old South African Party under General Smuts. Hertzog remained Prime Minister after a resounding victory in the general election, and this situation continued until the outbreak of the Second World War split the government. These years saw the country still in a depressed economic state, as well as witnessing the removal of African voters from the common roll and the development of the segregation policy with the passage of the Native Trust and Land Act of 1936 (see Ch VI).

General Smuts became Prime Minister for the second time in 1939 when he persuaded the majority of MPs to back his intention of taking South Africa into World War II on the British side: Hertzog wished to remain neutral. The war years were years of industrial expansion, the absence of white workers on active duty, and the consequent urbanization and "skilling" of large numbers of black workers. A massive strike by African mine workers in 1946 was crushed in the same way as earlier attempts at industrial democracy by white workers.

Dissatisfaction among returning soldiers and thorough organization by a rejuvenated National Party under Dr D F Malan led to a change of government in the 1948 general election. Within two years, the structures of the present "apartheid" state were being built upon the foundations laid in terms of earlier segregation policies.

This summarises, inadequately, the broad movements in (mainly white) politics over the period covered by this book. For even a superficial *understanding* of these events, readers must look elsewhere.

A NOTE ON TERMINOLOGY

For any writer on South Africa, a constant problem is caused by the different names given to race groups by the governing authorities, a matter which is exacerbated by changes in acceptability over time. The approach adopted here is that the name used is the one current at the time at which the event discussed took place. If no specific period is referred to, present-day nomenclature has been adopted. In this way, black South Africans will be called "kaffirs", "natives", "Africans", or "blacks"; Indian South Africans "Asians", "coolies", or "Indians"; and white South Africans "whites" or "Europeans". To distinguish "other-than-white" South Africans, when necessary, the labels "non-white" or "non-European" have been employed.

In general, such race terms have been written without quotation marks. This has been done for convenience, and by no means indicates acceptance of such arbitrary classifications. In addition, in matters of gender, "he", rather than"she", has been used when no particular gender is indicated, and should be taken to refer to both men and women. The overwhelmingly male subject-matter (all the judges and most litigants) of this book suggested the use of the masculine appellation.

Further, an explanation of judicial titles is required in order to avoid confusion. When first constituted, the Appellate Division consisted of a Chief Justice (abbreviated CJ), two ordinary judges of appeal (J until 1913, and then JA), and two additional judges of appeal (AJA after 1913, and before that given the abbreviated version of their provincial judicial position, e g JP for Judge President, or CJ for Chief Justice). Acting judges of appeal were entitled Actg JA or Actg AJA up till 1914, depending on whether they were replacing an ordinary or additional judge of appeal. The Acting Chief Justice has always been ACJ.

The Appellate Division Act 12 of 1920 substituted a new section 96 in the South Africa Act. Section 1 changed this rather complicated state of affairs by providing for four permanent judges of appeal (JA) presided over by a Chief Justice (CJ). Since then, acting judges of appeal have been given the title AJA, including those retired judges of appeal who return to act on the Bench. Judges of the provincial divisions are styled J in the singular, and JJ in the plural, and acting judges AJ. More than one appeal judge is called JJA.

In what follows, judicial titles and abbreviations employed *at the time the decision under discussion was reported* will be used. When the judges are written about out of the context of a particular case, *no titles* will be used.

ABBREVIATIONS

Apart from judicial titles, which are set out and explained in the foregoing note, and the standard form of referring to reports and journals, several names are commonly used in an abbreviated form in this book. An alphabetical list of these expressions follows:

A-G	Attorney-General
AD	Appellate Division
CMG	Commander of the Order of St. Michael and St. George
CPD	Cape Provincial Division
EDC	Eastern Districts Court
EDLD	Eastern Districts Local Division
GWLD	Griqualand West Local Divisin
HCGW	High Court of Griqualand West
IA	Rose Innes Archive, South African Public Library, Cape Town
JP	Judge President
KC	King's Counsel
KCMG	Knight Commander of the Order of St. Michael and St. George
MLA	Member of the Legislative Assembly
MLC	Member of the Legislative Council
MP	Member of Parliament
NPD	Natal Provincial Division
OFS	Orange Free State
OPD	Orange Free State Provincial Division
ORC	Orange River Colony
PC	Privy Council
QC	Queen's Counsel
SA	South Africa
SAC	South African College
SACS	South African College School
SALJ	*South African Law Journal*
SAR	South African Railways
SAR and H	South African Railways and Harbours
SWA	South West Africa
SWAHC	South West Africa High Court
THC	Transvaal High Court
THR-HR	*Tydskrif vir Hedendaagse Romeins-Hollandse Reg (Journal of Contemporary Roman-Dutch Law)*, also known as *Tydskrif*
TPD	Transvaal Provincial Division

TUC	Transvaal University College (Pretoria)
UCGH	University of the Cape of Good Hope
UCT	University of Cape Town
UG	Union Government
WLD	Witwatersrand Local Division
ZAR	Zuid Afrikaansche Republiek (South African Republic, which became the Transvaal)

CHAPTER ONE

INTRODUCTION

> "There was never a more sterile controversy than that upon the question whether a judge makes law. Of course he does. How can he help it?"
>
> —Lord Radcliffe[1]

Over the past two decades, the South African judiciary has been placed increasingly under the gaze of critical observers. The "accepted wisdom" which dominates assessments of judicial performance is that the courts are independent and impartial in ensuring equality before the law,[2] and that most of the blame for any apparent divergence from this condition should be lodged squarely at the door of Parliament and its discriminatory enactments.[3] There is, on the other hand, a vocal and growing school of opinion, both within the country[4] and abroad,[5] which maintains that the judiciary has failed to fulfil its role as the dispenser of justice equally to all litigants. These writers point out that the inherent injustice of the South African social structure cannot but affect the performance of the courts, whose personnel is drawn from the privileged group.

Two features are clear when these currents of opinion are juxtaposed. Firstly, almost all commentators concentrate on the period since the present government's accession to office in 1948, and tend to assume that the courts functioned actively as agents of justice and equality before that date. Secondly, almost all conclusions are based on vague impressions or limited samples of judicial pronouncements. There has been no systematic study of the role and attitudes of

[1] "Law and Order" 821.

[2] See, for example: Sampson *My Reminiscences* 123–4; May *The South African Constitution* 247; Broome *Not the Whole Truth* 266; Hahlo and Maisels "The Rule of Law in South Africa" (1966) 52 *Virginia Law Review* 1 at 10, 12, and 14; and Van der Vyver *Seven Lectures on Human Rights* 12.

[3] A clear example of such an attitude is found in Centlivres "Report of the US Commission on Civil Rights" 1962 *Acta Juridica* 1 at 10.

[4] Some examples of which are: Mathews and Albino "The Permanence of the Temporary—An Examination of the 90- and 180-day detention laws" (1966) 83 *SALJ* 16; Bamford "Aspects of Judicial Independence" (1956) 73 *SALJ* 380; Davenport "Civil Rights in South Africa 1910–1960" 1960 *Acta Juridica* 11; Beinart "The Rule of Law" 1962 *Acta Juridica* 99; Van Niekerk "Hanged by the neck until you are dead" (1969) 86 *SALJ* 457 and (1970) 87 *SALJ* 60; Milton "A Cloistered Virtue?" (1970) 87 *SALJ* 424; Van Niekerk "The Uncloistering of the Virtue" (1978) 95 *SALJ* 362 and 534; Dugard "The Courts and Section 6 of the Terrorism Act" (1970) 87 *SALJ* 289; Dugard "The Judicial Process, Positivism and Civil Liberty" (1971) 88 *SALJ* 181; Maister "Judicial Attitudes to Race in South Africa" (1969) II *Responsa Meridiana* 1; Dean "Whither the Constitution?" (1976) 39 *THR-HR* 266; Mathews *Law, Order, and Liberty*; *South African Outlook* (January 1981); and Spro-Cas *Law, Justice, and Society*.

[5] See for example: Millner "Apartheid and the South African Courts" (1961) 14 *Current Legal Problems* 280; International Commission of Jurists *Erosion of the Rule of Law in South Africa* (1968); Sachs *Justice in South Africa* and "The Instruments of Domination in South Africa" in Thompson and Butler (Eds) *Change in Contemporary South Africa*; Wallance "South Africa: Racism and the Death Penalty" *Race and Class* XIX Spring 1978 (4) 404; Carlson *No Neutral Ground*; and Jackson *Justice in South Africa*.

the judiciary, and even the important works of Dugard,[6] Sachs,[7] and Kuper[8] were based on the examination of a relatively narrow field of judicial activity.

These remarkable differences in opinion, the current discussion of the work of South African judges,[9] and the deficiencies in previous studies of the judiciary, among other things, prompted the undertaking of the present task.

Aims and Methods

The aim of this book is to provide an accurate account of appellate judicial performance in the period 1910 to 1950, as a basis for a critical assessment of the judges' approach to their work. In dealing with this subject, two main difficulties were encountered.

Firstly, the sensitivity displayed by the South African judges and authorities to investigations of this type,[10] and the aura of infallibility which, in the eyes of many observers, surrounds the South African judiciary, form considerable inhibitions for a South African researcher. The contempt of court prosecutions against Van Niekerk,[11] as well as various pessimistic passages in the work of both Dugard and Van Niekerk,[12] which outline the problems central to such a task, are indications of the pervasive atmosphere. As Van Niekerk once said:[13]

> "The effect of this self-imposed abdication of legal academics has been that the functioning of the members of the judiciary in South Africa for all practical purposes takes place in a sort of intellectual vacuum, where their actions, their attitudes and failings (both as individuals and as a group) remain unscrutinized amidst the sycophantic praise customarily piled on them—academics being among those who extol their attributes."

On the other hand, the mere fact that these and other writers were prepared to insist upon their right to subject the judiciary to critical investigation, and that some South Africans shared their view of the court's work, acted as incentives to the present research.

Secondly, the inevitable complication caused by the subjective nature of the endeavour constituted a formidable obstacle. There is

[6] *Human Rights and the South African Legal Order.*

[7] *Justice in South Africa.*

[8] "The Supreme Court and Race Relations in South Africa" (unpublished dissertation 1965).

[9] The frequent use of judges to head commissions of inquiry into national political events, such as the Mostert, Erasmus, M T Steyn, and Rabie Commissions of 1978–1982; the resignations of A Mostert and M King from the Bench in 1980; the use of Mr Justice M T Steyn as Administrator General of Namibia; and the Hoexter Commission of Inquiry into the structure of South African courts, have all contributed to greater public discussion of the judiciary, as well as disquiet within judicial ranks.

[10] See the South African government publication *South Africa and the Rule of Law* (1968), and the comments of Rumpff, CJ in a speech reported in "Centenary of the Orange Free State Supreme Court" (1974) 91 *SALJ* 529 at 534–5.

[11] See *S v Van Niekerk* 1970 (3) SA 655 (T); and 1972 (3) SA 711 (AD).

[12] See Dugard (1971) 88 *SALJ* 181 at 194; Van Niekerk (1975) 92 *SALJ* 298 at 299; Van Niekerk (1978) 95 *SALJ* 534 at 539, 551–2, 559, and 561; Van Niekerk (1978) 95 *SALJ* 589 at 590 for example.

[13] In a review of Shetreet *Judges on Trial* which appeared in (1978) 95 *SALJ* 589 at 592–3.

no doubt that research-methods and ways of evaluating judicial performance are directly coloured by the writer's values and experiences, no matter how firmly he attempts to suppress them. In this regard, some comfort can be drawn from the words of Professor J B Bury in his introduction to Gibbon's *Autobiography*, which are quoted by Mr Justice Broome:[14]

> "It is slowly being recognised that history is in the last resort somebody's image of the past, and the image is conditioned by the mind and experience of the person who forms it. Only such things as dates, names, documents, can be considered purely objective facts. The reconstruction, which involves the discovery of causes and motives, which it is the historian's business to attempt, depends on subjective elements, which cannot be eliminated."

As far as the focus of investigation was concerned, the Appellate Division was the obvious target, because of its national importance; its appellate function; its foundation as part of political union; the prominence of its members; and the avoidance of an invidious choice between the provincial divisions. In addition, the existence of comprehensive studies of the British appellate judiciary provided an invaluable comparative guide.[15] A distinct disadvantage of this choice was that some of the most illuminating cases (in the sphere of issues of public importance) came before the provincial and local divisions alone.[16] A second drawback was that the particular type of case which was likely to come on appeal, and the financial burden which an appeal to Bloemfontein imposed on the unsuccessful litigant, could combine to give an impression untypical of wider judicial activity.

Another problem was the selection of a time period for study. While it seemed natural to start with the creation of the court in 1910, limited research time meant that it would not be possible to incorporate what many people regard as the crucial decade of the 1950's.[17] A second constraint is to be found in the difficulties created for a researcher who is removed both in years and experience from the events and influences of the early days of the Union of South Africa. In some ways, though, concentration on the period before 1950 is an advantage. For it is an unsurveyed period, in regard to which the public has not acquired indestructible preconceptions, and in which the court is shown at work in "normal" conditions.

But the early years are also important in that the actions of the judges at that time set the limits for subsequent judicial action, and marked the level of their willingness to be involved in the type of

[14] *Op cit* 285.

[15] See for example: Blom-Cooper and Drewry *Final Appeal*; Stevens *Law and Politics*; and Shetreet *op cit*.

[16] Examples of which are: *R v Plaatjies* 1910 EDL 63; *Williams & Adendorff v Johannesburg Municipality* 1915 TPD 106; and *George v Pretoria Municipality* 1916 TPD 501.

[17] During which the court had for the first time to interpret the laws of the apartheid policy, particularly those dealing with the franchise which brought on the "constitutional crisis".

issues described in this study. The degree to which judicial attitudes before 1950 influenced the appeal court's reaction to the legislative roguery which precipitated the "coloured vote" cases of the 1950's[18] is difficult to gauge, especially as the "constitutional" nature of the events would have put it in a separate compartment in judicial thinking. Nevertheless, it is likely that the approach instilled in judicial style by the AD's attitudes in its early years has profoundly influenced the nature of the response of the present-day judiciary to legislative inroads in the fields of liberty, justice, and equality.

The change in international circumstances which followed the end of World War II; the rise of nationalism and decolonisation in Africa; the passing of the Privy Council Appeals Act;[19] and the coming to power of the National Party in 1948 pointed to the retirement of Watermeyer, CJ in October 1950 as a convenient and logical closing point for this investigation.

How, then, to assess judicial attitudes and role from 1910 to 1950? Few judges of appeal had written anything (except judgments), nor had more than the bare facts of most of their lives been published.[20] The only way which seemed to meet the requirements of availability and "manageability" appeared to be the law reports, which are likely to have included most of the more important disputes of the period. They were used with Professor Kahn-Freund's dire warning in mind:[21]

> "Once more (as so often) those of us who are lawyers were taught the elementary lesson that the law reports are the worst possible mirror of society. They convey to the beholder a distorted image in which that which is marginal appears as typical, and this may be one of the reasons why sometimes the judgments of lawyers on problems of social policy are so surprisingly warped and ill-founded."

Nevertheless, although judgments are to a great extent dictated by the facts and the law of the case, in reported form they provide an accurate memorial of judicial views on particular subjects, which satisfies the present purpose.

With case reports as the major source of materials, the next choice lay in the selection of those matters which would most clearly display judicial attitudes to issues crucial to South Africa (such as race, class, gender, civil liberties, human rights, and so on). In the end, every reported judgment had to be perused, for the clearest indication of judicial thought on these topics can often be found in the most unlikely forum. In general, however, discretion was guided by the concept of "issues of public importance". This involves a subjective evaluation, in which the repercussions of a decision for a larger group of persons than the particular litigants, and the significance for wider

[18] *Harris v Minister of the Interior* 1952 (2) SA 428 (AD); *Minister of the Interior v Harris* 1952 (4) SA 769 (AD); and *Collins v Minister of the Interior* 1957 (1) SA 552 (AD).
[19] 16 of 1950.
[20] See Ch II below.
[21] "Trade Unions, the Law, and Society" (1970) 33 *Modern Law Review* 241 at 242.

South African society of the "political" questions raised in a case, assume great importance. In addition, particular attention was paid to cases in which the litigants belonged to the classes excluded from full participation in the government of South Africa, such as those known as "poor whites" and "non-whites".

The use of the word "political" here demands some elucidation, as it forms an essential element in what follows. In general, unless the context dictates another meaning, "political" signifies the widest scope of the concept of "politics", along the lines of those "issues of public importance" referred to above. It does not indicate "party-political", and, in the few instances in which party affiliations of judges are mentioned, this is of concern only in so far as they could have affected the outcome of particular cases. In other words, judicial attitudes to a legal dispute have "political" overtones if the result of that dispute, or the issues raised by it, have the potential to affect the socio-economic, or power, relationships of larger societal groups, not directly involved in the litigation.

This concept includes the constitutional sphere, although no cases in the period 1910 to 1950 squarely confronted the judiciary with a challenge to its view of its position in the government of the country. Thus "political" here encompasses those matters which can be labelled as "legal-political" or "constitutional-legal", and not those seen as "party-political".

In the event, the cases selected came from private as well as public law fields, and fell with relative ease into the sections in which they appear below. They have been grouped as far as possible by similarity of feature, in order more conveniently to explain the wider socio-economic context of each set of disputes, and to determine whether judicial roles and attitudes vary in different fields. The final chapter sums up the trends in judicial actions over the entire period, both as a group, and individually.

There is also a chapter on the personal backgrounds of all those who sat permanently as judges of appeal in this period, so that we can have some idea of the type of person whom the government appointed, and better understand the possible motivations for judicial opinions. To this end, various biographical sources, including the small number of judicial autobiographies of the day, were used. In addition, most South African legal periodicals and textbooks were consulted, in order to track down any comment on judicial activity of whatever form. Similarly, any references to foreign journals and books which seemed likely to shed light on the subject were pursued, but it would be foolish to claim that the research has encompassed all possible sources of knowledge and inspiration.

The body of this book thus contains a foundation of fact from which readers can evaluate the reaction of the South African appellate judiciary to political issues, and, on this basis, can assess its contribution to the cause of judicial independence and impartiality in the period 1910 to 1950, and since. For the tradition established (or reinforced) at that time forms the foundation of subsequent judicial behaviour.

Before embarking on the substance of the work, it is important to examine the AD as an institution within the context of the South African social formation at the start of, and during, the period.

The Social Position of the South African Appellate Judiciary 1910–1950

> "Throughout the history of race relations in South Africa the judges of the Supreme Court, with very few exceptions, have shown themselves more liberal than either the Government or the local magistrates. . . . Judges in South Africa, even when South African born, are usually men of experience and culture. They have been to universities overseas and have a wider outlook than the average South African magistrate, policeman, or Member of Parliament."
>
> (Edward Roux)[22]

> "While I was sitting next to a Cabinet minister in London, that gentleman said to me that whatever criticism they may have had against the policies applied in South Africa, they certainly have no criticism to level against the Supreme Court of South Africa. I am told on good authority that the English judges, who are undoubtedly the most eminent judges in the world, consider only the South African judges as their equals."
>
> (Hon Mr Justice C J Claassen,
> Transvaal Provincial Division,
> Supreme Court of South Africa)[23]

> " . . . . "
>
> (Nelson Mandela)[24]

These three passages give a fair indication of the range of views concerning the role and attitudes of the South African judiciary which have been expressed over the years. As stated above, this book attempts to provide a factual basis for a firm conclusion regarding the performance of the AD during the first forty years of its life. It is important to indicate, and discuss briefly, the conditions under which the court has operated since Union, in order to situate the judiciary within its general social context and to determine whether the course adopted by it was the only one available in 1910. For the judges will, to a large extent, have seen their function in the government of the country by reference to the events and influences which they experienced.

In what follows, no attempt is made to summarise and debate the complex issues which surround the theory of judicial decision-making, nor to apply these to South African judges. Further, the general arguments for and against judicial activism do not fall to be

[22] *Time Longer than Rope* 228. Roux had been a communist, and had found himself before the courts (see *R v Roux & another* 1936 AD 271).

[23] "Retain the Bar and Side-Bar" (1970) 87 *SALJ* 25.

[24] Statement to magistrate's court of October 1962 set out in Mandela *The Struggle is my Life* 125–6. This has had to be excluded because of the Internal Security Act 74 of 1982. The gist of the statement is that white judicial officials cannot fail but be judges in their own cause.

discussed here. The purpose is, rather, to indicate various facts and trends which deeply affected the South African judicial process at that time, and to see what scope was available to a judge who felt duty-bound to pursue justice and equality, rather than the strict letter of the law, when their paths diverged.

Were there any social factors which would have allowed Lord De Villiers and his fellow judges to change their accustomed style of adjudication in favour of a more active approach as guardians of that majority of the population which was not part of the ruling group? Could the appellate judiciary realistically have assumed a more "political" stance, in the sense, not of party political affiliations, but of recognising the special difficulties caused by the colour or class of a particular litigant, and of being aware of the wider social implications of their judgments?

Several factors prevalent at the time, and since, suggest that the judges would have been able to justify their pursuit of a slightly unusual course of action, considering the times and their training, in order to dispense justice more equally under the law. These and other factors would simultaneously have produced strong pressures in favour of a continuation of the conventional manner of operating, so that they must be examined in some detail.

The Formal Structure

The constitutional framework of the South African state is of central importance in any consideration of the position of the judiciary in that society. For, without formal allocation of judicial power beyond that customarily assumed, the courts will be less willing to consider issues normally the preserve of the other departments of government.

Now the actual state structure which was approved by the National Convention, which led to the creation of the Union of South Africa in 1910, was that of a unitary constitution with a powerful central government. There had been a long-running agitation to secure a federal or confederal combination of the Southern Africa colonies,[25] and the Natal and some Free State delegates proposed such an arrangement at the first meeting of the Convention.[26] However, strong speeches by John X Merriman and General Smuts ensured that union was eventually adopted as the form of state organisation.[27] It is interesting to note that one of the main arguments used by opponents of federalism was the potential politicisation of an unelected judiciary, and the judicial role in the

[25] See *The Conference* (articles from *Cape Town Daily News* 1875); *Papers relating to a Federation of the South African Colonies*. Presented to both Houses of Parliament by Command of His Majesty 1907; and Haasbroek "Die Federasiebeweging in Suid-Afrika" 13 *Historia* (1968) 6.

[26] See Walton *The Inner History of the National Convention* Chapter III; and Thompson *The Unification of South Africa* 186–92.

[27] Only the Natal delegates supported federation to the end of the debate.

Australian and Canadian constitutions was cited as a development which should be avoided.[28] Consequently, the Convention agreed to grant only limited powers to provincial administrations to supervise education, roads, municipal affairs, and suchlike.[29]

This defeat for the federal concept had a direct effect on the judiciary, in that it was not faced with impetus for a change in its accustomed constitutional function. The transportation of a Westminster-style governing structure to Southern Africa ensured that the conventional attitude to the allocation of powers to the branches of government would continue unchanged on the British pattern, with any American influence firmly excluded. A marginal alteration in the judicial sphere came in the form of the court's ability to interpret those parts of the South Africa Act[30] which laid down procedures to be followed by Parliament in acting with regard to the "entrenched clauses",[31] and those which determined the powers of the Provincial Councils to levy taxation.[32] These changes alone were not sufficient to force the judges to review their position in government as a whole.

On the other hand, further provisions of the Act of Union are of interest here. Although the South Africa Act indicated that it was "expedient ... to define the executive, legislative, and judicial powers to be exercised in the government of the Union",[33] it failed specifically to lay down the limits of judicial authority.[34] Instead, it was content to create the Supreme Court of South Africa,[35] incorporating the existing colonial courts, and adding an Appellate Division, as an intermediate forum of appeals which would reduce reliance on the Privy Council in London.

What is important is that the Union Parliament was not created "sovereign" in the accepted sense of the Westminster model. Although it had "full power to make laws for the peace, order, and good government of the Union",[36] bills passed by Parliament could be disallowed by the King,[37] or reserved for his assent,[38] until the passage of the Statute of Westminster in 1931. Further, throughout the period under review, the Union Parliament remained procedurally bound to act unicamerally with a two-thirds majority if it wished to vary franchise or language rights.[39] This requirement

[28] See Malan *Konvensie-Dagboek* 72–7; 119–21; and 179–81; Walton *op cit* 60–1.
[29] South Africa Act, section 85.
[30] 9 Edw VII Ch 9 (1909).
[31] *Ibid* sections 35 and 137, shored up by section 152. A two-thirds majority of both Houses of Parliament sitting together was required to change the provisions relating to the franchise and language rights.
[32] Examples of legal challenges to Provincial Ordinances are to be found in *R v Williams* 1914 AD 460; *Middelburg Municipality v Gertzen* 1914 AD 544; and *De Waal, NO v North Bay Canning Co Ltd* 1921 AD 521.
[33] In the Preamble.
[34] There was no equivalent of the present Republic of South Africa Constitution Act 32 of 1961, section 59(2), which declares that no court of law shall be competent to pronounce on the validity of an Act of Parliament.
[35] In Part VI. [36] Section 59. [37] Section 65. [38] Section 66.
[39] The "entrenched clauses"—see note 31 above.

implied a duty on the court to check whether the correct procedure had been followed.

Thus, on a purely formal level, the judges were certainly not explicitly bound to adopt a position uncritical of unjust legislative or executive action.

THE CONSTITUTIONAL AND LEGAL HERITAGE

The official constitution was not imposed upon a region which had no past experience of politics and government, however. The Cape and Natal contributed overwhelmingly British ideas and conventions to the Union, but the constitutional past of the OFS and the Transvaal was of a different order. To a certain degree, recent Southern African history provided appropriate backing for the idea of a judiciary more involved in the "political" side of life.

To begin with, the Chief Justice of the Cape Colony had been *ex officio* President of the Legislative Council,[40] the colonial second chamber of Parliament. In practice, this had involved him in political intrigue and conflict. Then, the OFS constitution had entrenched several "political rights",[41] and had required a large majority of the Volksraad[42] in successive sessions to amend these rights.[43] The court had acted as a watchdog to ensure compliance with this stipulation by the legislature.[44]

In addition, the neighbouring ZAR had witnessed an intense struggle between executive and judiciary fifteen years before Union, in which Chief Justice Kotzé, under the influence of American Supreme Court practice,[45] had attempted to declare invalid a particular legislative procedure used by the Volksraad. Although President Kruger and his executive had triumphed over the judiciary, a strong case had been made out by the latter, and the issues had been widely and thoroughly canvassed.[46] All South African lawyers would, thus, have been confronted with questions and arguments as to their own relations with government and society, and would have been alive to possible problems. Whether this would have made them hesitant to take on the other departments of government again, or merely keener for further battle, is a matter for conjecture.

[40] This situation was first adopted with the grant of "representative" government in July 1853 (see Order in Council of March 11 1853, section 2 of the Schedule).

[41] Such as the right of peaceful assembly and petition (Article 20); of equality before the law (Article 58); and of property (Article 60).

[42] Literally "Peoples' Council", the national assembly of the Boer republic.

[43] This was originally fixed at a three-quarters majority for three successive annual sessions, soon reduced to two successive annual sessions.

[44] Even though there was no effective legal sanction for the enforcement of the limitations. See Thompson "Constitutionalism in the South African Republics" 1954 *Butterworths South African Law Review* 49 at 53.

[45] Kahn "The History of the Administration of Justice in the South African Republic" (1958) 75 *SALJ* 397 at 416.

[46] For a good account of these events, see Thompson "Constitutionalism" 57–73.

The eminent historian, L M Thompson, sums up the philosophy of the two republics succinctly:[47]

> "The constitutional history of these two nineteenth-century republics shows that there are two distinct and widely divergent Afrikaner constitutional traditions. On the one hand there is the tradition of the OFS, where the written constitution was rigid, the judiciary was in fact completely free and independent, and the legislature did not in fact exceed its proper powers—an admirable tradition in all these respects. On the other hand there is the tradition of the South African Republic, where the written Constitution was often ignored, the judiciary became the creature of the governments of the day, and the legislature passed laws on any subject, including constitutional amendments, in the simplest possible way."

Besides this constitutional legal background, South African law itself contained traces of support for a judicial approach which gave greater prominence to "justice" and less to the will of the legislature. Roman-Dutch authority displayed signs of "natural law" thinking,[48] and English law, while heavily influenced by positivism at the time, paid some attention to natural justice and equity. Although the struggle between the courts, the King, and Parliament in seventeenth-century England, and the constitutional teaching of John Locke had receded into the somewhat distant past, they figured large in the formation of the British and United States systems of government, to which South African judges were wont to refer for guidance. At the least, therefore, they were aware of such constitutional incidents, and their lessons for the judicial branch of government.

So it seems that the first incumbents of the appellate bench could have relied on a relatively broad range of reasons to justify the adoption of a changed role for themselves and future judges of appeal. Certainly, as far as "lawyers' law" was concerned, it seems to have been widely expected that the AD would pursue a policy of innovation in the creation of a "South African" common law. Professor R W Lee puts it thus:[49]

> "Seldom have the courts of any country enjoyed the opportunity which the courts of South Africa now enjoy, of moulding the laws to their will, inspired but not hampered by tradition, aided but not checked by the legislator. For . . . the task of directing the course of legal development has principally rested with the courts of justice. . . . The general impression . . . is of a system of law singularly rich in the sources that it draws upon, singularly unhampered in the use it makes of them; of a court which enjoys a liberty of action scarcely to be paralleled in the history of modern states."

This might describe the freedom of action a little too enthusiastically, but the author was prepared to repeat his basic theme in another article,[50] and little opposition to his views appeared in print. So it

[47] *Ibid* 73.

[48] For an acknowledgement of the natural law strain in Roman-Dutch law, see Carey Miller (1973) 90 *SALJ* 86.

[49] "Law and Legislation in the Union of South Africa" (1923) 40 *SALJ* 442 at 443, 448.

[50] In the *Law Quarterly Review*, reprinted as "Roman-Dutch Law in South Africa" (1924) 41 *SALJ* 297.

appears as if the judges had a relatively free hand in determining what the law should be, and were not subject to any specific statutory limitations on their relationship to the rest of government and society.

On the other hand, these influences must be weighed against the considerable force exerted by British imperial practice. In particular, it is important to note that the first forty years of Union witnessed no great constitutional disputes which would have challenged the judges to analyse and define their position in government, nor was the latter a major topic for academic debate. A brief sampling of some of the published writing will provide a taste of the atmosphere in those years.

Majority opinion in professional circles seems to have been firmly against the exercise by the judges of any right to criticise legislation according to standards such as fairness or equality, or in certain respects to innovate where the "law" was silent. Most of these comments were elicited as the result of particular judicial decisions,[51] though one was prompted by constitutional difficulties in other countries,[52] and another was the direct conclusion of a discussion on constitutional law.[53] The basic motivation of several of these writers seems to have been that judges should not become immersed in party-political controversies.[54] Nevertheless, there were a few writers who maintained that the judiciary was entitled to a more dynamic constitutional function, and that they should regard equality of treatment as the cornerstone of South African law.[55] An early note in the SALJ decried the concept of a "High Court of Parliament" in South Africa, and affirmed the power of the Supreme Court to decide the validity of an Act of Parliament,[56] while Melius de Villiers argued that "... it is an inherent power, and duty of the Court to interpret ... the constituting law ...".[57] Later in the period, Findlay stated bluntly that "[sovereigns] are fantasies flowing from the doctrine of Sovereignty and they obscure the fact that the Legislature is not almighty but a human and strictly limited part of our social organization".[58]

Notwithstanding these last remarks, the importance of a "constitutional crisis" in spurring lawyers to consider their position in society

[51] See for example Aquilius "Immorality and Illegality in Contract" (1942) 59 *SALJ* 16 and 333; anonymous note on "*Crimen Laesae Majestatis*" (1938) 55 *SALJ* 14; L I Coertze "Vonnisbespreking" (1937) 1 *THR-HR* 114. Aquilius (F P van den Heever in fact) maintained that the legislature was the bulwark between the executive and the liberties of the people.

[52] "T" "President Roosevelt and the Supreme Court" (1942) 59 *SALJ* 103.

[53] P U Rissik "The Legislative Authority of the Union Parliament" (1921) 38 *SALJ* 132.

[54] Unsigned note on "The Judiciary and Legislation" (1918) 35 *SALJ* 54.

[55] Unsigned note on "The 'Black Peril' Question" (1911) II *Union Law Review* 3.

[56] Unsigned note (1914) 31 *SALJ* 165.

[57] "The Court and the Constitution" (1919) 36 *SALJ* 365. The writer was a former Chief Justice of the OFS, which helps to explain his view.

[58] George Findlay "The Source of Law" (1948) 65 *SALJ* 497 at 502.

can be gauged from the reaction[59] to the controversy which surrounded the removal of coloured voters from the common voters' roll in the 1950's. Most articles at this time agreed on the existence of a limited "testing-right" in the courts' arsenal.

So it can be seen that, although there was some academic attention devoted to the question of the judicial role in the state in the years before 1950, there was no incident which forced lawyers to define their position, and that of the judges in particular, and little incentive to challenge the *status quo*. The judiciary exacerbated this state of affairs by its failure to discuss the issues at stake. Very few South African judges have written about, or been prepared publicly to debate, their own views of their role in wider society,[60] a reluctance which they justify on the ground of non-involvement in "politics". Of the twenty-three judges of appeal covered by this study, Rose Innes and Kotzé alone published autobiographical accounts, neither of which touched in any detail on their terms of judicial office.[61] Several other judges published books or articles after appointment to the AD,[62] but none focussed on the judicial process or the judiciary's part in government.

If they had been more forthright, would they have expressed the self-righteous indignation and self-adulatory justification so evident in more recent pronouncements?[63] The quotation of just two statements by Chief Justices will indicate the pervasive train of thought:

> "A measure of aloofness attaches to judicial office. . . . The public expression, and particularly in the news media, by judges of opinions on controversial issues, whether or not such issues have political overtones, is to be deprecated. . . . In South Africa a judge must interpret the enactments of legislatures and administer the law, not as he would like it to be, but as it is set out in the relevant statutory provisions."
>
> (Ogilvie Thompson, CJ)[64]

> "The task of our Courts—I would emphasize, their only task—was to ascertain the intention of Parliament as expressed in this enactment. . . . It is one thing, and a very proper one, for a judge to point out defects in a statute or to draw attention to results, in all probability not anticipated or appreciated, which work hardship or injustice, i e to matters which Parliament might presumably want to rectify. It is a very different thing, and in my view a very improper one, for a judge to rush into a political storm or into the wake of it, in a strongly contested matter in which

[59] Examples are: D V Cowen "The Entrenched Sections of the South Africa Act" (1953) 70 *SALJ* 238; E McWhinney "Court versus Legislature in the Union of South Africa: The Assertion of a Right of Judicial Review" (1953) 31 *Canadian Bar Review* 52; H W R Wade "The Senate Act Case and the Entrenched Sections of the South Africa Act" (1957) 74 *SALJ* 160; G A Mulligan "Judicial Criticism of Legislation" (1953) 70 *SALJ* 35.

[60] Two notable exceptions being Blackwell *Are Judges Human*? and Broome *Not the Whole Truth*.

[61] See Ch II below.

[62] Notably Centlivres, Feetham, Schreiner and Van den Heever: see Ch II below.

[63] See Claassen's remarks quoted at the head of this section; and those of Curlewis, J in *S v Mothopeng & others* 1979 (4) SA 367 (T) at 368–9.

[64] "Centenary Celebrations of Northern Cape Division of the Supreme Court" (1972) 89 *SALJ* 23 at 32–4.

Parliament has, by way of firm deliberate policy, knowing what it is about and in the valid exercise of its legislative powers, laid down what is to be done."

(Steyn, CJ)[65]

It is unlikely that the earlier judges of appeal would have adopted quite such a detached and isolated approach to "... controversial issues, whether or not such issues have political overtones". They seem to have drawn a clear distinction between their views on broad socio-economic matters (which can be termed "political"), which it was acceptable to hold, and any "party-political" loyalties, which were not tolerated. It is this latter sense which appears to have been central to whatever debate there was in the early years on the "political" position of the judiciary. As one commentator observed[66] in 1913: "... the profound truth ... that judges set aside their politics once they have reached the Bench cannot be questioned."

By way of summing up the pervasive trends of debate, it is important to refer back to the threefold division of the meaning of "political" outlined above. Now it is plain that legal opinion, from 1910 to the present, discards the possibility or desirability of any "party-political" part to be played by the judiciary. Authoritative South African constitutional law today denies the existence of a judicial capacity to test the substance of legislation in a "constitutional-legal" sense,[67] and most modern observers choose not to write about the judiciary's role in the wider "legal-political" field. Yet it appears that this state of affairs has not always held sway, and that the concentration on the exclusion of the "party-political" aspect of the judicial personality before 1950 implicitly recognised the ineradicable nature of judicial involvement in "legal-political" questions.

No doubt the absence of significant discussion of these wider issues and the fact of judicial security of tenure[68] contributed to an atmosphere which fostered judicial caution, and even conservatism. Further, in the early days of Union, the delicate balance of power in the white group would have acted as an additional discouragement from judicial participation in controversial debate in public.

So it can be seen that the intellectual climate in which the judiciary was operating provided firm support for the assumption of a conventional approach to the judicial function by the court, but with some pressure to the contrary.

The Judges Themselves

This leads on to a vital aspect of any consideration of judicial role, the traditions and training of the judicial character. In one sense, as

[65] "Regbank en Regsfakulteit" (1967) 30 *THR-HR* 101 at 106–7.

[66] Unsigned note on "The Training of Judges" (1913) 30 *SALJ* 324.

[67] See Hahlo and Kahn *The South African Legal System and its background* Ch II Part IV; VerLoren van Themaat (Wiechers) *Staatsreg* 510–13; Hosten, Edwards, Nathan, and Bosman *Introduction to South African Law and Legal Theory passim.*

[68] Except on an address of both Houses of Parliament on ground of misbehaviour or incapacity: South Africa Act, section 101; and Supreme Court Act 59 of 1959, section 10(7).

will be seen,[69] the personalities of those men appointed to the AD from 1910 to 1950 prompt the suspicion that a more active "political" function would not have been entirely unsuitable. Almost without exception, the judges were men of great conviction, highly esteemed in the white community, and educated more widely than most of their compatriots.

In addition, their roots were predominantly in the Cape, so that a more relaxed and urbane outlook on matters of race might be expected of them. A further factor which would have added to public acquiescence in a more active judicial role was the deep involvement of many of the judges of appeal in political affairs and government office before their appointment to the Bench. For this reason, people would have been accustomed to political utterances from the individuals concerned. Another tool for their use was the fact that the AD had no predecessor in Southern Africa,[70] so that there were no specific conventions limiting its activities. The rarefied atmosphere of appellate proceedings would have contributed further to an ability to see issues dispassionately, and to give expression to ideal values which judges in the lower divisions might have balked at. All these points suggest an authority, based on prestige and public confidence, to become involved in broad social issues in a way which had not been conventional in the past.

Another institutional factor which was relevant was the judicial oath of office, which most judges were required to take, and which laid down that they were to do right according to the law and usages of the country.[71] This exhortation certainly did not rule out an appeal to concepts such as "natural justice" or "equality before the law" by a judge who wished to justify his interpretations of a legal or factual situation. The important determinant in this formulation is what he understands by "right": should a judge consider the governing social group alone when applying these ideas, or should the welfare of the whole population be in his mind? The terms of the judicial oath would have supported the latter sense, had the judges wished them to do so.

However, ranged against these factors, which would have provided a way for the judiciary to assume a more active position in favour of justice and equality before the law, were the considerable inhibitions emanating from judicial history and training. Of great importance is the fact that all judges throughout the period of study were men, and were drawn from the group designated as "Euro-

[69] For further details see Ch II below.

[70] There had been a Court of Appeal for the Cape Colony alone from 1879–1886.

[71] See Kahn "The Judicial Oath" (1954) 71 *SALJ* 22. Strangely enough, until the Supreme Court Act, 59 of 1959, came into effect, only Cape and Natal judges took an oath of office, thus: "I . . . do swear that I will well and truly serve His Majesty . . . in the office of Judge . . ., and that I will do right to all manner of people after the Laws and Usages of this Colony without fear, favour, affection or ill-will. So help me God."

pean". There was no statutory reason for this, but various influences and practices ensured that only white men became eligible for appointment, and that they came from an élite section of that group.[72] The effects of such facts on judicial impartiality were clearly summed up in respect of the English judiciary by Lord Justice Scrutton:[73]

> "I am not speaking of conscious impartiality; but the habits you are trained in, the people with whom you mix, lead to your having a certain class of ideas of such a nature that, when you have to deal with other ideas, you do not give as sound and accurate judgments as you would wish. . . . It is very difficult sometimes to be sure that you have put yourself into a thoroughly impartial position between two disputants, one of your own class and one not of your class."

So, it was highly improbable that the interests and needs of the non-élite and non-white citizens of the country would have been foremost in the judges' minds, or even understood by them. This would have made it difficult for them to overcome prejudices and fill gaps in their knowledge when faced with cases whose outcome depended on features unique to blacks or women or workers, for example.

Again, a significant influence in the lives of all South African judges, but particularly those who held office in 1910 and soon afterwards, was their tradition and training. The dominant centre in terms of legal practice prior to Union had been the Cape, whose Bar had supplied most of the judicial personnel for Natal, the OFS, and the ZAR, as well as four of the first five appeal judges. The Cape courts were entirely wedded to the English system of procedure and practice, and studies of the English courts at the turn of the century show that the House of Lords, at any rate, was withdrawing from a political stance to a more declaratory and mechanistic approach to its judicial power.[74]

As well as the direct influence of the Cape legal tradition, most of those appointed as judges had been educated academically and professionally in England, where positivism was in the ascendancy. This doctrine would have discouraged overt judicial forays into "law-making" activity, especially in sensitive areas of policy, and would have stressed the subordination of judges to the legislature. In turn, this approach to law and its administration would not have inspired any judge to great feats of innovation in his constitutional role.

Moreover, when judicial character and tradition are considered, the dominance of Lord De Villiers in the Southern African legal world must be noted. He had been Chief Justice of the Cape for more than a generation; he had been closely involved in public affairs of great moment over the years; and he had been attempting, for at least two

[72] See Ch II below.
[73] "The Work of the Commercial Courts" (1923) 1 *Cambridge Law Journal* 6 at 8.
[74] See Stevens "The Role of a final Appeal Court in a Democracy: The House of Lords today" (1965) 28 *Modern Law Review* 509 at 513–6; Abel-Smith and Stevens *Lawyers and the Courts* 121–5; and Stevens *Law and Politics* 183–4.

decades, to set up a single court of appeal for all the territories in the sub-continent. In pursuit of the latter goal, he had encountered much political opposition to a powerful supreme court, which must have convinced him that only a court with a very limited constitutional role would be acceptable to all parties.[75]

The importance of Lord De Villiers's views becomes apparent when it is realised that he was the unanimous choice as chairman of the National Convention, as well as a member of several of its committees. His original proposals for the administration of justice[76] were referred to a committee, of which he was chairman,[77] in the deliberations of which they were substantially altered.[78] He claimed, nevertheless, when he presented the committee's report to the Convention, that only his caution, and fear of their non-acceptance, had prevented him from including the final recommendations in his initial ideas.[79] This is likely to have been the case, because the amended version gave more power to the AD and less to the ex-colonial courts, which he would have imagined to be an unpopular change. In fact, the lower expense involved seems to have been determinative[80] in swinging delegates' votes behind a scheme which was probably more in line with the desires of Lord De Villiers and the other judges.[81]

Lord De Villiers was also the undisputed choice as first Chief Justice of the Union, an office which he occupied until his death in 1914. He had received his legal education in London; he had built up the Cape courts on the English model; he had introduced many English legal concepts to South Africa; he had been a member of the Judicial Committee of the Privy Council since 1897; and he was made a member of the House of Lords at Union. In addition, his manner tended to intimidate those with whom he came into contact,[82] so that there can be little doubt that his views on the judicial function, predominantly shaped by his English legal experiences,[83] set the tone for the members of the first AD Bench, whose direct influence continued until 1932.[84]

With these forces, which strongly favoured an interpretation of the judicial function along the lines of the Westminster system, as a backdrop, it is clear that some other exceptional circumstances would

[75] For details of this aspect of his life, see Walker *Lord De Villiers and his times* Ch VI.
[76] Set out in *Minutes of the Proceedings* with Annexures (selected) of the South African National Convention 62–3.
[77] Other members being: Merriman, Sauer, Colonel Greene, Morcom, General Smuts, Lindsay, Fischer, General Hertzog, and Coghlan.
[78] *Minutes* 117–23.
[79] Malan *op cit* 119.
[80] Walton *op cit* 205.
[81] Of whom Rose Innes and Solomon, at least, were consulted.
[82] See for example James Rose Innes *Autobiography* 243–4.
[83] See a note on his life by Irene Rumpff in VI *Codicillus* 1 (1965) 39; and Walker *Lord De Villiers* 85–91.
[84] With the death of the last of the five original judges of appeal, J A J de Villiers.

have been necessary to produce a change in the judges' attitudes to their role in society. It is submitted that the political and social conditions in South Africa at the time afforded whatever further justification was necessary for a judge who felt obliged to follow the interests of justice when they conflicted with the law.

South Africa 1910 to 1950

The perception of most participants and observers over many decades has been that South Africa forms part of a politically volatile and highly unstable region. In 1910 in particular, the fragility of the single state created from what had, only eight years before, been the antagonistic factions in a bitter war was a reality of which all politically-conscious South Africans were acutely aware. The source of danger to this national arrangement was, until 1945 at least, seen as the strained relations between English- and Afrikaans-speaking whites, manifest in disputes in industry and over the nation's involvement in both World Wars, as well as the problems linked to economic depression and exploitation.

Intra-white group rivalries constituted the "race-problem" at that time, but the "native question" lingered as a major preoccupation, and came to be regarded as the chief danger to the *status quo* from the end of the Second World War onwards. All these social and political uncertainties combined to induce a judicial caution which would have inhibited any bold initiative in the field of judicial role, for fear of upsetting the delicate balance which was being engineered between English- and Afrikaans-speaking whites.

But there was a different aspect of this apparent instability, to be found in the franchise arrangements which obtained after Union. Now the South African population has been ruled since that time by a legislature and executive whose constituency is a mere fifth of the country's citizenry, a fact largely due to race discrimination. But this had not been the case in all four colonies which entered the Union. In the Cape, and, to a lesser extent, Natal, the franchise requirement had not been based overtly on race, and the Cape had followed a generally liberal tradition.[85]

However, political compromise at the National Convention had led to the domination of the racial attitudes of the former Boer republics and Natal, and the Cape liberals had had to be content with procedural safeguards for existing and future voting rights of non-whites within its boundaries.[86] But this capitulation did not mean that the struggle for a non-racial franchise had ended. It was assumed by many of those who had held out for greater rights for black South Africans that the entrenched provisions in the South Africa Act formed the mere minimum, from which the right to vote could be

[85] See Thompson *The Unification of South Africa* 212–26.
[86] See note 31 above.

generally extended in a non-racial manner. This hope was founded on the presumption that, with the passage of time, racial tension would ease substantially, and that the more liberal attitudes associated with the Cape would predominate over those of the other provinces.

The approach of the courts to race in the cases which came before them could have contributed in a not insignificant way, through the educational effect of their judgments on the public, to the eventual victory of one side. It might be expected, perhaps, that an AD composed of Cape men would have done its utmost to continue the liberal tradition when the opportunities arose, which they could have achieved by an enlightened attitude to questions of race in cases and statutes. The adoption of such a stance was plausible because of the dichotomy in historical approaches to racial affairs, but it was also constitutionally justifiable in pursuit of the goal of equality before the law.

The Options

In the light of this brief survey of the conditions and influences under which the AD operated in the period under consideration, the choice available to the judges of appeal must be defined. From some of the circumstances described, there seems little doubt that Lord De Villiers and his brethern could have found support in the constitution, the law, and the social history of South Africa for a more vigorous judicial stance, especially in the protection of that part of the population which had no access to the formal political process. Had they been inclined to take the initiative, for whatever motive, it is possible that the strength of their characters, allied with calls upon such concepts as justice and equality, would have won the day.

On the other hand, there can equally be no doubt that most of the forces of tradition, training, and structure, backed by the judges' sense of social and political reality, indicated the path of caution, formalism and reserve prescribed for the judiciary by British constitutional history and practice. It was obviously of little concern to the authorities at the time that the Union Parliament was governing an entirely different and heterogeneous population, compared with that in Britain. With the benefit of hindsight and as a result of tragic historical developments, it can be seen that they were misguided not to have allowed for the peculiar nature of Southern Africa's social complexities.[87]

The cases discussed in the body of this book give a fair sense of the direction chosen by the appellate judiciary. Indications can be sought in the judges' willingness to express an opinion on a controversial topic, to disapprove of unjust executive or legislative action, and in their adaptability to changes in one area, while remaining obdurate in

[87] In regard to judicial "choice" and "options" in general see the "Postscript" below.

another. These all provide clues to the
those who served on the appellate Benc

Before such a task is undertaken, it
facts about the court's history, an
members.

CHAPTER TWO

THE STRUCTURE AND JUDICIAL PERSONNEL OF THE APPELLATE DIVISION 1910–1950

"An Act to constitute the Union of South Africa. . . . And whereas it is expedient . . . to define the . . . judicial power [. . .] to be exercised in the government of the Union. . . . There shall be an Appellate Division of the Supreme Court of South Africa. . . ."[1]

In order to comprehend and comment upon the actions and pronouncements of the judges of appeal in the period under discussion, it is necessary to set out briefly various facts concerning the formation and functioning of the court, and the occupants of the Bench.

THE COURT

The Appellate Division was constituted as a court as a direct result of the process of political union of the four British Crown Colonies in Southern Africa: the Cape of Good Hope, Natal, Orange River Colony, and Transvaal. The latter two were formerly the Boer Republics of the Orange Free State and the Zuid Afrikaansche Republiek. As a prelude to Union, Britain had granted these ex-republics responsible government in 1907, and their elected representatives had conferred with those of the Cape and Natal in a National Convention in 1908 to 1909, the outcome of which was the enactment by the British Parliament of the South Africa Act.[2] This Act created a new colony, the Union of South Africa, and granted it a status in the Empire similar to that of Australia, Cananda, and New Zealand. Although the idea of closer relations between the colonies had been in circulation for some time, suspicions engendered by war, and markedly different views on matters such as the franchise, relationships between the colonies,[3] and language rights contributed to a fragile constitutional arrangement in political terms.

However, one issue upon which there had been comparatively little discussion and dissent was the creation of a central court of appeal for the whole of South Africa. This was due partly to the

[1] South Africa Act 1909, Preamble and section 96.
[2] 9 Edw VII (Ch 9).
[3] Renamed "provinces" after Union.

dominance of the Cape legal tradition,[4] and partly to the pre-eminence of its Chief Justice, Sir Henry de Villiers, who had been working strongly in favour of such a court for more than two decades.[5] Various questions, such as the status of the colonial courts after Union,[6] the composition of the appellate judiciary,[7] and the seat of the court[8] did cause slight difficulties, though only the last problem persisted for any time after Union.[9]

In the end, Part VI of the South Africa Act created a single Supreme Court of South Africa, with an Appellate Division at its apex, and provincial and local divisions at its foundations.[10] The Act provided for security of judicial tenure, the civil and criminal jurisdictions of the various divisions, rules of procedure, and the officers of the court.[11] The seat of the AD (whose jurisdiction was to run throughout the country) was designated as Bloemfontein, although cases could be heard elsewhere "at the convenience of suitors".[12]

The court having been constituted, much speculation surrounded the appointment of its judges.[13] There was little doubt that Sir Henry de Villiers would be the first Chief Justice of South Africa, and the elevation of Sir James Rose Innes and Sir William Solomon to the permanent positions of ordinary judges of appeal did not cause much surprise. C G Maasdorp's appointment to the Judge Presidency of the Cape and as additional judge of appeal was also expected, but there was some disquiet at the appointment of Jacob de Villiers as Judge President of the Transvaal as well as fifth member of the AD. It was regretted that no place could be found at appellate level for J G Kotzé, former Chief Justice of the ZAR.[14]

[4] This was true both before and after the Anglo-Boer War (1899–1902), the reason being that the educational institutions of the Cape were, in general, the only ones able to produce students of sufficiently high standard to attend university, and so to become qualified lawyers.

[5] He was also President of the National Convention. See Walker *Lord De Villiers and his Times* Ch VI "The Courts" 97–120.

[6] In particular, the status of the Eastern Districts Court at Grahamstown, which claimed for itself equal status with the courts at Cape Town, Pretoria, Bloemfontein, and Pietermaritzburg as a provincial division. See for example a letter from J G Kotzé to Sir James Rose Innes, dated 12 February 1909 (No 464, Innes Archive, SA Public Library, Cape Town—hereafter IA).

[7] Discussion focussed on the advisability of having two classes of Judges of Appeal (Ordinary and Additional) and of having acting Judges of Appeal. See letter of Sir Henry de Villiers to Rose Innes, dated 22 October 1908 (No 462 IA) and the latter's reply of 27 October (No 463 IA). Innes did not wish to confine appointment as Judges of Appeal to those already sitting as judges; having W P Schreiner in mind, he advocated the selection of those best suited to appeal work (James Rose Innes *Autobiography* [Ed B A Tindall] 236).

[8] The location of which depended absolutely on the Convention's choice of legislative and executive capital, a matter which was resolved at the last moment.

[9] Below.

[10] Sections 95, 96, and 98 of the Act.

[11] Sections 101, 103, 107–8, and 114–15. For a more detailed exposition, see G W Keeton (Gen Ed) *The British Commonwealth: The Development of its Laws and Constitution* Vol 5 *The Union of South Africa* Ch 6.

[12] Section 109.

[13] Power of appointment lay in the hands of the Governor General in Council, by virtue of section 100.

[14] See for example (1910) I *Union Law Review* 171–2 and 274–6.

The court sat for the first time on June 4 1910,[15] and from the start it was conscious of its consolidating function in reconciling different judicial precedents and practices in the courts of the four former colonies under its sway, and in moulding a broad South African law, adaptable to the requirements of the times.[16] The judgments and demeanour of the court were generally favourably received,[17] and it was not long before detailed articles on aspects of its operation began to appear in the *South African Law Journal*.[18] This general satisfaction with the court's operations has continued to the present, although Parliament has not hesitated to amend the legislation governing the number of judges and the powers of the court, acting as the result of judicial requests or of its own volition.[19] Nevertheless, two issues caused problems, and brought the AD into the public spotlight on several occasions.

Firstly, the question of the seat of the court was a constant source of irritation in the early years.[20] Bloemfontein had been adopted as a political compromise at the National Convention, but it was not viewed enthusiastically by the first incumbents of the Bench.[21] They did their best to ensure that as many cases as possible were heard in Cape Town,[22] by using the provision in the South Africa Act which allowed a case to be heard elsewhere "at the convenience of suitors".[23] This practice upset many Free Staters, among them General Hertzog, the Minister of Justice, and in 1912[24] Parliament amended section 109 to the effect that the court could sit elsewhere only in exceptional circumstances and on application by a suitor at Bloemfontein. This so annoyed Lord De Villiers that he threatened to resign. He had to be placated by a special plea from General Botha, the Prime Minister, and an arrangement whereby, during his own term of office, applications for a change in venue might be heard elsewhere than at Bloemfontein.[25]

[15] When Lord De Villiers, CJ (as he had become) laid down various rules of conduct for the AD: see 1910 AD ix–xi. Rule 14 required records of cases on appeal to be printed—only in 1936 was it amended to make typed or roneographed records acceptable: see (1937) 54 *SALJ* 77–8.

[16] See for example *Joubert v Enslin* 1910 AD 6, and *Marcus v Stamper & Zoutendijk* 1910 AD 58.

[17] See comments by "H J F" in (1911) II *Union Law Review* 324–7; although an anonymous note did appear which decried the ". . . portentous length of the collective judgments of the judges . . ." (see (1912) 29 *SALJ* 223).

[18] See "E R R" "The Jurisdiction of the Appellate Division" in (1915) 32 *SALJ* 20–33.

[19] For details of amendments up to 1959, see Keeton *op cit* 253–6. There is now a special statute The Supreme Court Act 59 of 1959, which regulates the functions of the superior courts.

[20] See Keeton *op cit* 250–1.

[21] Walker *op cit* 494–5; Rose Innes *op cit* 244–7.

[22] On average, about one third of the sitting-days of the court were held outside Bloemfontein in the period 1910–1919 (Department of Justice Annual Reports).

[23] Section 109. Many people thought that the judges interpreted this clause to mean "at the convenience of the judges". Indeed, Rose Innes, while not favouring a peripatetic tribunal, states that Lord De Villiers repeatedly declared that the National Convention had intended the court to have a free hand in the matter, and his view was supported by J X Merriman and J W Sauer (*op cit* 246).

[24] Administration of Justice Act 27 of 1912, section 16.

[25] Rose Innes *op cit* 247, and see section 16.

Even so, the court continued to spend some of its time outside Bloemfontein,[26] and few of the judges of appeal took up permanent residence there, despite the fact that the choice of Bloemfontein as judicial capital was confirmed by the construction of a new court building in 1929.[27] Matters came to a head in 1933 when the editor of the Bloemfontein newspaper *The Friend* was fined for contempt of court for publishing an anonymous letter which had sharply attacked the judges for hearing a case in Cape Town on the ground that the Free State summer conditions might damage their own health and that of counsel in the case.[28] The letter-writer (who is believed to have been none other than the Judge President of the OPD, Dr F E T Krause)[29] stated that this was no reason at all for moving from Bloemfontein, and called for the judges' resignations if they could not respect the spirit as well as the letter of the law. Since that time very few sittings have been held elsewhere than in Bloemfontein, though most judges have continued to live there only during court terms.

The second issue which has never been far from the forefront of public debate is that of the method of appointment of judges, and, more particularly as it affects the AD, their "promotion" to the appellate Bench and the Chief Justiceship. Until 1957, the most senior judge of appeal was invariably appointed Chief Justice, and the pattern appears to have been restored recently.[30] In the case of initial appointment to the provincial Bench, the power resided in the Governor General in Council,[31] and, with a few exceptions, his choice was always made from the ranks of those practising at the Bar.[32] In turn, judges of appeal have usually been appointed from the judges of the provincial divisions, though there have been some notable exceptions to this convention.[33]

Public concern has been aroused by the possibility of the abuse of this method of appointment for party-political ends,[34] but on the whole the public has been reassured by the selection of long-serving advocates. Training at the Bar tends to produce conservative

[26] Department of Justice Annual Reports 1920–1927.

[27] Keeton *op cit* 251, and see (1930) 47 *SALJ* 44–5.

[28] *In re Mackenzie* 1933 AD 367.

[29] See Keeton *op cit* 251 note 20; and Blackwell *Are judges human?* 182–3.

[30] See Kahn "Oliver Deneys Schreiner—The Man and his judicial World" (1980) 97 *SALJ* 574; and Keeton *op cit* 266.

[31] Section 100 of the South Africa Act. In practice there would seem to be some prior consultations with the Chief Justice in the case of appointments to the AD.

[32] There have apparently been eight appointments from outside the Bar since 1910, each greeted with protest from the organised Bar. See Kahn in (1971) 88 *SALJ* 512, and (1972) 89 *SALJ* 245. Three of these (D H Botha, L C Steyn and F P van den Heever) became appeal judges. Centlivres, although Parliamentary Draftsman for fifteen years, is not included, as he remained nominally at the Bar.

[33] On only two occasions have vacancies on the AD been filled by persons not judges of other divisions (T de V Roos and F W Beyers), neither of which was welcomed, and neither a success. (Keeton *op cit* 266 note 36.)

[34] See eg E Brookes "The Administration of Justice" Ch IV in *Coming of Age* section III, at 390–2.

attitudes, whatever the party affiliations of the advocates may be, and it ensures that successful practitioners (who will be candidates for judicial appointment) display an admirable blandness on controversial matters. Thus the executive has had a relatively "safe" field from which to choose its judges, including, if it wishes, those with strong political views, while it has maintained an impression of impartiality in the exercise of this choice.

In the period under review, the AD was for practical purposes the highest court in Southern Africa,[35] hearing civil and criminal appeals under certain conditions from all the provinces, Southern Rhodesia,[36] and the mandated territory of South West Africa (from 1920 onwards).[37] The size of a judicial quorum for the hearing of a case varied with time, and was dependent on whether the case was civil or criminal in nature.[38]

The Personnel

With this skeletal outline of the structure and functioning of the court in mind, it is important to shift attention to the type of person who occupied the Bench from 1910 to 1950, as this will aid a more accurate assessment of judicial utterances, within the social conditions of the time. Table I sets out the bare biographical details of the twenty-three judges of appeal who held permanent office at some time during that period,[39] and these are followed by a short paragraph of additional information on each of them, as well as a summary of any trends evident in this data.

Before proceeding, a point not immediately apparent must be noted. All judges of appeal in this period were male, and all were drawn from what is accepted in South Africa as the "white" (European) group. Although there was no statutory reason for this,[40] it is explicable in terms of dominant customs and prejudices, and the structure of the legal profession.[41] Against this background, the judges will be dealt with in the order of their appointment as permanent members of the appeal court.

[35] Up till 1950, appeals could still be taken to the Privy Council in London, with special leave from that body. (South Africa Act, section 106), but this freedom was seldom exercised (Keeton *op cit* 252).

[36] By section 103 of the South Africa Act, in civil cases only.

[37] By the AD Act 12 of 1920, section 3.

[38] Keeton *op cit* 253.

[39] Most of the information in the tables has been compiled from biographical sketches published in the SALJ; from Roberts *South African Legal Bibliography*; and from Comaroff *Judges of the AD and the Transvaal Bench from 1943 to 1970*. The major source will be indicated in the table, and any supplementary sources will appear when each judge is discussed below.

[40] No restriction was laid down as to type of person in section 100 of the South Africa Act. Today, the only qualification is that of "fit and proper person" in the Cabinet's view (Supreme Court Act 59 of 1959, section 10(1)*(a)*).

[41] Although section 20 of the Charter of Justice of 1828 (Cape) provided that "persons" could be enrolled as attorneys, the AD held that this must be interpreted to include only males—*Incorporated Law Society v Wookey* 1912 AD 623.

TABLE I

NAME:	DE VILLIERS, Henry	ROSE INNES, James	SOLOMON, William Henry
Date of Birth and Death	1842–1914	1855–1942	1852–1930
Place of Birth	Paarl, Cape	Grahamstown, Cape	Philippolis, OFS
Father's Occupation	Land Surveyor	Magistrate, Superintendent-General of Education	Missionary
Schools Attended	SA College, Cape Town	Bedford, and Gill College, Cape	Lovedale and Bedford, Cape
Universities Attended	Utrecht; London	Cape of Good Hope	Peterhouse, Cambridge
Career before Appointment as Judge	Inner Temple. Cape Bar, 1866 MLA and A-G, Cape Colony	Bank Clerk. Cape Bar, 1878 MLA and A-G, Cape Colony. QC, 1890	Inner Temple Cape Bar, 1877 Kimberley Bar
Date and Court of Initial Appointment	1873 Chief Justice, Cape Supreme Court	1902 Chief Justice, Transvaal Supreme Court	1887 HCGW
Years at AD	1910–1914 Chief Justice	1910–1914, JA 1914–1927, CJ	1910–1927, JA 1927–1929, CJ
Activities in Retirement	Died in office	Founded and organised Non-racial Franchise Association	
Approximate Period at Bar (Average 19 years)	7	24	10
at Provincial Level (Average 14 years)	37	8	23
at AD (Average 11 years)	4	17	19
Extraordinary Features	Knighted 1877; KCMG 1881; Privy Council 1897; Baron 1910; President of Cape Legislative Council, and National Convention	KCMG 1901	President of Special Court, during Anglo-Boer War; served in EDC (1896) and THC (1902)
Principal Sources of Reference	(1901) 18 *SALJ* 1; E A Walker *Lord De Villiers and his Times* Ch V, VI, XXVII	(1902) 19 *SALJ* 1; James Rose Innes *Autobiography* Ch XXI–XXVII	(1904) 21 *SALJ* 189

TABLE I (*contd*)

NAME:	MAASDORP, Christian George	DE VILLIERS, Jacob Abraham Jeremy
Date of Birth and Death	1848–1926	1868–1932
Place of Birth	Malmesbury, Cape	Fauresmith, OFS
Father's Occupation	Doctor	Deputy Sheriff
Schools Attended	Graaff-Reinet, Cape	Grey College, Bloemfontein
Universities Attended	Cape of Good Hope London	Victoria College, Stellenbosch Amsterdam
Career before Appointment as Judge	Inner Temple; Cape, Kimberley and Grahamstown Bars; A-G, Transvaal 1878–1880.	Middle Temple; Johannesburg Bar, 1894; State Attorney, OFS, 1896–1898; Minister of Mines & A-G, Transvaal, 1907–1910
Date and Court of Initial Appointment	1885, EDC	1910, JP, TPD
Years at AD	1910–1922, JA	1910–1929, JA 1929–1932, CJ
Activities in Retirement		Died in office
Approximate Period at Bar (Average 19 years)	14	16
at Provincial Level (Average 14 years)	25	0
at AD (Average 11 years)	12	22
Extraordinary Features	Served in Cape Supreme Court (1896–1910)	Fought for Boers in Anglo-Boer War, 1899–1902 Prisoner of war on Bermuda
Principal Sources of Reference	(1907) 24 *SALJ* 129	(1907) 24 *SALJ* 237

JUTA, Henry Hubert	KOTZÉ, John Gilbert	WESSELS, Johannes Wilhelmus
1857–1930	1849–1940	1862–1936
Cape Town	Cape Town	Cape Town
Publisher	Businessman	Solicitor
SA College, Cape Town	SA College, Cape Town	SA College, Cape Town
London	London	Cape of Good Hope Downing, Cambridge
Inner Temple; Cape Bar, 1880; MLA, A-G, and Speaker, Cape Colony; MP 1910–1914	Inner Temple Cape Bar, 1874 Grahamstown Bar, 1876	Middle Temple Cape Bar, 1886 Pretoria Bar, 1887
1914, JP, CPD	1877, ZAR, Chief Justice	1902, THC
1914–1923, JA	1922–1927, JA	1923–1932, JA 1932–1936, CJ
	Writing	Died in office
34 0 9	3 45 5	16 21 13
	A-G, Southern Rhodesia, 1900–1902; judge in EDC 1903–1913 (JP 1904); CPD 1913–1922 (JP 1919); Knighted 1913	Knighted, 1909 JP, TPD, 1920–1923 Writer on law
(1915) 32 *SALJ* 1	(1903) 20 *SALJ* 101. *Biographical Memoirs and Reminiscences*, vols 1 and 2	(1937) 43 *SALJ* 451

TABLE I (*contd*)

NAME:	CURLEWIS, John Stephen	STRATFORD, James
Date of Birth and Death	1863–1940	1869–1952
Place of Birth	Paarl, Cape	Port Elizabeth, Cape
Father's Occupation	Priest	Businessman
Schools Attended	Diocesan College, Cape Town	St Aidan's, Grahamstown, Cape
Universities Attended	Cape of Good Hope	Exeter, Oxford
Career before Appointment as Judge	Teacher Clerk in Master's office Prosecutor Transvaal Bar, 1887	Surveyor; Chancery Bar, London, 1898–1901; Transvaal Bar, 1901; KC, 1912
Date and Court of Initial Appointment	1903, THC	1921, TPD
Years at AD	1927–1936, JA 1936–1938, CJ	1927–1938, JA 1938–1939 CJ
Activities in Retirement		
Approximate Period at Bar (Average 19 years)	16	23
at Provincial Level (Average 14 years)	24	6
at AD (Average 11 years)	11	12
Extraordinary Features	JP, TPD, 1924–1927	Awarded Honorary LLD by University of the Witwatersrand, 1944
Principal Sources of Reference	(1925) 42 *SALJ* 121	(1921) 38 *SALJ* 248

ROOS, Tielman Johannes de Villiers	BEYERS, Frederick William	DE VILLIERS, Jean Etienne Reenen
1879–1935	1867–1938	1875–1947
Cape Town	Paarl, Cape	Cape Town
Businessman	Land Surveyor	Priest, MLC
SA College, Cape Town	SA College, Cape Town	SA College, Cape Town
Cape of Good Hope	Cape of Good Hope	Cape of Good Hope St John's, Cambridge
Articled Clerk Judge's Clerk Attorney Pretoria Bar MP, 1915 Minister of Justice, 1924	Side Bar, ZAR, 1888; Johannesburg Bar, 1904; MLA (Transvaal) 1907–1910; A-G, Transvaal, 1911–1914; A–G, Cape, 1914–1915; Cape Bar, 1915–1924; MP, 1918–1929; Minister of Mines, 1924–1929	Fellow, St John's, 1900 Cape Bar, 1900 KC, 1919 Water Court judge, 1913
Direct to AD	Direct to AD	1920, JP, OPD
1929–1932, JA	1932–1937, JA	1933–1939, JA
Returned to party politics	Returned to party politics	
27 0 3	28 0 5	20 13 6
Used AD as a refuge from political difficulties; died young of broken health	Wrote the first judgments in Afrikaans in the AD	Health declined, became a recluse, after brilliant academic career
(1930) 47 *SALJ* 169	(1924) 41 *SALJ* 417	(1920) 37 *SALJ* 1

TABLE I (*contd*)

NAME:	DE WET, Nicolaas Jacobus	WATERMEYER, Ernest Frederick
Date of Birth and Death	1873–1960	1880–1958
Place of Birth	Aliwal North, Cape	Graaff-Reinet, Cape
Father's Occupation	Farmer, MLC	Farmer
Schools Attended	Aliwal North Public School	Graaff-Reinet College Stellenbosch Gymnasium Bath College, England
Universities Attended	Victoria College, Stellenbosch; Cambridge (non-collegiate)	Gonville and Caius, Cambridge
Career before Appointment as Judge	Cape Bar, 1896; Transvaal Bar, 1896; MLA (Transvaal), 1907–1910; MP and Minister of Justice, 1913–1921; Senator and Minister of Justice 1921–1924; Senator 1924–1929; Pretoria Bar, 1931	London Bar, 1904 Cape Bar, 1905
Date and Court of Initial Appointment	1932, TPD	1922, CPD
Years at AD	1937–1939, JA 1939–1943, CJ	1937–1942, JA 1943–1950, CJ
Activities in Retirement	Leader of Torch Commando	
Approximate Period at Bar (Average 19 years)	36	18
at Provincial Level (Average 14 years)	5	15
at AD (Average 11 years)	6	13
Extraordinary Features	Fought for Boers in Anglo-Boer War, 1899–1902	A good sportsman
Principal Sources of Reference	(1914) 31 *SALJ* 369	(1923) 40 *SALJ* 99

TINDALL, Benjamin Arthur	CENTLIVRES, Albert van der Sandt	FEETHAM, Richard
1879–1963	1887–1966	1874–1965
Namaqualand, Cape	Cape Town	Penrhos, Monmouthshire
Priest	Businessman	Priest
	SA College School Cape Town	Marlborough
Stellenbosch	SA College, Cape Town New College, Oxford	New College, Oxford
Civil Servant, 1902 Private Secretary to Judge, 1903 Transvaal Bar, 1903 KC, 1919	Middle Temple; Cape Bar, 1911; Parliamentary Draftsman, 1920–1935; KC, 1927	Inner Temple; Deputy Town Clerk, Johannesburg, 1902–1905; Transvaal Bar, 1903; MLC (Transvaal), 1907–1910; MP 1915–1923; KC, 1919
1922, TPD	1935, CPD	1923, TPD
1938–1949, JA	1939–1950, JA 1950–1957, CJ	1939–1944, JA
	Opposed apartheid in Universities	Opposed apartheid in Universities; acted as JA
19	24	20
16	4	16
11	18	5
JP, TPD 1937–1938	Rhodes Scholar; Chancellor UCT (1951–1966); Honorary DCL, Oxford	Chairman, various commissions of inquiry; CMG, 1924; Chancellor, University of the Witwatersrand, 1949–1961.
(1923) 40 *SALJ* 245	(1935) 52 *SALJ* 409	(1928) 45 *SALJ* 179

TABLE I (*contd*)

NAME:	GREENBERG, Leopold	SCHREINER, Oliver Deneys
Date of Birth and Death	1885–1964	1890–1980
Place of Birth	Calvinia, Cape	Cape Town
Father's Occupation		Politician/Lawyer
Schools Attended	Grey College, Bloemfontein SA College School, Cape	Rondebosch Boys' High School, Cape SA College School, Cape
Universities Attended	SA College, Cape	SA College, Cape. Trinity College, Cambridge
Career before Appointment as Judge	Attorney, 1909 Advocate, 1911 KC, 1924	Inner Temple Fellow, Trinity College, 1916 Transvaal Bar, 1920. KC, 1935
Date and Court of Initial Appointment	1924, TPD	1937, TPD
Years at AD	1943–1955, JA	1945–1960, JA
Activities in Retirement		President, South African Institute of Race Relations
Approximate Period at Bar (Average 19 years)	13	17
at Provincial Level (Average 14 years)	19	8
at AD (Average 11 years)	12	15
Extraordinary Features	Very young when appointed a judge; 1938–1943, JP, TPD; Honorary LLD, Witwatersrand and UCT; Jewish	Chancellor, University of the Witwatersrand, 1962–1974; President, Special Court, World War II; Honorary LLD, Witwatersrand and UCT
Principal Sources of Reference	(1926) 43 *SALJ* 1	(1938) 55 *SALJ* 1

VAN DEN HEEVER, Francois Petrus	HOEXTER, Oscar Hendrik	FAGAN, Henry Allan
1894–1956	1893–1970	1889–1963
Heidelberg, Transvaal	Rouxville, OFS	Tulbagh, Cape
Farmer	Doctor	Lawyer
Ermelo, Transvaal	Rouxville	Somerset West, Cape
Transvaal University College, Pretoria	Grey University College, Bloemfontein; Emmanuel, Cambridge	Victoria College, Stellenbosch London
Teacher, 1917–1918; Civil Servant, 1919; Windhoek Bar, 1921; Senior Government Law Adviser, 1926; Foreign Affairs Law Adviser, 1928	Bloemfontein Bar, 1918 KC, 1929	Inner Temple; Cape Bar, 1914; Assistant Editor, *Die Burger*; Professor at Stellenbosch, 1920; MP and Minister for Native Affairs, 1933–1939; Cape Bar, 1939
1933, SWAHC	1938, SWAHC	1943, CPD
1948–1956, JA	1949–1963, JA	1950–1957, JA 1957–1959, CJ
Died in office	Acted as a JA	Stood for election as State President, 1961 Senator
12	20	29
15	11	7
8	14	9
Served in OPD, 1938–1948 (JP, 1948); SA Government delegate at Imperial Conferences; writer and poet; Secretary for Justice	Served in EDLD, 1944–1949 (JP, 1948)	Third most senior judge of appeal on appointment as Chief Justice; writer and poet; Chairman, Commission of Inquiry into Native Affairs
(1949) 66 *SALJ* 135	(1940) 57 *SALJ* 241	(1943) 60 *SALJ* 1

The First Court

Lord De Villiers was without doubt the dominant character of the legal world of Southern Africa from the last two decades of the nineteenth century until his death four years after Union. His initial appointment as Chief Justice of the Cape Colony at the age of 31, directly from the office of Attorney General, caused much gossip and even some resentment, so much so that he was forced to administer the oath of office to himself, as the other judges refused to do so.[42] But he soon overcame this uncertain start to his judicial career, and, though criticised for borrowing too heavily from English law,[43] he stands credited today with being the moulding architect of a broad "South African" law.

Notwithstanding his elevation to the Bench, he remained in the forefront of colonial politics in Southern Africa,[44] both through his Presidency *ex officio* of the Legislative Council (upper house) of the Cape government, and through his involvement in the settlement of many constitutional and political disputes.[45] He was often tempted to re-enter political life officially, never more so than in the first half of 1893, when he was requested to stand for election as President of both Boer Republics, and when C J Rhodes sounded him out with a view to De Villiers's forming a ministry in the Cape.[46] He was the automatic choice as President of the National Convention and first Chief Justice of the Union, and he died while fulfilling the duties of Officer Administering the Government.[47]

As a lawyer, he was well read in the Roman-Dutch works, especially Voet, but not as deeply versed in the civilian authorities as some of his brother judges.[48] He was extremely annoyed when overruled by the Privy Council or another court. This trait led to the celebrated *causa*—consideration dispute with J G Kotzé in the law of contract, finally resolved after De Villiers's death.[49] As a judge it is said that he was more suited to acting in a court of first instance than in an appellate capacity, his outstanding characteristic being an "extraordinary intuitive perception of the side on which equity lay and [a] determination to find a way out if the letter of the law seemed likely to do injustice".[50] He is said to have seen no distinction between justice and equity in his court,[51] and to have delivered

[42] See the account in (1901) 18 *SALJ* 1 at 3–4.

[43] In particular, in regard to consideration in contract. See Walker *op cit* 84–5.

[44] *Ibid* Ch XII. He was regarded as a liberal, being close to J X Merriman and J W Sauer (215).

[45] For example he was a Royal Commissioner to arrange for the retrocession of the ZAR at the end of the Boer War of Independence 1881; he represented the Cape at the Colonial Conference in Ottawa 1894; and he interceded in the dispute between Chief Justice Kotzé and President Kruger of the ZAR in 1897–1898. (see (1901) 18 *SALJ* 1, and Walker *op cit* Ch XVII).

[46] See a full account in Walker *op cit* 216–37.

[47] An office assumed by the Chief Justice in the absence of the Governor General.

[48] Walker *op cit* 81.

[49] *Ibid* 85–6; Rose Innes *op cit* 209–10.

[50] Walker *op cit* 83. See also Sampson *My Reminiscences* 54.

[51] Walker *op cit* 84.

judgment regardless of political consequences.[52] His manner in court was brusque and cold, and his brief opinions were delivered promptly.[53]

In his person, he suffered from frequent bouts of ill-health, and he was not know for his humour or expansiveness. He was an excellent counsellor, but was "debarred by his office, his aloofness and an excess of caution from becoming a leader of men".[54] He was popular with witnesses and counsel, and, above all else, he detested lying, sharp practice, and culpable ignorance.[55] He was widely mourned, both in Southern Africa and the British Empire, on his death.[56]

Apart from Lord De Villiers, the best known judge of the period was Sir James Rose Innes. The only appeal judge in the early years to have been educated entirely in South Africa, Rose Innes is widely regarded as the greatest judge to have served before 1950.[57] Although he had been deeply involved in party politics before his appointment as Chief Justice of the Transvaal in 1902,[58] he endeavoured to separate himself from political matters while a judge.[59] A liberal in the Cape tradition by persuasion, he retired from the AD while at the height of his ability and influence, and devoted the remaining fifteen years of his life to the cause of the Non-Racial Franchise Association in an unsuccessful attempt to stave off the actions of the government which resulted in the transfer of the 11 000 black voters in the Cape to a separate roll.[60] His influence continued on the Bench after he left it, through his life-long friendship with W H Solomon, and his close links with J W Wessels, both of whom served as Chief Justice after him.[61]

Rose Innes felt strongly that a judge should not return to party politics after leaving the Bench,[62] but he was not afraid to express his views on matters of public concern. Whilst a judge, he did this through his letters,[63] and, after his retirement, through the medium of his speeches and his autobiography, which was published only

[52] *Ibid* 94.

[53] *Ibid* 90–1; and Sampson *op cit* 54.

[54] Walker *op cit* 175.

[55] *Ibid* 91–2.

[56] He had achieved imperial renown through his membership of the Judicial Committee of the Privy Council from 1897, and his creation as a baron in 1910—the only South African to be honoured in this way.

[57] See F N Broome *Not the Whole Truth* 124; Blackwell *op cit* 20; and Dugard *Human Rights and the South African Legal Order* 385.

[58] See Rose Innes *op cit* Ch VIII–XVII, and (1902) 19 *SALJ* 1.

[59] He advised against his being made President of the Legislative Council of the Transvaal in the period of responsible government prior to Union—see Rose Innes *op cit* 200–1.

[60] *Ibid* Ch XXX and Appendix A.

[61] See Innes's tribute to Solomon (Appendix D of his *Autobiography*); and Wessels's tribute to Innes ((1931) 48 *SALJ* 459–63), as well as letters exchanged by them (eg No 498, 499, 501, 509, 738 and 897 IA).

[62] Rose Innes *op cit* 127.

[63] See letters to his wife and others (No 685, 687, 692, 702, and 714 IA) on political matters of current concern.

after his death.[64] He was very close to his wife and only daughter, and the latter's early death did much to hasten his own.[65]

Sir James's retirement left the Chief Justiceship vacant for his closest friend, Sir William Solomon, who is unusual as a judge of that time because of his lack of involvement in politics.[66] He had not been a great success at the Bar, but his detailed grasp of the law was, nevertheless, recognised by his appointment as a judge at the age of 34.[67] He was regarded as one of the soundest lawyers and best judges produced by South Africa,[68] and he had "... a direct and logical mind, a balanced judgment, an insight into character, and the faculty of firm, yet not hasty, decision—and those qualities were reinforced by a lofty character and a high standard of duty".[69] His ancestors were of Jewish descent, though his grandfather had become a non-conformist minister, and his family was well known in the Eastern Cape.[70]

C G Maasdorp was another of the early judges noted for his brief but unsuccessful foray into political life, and his early appointment to the Bench. His brother, Sir Andries Maasdorp, was Chief Justice of the OFS and acted as an additional judge of appeal. Maasdorp himself was a hard worker,[71] but he suffered from indifferent health and took little part in public affairs.[72]

The second De Villiers of the period, J A J ("Japie"), was not closely related to Lord De Villiers, and came from a very different background. Wounded during the Anglo-Boer War and imprisoned by the British for much of it, he re-entered politics after the grant of responsible government to the Transvaal, became a Minister, and was appointed straight to the AD at Union.[73] Although he was neither a hard nor a quick worker, he had a great ability to simplify complex matters. He died at a comparatively young age, while occupying the chair of Chief Justice.[74]

The five judges above were the original incumbents of the appellate Bench, and those that follow below were appointed in piecemeal fashion, as vacancies arose.

The Rest of the "Old Guard"

Lord De Villiers's death brought Sir Henry Juta to the appeal court, straight from a seat in the Union Parliament. He had served as an

[64] His strong views are apparent in: Rose Innes *op cit* 195–6, 232, 251–5, 285 and Appendix A.

[65] See "Introduction" to Innes's *Autobiography* by B A Tindall.

[66] See Rose Innes *op cit* 307; and letters from Solomon to Innes (No 499, 501, 507, 508 and 509 IA).

[67] (1904) 21 *SALJ* 189.

[68] Blackwell *op cit* 22; and (1930) 47 *SALJ* 44–5.

[69] Remarks of Innes at unveiling of bust to Solomon, in (1931) 48 *SALJ* 150 at 151.

[70] Blackwell *op cit* 22.

[71] Letter from W H Solomon to Innes dated 20 June 1911 (No 498 IA).

[72] (1907) 24 *SALJ* 129 at 131.

[73] (1907) 24 *SALJ* 237.

[74] See tribute to him by Wessels in (1932) 49 *SALJ* 488–9.

elected representative at the Cape for over twenty years, while carrying on a substantial practice at the Bar. He was likened to his predecessor in style and manner,[75] but Innes found him "rash".[76]

On C G Maasdorp's retirement, the "infallibles"[77] in Bloemfontein were joined by the longest-serving and most controversial of judges, Sir John Kotzé. He had accepted the Chief Justiceship of the ZAR in 1877, at the age of 27, and he retired from judicial office fifty years later.[78] His tenure of office in Pretoria was marked by vicissitudes which he could hardly have expected: his adopted country was annexed by the British while he was travelling north to take up his post, and he ended up by being dismissed from office by President Kruger just over twenty years later.[79] This occurred because, influenced by trends in the constitutional law of the United States,[80] he dared to hold that legislative sovereignty under the Grondwet (Constitution) of the ZAR lay with the people. In this way he denied validity as "law" to decisions of the Volksraad,[81] and incurred the wrath of the Executive.

This independence of mind,[82] though it proved his undoing in this case, was respected by many, and he soon found himself back on the Bench. He devoted much time to his researches and writing, which he treasured,[83] and he completed two volumes of biographical reminiscences in the thirteen years between retirement and death.[84]

One of those who read Kotzé's memoirs and found them "unutterably dull"[85] was Sir John Wessels, whom Innes described as carrying "heavier guns than any of us as regards Roman-Dutch Law".[86] He was author of *The History of Roman-Dutch Law*, and was a strong advocate of the codification of South African law in order to

[75] See (1915) 32 *SALJ* 1 at 6. His father was the founder of the foremost legal publishing concern in South Africa, his mother was a sister of Karl Marx.

[76] See letter to Lady Innes of 27 October 1922 (No 685 IA).

[77] In Kotzé's own words in a letter to Prof R W Lee, reprinted in (1950) 67 *SALJ* 174 at 183.

[78] Blackwell *op cit* 193 remarks that Kotzé became extremely deaf at the end and that his "limpet-like quality" of staying on the Bench helped to persuade the legislature to introduce a retiring age of 70 for the judges. This seems unlikely in view of the fact that no retiring age was laid down in the South Africa Act, but Parliament laid down a compulsory age of 70 for all judges appointed after 1912, by the Judges Salaries and Pensions Act 16 of 1912, section 6.

[79] Despite Sir Henry de Villiers's attempt to mediate in this famous dispute. See Walker *op cit* Ch XVII. Kotzé apparently held De Villiers partly to blame for his dismissal. (Walker *op cit* 320.)

[80] See Kahn "The History of the Administration of Justice in the South African Republic" (1958) 75 *SALJ* 397 at 416.

[81] In the case of *Brown v Leyds, NO* (1897) 4 Off Rep 17, and explained in further detail in Appendix I to Vol II of his *Biographical Memoirs and Reminiscences*.

[82] See his views against cigarette smoking (*Memoirs* Vol I 52); against an over-emphasis on sport (*ibid* 83); and strongly in favour of capital punishment (*Memoirs* Vol II 154).

[83] His view on the *causa*—consideration dispute with Lord De Villiers triumphed in *Conradie v Rossouw* 1919 AD 279. He also translated Van Leeuwen's work and compiled law reports while in Pretoria.

[84] Entitled *Biographical Memoirs and Reminiscences*. Volume I appeared in 1934; Volume II is not dated, but was edited by BA Tindall and appeared after Kotzé's death in 1940.

[85] Letter to Innes of 2 June 1927 (No 738 IA).

[86] *Op cit* 200.

protect its Roman-Dutch roots from the "insidious creeping" of English law ideas.[87]

Innes's rather indulgent view of Wessels was that, although "quick of apprehension and quick in decision, he was vehement in manner, but not obstinate; his vigorous intellect was always prepared to grapple with a new argument".[88] Unfortunately, his brilliance as an academic and at the Bar, and his impulsiveness and habit of thinking aloud sometimes led practitioners to believe that, once his mind was made up, no argument they used could change his opinions.[89] In private life a simple and kindly man, he died in harness, and was much lamented by his colleagues.

Wessels was succeeded as Chief Justice by one of his closest friends,[90] J S Curlewis, distinctive for his lack of involvement in politics, and the fact that he had not been educated abroad. His main features as a judge seem to have been his[91] "unbelievably meticulous" attention to detail,[91] his "plaintive and querulous nature" (as though he was anxious to understand just what the case was about, but could not),[92] and his hard work and monotonous conversations.[93] He was a frail man physically,[94] and there is a record of his wish for retirement fully five years before he actually did so.[95]

Curlewis's short term as Chief Justice was followed by that of an equally brief occupant, James Stratford, who had built on a great career as an advocate to achieve rapid promotion to the AD.[96] Reasoning, analysis, and masterly skill in cross-examination were said to be his strong points, but he was not regarded as a learned man, with little Latin, less Greek, and only a nodding acquaintance with Afrikaans.[97] He worked thoroughly and rapidly, yet Blackwell comments that "it is noteworthy how many of his judgments have since been dissented from . . .".[98] His poor health did not prevent him from attaining the age of 82, nor from living to receive an Honorary LL D degree from the University of the Witwatersrand in 1944.[99]

[87] (1937) 54 *SALJ* 451; and see his speeches on this subject published in (1920) 37 *SALJ* 265, and (1928) 45 *SALJ* 5. But this by no means indicates that he was anti-British, as his place of education and acceptance of a knighthood indicate.

[88] *Op cit* 200.

[89] See tribute by Stratford in (1936) 53 *SALJ* 462 at 463; and the reaction of Blackwell *op cit* 148, and Broome *op cit* 147, who were both intimidated by his demeanour on the Bench. Solomon seemed to regard Wessels's knowledge as less than encyclopaedic (see letter to Innes of 1 December 1911 No 509 IA).

[90] See (1937) 54 *SALJ* 451, where Curlewis is reported as being unable to deliver an address in memory of Wessels through being overcome by emotion.

[91] Blackwell *op cit* 191.

[92] Broome *op cit* 147.

[93] See letter from Wessels to Innes of 2 June 1927 (No 738 IA).

[94] See letter from Stratford to Innes of 24 September 1932 (No 859 IA) and Wessels to Innes of 9 January 1935 (No 926 IA).

[95] See letter of Wessels to Innes of 26 April 1933 (No 897 IA).

[96] (1921) 38 *SALJ* 248.

[97] (1952) 69 *SALJ* 1.

[98] *Op cit* 21.

[99] See report in (1944) 61 *SALJ* 258.

A Mixed Bag

This rather orderly and predictable stream of appointments was upset by the two which followed, the most controversial of the period. It is plain that Tielman Roos was using the AD as a safe refuge from which to plan his re-entry into party politics. Although an advocate by profession, with a large practice, he was first and foremost a politician in the Nationalist cause, and had been Minister of Justice and Deputy Prime Minister from 1924.[100] However, deteriorating health and a clash of personality and policy with his rival for the leadership of the National Party, Dr D F Malan, led to his resignation from the Cabinet and his acceptance of Sir William Solomon's seat on the Bench.[101]

Throughout Roos's three years in Bloemfontein, rumours circulated about his impending return to active politics, though he constantly denied that they had any substance. Nevertheless, following conversations with General Smuts, he resigned late in 1932, only to find that Smuts had joined General Hertzog, the Prime Minister, to form the United Party, and Roos was left out in the cold.[102] He died of ill-health soon afterwards. Although not known for his liberal ideas as regards the colour question,[103] Blackwell has described him as "that genial, much-loved Nationalist politician".[104] It is clear, however, that his cavalier treatment of the position of judge of appeal was not well received, and his return to formal politics was "deeply deplored" by Innes.[105]

Such expressions of dismay do not appear to have distressed the government unduly, as their following nomination indicates. They brought a former Cabinet colleague, F W Beyers, out of retirement, as an obvious reward for political services rendered. Although Beyers had been Attorney-General of the Transvaal and the Cape in the five years immediately after Union,[106] and had carried on a substantial practice at the Bar until 1924, his major interest had been in the fortunes of the National Party,[107] and only ill-health had curtailed his political career.[108] His judicial tenure lasted a mere five years, its

[100] (1930) 47 *SALJ* 169. A former clerk of Curlewis, he appointed him to the AD.

[101] See C M van den Heever *Generaal J B M Hertzog* 569–72.

[102] Van den Heever *op cit* 573–81, and 590–9.

[103] He is said to have remarked: "I would be insulted if a Native apologised to me." See Roux *Time Longer than Rope* 203.

[104] *Op cit* 117.

[105] *Op cit* 127. There is no direct reference to Roos, but there is no doubt that Innes was writing of him.

[106] Although his appointment as Attorney-General of the Transvaal was given a guarded welcome in public (see (1911) II *Union Law Review* 342), its party-political nature "shocked" Solomon, who saw it as an example of Hertzog's (Minister of Justice) patronage. (See letters to Innes of 20 June 1911 and 6 July 1911 No 498 and 499 IA.) Hertzog was Prime Minister when Beyers was elevated to the AD.

[107] See details in (1924) 41 *SALJ* 417. He stood for the party again in the OFS after leaving the AD at age 70. (Blackwell *op cit* 187.)

[108] See Van den Heever *op cit* 533. He retired in 1929.

peculiar feature being the extensive use he made of the Afrikaans language in his judgments, [109] despite being a "master of English". [110]

The appointments of Curlewis and Stratford in 1927, and the political motives underlying those of Roos and Beyers[111] had been bitter blows to the expectations of the next man to join the AD Bench, J E R ("Etienne") de Villiers. A brilliant academic sojourn at Cambridge had established him as a jurist rather than as a practitioner, and this justified his early appointment as the Water Court judge in the Cape, and his subsequent transfer directly to the Judge Presidency of the OPD.

The idea was that "Oofy", as he was known, [112] should be on hand in Bloemfontein to act as a judge of appeal, with a permanent position in the offing. As it turned out, "he had to suffer the mortification of seeing others, some of them lesser luminaries in the legal firmament, whatever might have been their standing in other walks of life, appointed to the place which was rightly his". [113] In addition, the death of his wife, his dearest companion, led to a breakdown in his health and an incapacity for sound work after his eventual appointment. He died, a sad recluse, eight years after an early retirement. [114]

A fascinating insight into the characters of those on the Bench in 1933 is provided by a letter written by Chief Justice Wessels to Innes, which is to the following effect:[115] The court has just completed a strenuous term. Wessels himself has lumbago, Curlewis ("Curly") a bronchial cold, and Stratford and De Villiers ("Oefie") "are always crocks". Beyers is chirpy ("he feeds on scraped carrots, lettuce, and lemon juice") but is a "curious card". He has some curious ways of interpreting statutes, and thinks as an attorney rather than a barrister. He insists on giving judgment in Afrikaans, though his language is "anything but clear", and he always addresses counsel who have Dutch names in Afrikaans, even if the entire case is in English. Wessels finds this all very disconcerting, as he can see from the language used that Beyers thinks in, and is better at, English.

"Oefie" is more jumpy than ever, and it is impossible to converse with him. "Curly" is as precise as ever with regard to detail, and is thinking of resigning again. If Wessels knew that Beyers's appointment would not be repeated it would be alright, but he does not want a court full of disgruntled politicians with no judicial experience. He ends with an outburst which gives a clear idea of his own forthright

[109] He was the first judge of appeal to do so: see *Souter v Norris* 1933 AD 41 at 48–50.

[110] According to Broome *op cit* 147, whose opinion of Beyers rose with time.

[111] See letter from Stratford to Innes dated 24 September 1932 (No 859 IA).

[112] Or "Oefie". Apparently a reference to his pronunciation of the name "Ovid". See tribute to him by Watermeyer, CJ in (1947) 64 *SALJ* 137–40.

[113] *Ibid* 140.

[114] *Loc cit*.

[115] Dated 26 April 1933 (No 897 IA). Although not a direct quotation, it is rendered in the style in which it was written.

views. Referring to the state of Europe after the First World War, he writes: "A stupid war and a stupid peace has made this stupid world much more stupid than it used to be, though heaven knows it was stupid enough even to begin the war."

THE PROFESSIONALS

Wessels's death led to the arrival in Bloemfontein of a former politician, N J de Wet, who had eschewed any direct move from Cabinet to Bench,[116] and had accordingly returned to serve his apprenticeship at the Bar and as a judge in the TPD. Like Japie de Villiers, he had fought for the Boer forces in the war of 1899 to 1902, and had been enticed into political life and the office of Minister of Justice through his close association with General Botha, who was the first Prime Minister of the Union.[117]

While Chief Justice, De Wet was offered the Governor Generalship of the Union, but he declined and acted instead as Officer Administering the Government for three crucial years in the mid-1940's.[118] In retirement, he was active as one of the leaders of the Torch Commando, an extra-Parliamentary group opposed to the policies of the Nationalist government after 1948.[119]

A second Chief Justice followed De Wet in 1937, but this time from one of the Cape's leading families. E F Watermeyer, who had much of his formal education in England, and was a great sportsman, turned out to be a champion of Roman-Dutch law, not averse to disregarding precedent where he thought it necessary.[120] He was not a controversial man, either on or off the Bench, and it is with the end of his term as Chief Justice that the focus of this research terminates.

Another non-controversial appointee at this time was B A Tindall, former private secretary to Innes in the Transvaal, and the editor of Innes's autobiography.[121] Tindall's manner was regarded as "unerringly . . . objective",[122] and he sat on the Bench as a permanent judge for 27 years before statutory retirement.

The circumstances surrounding the elevation of Albert v d S Centlivres to the court of appeal are worth recording, not only for the light which is shed on some of the considerations which play a part in this process, but also because of his subsequent career. Centlivres had become Partliamentary draftsman in 1920, after a slow start at the Bar, and, after some time as an acting judge, he was made a puisne judge in the CPD in 1935.[123] Despite being a junior judge in 1939, he

[116] On two occasions, in 1914 and 1924, it was thought natural that he should accept a seat on the AD. See (1960) 77 *SALJ* 133, and Innes *op cit* 257.
[117] (1914) 31 *SALJ* 369.
[118] (1943) 60 *SALJ* 275.
[119] Blackwell *op cit* 187.
[120] (1950) 67 *SALJ* 332.
[121] (1923) 40 *SALJ* 245.
[122] (1963) 80 *SALJ* 164—a tribute by Steyn, CJ on Tindall's death.
[123] (1935) 52 *SALJ* 409.

was promoted to the AD over the heads of Feetham and Greenberg, twelve and eleven years his senior in judicial experience respectively.[124] The reason for the passing over of Greenberg has never been revealed though his Jewish faith is likely to have figured prominently in the discussions.[125] But Feetham's claim was ignored because his place on the Natal Bench would have been filled by F N Broome, a sitting MP, and the government did not wish to risk a by-election at that time. Broome himself wrote subsequently that ". . . from an intellectual and judicial point of view there could be no comparison . . ." between Centlivres and Feetham, the latter's standing being vastly superior.[126]

Notwithstanding this rather inauspicious start to his appellate career, Centlivres served on the court for a longer time than any other judge except Solomon, during which he proved himself a very sound judge and gained a reputation for giving judgments in the "slowly-moving main stream of case law". He could not, in the eyes of one observer, be accused of excessive conservatism nor be called an arch-priest of legal positivism. Indeed, he always emphasised the great care with which the courts should scrutinise statutes granting the executive powers to invade individual liberties. But once Parliament's will had been made abundantly clear, he regarded it as the court's duty to give expression even to autocratic powers.[127]

Centlivres's Chief Justiceship is best known for the "constitutional crisis" over legislative attempts to remove coloured people from the common voters' roll,[128] and his retirement was characterised by his whole-hearted efforts to prevent the implementation of apartheid policy in the universities.[129] Modest, gentle, tall, and humane, his retirement and death were greeted with sadness and respect in most quarters.[130]

The political manoeuvres surrounding Centlivres's appointment were to no avail, as another vacancy soon occurred and Richard Feetham could not be ignored again. A member of Lord Milner's Kindergarten and the only judge of appeal to be born outside South Africa, Feetham had had considerable experience as a commissioner of inquiry in many parts of the Empire.[131] It was said of him on his

[124] (1966) 83 *SALJ* 387.

[125] *Ibid* 388. Blackwell opines: "But a large section of political South Africa, though willing to accept an occasional Jewish judge, could not, so it seemed, view with any favour the idea of a Jewish Chief Justice, and at the appropriate moment, another Judge much his junior was placed on the Court of Appeal ahead of him." (*op cit* 6–7).

[126] For a full account see Broome *op cit* 174–6.

[127] For all above, see anonymous tribute on his retirement in (1957) 74 *SALJ* 1–5.

[128] He delivered judgment in each of the three cases: *Harris v Minister of the Interior* 1952 (2) SA 428 (AD); *Minister of the Interior v Harris* 1952 (4) SA 769 (AD); and *Collins v Minister of the Interior* 1957 (1) SA 552 (AD).

[129] See writings of his on civil rights (1962 *Acta Juridica* 1) and on *Blundering into University Apartheid*, an address published by the Academic Freedom Committee of the University of Cape Town, of which he was Chancellor, 1951–1966.

[130] See (1957) 74 *SALJ* 1; (1966) 83 *SALJ* 387; and (1967) 84 *SALJ* 87.

[131] See details in (1928) 45 *SALJ* 179.

death that his only indulgence was the power to do what was right, and that no amount of unpopularity would deter him.[132] He served as chancellor of Witwatersrand University after retiring from the AD, during which time he performed a role similar to Centlivres's in fighting university apartheid. In particular, he took a leading part in the organisation known as The Defenders of the Constitution, for which he wrote a number of pamphlets in the 1950's, which contained forthright and courageous criticism of government policy as it affected voting rights and the courts.[133]

Leopold Greenberg, also passed over when Centlivres moved to Bloemfontein, had to serve six more years as Judge President of the Transvaal before being asked to fill the gap caused by De Wet's retirement. After achieving rapid prominence at the Johannesburg Bar, Greenberg was the youngest judge appointed since the Anglo-Boer War, and the first Jewish judge to go to the appeal court.[134] A man of humour, quick perception, thoroughness, and clarity,[135] his undivided devotion to his task led to expressions of regret when he had to retire on reaching the statutory age limit of seventy.[136]

Another man who was the youngest South African judge when first elevated to the Bench was Oliver Schreiner.[137] Having spent a comparatively short time in the TPD, he went to the appeal court as the last appointment of the United Party government. Like General Smuts, the Prime Minister, he had had a brilliant Cambridge career, but in political outlook he followed the liberal ideas of his father, W P Schreiner, sometime Prime Minister of the Cape Colony.[138] A man of strong conviction,[139] Oliver Schreiner was early a public advocate of the retention of a common voters' roll and a qualified franchise.[140] These views led him to be the sole dissident in the final case of the "constitutional crisis" of the 1950's,[141] and contributed to his international reputation. He was twice passed over when the chair of Chief Justice fell vacant while he was the senior judge of appeal, but he never discussed this in public or private.[142]

[132] (1966) 83 *SALJ* 1.

[133] See: *Crisis The Real Issues* (1952) 7–14; *The High Court of Parliament Act and the Rule of Law* (1953); *Political Apartheid and the Entrenched Clauses of the SA Act* (not dated); *The "Suspended" Bill* (not dated); *Then (1931) and Now (1955)* (1955); *Guarantees and National Unity* (1956).

[134] (1926) 43 *SALJ* 1. Blackwell *op cit* 6–7, a school friend of Greenberg, tells of how he urged Greenberg to accept the judgeship for his "own people", as in South Africa it was more difficult for a Jew to reach the Bench than a Christian.

[135] See (1964) 81 *SALJ* 405–7.

[136] See note by G A Mulligan in (1955) 72 *SALJ* 1–3.

[137] See (1938) 55 *SALJ* 1.

[138] See Kahn "Oliver Deneys Schreiner" (1980) 97 *SALJ* 566 at 579.

[139] Examples of which are his refusal to apply for a Rhodes Scholarship (because of his father's abhorrence of Rhodes and his activities); his refusal to sit on segregated park or bus benches; and his refusal of his nomination as patron of several charitable organisations because they served whites only. See Kahn *op cit* 569 and 580.

[140] See his letter to Innes dated 26 May 1929 (No 753 IA); and his chapter (written with W H Ramsbottom) "The Franchise" in *Coming of Age* 110–28.

[141] *Collins v Minister of the Interior supra.*

[142] Kahn *op cit* 574–5.

After retirement, Schreiner served three terms as President of the liberal South African Institute of Race Relations, and used his annual addresses to expound his ideas on topics such as nationhood, economic opportunity, and the franchise.[143] He became the first South African to deliver a series of Hamlyn lectures.[144] He succeeded Feetham as Chancellor of the University of the Witwatersrand, and continued to play an active public role until his much-lamented death in 1980.[145]

The appointment of F P van den Heever to the AD had a number of unusual features: he was the first judge of appeal born in the Transvaal; the first civil servant appointed; the first appointment of the National Party after 1948; and his appointment represented an increase in the number of appeal judges to six.[146] He had only practised at the Bar for four years, but had had wide experience as a judge at provincial level, and was a man of considerable literary ability.[147]

In the preface to his *Breach of Promise and Seduction*,[148] after pondering the propriety of publishing the book after his transfer to the AD, Van den Heever candidly admits that his time at the Bar, in the civil service, and in the provincial courts have determined his attitudes to various legal issues, an acknowledgment seldom openly made by South African judges. His judgments are marked by a profound knowledge of Roman-Dutch law and a literary quality in the use of both official languages, and only an early death[149] robbed him of the Chief Justiceship.

Like Van den Heever, Oscar Hoexter had originally been elevated to the Bench of the SWA High Court, preceded by a conventional career at the Bloemfontein Bar.[150] His judgment in *Radebe v Hough*[151] is often cited as conclusive proof of the "colour-blindness" of the South African judiciary, and he is believed to have refused the Chief Justiceship in 1957 and 1959, because in each case Schreiner was senior to him.[152]

Although none of his reported judgments is dealt with below, it is proper to include Henry Fagan in these biographical sketches, as he had acted as a judge of appeal in 1949, and was permanently appointed in October 1950. After a varied career as advocate,

[143] His addresses, with another article he wrote, were published in *The Nettle* in 1964.

[144] See *The Contribution of English Law to South African Law; and the Rule of Law in South Africa*, delivered in 1967. In 1982, Professor A M Honoré became the second South African lawyer to be accorded this honour.

[145] See Kahn *op cit* 584–9.

[146] (1949) 66 *SALJ* 135.

[147] He wrote in the SALJ under the name "Aquilius" (see (1942) 59 *SALJ* 16 and 333 and (1949) 66 *SALJ* 135) and published poetry as Toon van den Heever.

[148] Published in 1954.

[149] See tribute in (1956) 73 *SALJ* 117.

[150] See (1940) 57 *SALJ* 241.

[151] 1949 (1) SA 380 (AD) and (1963) 80 *SALJ* 165.

[152] Kahn "Oliver Deneys Schreiner" at 574.

journalist, and law professor, he entered party politics in the National Party colours, and achieved Cabinet status as Minister of Native Affairs in Hertzog's United Party government. He returned to the Bar at the outbreak of the Second World War, and was given a seat on the Cape Bench soon afterwards.[153] His appointment as Chief Justice in succession to Centlivres, and over the heads of Schreiner and Hoexter, was not enthusiastically received,[154] and he served for just over two years until statutory retirement.[155]

Thereafter Fagan again entered the political arena, presenting himself as a candidate for the State Presidency, accepting a seat in the Senate,[156] and writing two little books,[157] in which he pleaded for wider consultation and co-option of the black population without any fundamental change in the existing order. The following is typical of his views:[158]

> "... [W]e, the white people, must make every effort *to ensure that the consultations are effective*. . . . Let me take the analogy of a judge on the bench. He does not try to satisfy the litigants. He tries to do justice between them. For that purpose he makes an exhaustive study of all the facts of the case. He listens carefully to the evidence, he pays serious attention to the arguments submitted to him, he weighs the pros and the cons with a dispassionate and unprejudiced mind. That is all the litigants can demand from him. And that is all that the various groups can demand from the consultations."

Trends and Conclusions

With this outline of facts about the personalities of the judges as a basis, it is instructive to try to determine any basic trends and unusual features in the characters of those who served in the period 1910 to 1950. This might point to the type of person sought for the position of judge by the governments of that time, as well as providing part of the explanation for the judges' attitudes towards their own function and particular social questions, which would inevitably have been affected or even determined by their pre-judicial experiences. Despite the striking diversity of background which is apparent in the table and short sketches, certain similarities can be discerned.

Firstly, the dominance of the Cape as birthplace is noticeable. Eighteen of the twenty-three judges were born there, although many of them carved out their careers elsewhere. Indeed, if one looks at the court from which each judge was transferred to the AD, ten came from the Transvaal, and only seven from the Cape.

Secondly, in terms of their social background, the vast majority came from the middle classes, as will be seen from Table II:

[153] See details in (1943) 60 *SALJ* 1.
[154] (1957) 74 *SALJ* 6.
[155] (1959) 76 *SALJ* 117.
[156] (1964) 81 *SALJ* 127.
[157] *Our Responsibility* (1960) and *Co-Existence in South Africa* (1963). Fagan also published poetry in Afrikaans.
[158] *Co-Existence* 119 (emphasis in the original).

TABLE II

Judges of Appeal: Father's Occupation.

Professional	12
Commerce	5
Civil Service	2
Farming	3
Unknown	1

This fact is further reflected in the educational institutions attended, although here the lack of a sufficiently high standard in most of the secondary schools in Southern Africa and the absence of any teaching university of repute in the earlier years of this period, gives an exaggerated emphasis to the roles played by the South African College and its school; the Cape University; and universities abroad.

TABLE III

Education and Training.

Schools	*No*	*Universities*	*No*	*Professional Training*	*No*
SA College	11	Cape	10	Inner Temple	7
Local public schools	6	Stellenbosch	4	Middle Temple	3
Private schools	6	Cambridge	7	Chancery Bar	1
		London	4	Cape Bar	10
		Oxford	3	Transvaal Bar	11
		Other SA	2	OFS Bar	1
		Amsterdam	1	SWA Bar	1

This class background may have played a major part in shaping judicial attitudes to many social issues, but particularly those involving individual liberty, industrial relations, and the powers of groups or government. Thus, in accordance with the values of the time, a strong insistence upon individual freedom, a lack of full understanding of the position of labouring classes, and an inclination to support the government, should its base come under attack, can be anticipated.

Thirdly, in modern terms, a surprisingly high number of judges were formally involved in politics before moving to the Bench, [159] and eight returned to political involvement in one form or another after retiring.[160]

Fourthly, the approximate average age at death of these judges was 77 years and seven months (seven of them passing their 80th birthdays),[161] which would seem to lend weight to those who plead

[159] From information available, ten: Lord De Villiers, Innes, Maasdorp, Japie de Villiers, Juta, Roos, Beyers, De Wet, Feetham, and Fagan.

[160] Innes, Roos, Beyers, De Wet, Centlivres, Feetham, Schreiner, and Fagan.

[161] Innes, Kotzé, Stratford, De Wet, Tindall, Feetham, and Schreiner.

for the possiblity of judicial office being tenable beyond the age of 70, in cases where senility has not yet made its mark.[162]

Fifthly, as far as language affiliations are concerned, it is hard to draw any firm conclusions, except to note that, although many of the judges would have had Dutch or Afrikaans as their mother tongue, all except Beyers, De Wet, Van den Heever, and Hoexter preferred to use English in their judgments. This indicates the extent of the judicial hegemony of Britain at the time, and highlights the enormous strides made by Afrikaans as a legal language since 1950.[163]

Finally, the dominant aspect of what has appeared in the preceding pages is probably what can be termed the "broad South Africanism" which appears both in terms of individual experience and the collective characteristic of all those appointed as appeal judges. This means that those men selected were not drawn from one tightly-knit cultural, geographical, or political grouping, although the ethics and traditions of the Bar tended to produce a similarity in their judicial utterances. There is no *obvious* pandering to any particular point of view, and no rapid shift in the type of person appointed, consequent upon change of political power.[164] This can be seen in Table IV:

TABLE IV

Government in Power	*Years*	*Judges of Appeal appointed*
South African Party ... (Botha, Smuts)	1910–1924	Lord De Villiers, Innes, Solomon, Maasdorp, J A J de Villiers, Juta, Kotzé, and Wessels
National Party .... (Hertzog)	1924–1933	Curlewis, Stratford, Roos, Beyers, and J E R de Villiers
United Party......... (Hertzog)	1933–1939	De Wet, Watermeyer, Tindall, Centlivres, Feetham
United Party......... (Smuts)	1939–1948	Greenberg and Schreiner
National Party .... (Malan)	1948	Van den Heever, Hoexter, and Fagan

As for individual distinctive features, several judges stand out for their early appointment to the provincial Bench (Lord De Villiers, Solomon, Kotzé, Greenberg, and Van den Heever) or for their rapid

[162] See G A Mulligan in (1955) 72 *SALJ* 1 for example.

[163] Until 1949, the only other judgments delivered in Afrikaans, besides those of Beyers, was a single speech of Wessels (*R v Gertenbach* 1933 AD 119 at 120–1) and three by De Wet in *R v Van As* 1941 AD 361; *R v Vorster* 1941 AD 472; and *Unie Volkspers Bpk v Rossouw* 1943 AD 519. Van den Heever's first Afrikaans judgment reported is *Gleneagles Farm Dairy v Schoombee* 1949 (1) SA 831 (AD); and that of Hoexter is in *R v De Beer* 1949 (3) SA 740 (AD).

[164] Even the overtly political appointments of Roos and Beyers had been preceded by those of two of the most obviously English members of the court: Curlewis and Stratford, both promoted by a strongly Afrikaner Nationalist government.

move to the AD (J A J de Villiers, Juta, Stratford, Roos, Beyers, De Wet, Centlivres, Schreiner, and Fagan). Kotzé and Greenberg, on the other hand, had to wait abnormally long for the call to Bloemfontein. Another aspect which ought not to be ignored is the extensive use made of certain judges as chairmen of Commissions of Inquiry (Lord De Villiers, Maasdorp, Centlivres, Feetham, and Fagan), or as presiding officers in special courts set up in time of war (Solomon, Curlewis, and Schreiner).

The general impression which remains in the observer's mind is, therefore, one of a relatively wide range of human material drawn from a narrow élite, consisting of white male university graduates (often with overseas experience), channelled along respectable and conservative lines by the collective socialisation of life at the Bar. This would seem to have engendered a tolerant, and sometimes liberal, acceptance of views outside the conventional political spectrum, prompted by a basic sense of fairness, but always tempered by an acute awareness of the political reality of early twentieth-century Southern Africa. Such factors would seem to provide a guarantee for the continued stability of the political *status quo* and the established order in times of social stress.[165]

With this in mind, the focus of study shifts to consider how this body of men approached the legal and social problems which confronted them in the cases presented to them.

[165] In addition, see the discussion in the "Postscript" below.

THE HON SIR JAMES ROSE INNES
The second Chief Justice of South Africa 1914–27

B. A. Tindall, ed.: *James Rose Innes, Chief Justice of South Africa, 1914–1927: Autobiography.* Cape Town, Oxford University Press, 1949

THE HON SIR WILLIAM SOLOMON
The third Chief Justice of South Africa 1927–29

CHAPTER THREE

CIVIL LIBERTIES

One of those areas of the law which displays most clearly the political attitudes of the judges is that which encompasses the freedom of the individual to act according to his or her own principles, and the extent to which this freedom ought to be curtailed for the benefit of the social formation. This category is called "civil liberties" rather tentatively, as it includes a range of subjects, not all of which are normally regarded as such. It is dominated, though, by cases involving freedom of expression, and police powers, and so that title appears to be most appropriate.

The issue which probably presented itself most urgently to the judges in these cases would have been the creation of a balance between the interests of the individual and those of the state, when they came into conflict. This necessarily required an acute awareness of the need for protection of the individual, and for maintenance of public order by the state, both of which would have depended largely on the political and economic stability of society at the time. Judicial assumptions about the relative importance of individual and state concerns, and judicial perception of the stability of social conditions would, accordingly, have been largely determinative of their attitudes in disputes regarding such matters.

In considering what follows below, therefore, the observer should keep in mind the various historical events which dominated the period in SA, lending it a crisis-ridden flavour. These included the rebellion at the outbreak of the Great War, the war itself, insurrection by labour on the Rand, severe economic depression, organised protests by blacks, and the Second World War, all of which contributed to a feeling of extreme fragility in the social order. As a result, one might expect that the judicial tendency would have been to lean towards the authorities in their attempts to preserve peace and good government. The cases in this field which came before the AD will illustrate whether this was indeed the stance adopted by the judges.

Freedom of Expression

Those cases which concerned freedom of speech, of publication, and of religion are grouped within this section, as each depends upon a measure of protection for the holding and expression of unpopular beliefs. An important factor to note here is the identity of the parties involved and their position in the body politic, as any variation in approach by the courts could be ascribed to feelings of deference to authority or sympathy for rebels.

The first case in this field was *Hertzog v Ward*,[1] which saw the Minister of Justice appealing against the dismissal of an exception which he had brought against a defamation action, which, he claimed, disclosed no cause of action against him. Ward, who had filed the original suit against Hertzog, was President of the Medical Council of the OFS, and he maintained that the Minister had besmirched his name in a public speech, in which Hertzog was alleged to have accused the Council of adopting an anti-Afrikaner posture. In the event, the AD dismissed Hertzog's appeal on the evidence in a unanimous decision which is important for two reasons. Firstly, no special allowance was made for the fact that appellant was a Cabinet Minister making a speech at a political rally.[2] Secondly, Lord De Villiers, CJ (who gave the judgment of the court) stated that attacks on the conduct of public men were tolerable if made without imputing motives which would bring discredit upon them as members of the community.[3]

This strictly impartial approach of the court was repeated in substantial terms five years later in *Crawford v Albu*,[4] when the parties represented antagonists of a very different kind. After labour disturbances among white workers on the Witwatersrand in the period from July 1913 to January 1914, nine of the labour leaders had been summarily kidnapped and deported by the Government, which then proceeded to indemnify its actions retrospectively by Act of Parliament.[5] Soon afterwards Albu, a mine employer, spoke at a meeting of the Chamber of Mines and stated that: "All this strife has been caused by men who are fanatics—no they are not fanatics—they are criminals in the fullest sense of the word." Crawford was one of those deported, and, on his return to the country, he sued Albu to recover alleged damages of £1 000 for defamation. He was unsuccessful in the WLD,[6] and so came to Bloemfontein on appeal.

Albu's defence on appeal was that the words used by him constituted fair comment on a matter of public interest, but he raised no plea of justification. In a split decision, the judges of appeal upheld Crawford's allegation that he had been defamed, but awarded him only £5 damages, together with his costs in both courts. This finding shows the court's preparedness to support the claim of a person

[1] 1912 AD 62.

[2] This may be due in part to the fact that the Minister was not very populat at the time as he espoused attitudes to the language question which were regarded as extreme and were causing upheavals in the Cabinet. In addition, Solomon, at least, distrusted Hertzog as a result of the appointment of Beyers as A–G of the Transvaal. (See his letters to Innes in 1911 No 498 and 499 IA).

[3] At 70. On the same page he sets out his view in general terms, thus: "It is the policy of the law on the one hand to protect the right of full and free discussion of matters of public interest and on the other hand to protect the right which every person has to the maintenance of his reputation."

[4] 1917 AD 102.

[5] Indemnity and Undesirables Special Deportation Act 1 of 1914, section 4.

[6] The judgment of Bristowe, J is set out at 104–11 of the AD report.

unpopular with the authorities in an action against a member of the dominant group in the social order, but it also provides an illuminating insight into the thinking of the three judges involved.

Innes, CJ acknowledged[7] that the defence of fair comment rested on the "right of every person to express his real judgment or opinion honestly and fairly upon a matter of public interest". He dealt with the essential elements of such a defence, and maintained that ". . . any genuine expression of opinion is fair if it is relevant, and if it is not such as to disclose in itself actual malice".[8] The Chief Justice concluded that ". . . the defence . . . will cover imputations as to motive, if such imputations are reasonable inferences from the facts truly stated",[9] and he held that Albu's remarks had clearly been fact.[10] But he claimed that, even if they had been comment, they had not been fair, a quality which had to bear some relation to the mind of the speaker.[11] Therefore, the appeal as framed should succeed.

He was joined in this opinion of the matter by J A J de Villiers, AJA[12] who decided that Albu's remarks taken together constituted a comment, but that, as he had no factual evidence to support his allegations, they had not been fair.[13] While he noted that modern conditions ". . . demand the utmost freedom of criticism on all matters of public interest . . ."[14] he displayed an almost sympathetic attitude to Crawford, being of the opinion that ". . . though misguided . . . " there was nothing to show that he had not honestly worked for the cause he advocated.[15]

Solomon, JA found himself in the minority,[16] being in agreement with Bristowe, J in the court *a quo*. Against the background of the troublous times[17] and Crawford's leading role in the labour movement,[18] he found that Albu's remarks were recognisable as comment[19] (even though couched as a statement of fact) which was fair, in that it had been relevant and made honestly and without malice.[20] He gave Albu considerable latitude to adduce evidence in support of his remarks,[21] and held that the word "criminal" was popularly used in a sense wider than its primary meaning, thus eroding the basis of Crawford's argument.[22]

An interesting spectrum of judicial views emerges: starting from a basic agreement on the principles of law relevant to the arguments, Innes, CJ takes a strong line in favour of the underdog[23] (which here implies a restrictive conception of freedom of speech), as opposed to Solomon, JA who is prepared to tolerate quite harsh statements made

[7] See 112–22. [8] At 115. [9] At 117. [10] At 119.
[11] At 120. [12] See 135–40. [13] At 139. [14] At 138.
[15] At 140. [16] See 122–35. [17] At 124. [18] At 131.
[19] At 125. [20] At 133–4. [21] At 130. [22] At 127.

[23] In his *Autobiography* Innes expresses himself very forcibly on the issue of the deportations. He remarks that the attempt by the executive to hamstring the judiciary should be relegated to the category of things which "aren't done", and that the incident remained a blot on the page of South African history (225).

by one in authority (which indicates a liberal outlook concerning free speech). J A J de Villiers, AJA sits comfortably in the centre, displaying an indulgent attitude towards the making of the remarks, but taking a dim view of their contents. Academic comment at the time took issue with the judges for approaching the case on the basis of English law, and suggested that the decision of Solomon, JA was preferable in Roman-Dutch law terms.[24]

In 1922, the same court, along with C G Maasdorp and Juta, JJA, had to decide whether a conviction obtained in terms of a *placaat* (statute) of 1754 of the States of Holland and West Friesland should be quashed on the ground that the *placaat* was not, and never had been, in force as law at the Cape. In this instance,[25] they held unanimously that the *placaat* had merely been a local measure passed to meet particular conditions prevailing in Holland at the time, and, therefore, that its incorporation into Cape law could not be inferred.

What is important for present purposes is that the accused, Harrison and Dryburgh, had issued a leaflet in the name of the United Communist Party, which had accused the Union government of the brutal murder of various "unarmed strikers and natives" and had referred particularly to the massacre of several hundred Africans at Bulhoek in the Eastern Cape in 1921.[26] Thus they were expressing opinions which would have been extremely unpopular with the authorities at a time of great social instability, yet Innes, CJ, who spoke for the court,[27] was not prepared to let their actions be punished under the provisions of the *placaat*. In other words, he would allow the expression of vitriolic opinions in written form here, whereas in *Crawford's* case he had viewed freedom of expression in a more limited fashion. This might possibly be ascribed to the fact that Harrison and Dryburgh faced criminal charges, as opposed to the civil nature of the proceedings in *Crawford*, but it could more probably be seen as indicative of his deep concern at political developments concerning the treatment of black people and those who spoke out for them, as became evident in his autobiography some years later.

A further factor which might have played a part in the shaping of the court's decisions came to light in *Kimpton v Rhodesian Newspapers, Ltd.*[28] Here, a newspaper article had referred to appellant as a "non-entity", which the court held not to be defamatory as there was no element of *contumelia* present. Innes, CJ, who again gave judgment,[29] stated that he did not approve of the writing or style of journalism involved, but that if articles of the kind under review were held to be

[24] See Melius de Villiers (Lord De Villiers's brother) in (1917) 34 *SALJ* 202–7.
[25] *R v Harrison & Dryburgh* 1922 AD 320.
[26] See 327.
[27] See 327–37. The other judges concurred silently.
[28] 1924 AD 755.
[29] See 756–8. Solomon and Wessels, JJA concurred silently.

defamatory, the courts would be "flooded with libel actions".[30] This indicates the judges' awareness of the practical results of their decisions, and is a demonstration of the capacity of the AD to regulate the type of cause which came before it. In this instance, the scope of free expression was widened through the court's concern for the efficient functioning of the machinery of justice.

The strongly civil libertarian note sounded in *Harrison & Dryburgh* was repeated in very similar circumstances in *R v Roux & another*[31] in 1936. A completely different court[32] upheld an appeal by the accused against a conviction on a charge of *crimen laesae venerationis*, and so reversed a full Bench decision of the NPD. Roux and Ngedlane, the co-accused, were the editors of a newspaper *Umsebenzi*, which had published an extremely forceful article which had accused King George V of being the "figurehead of English and Boer imperialists" who were "robbing and exploiting the poor people and workers of SA". It had further exhorted the oppressed people of Durban not to kiss the boot that kicked them, and to unite "in protest against pass-laws, liquor laws and all other forms of oppression".[33]

The accused had been charged under the *crimen laesae venerationis* with dishonouring the Majesty of the King and his government in SA, and with injuring their dignity and power. They had been convicted and sentenced to several months' hard labour. They appealed on four grounds, their central argument being that the *crimen laesae venerationis* did not exist in South African law, and that, even if it did, the words complained of in the charge sheet did not constitute such a crime.[34] After an examination of the Roman-Dutch authorities, Curlewis, JA[35] assumed that the crime existed in South Africa, but agreed that the article did not fall within the definition thereof. In doing so, he said that the court, ". . . under the conditions of our modern civilisation and development and of our political liberty and freedom of thought and speech, cannot be expected to accept the narrow and restricted views . . ." of earlier centuries.[36]

In considering the article in detail, Curlewis, JA found the language "strong and stupid, coarse and distasteful",[37] but advised that ". . . we must remember that the natives of Durban have no voice or vote in the passing of [those] laws or in the government of the country, and that they can only protest against what may be regarded by them as grievances"; indeed, ". . . if the appeal is intended to be effective one can well imagine strong and extravagant language being used in order to influence natives". Taking these factors into account,

30 At 758.
31 1936 AD 271.
32 Composed of Curlewis, Stratford, Beyers, and J E R de Villiers, JJA.
33 See 274–6.
34 At 277.
35 See 274–85.
36 At 281.
37 At 282.

the article was not a "grave or aggravated calumny", and the appeals should succeed.[38]

Beyers, JA handed down a separate concurrence.[39] After a thorough review of Roman-Dutch law, he decided that the *crimen laesae venerationis* could never have existed in SA, and found nothing in the article which constituted an offence. His judgment affords great insight into his political attitudes as he pronounced that ". . . [d]ie Unie is 'n demokratiese staat . . ., waar die regering . . . gegrond is op die vrye en onbelemmerde volkswil, en waar dit iedere burger vrystaan om sy mening omtrent die openbare staat van sake en die politiek vrylik te uiter".[40] In addition, if the conviction here stood, he observed that anyone who might plead for a change in the form of government would be liable to prosecution, which would put the members of two political parties in jeopardy, as they were free to agitate for a republic rather than a monarchy.[41]

Finally, in a discourse on the concept of *majestas* in South African law, he maintained that its seat lay not with Parliament nor the King, but with "die volk".[42] In this way he expounded ideas typical of and central to the thinking of Afrikaner Nationalists of the time. He justified this attitude by stating that it was the duty of the judicial authority ". . . om wel deeglik kennis te neem van Konstitutionele ontwikkeling en met die veranderinge rekening te hou".[43]

In this way the AD reaffirmed its strong commitment to a tolerance of the lawful expression of views which were quite beyond the limits of accepted political debate in the country. The attitude of the majority of the judges is a logical development from earlier decisions, but it seems that Beyers, JA assumed his separate position because he had a particular statement to make on behalf of a definite constituency, Afrikaner Nationalist republicans. It is important, too, to note that in both *Harrison & Dryburgh* and *Roux*, the accused were charged with outdated common-law offences, which meant that the court was not faced with the interpretation of a contemporary statute. The judges could, accordingly, approach the problem free from the restrictions imposed by legislative intent, and more comfortably express their own opinions.

That the views of the judges were not universally welcomed is clear from a strongly critical but anonymous commentary in the SALJ.[44] The author accused Curlewis, JA of being "consciously

[38] At 284. Stratford and J E R de Villiers, JJA concurred.

[39] See 285–96.

[40] At 293. "The Union is a democratic state, . . . where the government is based on the free and untrammelled will of the people, and where it is within the rights of every citizen freely to express his opinion about the public state of affairs and politics." (My translation.)

[41] *Loc cit.* This probably referred to the "Purified" National Party, and the Communist Party (with which the accused were connected).

[42] "the people". At 294–5.

[43] At 296. ". . . to take careful notice of Constitutional development and to keep account of changes". (My translation.)

[44] (1938) 55 *SALJ* 14–22. The editor at the time was T G Duncan.

reformative" in taking note of the great political advances since Roman times, and that this was a trespass into the legislative sphere which ill suited the judiciary, "too sequestered and irresponsible a body to be entrusted with the making or modification of laws".[45] The court was further accused of pursuing a policy which ". . . load[ed] the scales against the Crown in public law and against the 'haves' in private law".[46] These remarks vividly demonstrate the type of convictions current in legal circles, and the extent to which the AD diverged therefrom.

The apparent trend of support for the "have-nots" in the decisions was confirmed by two cases in the mid-1940's. In *Molepo v Achterberg*[47] the appeal of the president of the Transvaal African Teachers' Association (TATA) in a defamation action against a government school inspector was upheld by a bare majority in the AD. The circumstances were that Achterberg had called Molepo a "rotten teacher" at a meeting of schoolteachers, at a time when relations between teachers and inspectors were "disturbed", and after Molepo had adverted to this state of affairs in his published presidential address to TATA. Molepo's action had been dismissed by Greenberg, JP in the TPD, who had recognised Achterberg's defence that the occasion on which he had made the remarks had been privileged.

After detailed consideration of the evidence, Watermeyer, JA, speaking for the majority,[48] held that the occasion was indeed privileged, by virtue of the common interest of Achterberg and the teachers in their relationship,[49] but that respondent's statement about Molepo's personal qualities as a teacher *prima facie* bore no relation to the subject of common interest.[50] Achterberg's statement (which he denied making, but which Greenberg, JP found had been made)[51] was one of fact, not comment, and so Molepo was awarded £100 damages.[52] Tindall[53] and Feetham,[54] JJA, in the minority here, asserted that the personal remark about Molepo was part and parcel of the privileged statement and relevant to it, as they felt that Molepo's personal grievance and incompetence were central to his attitude towards the education authorities.

Once more, then, the majority of the court showed itself prepared to curtail the right to speak out freely when the target of the attack, though a public figure, was not a member of the ruling social group. This is reminiscent of Innes, CJ's attitude in *Crawford v Albu*,[55] the minority here being the judicial successors to Solomon, JA in that case.

[45] At 15. [46] *Loc cit.* [47] 1943 AD 85.
[48] See 87–100. De Wet, CJ and Centlivres, JA concurred in his judgment.
[49] At 91. [50] At 98.
[51] At 92. [52] At 100.
[53] See 100–13. [54] See 114–17.
[55] *Supra.*

The second example of the court's willingness to allow verbal attacks by those representative of "unpopular" opinions is provided by *Basner v Trigger* in 1946.[56] Here appellant, a Senator[57] and an official of the African Mine Workers' Union (AMWU), had been found guilty of defaming respondent, the manager of the Chamber of Mines police department. The alleged defamation had occurred when Basner had cited Trigger's actions as typical of the "worst features of American labour racketeering and a disgrace . . ." in his evidence[58] to a public session of a government Commission of Inquiry into African employment on the mines.[59] An earlier appeal[60] by Basner, in which he had challenged the decision of Millin, J in the WLD, which had disallowed his exception to and application to strike out Trigger's suit for defamation, had been unsuccessful. Tindall, JA[61] had decided that the test to be applied in such a case was whether "a reasonable person of average intelligence and education with knowledge of the circumstances pleaded in the declaration *might* reasonably have understood [the words complained of] in the sense assigned to them in the innuendo",[62] which had been satisfied here.

In the present case, however, the decision turned on the possible presence of malice (*animus injuriandi*) in the mind of Basner when he had made his submission to the Commission, for malice would generally nullify any protection gained under the defence of privilege, which had been pleaded by Basner and was examined first by the AD. Schreiner, JA had no doubt[63] that the occasion was a privileged one, on the basis of the common interest which existed between Basner and the members of the Commission on matters within its terms of reference, and that the evidence led by Basner which related to Trigger's espionage activities was relevant to the issue of trade union recognition.[64]

This notwithstanding, Murray, J in the WLD had found that Basner had been prompted by malice in alleging that Trigger's activities had been tantamount to spying on MP's, because he had known that what he said, if taken literally and out of context, was untrue.[65] Schreiner, JA countered this by invoking the exception, "despite a dearth of authority", which was available to one arguing a case before some sort of tribunal on a privileged occasion.[66] He examined similar cases dealing with privilege accorded to counsel in courts of law, and extended this principle to excuse Basner's

[56] 1946 AD 83.

[57] Representing Africans of the OFS and Transvaal.

[58] Much of which is set out at 86–90 of the report.

[59] The Witwatersrand Mine Native Wages Commission, under the chairmanship of Mr Justice Lansdown.

[60] Reported in 1945 AD 22.

[61] See 26–38 with whom Watermeyer, CJ; Feetham and Greenberg, JJA; and Davis, AJA concurred.

[62] At 32.

[63] See 86–109.

[64] At 97. [65] At 98. [66] At 105.

"overstatement" of his case to the Commission. The court upheld Basner's appeal.[67]

This case would, therefore, seem to provide a further example of the AD's willingness to tolerate the forthright expression of unpopular views, even when defamatory, so long as they were expressed on a privileged occasion *by those who were not part of the ruling social group*. Foundation for the last submission is to be found in the striking difference in the treatment by the court of the utterances of Albu and Achterberg, on the one hand, as opposed to Harrison and Dryburgh, Roux, and Basner, on the other, who were all in some way representative of black opinion.

This proposition requires qualification in at least one respect, though, as it would appear from the following two cases discussed that the AD was less willing to decide in favour of those who had a realistic potential to disturb the balance of political power among whites.

In *Unie Volkspers Bpk v Rossouw*,[68] the respondent, a minister of the Dutch Reformed Church, had successfully obtained damages for defamation in the CPD from appellant, the publisher of a newspaper which had reported a speech which had named Rossouw as a "political priest". This, Rossouw claimed, indicated that he was misusing his office. The appeal was argued on the ground that the report was not defamatory, when standing alone, or in conjunction with previous reports[69] which had characterised "political priests" as pro-Nazi, anti-South Africa, and anti-Christ, *inter alia*.[70] De Wet, CJ[71] agreed with both these submissions, holding that in neither case was the report *prima facie* defamatory, and that Rossouw had produced insufficient evidence to prove that ordinary readers of the report would have understood a secondary, and defamatory, meaning.[72]

An interesting comparison can be made with *Hertzog v Ward*[73] as the report in question here concerned a speech made by a Cabinet Minister, Conroy, at a public meeting at which, by all accounts, he had used far stronger and more damaging language than had Hertzog of Ward in 1911.[74] Perhaps the difference lies in the fact that the present case concerns a newspaper report of the speech rather than a personal action against Conroy, yet it is hard to escape the conclusion that the members of this court were far more sympathetic to the views of Conroy than the judges of appeal had been to those of Hertzog earlier.

[67] At 109. Watermeyer, CJ and Greenberg, JA concurred.
[68] 1943 AD 519.
[69] At 523.
[70] At 524–5.
[71] With whom Watermeyer, Tindall, Centlivres, and Feetham, JJA concurred.
[72] See 522–30.
[73] Above.
[74] See 522.

Five years later the shoe was on the other foot, when Conroy personally succeeded in a defamation action against *Stewart Printing*. This company had published a book containing a statement concerning Conroy's activities as a company director, which, he alleged, was defamatory when taken in its primary sense. Stewart Printing appealed against the award of damages against them,[75] and claimed that the words used were not defamatory, but that, if they were so, they were true and had been published in the public interest.[76]

The AD rejected these arguments,[77] and concluded both that the statements complained of were defamatory (even if taken in conjunction with the rest of the book), for the average reader would have understood the innuendo, alleged by Conroy, that he had acted dishonestly, and also that appellants had failed to prove the substantial truth of the statements.[78] It is hard on the basis of the case report to find fault with this judgment (or, indeed, any of the other judgments above), but it does indicate a willingness by the court to protect the reputation of public figures, perhaps more assiduously than it had been prepared to in the past. This, in turn might point to a closer identity with the views of those public figures involved.

Two further cases which fall within the wide ambit of freedom of expression dealt specifically with the interpretation of early Acts of the Union Parliament. In *R v Malefane*,[79] the accused, who worked in the OFS, had posted an obscene letter from Basutoland to a person within South Africa. He had been convicted by a magistrate for a contravention of a statute which outlawed the "putting into any Post Office" within the Union of any indecent or obscene material.[80] The Crown's argument was that, although the initial posting had been outside the Union, subsequent movement of the offensive article through the Union's postal system had brought it within the scope of the prohibition. This contention had been rejected on appeal to the OPD, a view which was confirmed by Watermeyer, CJ,[81] who was at pains to adopt the natural meaning of the words in dispute. Of note here is the race of the parties: accused was a Basuto employee, while the recipient of the letter was a European small businessman in a rural village.

The second case could be seen as one concerning freedom of religion, in regard to which one might expect an open-minded judicial attitude, considering South Africa's diverse cultural antece-

[75] *Stewart Printing Co (Pty) Ltd v Conroy* 1948 (2) SA 707 (AD).

[76] At 711.

[77] See the judgment of Greenberg, JA (709–19) with whom Tindall, ACJ; Centlivres and Schreiner, JJA; and Davis, AJA concurred.

[78] See 712–16.

[79] 1946 AD 207.

[80] Post Office Administration and Shipping Combinations Discouragement Act 10 of 1911, section 96(1)*(c)*.

[81] See 209–14, concurred in by Tindall, Greenberg, and Schreiner, JJA; and Davis, AJA.

dents. *Commissioner of Customs v Watch Tower Bible & Tract Society*[82] was an appeal against a decision of the CPD which had required the Commissioner to allege in his declaration, when seeking condemnation of certain imported goods as "objectionable",[83] that the Minister of the Interior had decided that such goods fell within such description,[84] if he wished his declaration to disclose a cause of action. The events preceding this litigation had been the attempted importation by the respondent of certain printed matter, which had been seized by customs officials. If the AD had required a declaration incorporating the Minister's decision as an allegation, the Bible Society would have been able to attack the validity of such a decision on the basis of non-compliance with the *audi alteram partem* rule.[85]

Tindall, JA[86] held that section 96 of the Act threw the onus on the Society to prove that the printed matter was not objectionable and, therefore, that the Commissioner could state that it was objectionable without citing the Ministerial decision.[87] He acknowledged that the result of his finding would place the Commissioner in a "very favourable position, . . . but I am satisfied that it was the deliberate policy of the Legislature to do so".[88] The practical outcome was that customs officials could thenceforth seize any material they deemed objectionable on its arrival in the country, the only recourse available to the importer being a successful defence against the subsequent condemnation action under section 98.

The judge's remarks display an unusual degree of trust in the manner of exercise of official discretion. His approach was probably coloured by two factors outside the strict confines of the case: the Second World War was at its darkest point in Allied terms at the time, and the Society preached a message not wholly confined to religious dogma.[89] This latter point, which included an anti-war attitude, was unlikely to have been popular among the authorities in the tense internal atmosphere of SA during the early 1940's. Judicial approaches towards statutory interpretation continue the trend of impeccable fairness towards individuals, but they reveal a strong tendency to lean towards the state when the effects of the decision were likely to have a wider impact, and entail inconvenience and even disruption in social order.

Powers of Arrest and Detention

From the area of freedom of expression, the survey shifts to a number of cases which concerned the powers of the police (or, in one

[82] 1942 AD 203.
[83] Customs Management Act 9 of 1913, section 98.
[84] *Ibid* section 23*(c)*.
[85] At 205.
[86] See 204–11, concurred in by De Wet, CJ; Watermeyer, Centlivres, and Feetham, JJA.
[87] At 209.
[88] At 210.
[89] See the cases of *R v McGregor* 1941 AD 493, and *R v Arsenis* 1943 AD 55, involving a challenge to, and efforts to circumvent, a Defence Regulation in Southern Rhodesia under which the importation by Jehovah's Witnesses of anti-war pamphlets had been outlawed.

case, a citizen) to arrest or detain, and to use force in doing so. To an extent, this ties in with the judicial function, for arrest and detention often constitute the first step in a process leading to conviction by a court of law, so that judicial attitudes here will be affected by the judges' own views of their role in administering the law.

The first two cases within this field to reach the AD arose out of conduct which had hindered the police in the execution of their powers of arrest. *Burkett v Smith*[90] was a civil action which resulted from the alleged commission of the offence of obstructing the police in the execution of their duties by respondent, who had removed £2 from a third party who was being arrested by appellant, a police constable. Smith had been acquitted, whereupon he successfully sued Burkett for damages for false arrest and malicious prosecution in the EDLD. On the evidence on appeal, though, Innes, CJ[91] held that Smith had contravened the Act[92] and had been rightly arrested and prosecuted, as the money, which he had removed without physical force, might have been part of the *corpus delicti*. In the circumstances of the case as reported, the attitude of the AD would seem to be justifiable, but their reversal of the Local Division, with its superior knowledge of the facts and conditions of the offence, is significant, as they were normally reluctant to do so.

R v Wallendorf,[93] which was also reported in 1920, involved a good deal more physical force on the part of the accused than the mere receipt of money. Here a police constable, M, in plain clothes, had been attempting to remove a drunk man from a public house when Wallendorf and his co-accused had come to the aid of the arrestee by assaulting M. Wallendorf and the others had subsequently been convicted in a magistrate's court for hindering M in the execution of his duty,[94] and their appeal to the CPD had been turned down by a majority verdict.[95]

Before the AD the crucial question was the necessity of proof of knowledge, on the part of the person hindering the policeman, that the arrester was a policeman. The judges of appeal were unanimous in their rejection of the appeal, but three separate opinions were handed down. Solomon, JA[96] gave the leading judgment. In his *ratio decidendi* he side-stepped the question of *mens rea* by holding that, even if it was essential, it had been present, because the accused had been guilty of assaulting M, policeman or civilian.[97] Therefore, they had been correctly convicted. However, he went on to pronounce

[90] 1920 AD 106.

[91] See 107–11, concurred in by C G Maasdorp, JA and J A J de Villiers, AJA.

[92] The Police Offences Act 27 of 1882 (Cape), section 8(5).

[93] 1920 AD 383.

[94] The Police Offences Act 27 of 1882 (Cape), section 8(5).

[95] See judgments reported in AD decision, 384–92. Juta, JP and Kotzé, J dismissed the appeal, while Searle, J dissented. The majority did not require the proof of *mens rea*.

[96] See 394–402, concurred in by Innes, CJ and C G Maasdorp, JA.

[97] At 397.

upon the necessity of proof of *mens rea* by the Crown, and concluded that it was an essential element of the offence, albeit in the form of an intention to commit any crime whatsoever.[98] The prosecutor having proved the strict offence, the onus would be on the accused to show that his action was innocent.[99]

J A J de Villiers, AJA asserted that the intention of the legislature and not the words of the Act constituted the law.[100] For the offence under consideration, knowledge that the person resisted was a policeman was essential, and had to be determined from all the circumstances of the case.[101] Here, Wallendorf must, on the evidence before the court, have known that M was a policeman, and his appeal should be dismissed.[102]

J E R de Villiers, AJA likewise thought that *mens rea* was essential but that it was not necessary for the prosecution to give positive proof of such knowledge, which the law would presume from the physical act of resistance.[103] As no evidence had been tendered by Wallendorf to rebut the presumption here, his appeal could not succeed.[104]

These judgments seem to establish the following propositions: that *mens rea* is an essential ingredient of the statutory offence of hindering a policeman in the execution of his duty, and that proof of the presence of such a guilty state of mind, although resting on the Crown, can be inferred from the facts of the case, and will be presumed if certain conditions (such as physical resistance) are met. This gives with one hand and takes away with the other: the *mens rea* requirement alone is a definite safeguard of individual liberty as it provides an innocent resister of arrest with an escape from over-hasty prosecution. But the method of proof of the presence of a guilty intent which the AD laid down here was such that any accused would have had a mammoth task in attempting to prove his innocence. In practical terms, the effect of the judgment was that any physical act of resistance to arrest, no matter how innocent, would carry with it the danger of prosecution under the statute, a state of affairs which grants a licence for over-zealous police action at arrest.

The next case in this vein which confronted the AD was an application by a policeman, *Hartzer*, for leave to appeal[105] against his conviction on a charge of common assault.[106] This arose out of the shooting by him of an African, Matsipa, who had fled when Hartzer had demanded his pass. Under section 44(1) of the Criminal Procedure Act[107] any amount of force, including killing, might be justified by the circumstances in order to effect an arrest in cases

[98] At 398.
[99] At 401.
[100] See 402–5.
[101] At 404.
[102] At 405.
[103] See 405–7.
[104] At 407.
[105] *R v Hartzer* 1933 AD 306.
[106] For which he was fined £5.
[107] 31 of 1917.

which fell within a certain category. Hartzer maintained that Matsipa had fallen within this category because, by running away after Hartzer had caught him by the arm, he was escaping from lawful custody, which rendered him liable to a sentence of up to two years' imprisonment.[108]

Hartzer's application for leave to appeal was unanimously rejected by the court of appeal, but the judges' reasons varied slightly. Wessels, CJ[109] held that section 46(1), upon which Hartzer relied, demanded that the escaper must have been arrested *and in lawful custody* before he could be sentenced for an attempted escape. Here, although Matsipa might have been technically arrested through Hartzer's action of holding his arm, he had never been under the latter's control or custody. Thus section 44(1) did not apply, and the shooting was not justified, either under the Act or by the particular circumstances. Use of a firearm to procure an arrest should be a last resort: "In any case a policeman cannot shoot at a person arrested merely because he runs away."[110]

Curlewis, JA was not prepared to pronounce on the "lawful custody" question, as he maintained that, even if Matsipa had been in lawful custody, shooting had not been justified on the facts.[111] Beyers, JA,[112] after a thorough examination of the evidence, concluded that Matsipa had been in lawful custody by virtue of the arrest, but that Hartzer had acted "onverantwoordelik, onverstandig, en uiters onversigtig",[113] with the result that his application should be refused. These opinions comprise a strong stand by the judges against the use of excessive force by the police in making arrests, and provide a counter-balance to *Wallendorf*. They sound strangely out of date when juxtaposed with modern police methods of arrest in South Africa.[114]

The subject of shooting on arrest arose again just before the close of the period under review in *R v Britz*.[115] Here there was a further complication, in that appellant was a private individual who, in the exercise of his citizen's right of arrest,[116] had killed an African by

[108] *Ibid* by virtue of section 46(1).

[109] See 307–9. J E R de Villiers, JA concurred with Wessels, CJ with a brief statement at 317.

[110] At 309.

[111] See 309–10.

[112] See 310–17.

[113] ". . . irresponsibly, without understanding, and exceptionally carelessly" (my translation).

[114] The following statistics relate to persons shot by the SA Police in the execution of their duties (excluding the crushing of civil unrest):

1976..........Adults—195 (158) killed, 410 (334) wounded.
Juveniles—7 (6) killed, 29 (20) wounded.
1977..........Adults—138 (108) killed, 362 (242) wounded.
Juveniles—11 (3) killed, 41 (26) wounded.

Figures in parenthesis refer to the number of casualties which occurred as a result of "escaping from custody". Obtained from the *Annual Survey* of the South African Institute of Race Relations, 1977–1978.

[115] 1949 (3) SA 293 (AD).

[116] Under the Criminal Procedure Act 31 of 1917, section 31, which authorised arrest by a private person for Schedule One offences, ie usually crimes involving violence.

shotgun fire at close range after a half-hearted attempt at formal arrest of the deceased. Britz had been convicted of culpable homicide in the TPD, but Dowling, J had reserved two questions of law for decision by the AD: firstly, whether an accused under section 44(1) had to establish his defence on a balance of probabilities, and, secondly, whether Britz was entitled to an acquittal in the particular circumstances.[117]

Schreiner, JA answered both questions in favour of the Crown after a careful consideration of modern South African and English authority on the point.[118] He decided that, where a true interpretation of the words of a statute, governed by general considerations of fairness and convenience, demanded it, the burden of proof in a criminal case could be transferred to an accused; although section 44(1) did not expressly do so, the defence which it provided had obviously been designed to afford protection only in specific circumstances.[119] Bearing in mind the "emphasis which our law and customs have in general laid upon the sanctity of human life", as well as the dangers inherent in granting too wide an indemnity in favour of those making an arrest, he was satisfied that the onus lay on the accused here, and that the evidence did not discharge such onus.[120]

In this way the court again took a firm line against the abuse of force in the process of arrest, although the gruesome behaviour of Britz would have made it easier to arrive at the conclusion reached, despite support for the accused from Europeans locally.[121]

In other respects, too, the judges of appeal took decisive action to correct what they saw as excessive use of power by individual police officers, as the following two cases demonstrate. *Union Government & another v Bolstridge*[122] concerned the attempted arrest, without warrant, of the respondent whom a policeman had reasonable grounds to believe was in the possession of uncut diamonds. Unfortunately for the police officer such possession was not an offence at the time he made the arrest, and Bolstridge sued the Minister of Police for damages for wrongful arrest. The police authorities pleaded in defence that Bolstridge had been rightly arrested, to which he had excepted on the ground that no offence had existed at the particular time of arrest (although it had before, and had come into being again subsequently). The NPD upheld the exception, whereupon the police superiors appealed, but Wessels, JA dismissed the appeal,[123] stating that, if a policeman had any doubt

[117] At 298 of AD report.
[118] See 295–304. Watermeyer, CJ and Fagan, AJA concurred.
[119] At 300–3.
[120] At 304.
[121] Although no specific reference is made to them, they are likely to have been in favour of Britz, a school master in Potchefstroom, as there had been assaults in the neighbourhood, and the women students of the nearby Normal College had asked for protection.
[122] 1929 AD 240.
[123] See 242–4, with the concurrence of Curlewis and Stratford, JJA; and J E R de Villiers, AJA.

about the existence of an offence, he should obtain a warrant prior to acting.[124]

Again, in considering police power to search private property, the AD clamped down on police practices of doubtful legality. In *Minister of Justice v Desai, NO*,[125] respondent had obtained a rule from the EDLD, which instructed the police to return certain books and documents taken from his offices under the power given by a search warrant, and to pay his costs. The local division had confirmed the order on the ground that the onus lay upon the police to show that there were reasonable grounds for their belief that the documents seized would afford evidence of the commission of an offence, an onus which they had failed to discharge.[126]

Tindall, ACJ[127] did not need to rule on this issue, for he rejected the Minister's appeal on the basis of a fatal mistake *ex facie* the search warrant. Under the statutory power to grant search warrants, the issuing officer had to be satisfied that the documents sought to be seized *would* afford evidence as to the commission of the particular offence in contemplation, whereas the search warrant issued in *Desai* had used the word *may*, instead of *will*.[128] Not even specific instructions by senior police officers could cure this defect, which was not a mere matter of form, the judge said, because it had the effect of enlarging the inroad upon the rights of an occupier of premises beyond that contemplated by the section.[129] In addition, the Acting Chief Justice warned that it was undesirable for the immediate investigating officer to issue the warrant.[130]

Such willingness to interfere to ensure a fair and correct process of justice from time of arrest until after conviction reflects considerable credit on the appellate judiciary in this period.[131] Nowhere is this determination more categorically underlined than in *Whittaker v Roos & Bateman; Morant v Roos & Bateman*[132] in the early years of the court's existence.

Whittaker and Morant were tramway company employees who had been arrested during a strike after dynamite had been found on the tram tracks, and who had been kept in gaol while awaiting trial, as they could not afford to raise the bail set for them. After acquittal on a charge of wilfully attempting to endanger the lives and property of others, they had sued Roos (the Director of Prisons) and Bateman

[124] At 244.
[125] 1948 (3) SA 395 (AD).
[126] At 401 of AD report.
[127] See 398–406, with the concurrence of Centlivres, Greenberg, and Schreiner, JJA; and Davis, AJA.
[128] At 401.
[129] At 402–3.
[130] At 405.
[131] Particularly when the subject of such police excesses was on the political fringes of society, as was Desai, who was the secretary of seven non-European trade unions in Port Elizabeth, the scene of much labour unrest over the years.
[132] 1912 AD 92.

THE HON MR JUSTICE J A J DE VILLIERS
The fourth Chief Justice of South Africa 1929–32

THE HON SIR J W WESSELS
The fifth Chief Justice of South Africa 1932–36

(the governor of the prison in which they had been detained) for damages by reason of the illegal treatment they alleged that they had received in prison, through being kept in punishment cells and denied privileges for over a month. A full Bench of the TPD[133] had absolved Roos and had held that the £20 tendered by Bateman should have been accepted by Whittaker and Morant, who then appealed to Bloemfontein.

In three exceptionally forthright judgments,[134] Lord De Villiers, CJ,[135] Innes[136] and Solomon, JJ,[137] upheld the appeals and awarded substantial damages against both respondents. Some remarks made by the judges serve to indicate their insistence upon the strict observance of just procedures by the police and prison authorities. Innes, J said: ". . . I would remark that however reprehensible a man's views may be he is entitled to have his personal liberty adequately protected;"[138] and that: ". . . assistance in the detection of crime is dearly bought if it is obtained at the expense of an unnecessary interference with the liberty of men who are only in the power of the authorities because they cannot afford to supply bail."[139]

Solomon, J agreed that: "It would be a most dangerous doctrine to lay down that the police authorities are entitled to infringe upon the personal rights of liberty of any individual merely because in their opinion it is desirable to do so in the interests of public safety."[140] In fixing damages he considered that a man of bad character may suffer as much in body and mind as a man of good character.[141] What is even more remarkable here is that Parliament had subsequently acted to legalise just such treatment as that meted out to appellants,[142] a fact to which Innes, J adverted, in the hope that the legislature would reconsider its policy.[143]

From the above, therefore, it is apparent that, after a hesitant start, judicial attitudes to police powers display a determined desire to impress the judges' own high ethical standards upon all state officials involved in the machinery of justice. Indeed, the fact that the police and prison administrations fell under the aegis of the Department of Justice may well have acted as a spur to the judges to ensure that the courts were not tainted by any maladministration in those other branches.

[133] Wessels, Curlewis, and Ward, JJ.
[134] The two additional judges of appeal, C G Maasdorp and J A J de Villiers, JJP concurred at 135.
[135] See 109–19.
[136] See 119–27.
[137] See 127–35.
[138] At 125.
[139] At 126.
[140] At 129.
[141] At 135.
[142] By the Prisons and Reformatories Act 13 of 1911, section 25(3).
[143] At 127.

MISCELLANY

Several other cases heard by the AD from 1910 to 1950 which indicate judicial views on matters which might be classified as "civil liberties" are included within this last section.

Three cases concern the position of women in the social formation, and illustrate the very traditional character of judicial attitudes to the issue. *Incorporated Law Society v Wookey*[144] came to Bloemfontein because the CPD[145] had decided that respondent, a woman, could be registered as an articled clerk in an attorney's office, leading to her eventual qualification for practice at the Side-Bar. The Law Society argued that, although the Cape Charter of Justice[146] had provided that "persons" might be enrolled as attorneys, the common law and custom demanded that this be limited to males.

The AD agreed with this contention, pandering to what was without doubt the dominant sentiment both in society and the legal profession at that time.[147] Innes, ACJ based his conclusion on the common law of 1828, which had barred women from becoming attorneys, though he reached this hard result "with real regret".[148] Solomon, J relied almost completely on subsequent practice in his interpretation of the Charter,[149] while J A J de Villiers, JP said that the court should discover what the law was, rather than what it ought to be, and that prohibition on the basis of sex had not yet become obsolete.[150]

These findings are hardly surprising, and they received favourable comment in the SALJ,[151] but the lack of an adventurous spirit on the part of the court is a matter for regret, especially in the light of the CPD's initial move in ordering the registration of Wookey's articles, as well as the argument of D M Buchanan[152] that positions in the civil service which were formerly the exclusive preserve of men were being opened to women. In the event, the legislature had to act to cure this impediment in the law.[153]

This type of attitude towards women was borne out much later in the period in two cases involving sexual assault. In *R v Mosago & another*[154] the AD answered a question of law to the effect that it was a

[144] 1912 AD 623.
[145] *Per* C G Maasdorp, JP.
[146] Of 1828, section 20.
[147] There were no female solicitors in Holland or England at that time; see R P B Davis "Women as Advocates and Attorneys" (1914) 31 *SALJ* 383–6, and Melius de Villiers "Women and the Legal Profession" (1918) 35 *SALJ* 289–91. There was one anonymous note in support of women, however: see (1913) 30 *SALJ* 462–3.
[148] See 627–35.
[149] See 635–40.
[150] See 640–2.
[151] See note 147 above.
[152] Counsel for Wookey at 625–6. An additional point here was that section 7 of the Interpretation Act 5 of 1910, which stated that "male" should include female when used in a statute, could have been preferred by the court, as a more recent indication of legislative will.
[153] By the Women Legal Practitioners Act 7 of 1923, section 1.
[154] 1935 AD 32.

defence available to an accused on a charge of rape that he had honestly believed that the actions of the complainant had signified consent to the assault. In this case, an African woman had shouted and screamed in protest at sexual assault by eight men in a dark and lonely place. The latter claimed that they had believed complainant to be a prostitute who had shouted in ecstasy, and all the judges[155] accepted that her protest had been insufficient. It would be interesting to know how much more of a struggle the appeal judges expected of a woman faced with such odds before they would have been prepared to conclude that she had not consented, and if their attitudes would have been different had all the parties been Europeans.

In *R v M*[156] the evidence of the African complainant in a case of attempted rape was again disbelieved, even though her story had been accepted by the magistrate, whose decision the TPD[157] had refused to overturn on appeal. The conflicting evidence of both complainant and accused had been corroborated by a friend of each, yet the majority of the AD[158] preferred that of the accused, a coloured school teacher, that complainant had provoked him to assault by insulting him. Within South Africa's social hierarchy, it is again of interest to speculate on the court's possible attitude had the racial roles of complainant and accused been reversed. A civil libertarian note was struck here by the sympathetic dissent of Tindall, JA[159] who was not prepared to disturb the magistrate's finding on the credibility of the witnesses, and who displayed an understanding of the plight of the female complainant in such cases which would bring praise upon a court even today.

Revealing attitudes to corporal punishment came to light in *R v Scheepers*,[160] in which a headmaster appealed against his conviction on a charge of common assault which resulted from his beating an eleven year old girl pupil twice in one morning. While Innes, CJ, admitted[161] that the teacher–pupil relationship justified the infliction of moderate and reasonable corporal punishment, he felt strongly that male teachers should not punish female pupils in this way and was not prepared to interfere with the magistrate's finding of excessive and illegal treatment in this instance. C G Maasdorp, JA agreed with this view,[162] but Solomon, JA thought that the punishment was merely severe, and not cruel, and he would have allowed the appeal, although he did agree that males should not beat females.[163]

[155] Judgments of Wessels, CJ (33–5); Beyers, JA (35–6); and J E R de Villiers, JA (36). Curlewis, JA concurred.
[156] 1946 AD 1023.
[157] Murray and Roper, JJ.
[158] Judgment of Davis, AJA (1023–9) concurred in by Watermeyer, CJ; Greenberg and Schreiner, JJA.
[159] See 1029–32.
[160] 1915 AD 337.
[161] See 338–40. [162] See 343–4. [163] See 341–3.

It is perhaps surprising that the language question, which so vexed the minds of European politicians in this period, should have surfaced in the AD on only one occasion. In *De Bruin v Director of Education*,[164] the AD decided that the "home language" of a pupil was that which was habitually spoken in the pupil's household, rather than that "best understood and most easily used", which was the test applied by the Transvaal Director of Education.[165] This decision struck a blow for parental choice as opposed to official discretion, which would probably have been to the benefit of Afrikaans, although in De Bruin's case his right to the education of his daughter in English was upheld.

Finally, in this civil libertarian miscellany, the AD ended on a tolerant note by upholding the right of passive political protest even during the sensitive period of the Second World War. In *R v Alberts*[166] the accused had been convicted of doing an act which he intended "should have the effect of preventing, interfering with, or disturbing any lawful gathering",[167] in that he had refused to stand during the playing of "God Save the King" at the end of a cinema performance in Tzaneen. This had caused a commotion in the rest of the audience, but there had been no actual breach of the peace, and De Wet, CJ[168] exploited a difference in meaning between the English and Afrikaans versions of the regulation so that he could adopt the narrower Afrikaans meaning. On this reading of the regulation, the cinema performance was held not to have been a "gathering", and Alberts's appeal succeeded.

This decision shows how aware the members of the court were of divisions of opinion and tensions within the white group in SA over participation in the war, and it represents an attempt to reconcile conflict rather than to bow to what was the sentiment of the majority of the élite, and, no doubt, the members of the Bench themselves, at that time.[169]

Summary and Conclusions

By way of summary, it must be asked how successfully the AD fulfilled its role as protector of the civil liberties of South Africa's citizenry, while simultaneously ensuring continued social stability and maintaining public order. If one takes all the cases which have been discussed above, it seems a fair assessment to say that the appeal judges struck a remarkably fine balance between the interests of the

[164] 1934 AD 252.

[165] See judgment of J E R de Villiers, JA, concurred in by Wessels, CJ; Curlewis and Stratford, JJA at 253–7; and Beyers, JA at 257–60.

[166] 1942 AD 135.

[167] A contravention of the National Security Regulations, section 9(1)*(a)*.

[168] See 138–40 concurred in by Watermeyer, Tindall, Centlivres, and Feetham, JJA.

[169] For a detailed account of feelings in the Afrikaner group at the time, see for example Moodie *The Rise of Afrikanerdom* Ch 11, and the cases in the next chapter.

individual and those of society with, perhaps, a slight bias in certain areas towards those who were deprived in some way.

Certainly, in the spheres of freedom of expression and the proper administration of justice, the court throughout assumed a role staunchly in favour of individual freedom, and restrained unjust action on the part of officialdom. The only category in which the judges appeared to succumb to the predictably mundane opinions of the early twentieth-century social élites was that of the status of women in the social formation. To a certain extent, these attitudes flow naturally from the generally liberal, middle-class backgrounds of the judges.

Nevertheless, it is significant and redounds to its credit, that the Bench was prepared to hold to its views, and to take a progressive lead in attempting to engender a more tolerant and cohesive social order in the Union. The power of judicial proceedings and pronouncements as an educational and opinion-making force should not be underestimated, and the AD would seem to have played a large part in the respect for whatever civil freedoms have existed in SA from time to time.

One slight blemish on the judicial record is the apparent willingness to tolerate extreme ideas which had little popular appeal, while adopting a more restrictive and less tolerant stance in respect of those ideologies or organisations which had a realistic prospect of changing the social framework in a way not approved of by the judiciary. To a degree the court appears to have been anxious to provide a forum through which those, who had no other means of formal political expression, could release their energy and frustration in a controlled manner, which involved no threat to the public order. Examples of this approach are found in the cases of *Crawford, Harrison, Roux, Desai*, and *Whittaker*, on the one hand, and *Hertzog, Rossouw*, and *Stewart* on the other.

A further distinctive feature is the constancy with which the AD approached issues of civil liberty over the years, as there appears to be no noticeable variation with changes in judicial personnel. This serves as an example of the self-generating character of the judicial ethos, the method whereby the length and form of apprenticeship at the Bar and the provincial Bench act to impose a uniform mould on judicial creativity and thought.

As far as individuals are concerned, a total of eighteen judges sat in the twenty-five cases surveyed above,[170] Innes, Watermeyer, and Tindall each having been on the Bench in nine cases. Certain judges—Lord De Villiers, Innes, Solomon, Beyers, and J E R de Villiers—were wont to speak out and give their views, even as separate concurrences, and there were five dissents delivered—

[170] Of those noted in Ch II, only Kotzé, Roos, Van den Heever, Hoexter, and Fagan did not sit in any of the cases.

Solomon in *Crawford* and *Scheepers*, Tindall in *Molepo* and *M*, and Feetham in *Molepo*. After 1920 there was an increasing trend towards a single judgment for the whole court, though Beyers did his best to change this, handing down a judgment in each of the four cases in which he sat.[171] In addition, it is noteworthy that only nine appellants in the cases discussed were not successful in their appeals,[172] connoting an inclination to overrule the provincial courts rarely present to so marked a degree in other groups of cases.

The overall impression, therefore, is one of a court invariably on its guard in an effort to protect the individual from state actions which tended to curtail liberty, with an emphasis on liberal values as a frame of reference, and with an ability to speak critically of official excesses when they occurred.

Judicial attitudes within the closely-related field of extra-Parliamentary resistance to government policy will now be reviewed, in order to see whether this pattern is repeated or altered.

[171] *Roux, Hartzer, Mosago*, and *De Bruin supra*.

[172] Hertzog, Kimpton, Stewart Printing, Wallendorf, Hartzer, Britz, the Minister of Police in *Bolstridge* and *Desai*, and Scheepers.

CHAPTER FOUR

RESISTANCE AND REBELLION

The racial factor has for so long been assumed to be the dominant characteristic of the South African "problem", connoting a homogeneity in the European group and the absence of economic class as a relevant consideration, that it comes as rather a surprise to discover that almost all the cases which fell within the category "resistance and rebellion" from 1910 to 1950 involved violent activities by whites against their own elected government. Although black resisters may have used other methods more readily than struggle through the courts,[1] and although some cases of organised opposition to government by blacks are dealt with under the title "Race Relations" below,[2] there is no doubt that the AD's attention was concentrated on the reconciliation of intra-white conflict, and that the "racial problem" was conceived of in Afrikaans–English terms in this period.

The court had ample opportunity to make its feelings known in this sensitive area, for at least eighteen cases dealing with rebellion and labour disturbances came before it from 1910 to 1950. They arose out of three major events: Afrikaner opposition to Union participation in each of the world wars in the Allied cause, and the "Rand Revolt" among white workers in 1922. Some of the cases bear a close relationship to the issues of civil liberty discussed above, but an important distinction in many of the following cases is the use of violent methods by protesters to make their point more effectively. The way in which the judges approached the parties and issues in dispute clearly manifests their concern at these developments, as well as their endeavour by their approach to contribute towards a solution, at best, or a containment, at worst, of the sharp conflict.

Although most of what follows is devoted to a description and analysis of cases involving whites, four cases which arose from efforts of blacks to fight government initiatives, two of which were non-violent in nature, will be dealt with first. As has been said, this is by no means the sum total of cases involving black opposition, nor was the legal system seen as a medium through which concessions could be wrung (as it has appeared to be in the United States). For it is a feature of South African legal history that the courts have only been resorted to in order to nullify state action against a particular individual, or to mitigate the consequences of "illegal" action against

[1] See Roux *Time Longer than Rope passim*.
[2] See for example *R v Herman* 1937 AD 168, and *R v Abdurahman* 1950 (3) SA 136 (AD).

the state by protesters themselves, through appeals against criminal convictions and sentences.

Black Resisters

Union Government v Montsioa[3] provides an early example of an unsuccessful attempt by a black leader to retain a certain measure of self-government in the face of increased local control after Union. The immediate issue in dispute was the power of the Divisional Council of Mafeking to levy a dog-tax in the Molopo Reserve, an area where Chief Montsioa held sway, but the case was in fact the outcome of a complicated series of negotiations and proclamations which had regulated the status of the Reserve.[4] Montsioa's principal contention, which had won the day in the CPD,[5] was that the colonial powers had given assurances to his ancestors, when they had annexed the British Bechuanaland Area in 1885 to 1886, that the Reserve would remain the inalienable possession of the chiefdom, and that subsequent government proclamations which purported to include the Reserve within the fiscal division of Mafeking were *ultra vires* by that token. The government and divisional council argued on appeal that the power given to the colonial Governor of the Cape to "alter boundaries" of fiscal divisions included the power to incorporate the Molopo Reserve, which had never before been part of a magisterial district.

The AD unanimously[6] upheld the government's appeal in three detailed judgments, which form prototypes of the judicial styles of Lord De Villiers, CJ,[7] Innes[8] and Solomon, JJA.[9] What is important here is not so much the fact that the court found for the government, but the assumptions which the judges made, and the manner in which they dismissed the cogent arguments of W P Schreiner, KC, counsel for Montsioa. The Chief Justice said[10] that no great hardship would be caused to Montsioa, as the form of local government to be imposed was regarded as a privilege in the rest of the Cape Province, and as the dog- and any road-taxes which might be imposed were not a grievous burden. Innes, JA, who had been a member of the Cape Parliament or Cabinet when much of the disputed government activity had taken place, insisted that any undertakings given by the administration on annexation of British Bechuanaland had not been broken by the extension of fiscal control over the Reserve.[11]

[3] *Union Government (Minister of the Interior) & Divisional Council of Mafeking v Montsioa* 1914 AD 42.

[4] For the clearest exposition of the facts see Innes, JA at 55–60.

[5] *Per* Buchanan and Kotzé, JJ at 46–7 of the AD report.

[6] J A J de Villiers, AJA concurred with Lord De Villiers, CJ, while A F S Maasdorp, AAJA agreed that the appeal should be allowed at 68.

[7] See 51–5.

[8] See 55–65.

[9] See 65–7.

[10] At 55.

[11] At 64.

None of the judges was sensitive to the wider ramifications of their decision to impose "civilized" (ie European) control over the region. The levy of taxes on huts, dogs, or individuals was the means whereby the government had forced much of the rural black population (which until then had been able to survive reasonably well on the product of subsistence farming) into the cash economy of the country, as the taxes had to be paid in cash, which could only be obtained by selling surplus produce or by labouring work on the European-owned farms or mines (a more likely option).[12] In addition, this local control exercised by a European-elected and -composed authority would greatly diminish the traditional powers of the tribal chiefs, who were often the focus of opposition to the government. Although the judges can hardly have been expected to encourage such opposition, and although Montsioa did not argue such points in his submission, the failure of the court to refer to these matters points to judicial identity with both the thinking of the government of the day, and the judge's accepted role in refusing to consider "extraneous" factors in deciding a case.

A second instance of a non-violent attempt to negate a government enactment came in the form of an application for leave to appeal by one *Vezi*[13] against his conviction[14] for unlawfully ploughing a portion of a "native trust farm" which had been set aside as commonage.[15] His rather ingenious argument at Bloemfontein was that the Proclamation under which he had been found guilty was of no force and effect, as it had not been laid before the Native Representative Council (NRC)[16] before promulgation, as required by the Representation of Natives Act.[17]

Now, the NRC had adjourned indefinitely during the African miners' strike of August 1946, in protest against the government's breach of faith.[18] Therefore, if Vezi's contention had been upheld, all legislation relating to Africans since that time would have been null and void. Not surprisingly, the court rejected the argument, Centlivres, JA,[19] pronouncing that there was nothing in the Act from which it could be inferred that Parliament had intended that the NRC's consideration was necessary for the validity of legislation affecting Africans: indeed, several provisions[20] of the Act pointed the

[12] See Bundy *The Rise and Fall of the South African Peasantry* Ch 4; and Wilson and Thompson (Eds) *Oxford History of South Africa* Volume II 65.

[13] *R v Vezi* 1947 (4) SA 551 (AD).

[14] For a contravention of Proclamation 12 of 1945, section 24(1)*(b)*, read with sections 2, 6(1), 6(5), 26, and 27, issued under section 25(1) of the Native Administration Act 38 of 1927, read in conjunction with section 21 of the Native Trust and Land Act 18 of 1936.

[15] Reserved in terms of Proclamation 12 of 1945, section 6.

[16] Set up by the Representation of Natives Act 12 of 1936, section 20.

[17] Section 27(1) of which provided that the NRC should consider and report upon proposed legislation in so far as it might affect the native population.

[18] See Roux *op cit* 340.

[19] See 553–6, speaking for Watermeyer, CJ; Tindall, Greenberg, and Schreiner, JJA.

[20] Such as sections 27(3) and 28.

other way. This case, then, provides an example of the ease with which the court accepted the government's version of the dispute under review, and ignored the wider "political" aspect of the legal challenge.

Violent action taken by blacks in opposition to government was the basis of two cases heard by the court of appeal. *R v Mpeta*[21] had its roots in the last major act of defiance by a tribal group before Union, the Bambata rebellion under Dinizulu in 1906.[22] The accused here had been tried and acquitted twice on a charge of murder arising from the killing of a magistrate during the uprising. He was eventually convicted of "assault with intent to commit murder" in 1911, but the AD, although "slow to interfere with the findings of experienced judges and magistrates upon questions of fact", overturned this decision on the basis that the evidence was conflicting and insufficient.[23] Innes, ACJ[24] remarked that it was good that criminals should be brought to justice, but better that a guilty person should go free, rather than an innocent person be convicted.[25] This can be regarded as an important affirmation of judicial policy in criminal cases, especially when the wider implications of Mpeta's alleged misdemeanour are taken into account.

The imposition of a dog-tax and other measures taken against the Bondelswarts people of southern South West Africa had slightly bloodier consequences than those in Montsioa's case. The Bondelswarts were "Hottentots", originally from the Cape Colony, who had been in constant rebellion against German authority, and who had helped the South African forces against the Germans in the First World War. Their "fighting chief", Abram Morris, had returned to his people from exile in the northern Cape, against the wishes of the Union Government. The South West African authorities attempted to arrest him, whereupon long-simmering discontent boiled over into open rebellion by the six hundred or so Bondelswarts. A large police and volunteer force (including future appeal judge Van den Heever), aided by aerial bombing and scouting by the infant Air Force, crushed the spirit of resistance, and killed at least fifty rebels.[26] The surviving hereditary chief, Jakobus Christian, was convicted on two charges of high treason, but, in view of the uncertain status of South West Africa as a mandated territory placed under South Africa's tutelage by the League of Nations, the SWAHC reserved a question of law for the AD as to whether the charge as laid had disclosed the crime of high treason.

[21] 1912 AD 568.
[22] See Roux *op cit* 94–6; Wilson and Thompson *op cit* 345; and Marks *Reluctant Rebellion.*
[23] See 575, *per* Innes, ACJ.
[24] See 568–76 with whom Solomon, J; C G Maasdorp, JP; Laurence, AJP; and J A J de Villiers, JP concurred.
[25] At 575–6.
[26] See R Freislich *The Last Tribal War* for a detailed account.

The issue which was central to the decision was whether the crime of high treason could be committed against a state which possessed internal sovereignty, even though its external powers had been limited in certain respects. In this regard, the mandate for SWA had been conferred on Great Britain by the Council of the League of Nations, to be exercised by the government of South Africa, which was to have full power of administration and legislation over the territory as an integral portion of the Union.[27] Thus, the judges had to determine whether the South African government was the seat of sovereignty with respect to SWA, such that the taking up of arms against South Africa with hostile intent would constitute the crime of high treason.

In four careful judgments,[28] the court considered the law relating to sovereignty and high treason, and the peculiar status of SWA in international law. The AD concluded that South Africa possessed sufficient internal sovereignty to warrant a charge of high treason against an inhabitant of SWA who took up arms against it with hostile intent. All the judges returned to the Roman and Roman-Dutch roots of the concept of sovereignty, and decided that it could be split into external and internal aspects, that its existence was a matter of degree of control, and that the limitation of sovereign rights would not deprive a claimant of sovereignty, so long as sovereignty was not abdicated in favour of another. After the court had studied the details of the mandate, and had discarded the idea that sovereignty might have resided in the Principal Allied and Associated Powers, or the League of Nations, it decided that the South African government had assumed the role of sovereign power. Kotzé, JA probably summed up the reasoning which led the members of the court to favour South African sovereignty when he said that ". . . all right thinking minds must welcome, with sincere approbation, this international attempt to promote and maintain the sacred cause of peace and the uplifting of public morality in the interest of humanity".[29] He recognised, too, that law was not so stereotyped that "well-settled and generally-acknowledged principles could not be applied to new circumstances".[30]

Besides being a clear insight into the South African attitudes to the mandate in its very early days, this decision is significant because of the harsh attitude displayed by the judges towards the acts of the accused when compared with their relatively lenient approach to the misdeeds of white rebels in the preceding eight years. *Christian* is on a slightly different footing when compared with these other cases, as

[27] At 110–11.

[28] *R v Christian* 1924 AD 101. The following judgments are reported: Innes, CJ (104–14), with whom Solomon, JA concurred; J A J de Villiers, JA (115–22); Kotzé, JA (122–34); and Wessels, JA (135–7).

[29] At 129.

[30] At 130.

Innes, CJ made it clear that the AD was concerned here only with the question of law as to sovereignty, and not the facts of the case. None the less, it is interesting to speculate whether the court would have been as willing to impute sovereignty to South Africa if the rebels had been German or white Afrikaner malcontents, rather than "natives".

It is submitted that it was possible, on the law as it stood, to have answered the question of law in Christian's favour, which would have resulted in a trial for a less serious offence. The likelihood of such a finding would have been greater had Christian been a white person, a proposition which is derived from a consideration of the treatment of Afrikaner rebels in World War I, to which the focus now shifts.

White Rebels

Although there had been minor ructions in the political sphere almost from the day of Union in 1910, the will of the politicians to remain united in one South Africa first came under severe strain with the outbreak of the First World War in 1914. Naturally, many of those who had fought and suffered for the Boer Republics from 1899 to 1902 still cherished the idea of an independent Afrikaner republic. They resented the Union's entry into the war as an ally of the British, especially as the campaign was directed against their erstwhile friend, the Kaiser (albeit in the guise of his colony in South West Africa). Dissension centred on various Boer War generals, both in the Defence Force and in Parliament, and the latter part of 1914 witnessed a widespread rebellion among Afrikaners in the Defence Force and in the countryside. However, General Botha, the Prime Minister, retained the loyalty of the larger part of Afrikanerdom, and he used these elements to crush the rebellion, before setting out to defeat the German garrison and occupy South West Africa.[31]

Most of the rebels were dealt with by a special criminal court,[32] and were not heavily punished, to avoid creating martyrs.[33] Nevertheless, several civil actions reached the AD, allowing the judges to express their views on the culpability of the rebels, as well as the general topic of martial law, with which this discussion begins.

Krohn v Minister of Defence & the Special Court[34] was an appeal by a rebel against the dismissal by the TPD of his application for an interdict to restrain the Special Court from proceeding with his trial on a charge, under the martial law regulations, of using seditious

[31] For an account of the events, see Moodie *op cit* 37–8 and 82–3; and Walker *A History of Southern Africa* 563–4.

[32] Set up under Government Notice No 1949 of 1914.

[33] There was one major exception to this trend in the case of Jopie Fourie, a Defence Force officer who was executed for his part in the rebellion and instantly became a folk-hero.

[34] *Krohn v The Minister for Defence of the Union of South Africa & the Special Court under Martial Law Regulations, Pretoria* 1915 AD 191.

language. His argument[35] before the AD was that the declaration of martial law was only justified by necessity, which was not the case here, and that there was no need for a Special Court, as the ordinary courts were operating normally. His appeal was dismissed by the court, which held itself entirely bound by *Ex parte Marais*[36] and *Van Reenen & Smit v A-G.*[37] In these cases, the Privy Council had established that, when an actual war was raging, acts done by the military authorities were not justiciable by ordinary tribunals; that the fact that ordinary tribunals might continue to operate was not conclusive that war was not raging; and that the Supreme Court had no jurisdiction to review the judgments of martial law courts.[38] Applying these principles to Krohn's case, the judges[39] decided that a state of war existed in South Africa as a consequence of which the civil tribunals could not enquire into the propriety of military actions. But, in doing so, they made some remarks which emphasised their commitment to the rule of law and their varying degrees of unease at its suspension during martial law.

Innes, CJ[40] began by affirming the absolute supremacy of the law, and that no one could be punished save by properly constituted legal tribunals, except when the force upon which the courts depended and the constitution was based (i e the state) was itself challenged, by war, rebellion, or civil commotion. Under such circumstances, he maintained, the state could be compelled for a time to disregard the ordinary safeguards of liberty in defence of liberty itself, but the proclamation of martial law, being an inherent right, could grant the state no authority or power which it had not previously possessed.[41] After dismissing the appeal, he added, "In no respect can Martial Law be regarded as good thing; it is at best a lamentable necessity. It imposes a great responsibility on the executive Government; it operates with inevitable harshness in certain cases, and it saps the political fibre of the people."[42] He ended with a plea for a regularisation of the system in certain localities in order to lessen the burden on the government and the people.[43]

Solomon, JA,[44] by contrast, confined himself to the relevant facts and law, but found it awkward that Krohn had relied in his submission on some remarks of Solomon's in *R v Bekker,*[45] which had preceded the Privy Council decisions. He maintained, though, that they should be regarded as erroneous in the light of the subsequent Privy Council decisions,[46] and he proceeded to dismiss the appeal without further comment. J A J de Villiers, AJA[47] pursued

[35] As outlined by his counsel, G van Pittius, at 193–4.
[36] [1902] AC 109. [37] [1904] AC 114.
[38] See Innes, CJ at 199–200.
[39] Innes, CJ; Solomon, JA; and J A J de Villiers, AJA.
[40] See 195–202. [41] At 197. [42] At 202.
[43] *Loc cit.* [44] See 202–7. [45] 17 SC 340.
[46] At 203. [47] See 207–12.

much the same line as Innes, CJ, traced the doctrine of the supremacy of the law back to Charles I, and considered Dicey's writing on the rule of law in detail.[48] The foundation of martial law was self-defence and necessity, he said, and both the justification for and exercise of martial law authority were strictly limited by the necessities of the situation.[49] Although he found it difficult to believe that the military and executive authorities were the final judges of the necessity for martial law, the Privy Council decisions were conclusive in this respect and the appeal had to be dismissed.[50]

The attitudes of the three judges are in many ways reminiscent of those which they displayed (to the issue of freedom of speech) in *Crawford v Albu*.[51] It is significant that Innes, CJ and De Villiers, AJA, felt obliged to make the warning remarks which they did here, as they constituted a firm reminder to the authorities that, in any future action which they wished to take, they would have to reckon with the watchful eye of the appellate judiciary.

Three other cases which stemmed directly from acts of rebellion reached Bloemfontein, and each concerned the liability of rebel leaders for acts performed by their subordinates which had resulted in harm to others, who had then sought damages as compensation. *Naùde & Du Plessis v Mercier*[52] took the form of an appeal by two rebel officers against the award by the OPD of damages to the respondent for wrongful arrest and detention, in that he had been captured and interrogated by men under appellants' command. Among other grounds of appeal, Naude and Du Plessis contended "with evident earnestness"[53] that their actions had been justified by self-defence. To this Innes, CJ replied that the government might put down rebellion by armed force, employing its army as well as its police, and that those who went into rebellion and took the field with organised bodies of armed men had no legal right to complain if they were attacked, resistance to which would not be legitimate self-defence.[54] As a result, the appeal was dismissed with firmness.

In *McKenzie v Van der Merwe*,[55] however, the rebel was successful in both the OPD and AD. The judges decided that, where a rebellion had taken place, it was not the case that every rebel was liable for the delict of every other rebel if done in furtherance of the common purpose and not foreign to it, in the absence of any other connection by way of command, instigation, advice, assistance, or participation in the particular delict.[56] Here, McKenzie, a non-rebel farmer, had sued a rebel commander, Van der Merwe, for the value of certain stock forcibly removed from his farm by rebels, but as there was no

[48] At 207. [49] At 210. [50] At 211–12.
[51] Above, Ch III. [52] 1917 AD 32. [53] Innes, CJ at 37.
[54] *Loc cit.* Innes, CJ (see 35–40), was joined in his judgment by Solomon and C G Maasdorp, JJA; and J A J de Villiers and Juta, AJJA.
[55] 1917 AD 41.
[56] *Per* Innes, CJ at 47–8.

evidence to implicate Van der Merwe directly, a majority[57] in the AD dismissed his claim, after a thorough examination of the law relating to criminal common purpose and the evidence of the case. Only C G Maasdorp, JA[58] was prepared to support McKenzie, on the ground that the supply by one of Van der Merwe's subordinates of a cart in which the rebels had removed the stock was sufficient to establish his liability.

A year later, the same judges were unanimous in holding a rebel commander liable in damages for the shooting by one of his men of a soldier serving in the Defence Force, in the process relying upon the principle laid down in *McKenzie v Van der Merwe*. In *Mouton & others v Beket,*[59] the field cornet of a small rebel commando and the fellow scouts of one D, who had attached himself to the commando, appealed against a substantial award of damages against them by the OPD, as the result of the wounding by D of Beket. D had soon thereafter been killed, and Mouton relied on arguments[60] that he himself had not been present at the shooting, at a time when the commando had taken cover in order to keep away from government troops in the area.

Innes, CJ rejected this claim,[61] and found on the facts that the commando had been militant, that D had been a member, and that Mouton was liable for D's actions as the probable and natural outcome of his exercise of authority in sending out the scouts. The rest of the judges[62] agreed with this view of the case.

What is apparent in these cases is a firm yet understanding application of the ordinary principles of delictual liability. While stressing that their victims had been acting on behalf of the state, the court treated the rebels' acts as conventional delicts, in an endeavour to minimise the political aspects of the Rebellion, and to heal the rifts opened thereby. This can be contrasted with the approach in *Christian,* in which armed resistance to a government act which directly affected the appellant was construed as an act of treason, rather than criminal disobedience. The cases which follow will determine whether this judicial magnanimity extended to a different sort of rebel, the general striker of 1922.

White Labour Revolts

After years of simmering discontent, white labour on the Witwatersrand, particularly in the mines, erupted in 1922, bringing much of the economy to a standstill, and forcing a confrontation with

[57] Innes, CJ (44–9); Solomon, JA (49–58); J A J de Villiers and Juta, AJJA who concurred silently.
[58] See 58–66.
[59] 1918 AD 181.
[60] Through his counsel, J B M Hertzog, at 187.
[61] See 187–92.
[62] Solomon (193–7) and C G Maasdorp (197–200), JJA gave separate opinions, while J A J de Villiers and Juta, AJJA concurred silently at 200.

the government of General Smuts, which intervened brutally on the side of the employers to smash the revolt.[63] Again a Special Criminal Court was set up to try the strikers for various offences, and this court reserved several questions of law for consideration by the AD. This forced the court to define the requirements for the commission of various crimes against the state, which were to prove important in the future.

In *R v Erasmus,*[64] the accused, a strike leader, had been convicted on five counts of high treason, but the Special Court asked the AD to consider, *inter alia,* whether the facts, as found by the court, disclosed that Erasmus had committed the crime of high treason. Innes, CJ[65] rephrased this to ask whether Erasmus's conduct in instigating and perpetrating acts of warfare against the forces of the Crown amounted to high treason, in view of the fact that his intention had not been wholly to subvert the government, but to coerce it with regard to its attitude to the industrial dispute. The court [66] answered the question in favour of the Crown, and held that Erasmus had been properly convicted of high treason.

Both Innes, CJ[67] and Kotzé, JA,[68] who handed down judgments on behalf of the court, surveyed the Roman and Roman-Dutch law roots of the crime of hoogverraad[69] in detail. In the Roman and most of the Dutch authorities[70] they found that the distinctive feature of the crime was the presence of a hostile intent against the state, to be deduced from all the circumstances. Voet and Matthaeus, however, limited high treason to those cases where there was not only hostility towards, but also a definite intention to overthrow, the state, which, if adopted here, would have absolved Erasmus, as had been argued by his counsel, Tielman Roos.[71] The AD was not prepared to accept this narrow ground for establishing high treason and preferred to hold that: "It is clear from an examination of the authorities that armed attacks on the State or Government, perpetrated with hostile mind or intent, constitute treason."[72]

By adopting this approach, the court was interpreting the common law in an extensive fashion in cases where human liberty was involved, which was contrary to their professed policy in regard to construction of statutes,[73] in which they assumed a restrictive

[63] For an account of the events, see Roux *op cit* Ch XIV; Wilson and Thompson *op cit* 27; and Walker *History* 590–2.

[64] 1923 AD 73.

[65] At 79.

[66] Consisting of Innes, CJ; Solomon, J A J de Villiers, Juta, and Kotzé, JJA.

[67] See 76–82.

[68] See 82–90.

[69] The Dutch equivalent of Roman *perduellio* and the English *high treason*.

[70] For example Damhouder (*Prac Crim cap* 62), Van Leeuwen *(Cens For Lib* 5 *cap* 2), Huber (*praelect ad Inst* 4.18), Van der Linden (2.4.2), and Moorman (*Misdaden* 1.3.2).

[71] At 74–5. See Voet (48.4.2), and Matthaeus (*de Criminibus* 48.2.2).

[72] *Per* Kotzé, JA at 88. He confessed himself disappointed with Voet's writing at 87.

[73] See for example *Ritch & Bhyat v Union Government* 1912 AD 719 at 740.

approach in such cases. This appears to be an example of an occasion on which the judges of appeal could quite feasibly, by means of arguments of "moving with the times and advances of political civilization",[74] have accepted Voet's writings as authoritative, had they wished to do so. Their failure to do so is indicative of their inability either to understand or to tolerate the actions of Erasmus and his co-workers at that time, which were potentially no more dangerous than those of the World War I rebels.

The same issues were raised by the questions of law reserved in *R v Viljoen & others,*[75] and the court applied the test for high treason established in *Erasmus* to uphold Viljoen's conviction on such a charge.[76] But this time they had further to consider whether the Special Court was competent to convict an accused for sedition when he had been charged with high treason, because Maré and Coetzee, Viljoen's co-accused, had not committed acts of treason. The same judges answered this in favour of the Crown, and again Innes, CJ,[77] and Kotzé, JA[78] were the court's spokesmen.

In substantially similar opinions, the judges admitted the imprecision of the definition of sedition by the Dutch authorities,[79] but averred that the test applied by the Special Court (which had required a hostile intention to be present for both high treason and sedition, the distinction being merely a question of the degree of hostility), was wrong.[80] Instead, Innes, CJ adopted a definition of J A J de Villiers, JP in *R v Endemann,*[81] that sedition was constituted by "a gathering in defiance of the authorities and for an unlawful purpose", with no implication of the existence of a hostile intent.[82] The court decided that the accused's conduct had been seditious (despite the actual finding by the Special Court of a hostile intent), and, on the general principle that the greater crime includes the less, they confirmed Maré and Coetzee's conviction for sedition.[83]

In other words, having decided that a hostile intention was the hallmark of the crime of high treason *alone,* they proceeded to allow the conviction of two accused, who had been found to have displayed such an intention, for *sedition*. In addition, by adopting such a wide definition of sedition when the lack of authority gave them an almost free hand to curtail the scope of such a serious crime, had they wished to, the judges dealt a further ace to executive capability to limit civil freedoms, including peaceful protest.

[74] As in *Crawford v Albu*; and *R v Roux & another, supra,* Ch III.
[75] 1923 AD 90.
[76] At 91–2 and 96.
[77] See 91–6.
[78] See 96–100. Solomon, J A J de Villiers and Juta, JJA concurred.
[79] At 94 and 97.
[80] At 92.
[81] 1915 TPD 142 at 149.
[82] At 93.
[83] At 94–5 and 98–9.

Many problems were caused by the fact that only certain named offences could be tried by the Special Court, and this factor led directly to the questions of law reserved in *R v Jolly & others.*[84] Here the accused strikers had been convicted of assault with intent to murder (one of the listed offences) which followed from their derailment of a train at a particular locality, the nature of which had made it unlikely that the train's occupants would be maimed or killed. The appeal judges[85] found it a simple matter to affirm the Special Court's finding that the derailment constituted an "assault" on the passengers,[86] but they confessed to some difficulty in establishing an "intent to murder" from the evidence.[87]

In the result, the AD decided that there was some evidence of murderous intent to be inferred from the facts, but neither Innes, CJ[88] nor Kotzé, JA,[89] although they answered the questions of law in favour of the Crown, was prepared to state categorically that this evidence was sufficient to establish intent, when this was precisely the question asked by the Special Court! Innes, CJ and Kotzé, JA maintained that it was solely within the power of the trial court to judge of the sufficiency of the evidence, and that the AD should only have been asked whether there was *any* evidence for such a finding. The judges hinted that the sentences imposed on the accused had been too harsh[90] (especially as they would not have been charged with assault to murder had a particular statutory offence[91] been within the jurisdiction of the Special Court), and J A J de Villiers, JA seemed to take a sympathetic view of the personal motives of Jolly and the others in the abnormal circumstances of the time.[92]

The somewhat unsatisfactory treatment of the legal questions which surfaced in these three cases raises questions about the judicial capacity for understanding the situation, motives, and actions of the strikers. There appears to be less anxiety to placate white workers than was evident in the court's treatment of the 1914 rebels. This indicates an unthinking partiality in judicial approach, for the actions of the strikers were no more subversive of state authority than those of the rebels had been. Whether this is a fair assessment can be gauged from a consideration of the cases which arose from treasonous activities by Afrikaners in World War II, which follow below.

The Second Rebellion

The rapid growth of National Socialist ideology in Germany between the wars had an echo in several Afrikaner groups in South

[84] 1923 AD 176. [85] Innes, CJ; Solomon, J A J de Villiers, Juta, and Kotzé, JJA.
[86] See Innes, CJ at 180 and Kotzé, JA at 185.
[87] See Kotzé, JA at 185 for example.
[88] See 177–82 at 182. [89] See 183–90 at 190.
[90] See Innes, CJ at 182; and De Villiers, JA at 182–3.
[91] Railways Regulation Act 22 of 1916, section 37 of which imposed a maximum penalty of two years' imprisonment or a £200 fine.
[92] At 183. He displayed a similar attitude in *Crawford v Albu supra.*

Africa. The German invasion of Poland and the Union's mooted participation in another European war in 1939 prompted a further political crisis in Parliament, and a perceptible rise in tension throughout the country. Certain Afrikaner organisations decided that active support for Hitler and agitation against the Imperial war effort were called for, in the form of propaganda, espionage, and sabotage, and the consequent prosecutions of the perpetrators of these deeds led to a number of appeals to the AD in Bloemfontein.[93]

The first three cases which confronted the court concerned offences committed by individuals in order to lend emphasis to their views on the war issue. In *R v Le Roux,*[94] the accused had been convicted[95] of being in possession of a "bomb or similar missile" following on the discovery in his room of a tin of explosives fitted with a fuse and detonator. He appealed on the ground, *inter alia,* that the article was not a "missile" because the length of the fuse would result in the elapse of five minutes between ignition and explosion. This rather absurd contention was rejected by De Wet, CJ,[96] who held that the words "bomb or similar missile" should be interpreted in their popular sense, and that, as the contraption was capable of being thrown and the fuse was capable of being shortened, Le Roux's conviction should stand.

R v Van As,[97] which followed soon after, concerned the admissibility as evidence of a confession made by the accused which had provided the foundation of his conviction[98] on a charge that he had caused an explosion which had damaged certain shops in Bloemfontein in August, 1940. On arrest, Van As had given a statement on oath to a magistrate, and at his trial he maintained that he had understood that the taking of the oath was a prerequisite to the making of a statement. Van den Heever, J, in the OPD, had admitted the statement as evidence, without which the Crown would have had insufficient proof to convict Van As, but had reserved two questions of law relating to the admissibility of the confession for decision by the AD.

De Wet, CJ[99] decided that, provided the statutory safeguards as to proper warning of the accused had been proved by the Crown (as they had here), the taking of the oath was not material,[100] and that there was sufficient evidence in the confession to convict the accused.[101] Thus the court indicated that it would not allow technical arguments on criminal procedure to absolve proven saboteurs.

[93] For a detailed account of events in this sphere, see Moodie *op cit* Chapter 11; and Walker *History* 716–17.
[94] 1941 AD 247.
[95] Under the Arms and Ammunition Act 28 of 1937, section 1(1)*(b),* read with section 30(i).
[96] See 248–50 concurred in by Watermeyer, Tindall, Centlivres, and Feetham, JJA.
[97] 1941 AD 361.
[98] Under the Explosives Act 8 of 1911, section 27(1).
[99] See 362–5 concurred in by Watermeyer, Tindall, Centlivres and Feetham, JJA.
[100] At 364. [101] At 365.

This strict line was confirmed in the next case reported, *R v Viljoen,*[102] which is significant, for this time the accused was an Afrikaner soldier who had set fire to a warehouse of the Afrikaanse Pers Bpk, a company which published newspapers which took an anti-war line. Viljoen had been convicted of arson, but evidence had been admitted, although not as a confession, of a statement he was alleged to have made without prompting, or compliance with the statutory formalities. The AD was asked whether this should have been admitted in evidence, but Feetham, JA[103] decided that the words used were not an unequivocal acknowledgment of guilt and, therefore, not a confession, so that they had been properly admitted. Viljoen's conviction and sentence were confirmed.

These first three cases indicate a tough but scrupulously fair treatment of people on both sides of the war issue who took the law into their own hands. They were followed by similar attitudes in two cases involving a different form of rebellion, espionage.

In *R v Vorster,*[104] a minister of the church and a general in the Ossewa Brandwag,[105] asked for three questions of law to be reserved for consideration by the AD, after his conviction under the Official Secrets Act[106] for obtaining information about South African military preparedness which might have been useful to the enemy. The court had to decide whether the Act was valid and binding in South Africa, whether the burden of proof rested on the defence, and whether there had been any evidence to support Vorster's conviction.[107] Fagan, KC, counsel for Vorster, pleaded especially that the changed constitutional relationship between Britain and South Africa since 1911 had made the Act impossible of application to South Africa as a Dominion.[108]

The AD[109] answered each question in turn in favour of the Crown. De Wet, CJ[110] held that South Africa as a Dominion had succeeded the British Empire as the "State" in the Act, and that enough evidence had been led by the Crown to have convicted Vorster. In addition, the court refused an application for special leave to appeal, and Vorster's sentence was confirmed.

Secondly, in *R v Hennig,*[111] the court was faced with the interpretation of a problematical proviso to section 284 of the Criminal Procedure Act.[112] This section laid down that a court was

[102] 1941 AD 366.
[103] See 366–9 with the concurrence of De Wet, CJ; Watermeyer, Tindall, and Centlivres, JJA.
[104] 1941 AD 472.
[105] Literally "ox wagon sentinel", a national socialist group of Afrikaners which arose out of the centenary celebrations of the Great Trek in 1938 and which opposed the war effort.
[106] Of 1911, section 1(1)*(c)*. The British Act (1 & 2 Geo 5, Ch 28) was taken over in South Africa.
[107] At 477.
[108] At 473–6.
[109] Consisting of De Wet, CJ; Watermeyer, Tindall, Centlivres, and Feetham, JJA.
[110] Who gave the court's judgment, 477–84.
[111] 1943 AD 172.
[112] Act 31 of 1917, section 284(2).

not competent to convict an accused on a charge of high treason except on the evidence of two witnesses, where one overt act had been charged in the indictment, or, where two or more such overt acts had been charged, on the evidence of one witness to each such overt act. Hennig had been convicted of high treason in the WLD where it was alleged that she had attempted to convey information to the German Consul in Lourenço Marques about the sailing of a convoy of ships from Cape Town to the Far East. In fact, L, through whom she had attempted to procure a messenger, had obtained a police sergeant instead, and Hennig had been tricked into handing over the message to L in the "messenger's" presence.

The difficulty for the Crown case was that the policeman's evidence did not relate either to the identity of the documents handed by Hennig to L or to the nature of the information to be conveyed. Van Blerk, counsel for the accused,[113] contended that the meaning of the proviso outlined above was that the evidence of each witness had to be such that, standing alone, it would be adequate to establish the commission of the overt act of treason by Hennig, and that the Crown had not complied with this proviso in the court *a quo*. De Wet, CJ,[114] after reviewing the English and American law applications of the proviso,[115] agreed with Van Blerk in his interpretation of the proviso, and that the policeman's evidence did not establish the treasonable character of Hennig's message. The court set her conviction aside accordingly.

Vorster and *Hennig* both deal with unsuccessful but potentially devastating acts of espionage, and provide nice examples of the court's dispassionately fair approach to arguments of a technical nature. For the temptation must have been strong in *Hennig* for the same judges who had rejected Vorster's appeal to gloss over the statutory requirements for the proof of high treason in view of the war situation. That they refrained from travelling this road, after Schreiner, J in the WLD had decided that it was possible, substantiates the impression of impartiality and reconciliation generated by the "first rebellion" decisions,[116] while it leaves little doubt that the court would not allow itself to be hoodwinked into absolving proven criminals through obscure and far-fetched legal niceties.

Evidence of the AD's tough attitude to organisational efforts to subvert the war effort was provided by the next two instances. *R v Van Schalkwyk & others*[117] arose as the result of a jeug-front kamp[118] on a farm near Bloemfontein in January, 1943, at which about fifty

[113] And later a judge of appeal; see 172–3.
[114] Who gave judgment at 173–81 for the court consisting of Watermeyer, Tindall, Centlivres, and Feetham, JJA.
[115] At 178–80.
[116] See *Naude v Mercier*; *McKenzie v Van der Merwe*; and *Mouton v Beket supra*.
[117] 1943 AD 469.
[118] Literally "youth-front camp".

young Afrikaners had participated in drilling and other outdoor activities, religious services, and lectures under the instruction of the Ossewa Brandwag. Those arrested had been convicted of the contravention of a war regulation[119] which outlawed unauthorised gatherings of more than five persons at which those present took part in military, drilling, or other physical exercises.

Van Schalkwyk and twenty-one others appealed against their convictions on the ground that there had been two independent gatherings, and that they had not been present at the gathering at which drilling had taken place. This unlikely story was rejected by Tindall, JA[120] on the evidence before the court, which indicated that the drilling, which had occurred only seventy yards from the main encampment and had been surrounded by guards, had been organised by those who had convened the camp, and the appellants' convictions and fines stood.[121]

The following case, *R v Leibbrandt & others*[122] was probably the most emotive and divisive of the whole war period,[123] in which the court[124] was once again confronted with difficult questions of proof and admissibility of evidence in regard to the commission of overt acts of treason by the accused. Leibbrandt had been a member of the SA Police until 1937, and had represented South Africa as a boxer at the 1936 Olympic Games in Berlin, after which he had converted to national socialism and trained as a parachutist in the German Army. He had been put ashore on the Namaqualand coast by a German submarine in 1941, equipped with a wireless transmitter, codes, and a large sum of money. He had headed for Bloemfontein, where he had attempted to infiltrate the SA Police and the Ossewa Brandwag in order to use their organisations as a basis for his planned setting up of a National Socialist state for Afrikaners in South Africa. When these efforts were rebuffed, he had created a military organisation whose members had to sign a blood oath swearing absolute loyalty to the organisation, Leibbrandt himself, and God.[125]

Leibbrandt had further attempted to transmit radio messages to Germany and had written various anti-Semitic and anti-British propaganda leaflets which had exhorted rebellion. He also recruited his two co-accused, Le Roux, a science lecturer from Potchefstroom, and Olwagen, a steelworker from Pretoria. But his efforts were in

[119] War Measure 4 of 1941, regulation 10(1)*(b)*(i) and (ii).

[120] See 469–74 with whom Watermeyer, ACJ; Centlivres and Feetham, JJA; and Greenberg, AJA concurred.

[121] A significant point for modern comparison is that those convicted were sentenced to fines of only £25 each.

[122] 1944 AD 253.

[123] The Director of Prisons was not prepared to allow Leibbrandt to travel to Bloemfontein to prosecute his own appeal, as this was not in the public interest: instead, the court had to travel to Pretoria, where he was being held. See *Ex parte Attorney-General, Transvaal: R v Leibbrandt & others* 1944 AD 105.

[124] Consisting of Watermeyer, CJ; Tindall, Centlivres, Feetham, and Greenberg, JJA.

[125] For all these facts and those that follow, see 263–76.

vain, as the police remained loyal and few Afrikaner organisations were prepared to have anything to do with him, and he had eventually been arrested and charged with committing acts of high treason, as had Le Roux and Olwagen. Leibbrandt was convicted on the proof of three overt acts of high treason, Olwagen was found guilty of high treason, and the case against Le Roux was confined to conspiracy with hostile intent to overthrow the government, on which he was convicted.[126] Schreiner, J, in the Special Criminal Court,[127] reserved six questions of law in regard to Leibbrandt, and four each in regard to the others, for the opinion of the AD.[128]

Watermeyer, CJ, after a detailed exposition of the facts as found by the Special Court, divided the arguments broadly into two categories:[129] one dealing with the essential elements of the crime of high treason, and the other with the evidence by which the commission of the crime could be proven. In considering each of these issues, he did not have the benefit of counsel's argument on Leibbrandt's behalf, as the latter had conducted his own appeal, but he made use of the argument of Ludorf and Cillie, who had appeared for Le Roux,[130] and the reasoning of Schreiner, J in the court *a quo*.[131]

As far as the essential parts of high treason were concerned, the Chief Justice maintained that all doubts were disposed of by the decisions in *Erasmus, Viljoen* and *Christian* above. As a result, the AD accepted that hostile intent against the state was the hallmark of treason,[132] which need not go so far as to include the entire overthrow of the government, and which was easier to establish in time of war when there was a foreign enemy with whom the accused could identify.[133] Any action to help the enemy or weaken the government forces necessarily implied such a hostile intent, he said, and the government was identified with the state in the field of treason. Although not all expressions of anti-war opinion necessarily disclosed such hostile intent, he claimed that sabotage, furnishing information to the enemy, and anti-war propaganda would do so, especially in a situation of "total war".[134]

Watermeyer, CJ next dealt with Ludorf's contention that *Hennig*[135] and the Criminal Procedure Act[136] demanded proof of this hostile intent by two witnesses, which he rejected on the ground that intention was a subjective state of mind, incapable of direct proof by witnesses, which could only be inferred from the accused's acts and

[126] *Ibid.*
[127] Parts of Schreiner, J's judgment are set out at 254–8.
[128] Details of the questions appear at 277.
[129] At 278.
[130] See 258–9.
[131] See note 127 above.
[132] At 279.
[133] At 280.
[134] At 281–2, adopting the reasoning of Schreiner, J in the Special Court.
[135] *Supra.*
[136] 31 of 1917, section 284(2).

surrounding circumstances.[137] In addition, both the Act and *Hennig* referred to parts of an overt act, and not to proof of intention: "[T]o hold otherwise would make it impossible to prove the crime of high treason. . . ."[138]

Ludorf had also averred that certain evidence as to the commission of overt acts of treason had been improperly admitted by Schreiner, J in terms of section 302 of the Act, which laid down that evidence of any overt act not alleged in the indictment could not be admitted unless relevant to prove some other act alleged therein. Watermeyer, CJ again disposed of this ground,[139] holding that, even if the evidence objected to had been excluded, Leibbrandt's case would not have been helped. Therefore, he answered all questions of law in favour of the Crown as regards Leibbrandt,[140] and did the same as regards Le Roux and Olwagen, after he had reviewed the points put forward on their behalf.[141]

The comprehensive and meticulous way in which the court approached this case shows the judges' awareness of the importance of the decision; for a man's life,[142] as well as the unity, such as it was, of white South Africa were in jeopardy. Although Schreiner, J had made detailed remarks about the way in which overt acts could be proved as required by the Act,[143] the AD did not have to pronounce upon this, but by implication they stamped their approval on his remarks, and the whole question of high treason, its definition and proof, was thus clarified and simplified. In doing so, there was no need to break new ground as the judges' task was more one of consolidation of prior trends. It is important, though, that the judicial spirit which was to the fore in this case was that seen before in *Christian* rather than *Hennig*.

The line of cases arising out of "un-South African" activities during World War II ends with three decisions in early 1948 which all related to acts of hostility performed outside South Africa and which served further to elaborate the concept of high treason and its proof in a court of law. *R v Holm; R v Pienaar*[144] was an appeal from a conviction in the Special Court on a charge of high treason arising out of the preparation and broadcast of propaganda to South Africa by the accused on behalf of the German Reich. The question of law reserved by the Special Court and argued by V G Hiemstra[145] for the appellants was whether the court had been correct in finding that it

[137] At 284.
[138] At 285.
[139] At 286–7.
[140] At 289.
[141] At 291–2. The other judges concurred silently.
[142] Leibbrandt had been sentenced to death. This was later commuted to life imprisonment, and he was released from prison on the accession to power of the National Party in 1948. See Walker *History* 775.
[143] At 254–8.
[144] 1948 (1) SA 925 (AD).
[145] See 925–6; Hiemstra is today Chief Justice of the Bophuthatswana homeland.

had jurisdiction to try the accused for acts committed outside the Union. Hiemstra contended that, as criminal jurisdiction was solely territorial and the only jurisdiction entrusted to the Special Court was that possessed by the TPD, it had no jurisdiction to try a person for an act committed outside the Transvaal.

Watermeyer, CJ[146] would have none of this, holding that, where high treason was concerned, there existed no international custom or comity which debarred a state from trial and punishment of an offending subject, no matter where the offence had been committed, because high treason was an offence only against that particular state.[147] As the criminal jurisdiction of the TPD covered all offences "triable" in the Transvaal, and as section 4 of the Criminal Procedure Act[148] provided for the trial of any person committed for trial, the Special Court had jurisdiction to try Holm and Pienaar, who had been committed in the Transvaal.[149] He further decided that, as the broadcast by the accused had intentionally caused an atmospheric disturbance in the Union, their unlawful conduct had been partially committed within the country.[150]

This decision slightly widened the scope of conduct which could be described as treasonable, as did the similar case of *R v Strauss,*[151] concerning another South African employee of the Reich Broadcasting Corporation. Three questions of law were reserved in his case, the first two being answered in favour of the Crown on the basis of *Holm and Pienaar*. As regards the third, Dönges, KC,[152] counsel for Strauss, urged two propositions: first, that direct and not circumstantial evidence of a witness was required to prove perpetration of an overt act by the accused, and, second, that it was not reasonable to impute a "hostile intent" to Strauss's activities.

After discoursing on different types of evidence at length, Watermeyer, CJ[153] stated that the line between direct and circumstantial evidence was extremely hard to determine and that, if his remarks in *Leibbrandt* were taken to suggest that direct evidence was required, they had been wrongly interpreted.[154] He construed section 284 of the Act as had Schreiner, J in the court *a quo* in *Leibbrandt,* to the effect that circumstantial evidence was sufficient to prove the commission of an overt act.[155] With regard to Strauss's intent, counsel claimed that his motives were for the good, in that he thought that non-participation in the War was best for the Union.

[146] See 928–34 joined by Tindall, Centlivres, Greenberg, and Schreiner, JJA.
[147] At 930.
[148] Above.
[149] At 934.
[150] At 929.
[151] 1948 (1) SA 934 (AD).
[152] At 935–6 assisted by V G Hiemstra. Dönges was later a senior Cabinet Minister and State President-elect.
[153] See 936–42 concurred in by Tindall, Centlivres, Greenberg, and Schreiner, JJA.
[154] At 939–40.
[155] At 940–1.

This, too, was rejected by the Chief Justice, who decided that assistance to the enemy meant "hostile intent" in time of war.[156] As a result, the questions of law were answered in favour of the Crown,[157] and the net of high treason could be cast more widely.

The last part of the judgment in *Strauss* was reiterated in *R v Mardon,*[158] in which the question of law reserved by the Special Court related specifically to the accused's intention when he, while a prisoner of the Germans, had joined the "British Free Forces" set up by Germany to fight the Russians on the Eastern front. Mardon's claim, which the Special Court accepted, was that he believed that, in holding back Russia, he was allowing Britain a greater chance to gain control of Europe. Nevertheless, he was guilty of high treason, for "[o]ne who in time of war intentionally helps the enemy to wage war against his own State intends to harm his State and has a hostile intent".[159] The AD agreed with this conclusion and Mardon's conviction stood,[160] but it is significant to note that his obvious predicament was reflected in his sentence of a mere £75 fine. The total disregard of motive by the court when establishing guilt, though, must inevitably have caused a widening of the ambit of high treason as a crime.

Summary and Conclusions

In the light of the decisions set out above,[161] what can be said about judicial attitudes towards acts of resistance to, and rebellion against, the government of the day?

Several common features are immediately apparent when the judgments are considered together. The fifteen permanent judges of appeal who variously heard these cases fall, by virtue of the distribution of the cases over time, into two easily definable groups. All cases resulting from black resistance (except *Vezi*), First World War rebellion, and strikes were heard by a solid core of judges, consisting of Innes, Solomon, C G Maasdorp, J A J de Villiers, Kotzé, and Juta, with Lord De Villiers and Wessels sitting in one case each. In the second group, consisting of all the Second World War cases, plus *Vezi,* Watermeyer, Tindall and Centlivres were on the Bench in every single case, while De Wet, Greenberg, Feetham, and Schreiner each sat in several decisions. The tendency noticed in the previous chapter, for a single judgment to be given on behalf of the court, was observed in every case heard by this second group.

[156] *Ibid.*

[157] At 941.

[158] 1948 (1) SA 942 (AD).

[159] At 945, adopting the words of Ramsbottom and Clayden, JJ in the Special Court.

[160] At 946 *per* Watermeyer, CJ, who spoke (944–6) for Tindall, Centlivres, Greenberg, and Schreiner, JJA.

[161] Several cases, more accurately seen as exposing attitudes to executive power, have not been included here. Examples are: *Winter v Minister of Defence & others* 1940 AD 194; *Haak & others v Minister of External Affairs* 1942 AD 318; and *R v Harmse* 1944 AD 295.

Within this area, too, the leading judgment seems to have been the prerogative of the Chief Justice of the time: Innes, De Wet, and Watermeyer handed down judgments in eighteen of the twenty-two cases surveyed. The only other judge who, it appears, had to have his opinion recorded was Kotzé, who concurred separately in all four cases in which he sat. This would seem to indicate an awareness by the judges of the importance of the issues which they were being called upon to decide. This factor was probably also a major incentive for the unanimity displayed by the AD: in all the cases, there was only one dissent, that of C G Maasdorp in *McKenzie*. In addition, it is remarkable to find that, in contrast to the civil liberties field, the court was very reluctant to upset the decisions of the provincial or special courts: in only three instances was the appellant successful in this area.

These facts certainly point to a desire on the part of the judges to present a united and firm front in the face of the division and discontent which was present in the white group when each set of cases arose.

Moving from the superficial similarities to those of judicial attitude and approach, the task becomes more exacting, but the following conclusions appear to emerge from the discussion above.

Firstly, although the sample of cases dealing with blacks is not large enough to warrant speaking with any conviction, for the present it is fair to say that the judges displayed lamentably little understanding or knowledge of the plight of the blacks in South Africa. This is especially so when contrasted with the strong sense of reconciliation evident in the first rebellion, and, to a lesser extent, second rebellion cases.

Secondly, if only the cases dealing with whites are taken into account, they fall neatly into three categories: those arising from the first rebellion, from the labour disturbances, and from the second rebellion. The first rebellion cases, all civil in nature, were characterised by the sympathetic treatment meted out to the rebels, the court disregarding the political side of their violent conduct. The labour cases, all criminal, show the same group of judges assuming a strongly disciplinarian role, and adopting a wide definition of the "crimes against the State" of high treason and sedition in order to reject the strikers' appeals.

The second rebellion cases, also all criminal, expose a new body of judges, more removed in language and feeling from the disputes of the time, who take a firm but impartial line in dealing with questions concerned mostly with legal-procedural challenges to convictions by the Special Court. The court seems here to have adopted the middle ground as its most comfortable position: it allowed *Hennig's* appeal on the one hand, but showed no leniency to *Vorster, Van Schalkwyk,* and *Leibbrandt* on the other. In the last three cases discussed, the effect of its decision further widened the field of actions indictable as high treason. Although the definitions adopted by the court received approval in the *Tydskrif* soon after the Second World War,[162] they have come under scrutiny again in cases arising out of the civil rebellions and resistance of the last five years.[163]

Perhaps this movement in judicial attitude over time can be discerned more clearly in the line of cases in which the charge against the accused was that of high treason. *Krohn,* from the first period, saw the court taking a critical, civil libertarian position. *Christian, Erasmus, Viljoen,* and *Jolly* led to a relatively harsh and punitive approach by the judges; whereas the Second World War cases reveal a judiciary, divorced from the arena of struggle, pursuing a "tough, but fair" policy to dissidents. Further, if the cases are split into those in which individuals, on the one hand, and individuals representative of groups, on the other, were involved, a more sympathetic stance is perceived in the former than the latter instances.

As a tentative proposition, therefore, it is contended that the judges were unwittingly more inclined to treat peace-time black resisters and white strikers less sympathetically (especially when they formed part of a group) than white rebels who resisted government in time of war. That they were not prepared to tolerate far-fetched legal arguments on appeal is clear throughout: *Naude* and *Le Roux* bear witness to this.

One way of testing this proposition is to outline and analyse judicial attitudes to labour and race matters, which are set out in the next two chapters.

[162] See H L Gonin "*Perduellio*" (1951) 14 *THR-HR* 1, at 30–3.

[163] See C R Snyman "Sedition Revived" in (1980) 97 *SALJ* 14 and the judgment of Van Dyk, J in *S v Hogan* 1983 (2) SA 46 (W).

CHAPTER FIVE

INDUSTRIAL RELATIONS

The cases which form the stuff with which this chapter of judicial views is concerned embrace many disputes, the common feature of all of which is their well-spring in the employer–employee relationship, on an individual or a group basis. For this reason, problems arising from the common law master and servant contract, from the statutory rights created by the Workmen's Compensation, Industrial Conciliation, and Wage Acts, and from the collective bargaining manoeuvres of trade unions and employers' organisations are all commented upon in what follows below.

This area has been selected as one of those deserving of special attention for a number of reasons. Firstly, it provides a means to test the hypothesis that the judges of appeal, being men drawn from a non-working-class background, were unable fully to comprehend the position in which labouring people found themselves in the changing conditions of the years 1910 to 1950. Certain attitudes displayed in the strikers' cases discussed in the preceding chapter have created the impression that this was the case.

Secondly, the course of industrial relations in Southern Africa in the period under review was one of such upheaval and rapid change that the judges were presented with a stiff test of their ability to move with the times, and to adapt both the law and their interpretation of factual situations to meet the exigencies of the day. Thirdly, the sheer volume of cases dealing with this subject which came on appeal ensured that industrial relations occupied much judicial time and thought.

Finally, the various employment laws which confronted the court provided good material from which the judges could develop rules for the interpretation of statutes. The fact that some canons of construction evolved in this area, and that these were then applied to statutes of a different nature, ensure the importance of a detailed consideration of labour cases in the present study of judicial attitudes. But before discussing the litigation, it is vital to set out the bare bones of Southern African labour history in this period, for, without an understanding of some of the events which gave rise to the disputes and the legislation, the evaluation of judicial performance can be only superficial and curtailed.

The unification of South Africa in 1910 provided a relatively solid commercial basis for the pursuit of industrial expansion consequent upon the major developments in the mining and agricultural sectors which had occurred in the preceding few decades. However, the maintenance of profitability of the mines depended largely on the procurement of a massive, unskilled, and, above all, cheap labour force. This was achieved in several ways, such as migrancy, compound housing, resort to labour from outside South Africa's borders, and legislation which drove blacks from the rural districts and forced them to seek work in the towns. This movement, in turn, caused shortages in the labour supply of rural employers, who could not compete as regards wages with industrial employers in the cities. The latter, for their part, resented the instability produced by migrancy, and wished to have a pool of unemployed but employable workers readily available to take advantage of any sudden increase in economic activity.

On the employee side, severe problems emanated from the difference in skills which existed between the white (and mainly English) artisans, and the black and white (mainly Afrikaner) unskilled workers. There were constant labour disturbances by both these groups in the first decade of Union, which came to a head in the "Rand Revolt" of 1922, an insurrection by white workers which paralysed the hub of South Africa's economy and which was subdued by the armed forces of the government. The workers' defeat was transformed into the victory of the National and Labour Parties' Pact in the 1924 general election, however, which led directly to the enactment by Parliament of comprehensive industrial legislation. These laws ensured a state-controlled and tightly regulated system of collective negotiations between employer and employee, but another prominent feature was the legal entrenchment of the supreme position of white workers in the field of industrial relations.

For white workers, as a result, the rest of the period until 1950 saw a gradual and comparatively peaceful improvement of their position, despite the catastrophic effects of world economic depression, drought, war, and difficulties for the mining industry caused by the gold standard crisis of the early 1930's. The only substantial upheavals in the white trade union movement came in the 1940's with the attempted take-over of the mining and railway unions by Afrikaners, who until that time had been largely shut out of organisational influence by English-speaking officials.

The trade-off for black workers after 1924 was uniformly of a different complexion, and their lot worsened steadily, until the Second World War robbed industry of many of its white workers and simultaneously produced a surge in economic activity. Black labour moved rapidly to the cities, and assumed skilled positions on a scale not contemplated before. Extensive trade union organising took place, often under the leadership of whites, and this formed the basis of the 1946 black miners' strike (which met a fate similar to the Rand Revolt), as well as many of the struggles in opposition to the National Party government elected to power in 1948.[1]

[1] For a general discussion of these events see Walker *History* 763–4; Wilson and Thompson *op cit* 22–31; and Roux *op cit* Ch XIV, XVI and XXVI.

This briefest of introductions should serve to alert the observer to the unsettled and bitter character of labour relations in South Africa from 1910 to 1950, and the multiplicity of conflicting pressures which strained to gain the upper hand in the employer–employee nexus. It is against this backdrop of exploitation and struggle that the cases which are outlined below should be assessed.

General Conditions of Employment

This section contains those cases which arose from individual contracts of employment and which related to such matters as payment of wages, sick and leave pay, dismissal, pensions, and liability of the master for actions of his servants. Due to the diverse character of the subject-matter covered by these cases, they have been incorporated into this study more for the way in which isolated judicial attitudes are exposed, than for any general trends or particular policies.

The racial character of South African labour law came to the notice of the AD early in its life, in *New Rietfontein Estate Gold Mines Ltd v Misnum.*[2] Under the Native Labour Regulation Act[3] it was unlawful to pay all or part of any wages due to a native labourer to any person other than that labourer. Misnum was the purported cessionary of all the wages of one of appellant company's native employees as a result of selling the latter certain goods, and, although cession was not specifically mentioned in the statute, the AD held that it was inconsistent with the Act's objectives, and so of no effect.

This conclusion is notable as Innes, ACJ[4] showed that the court was not prepared to allow sharp dealers to defeat the aims of legislation by clever legal arguments where the consequences, while insignificant in an individual case,[5] would affect a much wider group of people. As far as the court was concerned, the clause was clearly aimed at saving the native from himself, and protecting him against his employer and others with whom he might deal:[6] if the language used was ambiguous, it should be interpreted so as not to lead to absurdity or inconvenience, he said.[7] The awareness of the social implications of the Act shown by the judges here is an indication of their willingness to invoke such factors in support of their judgments when they felt it necessary; its absence in other circumstances is, by the same token, a point to be noticed.

Two other early cases serve to display the strict, indeed rigid, adherence of the judges to the law despite their express statements that the result would be inequitable for the workman concerned. In *Boyd v Stuttaford & Co,*[8] the appellant sued his employer, the

[2] 1912 AD 704. [3] 15 of 1911, section 15.

[4] See 707–12 concurred in by Solomon, J; C G Maasdorp, JP; Laurence, J; and Dove Wilson, JP.

[5] The amount at stake here was a mere £1 0s 6d.

[6] At 709. [7] At 710. [8] 1910 AD 101.

respondent, for wages for a period during which he had been unable to work through illness. This claim was rejected by the AD, which maintained that employees in the position of Boyd could recover their wages only *pro rata parte*, according to the amount of services actually performed.

In reaching this conclusion, the judges[9] relied on the authority of Voet[10] (who recognised the unique position of domestic servants as the sole exception to this rule) and other Roman and Roman-Dutch writers. Nevertheless, while Solomon, J felt bound to dismiss the appeal, he said:[11]

> "Personally I should have been glad if we could have . . . [laid] down the law on the subject in terms somewhat more favourable to the servant. . . . But the authorities on the Roman-Dutch law have forced me to agree with the conclusion arrived at. . . . I could have wished that it had been possible to hold that the exception mentioned by Voet . . . could be extended to apply to all servants or employees. . . . Our duty, however, is not to say what the law should be, but what it is. . . ."

The court echoed these sentiments in *Fichardt Ltd v Faustmann*[12] in which appellant objected to an order of the High Court of the ORC which had required it to pay a pension to respondent in consideration of his past services as an employee. The problem was that these services had been rendered to Fichardt and Company, a different legal entity from present appellant, although the latter pursued the same business as the former.

Lord De Villiers, CJ held[13] that, although the promise given by Fichardt and Company to pay a pension to Faustmann amounted to a remuneratory donation which could be enforced, Faustmann's action here did not lie against appellant, but rather against the deceased estates of the previous partners of Fichardt and Company. In arriving at this conclusion, the Chief Justice felt constrained to remark[14] that: "It would have been a great satisfaction to me if I could consistently with legal principles have confirmed to the plaintiff a pension which he so well deserves."

Besides the fact that these decisions show the judges abiding strictly by legal principle rather than the equities of the case, their open expressions of regret evince a frankness which is significant for its apparent absence in other cases of this type, and for the influence which it would have had in future developments in this area of the law. Indeed, *Boyd* evoked a comment in the SALJ,[15] which called for legislation along the lines of Voet's exception to cover all servants.

[9] Lord De Villiers, CJ at 114–15; Innes, J at 116–21; and Solomon, J at 121–4.
[10] 19.2.27
[11] At 121.
[12] 1910 AD 168.
[13] See 174–7. Innes and Solomon, JJ; C G Maasdorp and J A J de Villiers, JJP concurred.
[14] At 177.
[15] A note by C J Sutton in (1910) 27 *SALJ* 581.

Ten years later, the decision in *Spencer v Gostelow*[16] showed that the court was prepared to adapt the common law to suit modern conditions. Here the question for decision[17] was whether a servant, Gostelow, who had been dismissed for misconduct during the currency of his employment, was entitled to be paid for services rendered to Spencer, his employer, prior to dismissal, or whether his misconduct entailed forfeiture of his right to remuneration. No modern statute governed the position, but in the common law authorities several Dutch *placaaten*[18] had prescribed forfeiture in certain circumstances. The court[19] upheld the master's right to dismiss his servant for serious misconduct, but decided that, under modern conditions, he was not entitled to refuse the payment of arrear wages in so far as he had benefited by the work of the dismissed servant.

Innes, CJ, who gave the leading judgment,[20] denied the validity of the Dutch statutes in South Africa, as they had never been enforced,[21] and based his finding on the general principle that no one should be enriched at the expense of another.[22] Mason, AJA carried out an exhaustive review of historical authorities and modern precedent, both local and foreign,[23] before he decided that the *placaaten* did not apply in South Africa, and, therefore, that the TPD had been right in ordering the payment to Gostelow of his wages earned to the date of his dismissal.[24] This demonstrates the judges' ability to mould the common law to meet contemporary needs, if they thought such changes necessary: once more, the conditions under which they were prepared so to act contain important clues as to their social priorities.

In the sphere of employer–employee disputes in terms of statutory provisions, the court gave no indication that it favoured the side of the employer (usually the state or a state corporation here).[25] On the contrary, it assumed an attitude which created the impression that it was anxious to help the claim of the servant, even in the face of considerable provocation to do the opposite, in the form of a gross contempt of court by the litigant.[26] The reaction of Innes, CJ to such an attack upon the integrity of the court and the judicial honour of its members is typical: "We think that we shall best consult the dignity of the court, and further the interests of justice, by merely issuing

[16] 1920 AD 617.
[17] As outlined by Innes, CJ at 625.
[18] Or "statutes".
[19] Consisting of Innes, CJ; J A J de Villiers, AJA; Mason, Lange and J E R de Villiers, AJJA.
[20] See 625–32.
[21] At 628.
[22] At 627.
[23] See 632–43.
[24] At 643. The other judges concurred silently.
[25] See for example *Leibbrandt v SAR* 1941 AD 9; *Leibbrandt v SAR* 1943 AD 14; *Schierhout v Minister of Justice* 1925 AD 417; and *Schierhout v UG (Minister of Justice)* 1926 AD 286, and 1926 AD 295.
[26] *Union Government (Minister of Justice) v Schierhout* 1925 AD 322. Respondent had written various letters critical of the court as a result of his earlier dealings with it.

now [a] grave and public warning. But it must be understood that we have neither overlooked nor condoned the outrage."[27]

Changing social attitudes were reflected in the AD's treatment of the question of an employee's entitlement to be paid for leave which had accumulated, at the termination of a period of service. In 1923, in *Reed v Richmond Local Board*,[28] Innes, CJ[29] maintained that there was no proof of any custom of a cash payment in lieu of leave in the civil service, with the result that appellant was refused leave to appeal against the denial of payment for the fourteen days on which he had worked instead of taking a holiday.

Some years later, in *East London Municipality v Thomson*,[30] a different Bench[31] interpreted the municipal leave regulations to the effect that an employee who had accumulated vacation leave could not be required to take such leave, and that, on his retirement by superannuation, he was entitled to be paid for the period of leave accumulated up to 150 days.[32] Although the municipality had relied on the common law to back up its interpretation of the regulations,[33] Feetham, JA took no heed of this, and displayed instead a capacity to move away from an outdated approach to the contract of employment.

Two cases in this period are worthy of note for the light which they shed on the parlous position of black labourers on white-owned farms. In *Sillo v Naude*[34] the appellant, a black farm-worker, had entered into a contract of service with respondent, a white farm-owner, whereby he and his family could reside, graze their stock, and cultivate certain lands on the latter's farm in return for services rendered. Naude had summarily dismissed Sillo, and had given him 24 hours to leave the farm, when he heard that Sillo had joined a trade union.[35] Sillo had gone off to seek legal advice, whereupon Naude had impounded his stock which was grazing on the farm, and ordered his family off his property. Sillo had then applied unsuccessfully for a spoliation order in respect of the stock. On appeal, the AD confirmed the decision of the lower courts.[36]

In doing so, J A J de Villiers, ACJ[37] held that Naude had not taken the law into his own hands in impounding the animals, as he had merely invoked the machinery of the Pounds Ordinance,[38] and that

[27] At 323.
[28] 1923 AD 50.
[29] In a curt judgment only 13 lines long at 51. Solomon, J A J de Villiers, Juta, and Kotzé, JJA concurred.
[30] 1944 AD 56.
[31] Watermeyer, CJ; Tindall, Centlivres, Feetham, and Greenberg, JJA.
[32] *Per* Feetham, JA at 60–7.
[33] At 59–60, *per* Reynolds, KC and G Duncan, KC.
[34] 1929 AD 21.
[35] The Industrial and Commercial Workers Union, which achieved a remarkable level of organisation nationally in the mid-1920's, before being broken by dissent.
[36] Both the magistrate's court, and the OPD (McGregor, J).
[37] See 24–7 joined by Curlewis and Stratford, JJA.
[38] 3 of 1912 (OFS).

Sillo's remedy lay in an action for damages. He maintained that it was not necessary to pronounce upon the legality of Sillo's dismissal,[39] and so he made no comment on this aspect of the case.

A similar situation preceded the litigation in *De Jager v Sisana*,[40] in which the AD reversed a decision of the NPD,[41] and so upheld the right of a farm-owner to evict a black "squatter". The facts were that Sisana had entered into an agreement with the previous owner of De Jager's farm, Van der Westhuizen, and he had refused to recognise the transfer of ownership to De Jager. He maintained that he was willing to render services to Van der Westhuizen alone in return for his right of occupation of land. Despite De Jager's willingness to allow him to remain while giving services to him, Sisana was adamant that only a personal instruction from Van der Westhuizen would suffice to transfer his allegiance.

Not surprisingly, Curlewis, JA[42] was unwilling to condone such obstinacy on the part of Sisana. He agreed that Sisana could not be compelled to serve De Jager, but stated that, if in equity he had been allowed to continue to occupy the farm, then in equity he was bound to render services.[43] He expressed regret that Sisana's "child-like simplicity or perverseness" had led to ejectment, but was satisfied that De Jager had displayed no lack of consideration or patience in dealing with Sisana.[44] Wessels, JA gave judgment in similar vein, but added a detailed exposition on the status of a "squatting" contract and the rights of the parties to such a contract after a transfer of ownership of the property, in which he effectively ascribed absolute power of ejectment of "squatters" to the new owner.[45]

Besides providing a brief glimpse of farm-labour conditions at that time, the judicial attitude to the plight of the labourers is evidence of an overly legalistic and unrealistic approach to the issues at stake. While in purely legal terms there is little doubt as to the correctness of the decisions, there is little indication in the judgments of an attempt to comprehend the tenuous position in which blacks on farms found themselves, nor is any allowance made for the inappropriateness of Western legal procedure in the circumstances raised in the case. There should be little wonder, therefore, that there were so few challenges by blacks, in the form of litigation, to unlawful actions of whites in this period. For, in addition to the formidable obstacles presented by ignorance, indigence, and unfamiliarity with this legal process, blacks were faced with judges unable through their upbringing, as here, to understand, or even imagine, the conditions under which they lived.

[39] At 25.
[40] 1930 AD 71.
[41] A full Bench of Dove Wilson, JP; Tatham and Matthews, JJ.
[42] See 73–7 with whom J A J de Villiers, CJ and Stratford, JA concurred briefly at 78.
[43] At 76.
[44] At 77.
[45] See 78–86.

This review of general conditions of employment closes with a brief description of two cases which concerned the master's liability for his servant's delictual acts, which occurred in the performance of the latter's duties. In *Union Government v Hawkins*,[46] appellant had been held liable for the negligent killing of respondent's husband in an accident involving a Defence Force troop carrier. The AD[47] rejected the contention that the soldier-driver was not a "servant of the Crown", as defined in the Crown Liabilities Act,[48] on a procedural ground. Centlivres, JA[49] also firmly rejected appellant's attempt to escape liability on the basis of the soldier's disobedience of certain orders, and he displayed a clear understanding of the equities of the case in upholding the decision of the TPD.[50]

SAR and Harbours v Marais[51] saw the exoneration of appellant, a state corporation, from liability for the death of one of its passengers, who had certainly contributed to his own demise by travelling in a forbidden part of the train. Watermeyer, CJ[52] and Greenberg, JA[53] differed as to the basis for their conclusion that respondent should be denied leave to sue for damages *in forma pauperis*, but the Railways' success here indicates that the court was not yet willing to impose strict liability on the actions of a public carrier.

After this cursory survey of a variety of aspects of employment, specific issues will be concentrated on, starting with an analysis of those cases which arose from industrial conflict between 1910 and 1950.

Strikes and Lock-outs

As indicated above, the period from Union until 1924 saw enornous industrial unrest on the Witwatersrand.[54] The 1922 revolt led to criminal charges of high treason against those seen as the strike leaders,[55] as well as legal actions by employees which arose directly from the events of early 1922, two of which reached Bloemfontein.

In *Johannesburg Municipality v O'Sullivan*,[56] appellant sought to overturn a decision of the TPD[57] which had ordered it to pay wages to respondent, a tramway motorman employed by the Municipality, in respect of a period during which the trams had not run, owing to the strike. The challenge of the Municipality rested on certain

[46] 1944 AD 556.
[47] Watermeyer, CJ; Tindall, Centlivres, and Feetham, JJA; and Davis, AJA.
[48] 1 of 1910.
[49] Who gave the judgment of the court, see 559–71.
[50] Ramsbottom, J.
[51] 1950 (4) SA 610 (AD).
[52] See 614–20 with whom Centlivres, JA concurred.
[53] See 621–3.
[54] A graphic account of the 1913–1914 "civil commotion" is rendered in the report of *Lindsay & Pirie v The General Accident Fire & Life Assurance Corporation Ltd* 1914 AD 574.
[55] See "Resistance and Rebellion" above.
[56] 1923 AD 201.
[57] Gregorowski and Stratford, JJ; De Waal, J dissenting.

conditions of service and rules under which O'Sullivan had been employed, which stated that wages should only be payable for such days as the employee was actually on duty by order of the management,[58] and that all motormen were guaranteed a minimum-duration shift each day.[59]

Solomon, JA[60] refused to accept that these stipulations governed O'Sullivan's contract of employment expressly, and he fell back on what he regarded as an implied obligation on the Municipality to pay O'Sullivan during the strike, during which he had not been free to go and sell his labour elsewhere. This sympathetic interpretation of the employment contract in favour of an employee who had not been on strike, notwithstanding a written rule which seemed to imply a contrary meaning, can be taken as judicial endorsement of the actions of the non-striker, which was founded upon a keen perception of the forces at work in the field of industrial conflict.

The latter quality is again apparent in *Matthews & others v Johannesburg Municipal Pension Fund*,[61] but this time appellants were three stikers who were appealing against the refusal of the WLD[62] to order respondent to pay them special benefits. They alleged that these were due to them because they had been dismissed as the result of a strike[63] or, alternatively, a reduction in staff or reorganisation or abolition of office.[64] All three appellants (Matthews, Foster, and Hewitt) claimed to have been dismissed as the result of a strike, but regulation 18 of the Pension Fund rules provided that the strike must have been "called and continued by an association or trade union recognised by the Council of Federation of Trades", and non-compliance herewith had been the basis of the WLD's dismissal of their claim.

On appeal, Wessels, JA[65] held that three questions had to be resolved: firstly, whether or not the appellants had been dismissed as the result of a strike; secondly, whether the strike was of the type contemplated in regulation 18; and, if either of the first two was answered in the negative, whether appellants were entitled to the benefits consequent upon dismissal due to reduction of staff, reorganisation, or abolition of office.[66] In Matthews's and Foster's cases, after a review of the details of the strike, the judge held that their dismissal was because of strike action,[67] but he was not prepared to acknowledge that the strike had been of the type contemplated in the regulations.

[58] Rule 5 of the Municipal Tramway Department.
[59] Clause *(e)* of the employees' Conditions of Service.
[60] See 202–6 with the silent concurrence of Innes, CJ and J A J de Villiers, Juta, and Kotzé, JJA.
[61] 1924 AD 532.
[62] Gregorowski and Tindall, JJ.
[63] In terms of Regulation 18 of the Pension Fund regulations.
[64] In terms of Regulation 15 of the same regulations.
[65] See 534–49 concurred in by Innes, CJ and J A J de Villiers, JA.
[66] At 535. [67] At 538 and 546.

Wessels, JA adhered to this view on two grounds: firstly, on the evidence, that the strike committee which had called out the workers had not been recognised by the Council, even though it had acted with the full approval and consent of the trade union of which appellants were members, and which had been so recognized.[68] Secondly, he said that the "strike" comtemplated by regulation 18 must have been lawful: here, as the full statutory disputes procedure[69] had not been followed, the "strike" was accordingly unlawful.[70] The third question was not considered, as dismissal was held to have been caused by strike action alone.

Hewitt had not been on strike, but had been refused a job on re-application, as, when the strike had ended, fewer men had been employed at lower wages for longer hours.[71] This would appear to fall squarely under the "reduction, reorganisation, or abolition of office" contemplated by regulation 15, but Wessels, JA would have none of this. He concluded that there had been no intention to retrench any individual employee, even though fewer men had been required, while there had been an intention to get rid of certain undesirable employees who had sympathised with the strike, and this was the reason for Hewitt's dismissal. "[He] was not retrenched because he was superfluous, he was dismissed because of his participation in the strike", he said. Because the Council could always have done this with 48 hours' notice, Hewitt's appeal should fail.[72]

This judgment can be attacked on several grounds. Firstly, the evidence as to the relationship between the strike committee and the Amalgamated Union of Engineers (AUE), of which Matthews was a member, was far from conclusive in support of Wessels, JA's interpretation; indeed, as presented in the report,[73] it implies that the AUE identified completely with, and was absolutely prepared to work through, the committee which called and organised the strike. Secondly, as argued by Lucas, counsel for the strikers,[74] the closed-shop agreement between the AUE and the Council meant that any future employment opportunities would have been jeopardised by Matthews's refusal to join the strike. This contention was rejected by the judge of appeal as "more specious than true".[75]

Thirdly, there is no evidence at all that the "strike" referred to in the Fund regulations meant a "strike" as defined in the pre-Union law of the Transvaal. Finally, the process of reasoning adopted by the court to avoid the conclusion that Hewitt's dismissal fell within the

[68] At 539–44.
[69] Prescribed by the Industrial Disputes Prevention Act 20 of 1909 (Transvaal), section 6(1)*(b)*.
[70] At 545.
[71] At 547–8.
[72] At 549.
[73] See 535–44.
[74] At 539.
[75] *Ibid.*

terms of regulation 15 is nothing short of remarkable. It is difficult not to suspect that judicial attitudes here were influenced by a desire to punish the strikers for their actions by denial of their claim for financial benefits from the Fund.

The only other case concerning a strike which came before the AD in this period was in the form of an appeal against a conviction under the law which prohibited the threat or use of violence against employees to encourage them to strike.[76] *R v Herschel*[77] arose from the use of unambiguous language by the accused in an attempt to make two building workers join in a strike in the East London area, but Innes, CJ[78] felt that he could not interfere with the findings of the court *a quo*,[79] and so dismissed the appeal.

An important question of interpretation of the Industrial Conciliation Act[80] provisions relating to industrial action was decided in *Walker, NO v De Beer*,[81] the final case in this category. Here a dispute between an employers' organisation and a trade union had resulted in a cessation of work, the events preceding which appeared to show signs of both a strike and a lock-out, according to their statutory definitions.[82] It was important for the employees to know which it had been, as they would have been classified as "unemployed" and so become entitled to draw money from a provident fund set up on their behalf some years earlier, in the case of a lock-out, but not a strike.[83]

Centlivres, JA[84] weighed the facts carefully and decided that the legislature could not have intended one set of circumstances to constitute both a strike and a lock-out.[85] Here, in fact, the dispute which led to the cessation of work had been the proposed reduction of wages, which had been initiated by the employers, he said, with the result that a legal lock-out had occurred, and the employees had been genuinely unemployed.[86]

This decision constitutes a good example of the agility of the judges in interpreting complicated statutory and factual formulae, born of much practice, particularly in the field of industrial law, which will appear from the sections which follow. But before setting out into the maze of construction of statutes, those cases which were related to industrial action, in that they concerned the status and affairs of trade unions, will be reviewed.

[76] The Riotous Assemblies and Criminal Law Amendment Act 27 of 1914, section 8*(a)*.
[77] 1920 AD 575.
[78] See 576–82 speaking for J A J de Villiers and Juta, JJA; and Mason and J E R de Villiers, AJJA.
[79] The EDLD, *per* Hutton, J and Gane, AJ.
[80] 36 of 1937.
[81] 1948 (4) SA 708 (AD).
[82] Section 1 of the Act.
[83] See details at 711–12.
[84] See 711–16 with the concurrence of Watermeyer, CJ; Greenberg and Van den Heever, JJA; and Hoexter, AJA.
[85] At 715.
[86] At 716.

Trade Unions and the Law

Most trade unions in South Africa grew out of the various craft unions which migrated from Britain with the skilled workers on the gold and diamond mines.[87] Some of the unions retained links with their parent organisations in the United Kingdom, and it was only with the heavy influx of unskilled whites on to the mines after the Anglo-Boer War, and again in the depressions of the 1920's, that large-scale unionising took place among semi-skilled and unskilled workers, including many coloured people, but few blacks. Nevertheless, there were several attempts to form unions among black workers, and two significant achievements in this area were the Industrial and Commercial Workers' Union of the 1920's, and the African Mine Workers' Union, which developed during the Second World War. Most of the trade-union cases which came before the AD up till 1950, as a result, emanated from organisations of white workers.

As with any group of persons gathered in a voluntary association, disputes within the group were bound to surface, and several cases concerned legal actions by members against their unions, especially in instances in which the trade union had negotiated a closed-shop agreement with the employer so that loss of a union card connoted loss of a job. This was the situation which underlay *Matthews & others v Young*,[88] in that respondent had been expelled from the Amalgamated Engineering Union (AEU) (and so had lost his job) because he had drawn increased pay while the question of acceptance of the employers' offer was still under consideration. Young had in fact successfully claimed a *mandamus* which required his reinstatement as a union member because there had been procedural irregularities in his dismissal, but he had still been without a job. As a result, he had sued appellants, who constituted the SA Council of the AEU which had expelled him, for damages in their personal capacities. Ward, J in the WLD had awarded him a small sum in damages. Matthews and the council members appealed to the AD.

J A J de Villiers, JA[89] regarded Young's action as an attempt to gain compensation for intentional violation of his legal rights as a member of the AEU based on the *lex Aquilia*, which issue had to be resolved in the light of the rules of the Union.[90] As far as the liability of the executive was concerned, he stated that:

> "[W]here, under the rules of an association, there is a duty imposed on a body of persons under certain circumstances to consider the conduct of a member and in their discretion to take appropriate action, such persons are not liable so long as they, in good faith, act or purport to act under the rules of the association in the

[87] For details of SA labour history see references cited in note 1 above.
[88] 1922 AD 492.
[89] See 498–511 who spoke for Innes, CJ and Kotzé, JA.
[90] At 505.

interests of the association but through *imperitia* err in following the rules or in their proper application. To put the duty higher is neither warranted in principle nor would it be in the interests of the associations themselves."[91]

As there had been no malice or improper motive on the part of the appellants in this instance,[92] they could not be held liable and their appeal was upheld.

This ready acceptance of the status and powers of trade unions as representative of their members was echoed some years later in *Crisp v South African Council of the AEU*,[93] but the appeal court here stated its intention of keeping a watching brief on the disciplinary activities of trade unions. Crisp, a former organiser of the AEU, had been declared ineligible for re-election to such a post by respondent on instruction of the Executive Council in Britain, because of certain financial irregularities. The rules of the union provided for an appeal from the Council's decision to the Executive Council, and finally to the Society's court of appeal, but the jurisdiction of the ordinary courts of the land was excluded by the contract of union membership. Appellant had obtained relief against the Council from the WLD,[94] but the Council had then appealed successfully to the TPD.[95]

Wessels, JA[96] considered the question of the ousting of the court's jurisdiction by contract, but stated that the courts ". . . [would] not consider their jurisdiction as ousted, even if the rules of the Society should say so, where the act complained of [was] *ultra vires* the Society or against the principles of natural justice, for in the last resort the law courts [could] always be appealed to".[97] On this basis, he averred that the AEU had not acted in accordance with their rules or with natural justice, so that Crisp was not bound to exhaust the domestic remedies and was quite entitled to seek relief from a court of law.[98] This assertion of the overall competence of the courts to intervene in the affairs of voluntary associations is in keeping with the judges' insistence on proper procedures in the administration of justice,[99] and the AD's attitude here does not seem to be improper interference in union activities: on the contrary, it reinforces the impression of the judges' tolerant adaptability to the concept of workers' organisations.

A further case which arose from the alleged dismissal of an employee after coercion by a trade union was *Tramway & Omnibus Workers' Union (Cape) v Heading*.[100] Respondent, a former bus conductor, had sued appellant for damages as a result of its "unlawful threats, acts of violence and declaration of a strike" in an attempt to force his employers to dismiss him. In their plea in defence, the trade

[91] At 508. [92] At 510. [93] 1930 AD 225. [94] De Waal, JP.
[95] Feetham, Barry, and Gey van Pittius, JJ.
[96] See 233–42 concurred in by J A J de Villiers, CJ; Curlewis and Stratford, JJA.
[97] At 236. [98] At 238–240.
[99] See "Civil Liberties" above. [100] 1938 AD 47.

union maintained that, as it was constituted under the Industrial Conciliation Act,[101] which limited its powers, and as the law prohibited it from participating in a strike,[102] any threat to strike on its part would have been *ultra vires*. Heading excepted to this plea as being "bad in law", and the CPD[103] upheld his exception, which resulted in the union's appeal to Bloemfontein.

Stratford, JA[104] carefully examined the arguments and reasoning of the provincial division with regard to the union's powers, and concluded that ". . . [i]n each case it is a question, to be determined by construction, whether the incorporating Act intends to recognise pre-existing functions of the unincorporated body, or intends to curtail them or to supplant them, or, indeed, to bring into being a pure creature of its own devising".[105] He said that a distinction should be made between the absence of a right, and the denial of a power, and he decided that unions engaged in "essential services", like appellant, were not expressly prohibited from striking in all circumstances, but that the penalty prescribed by statute for striking in certain circumstances was an implied recognition of the right to do so.[106] On this ground he confirmed that the plea was embarrassing in its procedural sense, and dismissed the appeal.

This rather remarkable argument (akin to: because an act is penalised by law, everyone has a right to perform it, but such action will be punished anyway) certainly made it clear that the court would not endorse what it perceived as unfair union pressure on an individual. But it also inadvertently lent some flavour of legitimacy to strike action by unions engaged in the provision of essential services, which was quite contrary to legislative intent.

The court's insistence on fairness in a union's dealings with its members was further underlined in *Stuart v Ismail*,[107] in which the AD confirmed the CPD's order[108] to appellant, the secretary of a union, to disclose to respondent, a member of that union, the names and addresses of the executive committee members of the union. Ismail needed these in order to bring an action against the committee for alleged improper conduct of union affairs, and Centlivres, JA[109] held that Stuart's refusal to disclose the names would result in a defeat for justice, which necessitated the invocation of the "very large powers" of the Court to order disclosure, powers which were not confined to unincorporated bodies.[110]

[101] 11 of 1924, section 15.
[102] *Ibid* section 12(1) and 12(2).
[103] Watermeyer and Centlivres, JJ.
[104] See 50–7 with the concurrence of Curlewis, CJ; Beyers and De Wet, JJA.
[105] At 52.
[106] At 55. Section 12(3) of the Act laid down that "Nothing in this Act contained shall render lawful any lock-out or strike of employees . . ." in a service such as transportation. See also Riotous Assemblies and Criminal Law Amendment Act 27 of 1914, section 12.
[107] 1942 AD 327.
[108] *Per* Jones, Sutton, and Davis, JJ.
[109] See 330–5 with the concurrence of De Wet, CJ; Watermeyer, Tindall, and Feetham, JJA.
[110] At 332.

In the same vein, the court was not prepared to countenance any hint of dishonesty on the part of union officials which might have resulted in harm to the union's members. *Mine Workers' Union v Brodrick*[111] was an appeal against an order[112] to pay damages to respondent, formerly general secretary of appellant, for dismissal without the required period of notice. The AD[113] felt strongly enough about the alleged financial misdeeds of Brodrick to overrule the conclusions drawn from the evidence by the court of first instance, and maintained that, because Brodrick's conduct had justified summary dismissal, the onus lay on him to allege and prove further facts excusing his conduct. As this had not happened here, the union had rightly dismissed him, and its appeal was sustained.[114]

As to the broader operations of trade unions, inter-union disputes rarely surfaced in the AD before 1950, and only two need be noted. *Garment Workers' Union of the Cape & another v Garment Workers' Union & another*[115] was the outcome of an attempt by respondent to move in on the field of appellant's organising sphere of influence.[116] Appellant sought to block this by an insistence upon strict compliance with statutory procedures.[117] Although this had been successful in the WLD, the TPD had overturned this decision, and the AD held that no further appeal lay to it, as the issues raised in the appeal were not of sufficient importance to justify the granting of leave to appeal.[118]

Similarly, *Minister of Labour & another v AEU*[119] came about because of the decision of the Industrial Registrar to allow a rival union to organise workers in respondent's traditional area,[120] against the latter's objections, whose ultimate appeal to the TPD had been upheld.[121] The Minister of Labour and the union excluded by the latter decision then attempted to appeal to the AD, but Centlivres, JA[122] struck the appeal off the roll, on the ground that reconsideration of the provincial decision was prohibited by the terms of the Act, and precedent.[123]

[111] 1948 (4) SA 959 (AD).
[112] By the WLD *per* Roper, J.
[113] Through Greenberg, JA (960–85), with whom Schreiner, JA and Hoexter, AJA concurred.
[114] See 975–80.
[115] 1946 AD 370.
[116] Respondent, based in Johannesburg, had sought permission to organise millinery workers in appellant's area, Cape Town.
[117] See Industrial Conciliation Act 36 of 1937, section 77, which laid down a time limit of 30 days for the filing of an appeal in the Supreme Court against the Minister's decision under the Act, a requirement which appellants maintained had not yet been complied with.
[118] Judgment of Schreiner, JA (373–81), concurred in by Watermeyer, CJ; Tindall and Greenberg, JJA; and Feetham, AJA. Grindley-Ferris, J sat in the WLD; Barry, JP, Blackwell and Neser, JJ in the TPD.
[119] 1950 (3) SA 383 (AD).
[120] The rival was the Suid-Afrikaanse Yster en Staalbedryfsvereniging, which wished to organise white workers in the Thabazimbi Iron Mines.
[121] *Per* Murray, J and Grindley-Ferris, AJ.
[122] See 387–92 concurred in by Greenberg, Schreiner, Van den Heever, and Hoexter, JJA.
[123] The Industrial Conciliation Act 36 of 1937, section 77 provided only for an appeal to a provincial or local division, which was confirmed in *Minister of Labour v Building Workers' Industrial Union, infra.*

The question of the legal status of trade unions, as far as the actions of their members were concerned, was raised more often. A handbill issued by a trade union which alleged that an employer failed to pay a living wage, though financially able to do so, led to a defamation action against the former, and the appeal in *National Union of Distributive Workers v Cleghorn & Harris Ltd.*[124] The AD[125] accepted without question that the trade union could have been guilty of defamation, but decided here that a non-defamatory interpretation of the words used was possible, and so rejected the respondent's exception to the defendant union's plea, and upheld the appeal. In *The Mine Workers' Union v J J Prinsloo; v J P Prinsloo; v Greyling,*[126] the AD[127] extended the rule in *Royal British Bank v Turquand*[128] to cover the operations of registered trade unions, which in SA were bodies corporate. The result of this decision was that the appellant union suffered financial loss because of its purported purchase of portions of a farm belonging to respondents without having first carried out all the internal steps required by its constitution.

The ability of trade unions to act on behalf of their members was fully considered in the important decision in *Amalgamated Engineering Union v Minister of Labour.*[129] Here the appellant union, representative of certain municipal transportation employees in Durban, had applied to the Minister for the appointment of a Conciliation Board to settle a labour dispute with the Municipality. The Minister appointed such a board, but withdrew this appointment a month later, on the ground that the dispute existed between the employers and the union, rather than the employees, as was required by statute.[130] The NPD[131] upheld the correctness of the Minister's action on the basis of precedent, which stipulated that a union, as a body corporate distinct from its employee members, could not be in a dispute with employers on their behalf.[132]

Centlivres, JA[133] decided that this was an incorrect statement of the law: there *could* be disputes between trade unions and employers, but here the union had acted on behalf of its members.[134] He contended that substance rather than form should be determinative in such situations, and that the whole idea underlying the trade union system was that unions should act as spokesmen of their members in disputes, so that industrial relations could be regulated, and the

[124] 1946 AD 984.
[125] See judgments of Tindall, JA (986–90); Greenberg, JA (990–7); and Schreiner, JA (997–8).
[126] 1948 (3) SA 831 (AD).
[127] See Tindall, ACJ (837–40), and Greenberg, JA (840–52); Schreiner, JA concurred without comment.
[128] 119 ER 474, 886.
[129] 1949 (4) SA 908 (AD).
[130] Industrial Conciliation Act 36 of 1937, section 35.
[131] Broome and De Wet, JJ.
[132] See *Durban City Council v Minister of Labour & another* 1948 (1) SA 220 (N).
[133] See 908–16 concurred in by Watermeyer, CJ; Schreiner and Van den Heever, JJA.
[134] At 910.

interests of employers and employees furthered.[135] In upholding the appeal, he overruled an earlier TPD decision,[136] and he displayed a clear appreciation of the aims and methods of the process of industrial conciliation as it existed in South Africa.

This case led to an exchange of views in the SALJ which related to the interpretation of sections 35 and 64 of the Industrial Conciliation Act, and the conditions under which, and the means whereby, a conciliation board could be appointed.[137] In the first of these articles Caney and Bizzell took the courts to task for their tendency to see the sections as social legislation, which appeared at times to have been "conned . . . through what one may call social-security spectacles". They thought that "a sort of tender-heartedness towards employees ha[d] found its way into the courts, despite the fact that labour [was] quite well able to look after itself with the aid of its powerful trade unions". The authors expressed the hope that the case just outlined would be the turning-point in this tendency,[138] though the writer of the reply saw nothing in the case to support the arguments advanced by them.[139]

If the attitudes of Caney and Bizzell can be regarded as typical of at least one section of the legal fraternity, it is obvious that the courts had by 1950 achieved a reputation for being progressive in their interpretation of industrial legislation. That is to say, their reading of the law was seen to be in favour of employees rather than employers, and to be keeping pace with, if not outrunning, social change and ruling public opinion. In an endeavour to determine whether these assertions were warranted, judicial interpretation of labour statutes, mainly in connection with accident compensation, industrial conciliation agreements, and wage determinations will be set out at some length.

Workmen's Compensation

The award of financial compensation for damages suffered by workers in the course of their employment was one of the first aspects of industrial relations to receive legislative attention, and several Acts regulating procedures and supplanting the common law were passed before Union. The Union Parliament itself passed a consolidating Workmen's Compensation Act (hereafter the WCA) in 1914.[140] In applying these statutes, the AD was faced with having to adapt its approach to accident compensation in the light of the new rights, procedures, and duties created by the legislation, to the

[135] At 912.
[136] *OK Bazaars (1929) Ltd v Madeley, NO & another* 1943 TPD 392.
[137] See L R Caney and H V Bizzell "Some Observations upon Sections 35 and 64 of the ICA, 1937" (1951) 68 *SALJ* 30; and M Schaeffer "Some further considerations on sections 35 and 64 of the ICA" (1951) 68 *SALJ* 314.
[138] Caney and Bizzell *op cit* 32.
[139] Schaeffer *op cit* 315.
[140] 25 of that year.

exclusion of the common law. As the cases below will demonstrate, the court seems to have managed remarkably well.

A number of disputes came on appeal in the form of attempts by employers and employees to overturn the award or refusal of compensation by the lower courts, and concerned the direct application of phrases in the Act to the facts of the cases. In general, the AD adopted an interpretation sympathetic to the employees' interests here. For instance, they upheld the claim of a workman who had been drunk when the accident had occurred,[141] because there was no proof that this constituted the "gross carelessness" which had caused the accident.[142] Similarly, in *Vermeulen v Heyne*,[143] the appellant workman succeeded in his claim against his employer even though the accident had been caused by his use of different, and less safe, equipment from that which his employer had supplied. Solomon, J[144] decided that this was not enough to qualify as "serious and wilful misconduct", and he warned against the temptation to strain unduly the language of the Act[145] in cases of hardship (presumably to the employer).

Likewise, in *South African Railways v Estate Walton*,[146] Watermeyer, JA[147] did not hesitate to confirm the award of additional compensation on the ground that the accident which caused the workman's death had been due to the negligence of the employer,[148] which took the form in this case of the failure to provide adequate safety precautions when shunting trains at night in a railway yard.

On the other hand, at least one appeal under the WCA led the appeal court to take a less sympathetic attitude to the conduct of a workman which had resulted in his death. In *Van Breda, NO v Victoria Falls & Transvaal Power Co Ltd*[149] the executor of the deceased estate of Schurmann, an electrician in the employ of respondent, sought to overrule the decision by the TPD,[150] which had reversed an award of compensation made by a magistrate. Schurmann had died after entering a "live chamber" at a power station while his foreman was collecting the permit authorising entry, and after six of the seven safety steps required by company regulations had been carried out. He had touched a low-tension cable, which was dead, but had then

[141] *Sanders v Eddy Brothers* 1912 AD 558. Judgment of Laurence, J (560–7) with the concurrence of Innes, ACJ; Solomon, J; C G Maasdorp and J A J de Villiers, JJP.

[142] A ground of exemption available to the employer under the WCA, 40 of 1905 (Cape), section 6.

[143] 1913 AD 542.

[144] See 544–50 concurred with by Lord De Villiers, CJ; Innes, J; A F S Maasdorp, CJ; and Buchanan, AJP.

[145] WCA, 36 of 1907 (Transvaal).

[146] 1940 AD 321.

[147] See 325–33 with the concurrence of De Wet, CJ; Tindall, Centlivres, and Feetham, JJA.

[148] As provided in the WCA 59 of 1934, section 5.

[149] 1916 AD 325.

[150] Bristowe, Wessels, and Gregorowski, JJ.

put his hand on a live high-tension cable and had died instantly. The respondent and the TPD asserted that this had been "serious and wilful misconduct", enough to deny a compensation claim, whereas the magistrate had held that such misconduct had not been proved.

In the AD, all five judges gave opinions, but only J A J de Villiers, AJA felt that the judgment of the magistrate should be restored. Innes, CJ[151] Solomon [152] and C G Maasdorp,[153] JJA, and Juta, AJA[154] all expressed considerable regret that they could not allow the appeal,[155] but none of them could find anything in the circumstances which showed that the deceased had reasonable grounds for a belief that the chamber was safe. De Villiers, AJA's[156] dissent was based on his conclusion that the Company had not discharged the onus of proving misconduct by Schurmann. On reading the judgments, it is apparent that this decision could have gone either way, and the fact that Innes, CJ suggested that respondent should pay out compensation in any event[157] perhaps best sums up the feelings of the judges.

In addition to these appeals on the interpretation of the law as it related to the facts, several cases were fought on the interpretation of the procedures laid down by the WCA. Thus, in *Paine v Randfontein Central Gold Mining Co Ltd*,[158] the AD[159] refused to allow an injured workman to pursue his claim under common law because it considered that he had "recovered" compensation under statute. The evidence disclosed that Paine had signed a claim form while in hospital two days after his accident, but had subsequently refused a lump sum compensation and drawn three months' half-pay due to him. He contended that he had thought this was the customary sick pay, although he had signed a receipt "for account accident compensation". Even though it was desirable that there should be no duplication of claims here, it does seem that the court imposed too high and unrealistic a standard of caution on the actions of an ordinary workman in this case.

Cape Town Council v Jacobs[160] affirmed the court's reluctance to tolerate a long-running legal battle between employer and employee, by quashing an attempt by respondent to have a magistrate's order for compensation declared provisional where the evidence pointed to its finality.[161] A similar issue arose in *Neethling v Estate Burger*, [162]

[151] See 327–37.
[152] See 337–43.
[153] See 343–7.
[154] See 347–50.
[155] For example at 337, 343 and 350.
[156] See 350–7.
[157] At 337.
[158] 1912 AD 576.
[159] Judgment of Solomon, J (580–6) concurred in by Innes, ACJ and C G Maasdorp, JP.
[160] 1917 AD 615.
[161] Judgments of Solomon, JA (617–24) and Juta, AJA (624–30). Concurrence of Innes, CJ; C G Maasdorp, JA; and J A J de Villiers, AJA.
[162] 1942 AD 73.

where appellant had entered into an agreement with his employer for full and final settlement of his claim for accident compensation, which agreement had been made an order of court.[163] Neethling applied for a variation of this order under section 34(2)*(c)* of the Act (which allowed revision of an award if the agreement had been entered into in ignorance of, or under a mistake as to, the nature of the injury suffered) on discovering that he was more seriously ill than had originally been thought. Despite the statutory provision, De Wet, CJ[164] decided that an agreement was no longer such if it had been made an order of court, and he refused the application in the interests of finality.

The inability of a "native labourer" to claim compensation under the WCA[165] was confirmed, and the scope of the definition of such a person was widened by *Ngcema v Gilbert Harmer & Company Ltd.*[166] Here, Curlewis, JA[167] held that a native employed on any mine or works was a "native labourer" within the meaning of the Native Labour Regulation Act,[168] whether recruited under the Act or not. This meant that most natives could thenceforth claim injury compensation only under section 22(1) of this Act, rather than under the WCA, and that their benefits would accordingly be much lower. *Wagenaar v Thomas*[169] excluded once and for all the chance of suing a third party who was legally liable to pay damages as the result of an accident, after the injured workman had accepted statutory compensation. This was the court's interpretation of the Act[170] even where, as in this case, appellant had repaid the compensation received to his employer.

Nevertheless, the AD did seem to depart from its aim of achieving finality with its judgment in *Fred Saber (Pty) Ltd v Franks.*[171] Here, Centlivres, JA[172] confirmed the jurisdiction of the appeal court to hear appeals from a provincial or local division "as of right, after leave ha[d] been granted". He did so despite the point raised *in limine* by respondent's counsel, Quenet, KC, that the WCA[173] laid down that "any decision given by the [workmen's compensation] Commissioner shall be final and not subject to review or appeal in any court of law on any grounds whatsoever, save review or appeal as prescribed

[163] By virtue of the WCA 59 of 1934, section 15(2).

[164] See 75–9 concurred in by Watermeyer, Tindall, Centlivres, and Feetham, JJA.

[165] 25 of 1914, section 2(1)*(f)* of which defined those covered by Act 15 of 1911 as not being "workmen".

[166] 1928 AD 34.

[167] See 35–43 concurred in by Solomon, CJ; Wessels and Stratford, JJA.

[168] 15 of 1911, section 2 of which defined "native labourer" as a native employed upon any mine or works or recruited under the Act or a prior law for labour on any mine or works.

[169] 1930 AD 465. Judgment of Wessels, JA (467–74) concurred in by J A J de Villiers, CJ and Roos, JA.

[170] WCA 25 of 1914, section 38.

[171] 1949 (1) SA 388 (AD).

[172] See 394–408 with concurrence of Watermeyer, CJ; Schreiner, and Van den Heever, JJA; and Hoexter, AJA.

[173] 30 of 1941, section 25(7)*(a)*.

THE HON MR JUSTICE J S CURLEWIS
The sixth Chief Justice of South Africa 1936–38

(By courtesy of Legal & Financial Publishing Co (Pty) Ltd)

THE HON MR JUSTICE JAMES STRATFORD
The seventh Chief Justice of South Africa 1938–39

in this subsection". Now section 25(7)*(b)* allowed a review or appeal to a provincial or local division alone, with no mention of any recourse to Bloemfontein. But, even though the previous WCA (of 1934) had provided specifically for an appeal to the AD, the learned judge contended that absence of such a provision in the present Act should not be taken to indicate that there was no right of appeal, and he overruled the objection.[174]

On the merits of the appeal, however, the court displayed a realistic awareness of the conditions and problems faced by workers in the situation of respondent, and they refused to regard his customary action, which had led to the accident, as negligent or an error of judgment.[175]

This sympathetic view of the workman's task was not a uniform feature of AD decisions, though, as some of the following cases which all deal with accident compensation outside the scope of the WCA will demonstrate. *UG (Minister of Justice) v Scales*[176] took the form of a claim by a policeman, who had lost the use of an arm in the course of his duty, that he was incapable of earning a living, and was, therefore, entitled to a higher pension than that which he had been awarded.[177] Respondent submitted evidence that he had attempted to obtain a job over a wide area with only temporary success, and the OPD[178] had accepted his argument.

Lord De Villiers, CJ[179] upheld the government's appeal against this finding, as he maintained that Scales was capable of doing clerical or farm work. He said that ". . . it does not seem as if he has been looking for work for a sufficient time to show that he is incapable of obtaining it. We know of thousands of people who have lost one arm and are still able to earn a livelihood".[180] In addition he asserted that "[t]he effect of supporting the judgment would be to establish the principle that the mere fact of a person partially losing the use of an arm would render him incapable of earning a livelihood".[181]

This somewhat imperious approach, totally unsubstantiated by empirical data, was repeated in milder form some years later in *Du Preez & another v South African Railways*,[182] where the court refused to sustain the damages claims of two widows of railway workers who had died after being struck by a passing train. The evidence disclosed that warning of the approach of a train had been given and that deceased had returned to work after it had passed, but that a second

[174] At 398–400.
[175] At 407–8.
[176] 1913 AD 333.
[177] Under the Police Pension Act 2 of 1910 (ORC), section 5(1).
[178] A F S Maasdorp, CJ and Ward, J.
[179] See 335–7 with the concurrence of Solomon, J; J A J de Villiers, and Dove Wilson, JJP; and Buchanan, AJP.
[180] At 336.
[181] At 337.
[182] 1931 AD 40.

train had struck them and killed them. Although Roos, JA[183] found that the workers had probably become accustomed to a certain form of danger, which might explain the accident, this factor was not enough to disprove negligence on their part in disobeying certain work regulations. The court dismissed the claims, despite the long-established principle of workmen's compensation statutes (which provided for compensation for injury suffered even as a result of negligence), and despite the ability of the employer here, a public utility corporation, to absorb the losses through a marginal increase in railway tariffs.

Judicial attitudes to safety at work were expressed in straightforward fashion in *Van Heerden v South African Pulp & Paper Industries Ltd.*[184] This was an application for leave to appeal *in forma pauperis* against the dismissal by the WLD[185] of applicant's action for damages against his former employer, on the basis of permanent impairment of his health through inhalation of chlorine gas. Schreiner, JA[186] held that, in order to succeed, Van Heerden would have to show a reasonable prospect of proving negligence on his employer's part, and, in estimating his chances of doing so, the judge made several remarks about health standards in factories.

Schreiner, JA thought that it was not negligent *per se* to have an imperfect industrial plant in use, especially where it was new and the country was at war (as here), and that ". . . industrial plant should be safe but should also be economically workable". He clearly stated his view of the limitations of the judicial function in this regard when he maintained that: "Modern legal systems recognise the need to provide adequate protection for the health of workmen employed in industrial production. But for such protection to be as complete as is considered socially desirable, legislation is often necessary."[187] In the event, Van Heerden's reliance on the danger of sub-perceptible concentrations of chlorine to found negligence was supported by insufficient evidence, and his application was refused.[188]

On the other hand, two cases which concerned injury compensation but which fell outside the scope of the WCA do redress the balance to a degree. *Cele v Hunt, Leuchars & Hepburn Ltd*[189] showed the court's willingness to impose liability for negligence on an employer where it seemed that the absence of a customary warning signal had resulted in the appellant worker losing his hand in a machine which he was cleaning.[190] In addition, in *City Deep Ltd v Silicosis Board*,[191] the appeal court adopted a generous interpretation

[183] See 40–4 concurred in by J A J de Villiers, CJ and Wessels, JA.
[184] 1946 AD 382.
[185] Blackwell, J.
[186] See 382–9 with which Tindall, JA and Davis, AJA concurred.
[187] At 385. [188] At 386–9.
[189] 1927 AD 498.
[190] See judgment of Solomon, CJ (498–501) concurred in by Wessels and Curlewis, JJA.
[191] 1950 (1) SA 696 (AD).

of the words of a statute which governed compensation to be awarded to tuberculosis sufferers, where a black miner, T, had worked for only 27 days for appellant before becoming ill and being hospitalised. As T's contract had been terminated only a month later, Watermeyer, CJ[192] and Centlivres, JA[193] held that his time in hospital fell within his continuous period of service. This finding was crucial to the success of T's claim, as the statute[194] prescribed a minimum of 30 days' service before a worker was entitled to receive benefits. The judges took great care in reaching this conclusion, in spite of possible absurd results, but they preferred a liberal interpretation in order more fully to give expression to legislative intent.[195]

In sum, therefore, the judges of appeal appear to have adapted themselves well to legislative initiatives in the field of workmen's compensation, and to have been prepared on most occasions to apply the law in a spirit of goodwill, which benefited the employees rather than their employers. An analysis of further cases, the outcome of which depended upon the construction of labour statutes, will determine whether the judiciary pursued such a course in other aspects of the labour process.

Challenges to the Validity of Industrial Council Agreements and Wage Determinations

The statutory foundation of industrial relations in SA from 1924 to 1950 rested on two related laws, the Industrial Conciliation Act,[196] and the Wage Act[197] (hereafter ICA and WA, respectively). For the purpose of the review of cases which appears below, it is essential that the skeleton of the machinery created by those Acts[198] should be set out.

The ICA provided for the constitution of an Industrial Council for each industry, to consist of an equal number of representatives of the employers' organisation and trade unions in that industry. The rights and duties of both employers' organisations and trade unions were prescribed, and considerable powers were granted to the Industrial Registrar and the Minister of Labour to regulate employers' and employees' affairs and to determine whether their associations were "representative" of the participants in their particular industry. A lengthy internal disputes procedure was mandatory, and various methods, such as conciliation, mediation, and arbitration, had to be resorted to in certain circumstances before a legal strike could be called.

[192] See 700–7.
[193] See 707–13 with which Greenberg, Schreiner, and Van den Heever, JJA concurred.
[194] The Silicosis Act, 47 of 1946 section 71(2), read with section 92.
[195] See Watermeyer, CJ at 700 and 706 for example.
[196] 11 of 1924 as amended until a new Act 36 of 1937 was passed.
[197] 27 of 1925 as amended until a new Act 44 of 1937 was passed.
[198] As there were two major Acts during the period under review, section numbers will not be referred to in what follows, but the main features of each Act will be outlined.

The function of an industrial council was to draw up an agreement on all matters concerning the employer/employee relationship, and to submit such an agreement to the Minister for his approval and promulgation, after which it would carry the force of law. The terms of such agreements would bind all employers and employees in the industry as defined therein, whether represented on the industrial council or not. Pass-bearing (ie most male) Africans were excluded from the definition of "employee" in the Act, with the result that they could neither belong to trade unions recognised by the Minister nor be a party to the negotiation of agreements, although the Minister could extend the operation of an agreement so as to cover African workers in the industry.

The Wage Act was intended to regulate the wages and working conditions of all employees not subject to industrial council agreements. A Wage Board was set up to investigate, receive representations from, and report on those spheres of employment which escaped the ICA net, and the Minister was once more empowered to promulgate such a report as a wage determination. This action would bind all employers and workers to observe the terms of the determination, which customarily laid down minimum wages and conditions of work within a defined area, both regional and industrial. Although the Wage Board was forbidden to discriminate between the races when making a recommendation, farm workers, domestic servants, and gold and coal mine employees were excluded from its brief, with the result that large numbers of black workers were not affected by its determinations.

Several cases which reached the AD arose from conflicts over the meaning of the provisions of the ICA. For instance, *Minister of Labour v Building Workers' Industrial Union*[199] confirmed that the Act limited the right of appeal to the level of a provincial court, with no further appeal to the AD; and *Bethlehem Municipality v Minister of Labour*[200] established that a white person whose contract of employment was regulated by the Native (Urban Areas) Act[201] was not included as an "employee" by the ICA. *South African Welders' Society v National Industrial Council for the Iron, Steel, Engineering, & Metallurgical Industry & another*,[202] while it instructed industrial councils to include in their constitutions a provision which would enable them to admit trade unions or other persons as members, laid down the rule that a registered trade union was not entitled as of right to admission to the industrial council which covered the interests represented by it. In

[199] 1939 AD 328, *per* Centlivres, JA (330–4), with the concurrence of Stratford, CJ; De Wet, Watermeyer, and Tindall, JJA.

[200] 1943 AD 75, *per* De Wet, CJ (76–80) with the concurrence of Watermeyer, Tindall, Centlivres, and Feetham, JJA.

[201] 11 of 1923.

[202] 1947 (2) SA 841 (AD) *per* Greenberg, JA (845–51) with the concurrence of Tindall, JA and Hathorn, AJA.

addition, the court decided in *Garment Workers' Union v Schoeman, NO & others*[203] that the fact that the ICA empowered the Industrial Registrar to ask the Minister to appoint a commission of inquiry[204] into a matter of public concern in no way limited Ministerial power to request the Governor-General to appoint such a commission under the Commissions Act.[205]

But many employers attempted to evade conviction under these Acts by challenging the *validity* of the agreements or determinations made thereunder (non-compliance with which was a criminal offence), and it is to these cases that this section is devoted. In the last section, those cases which came on appeal as the result of disputes concerning the *meaning* of those determinations and agreements which were held to be effective will be examined.

Two cases which reached Bloemfontein in the 1940's were in the form of appeals by employers against their criminal convictions for the breaking of industrial council agreements which, they claimed, were irregular and thus invalid. In *R v Chadwick*,[206] appellant contended that an agreement,[207] which prescribed minimum wages in the following words: "All other operations in the manufacture and/or erection of tubular wrought iron domestic and farm gates and fences—repetition work 1s 9d per hour", was so vague that it could not be understood and enforced, and that the agreement was invalid because minimum wages had not been laid down for every branch of the industry. Centlivres, JA[208] rejected both of these arguments by extracting a sensible interpretation of the wage formulation, and by holding that it was absurd to view a whole agreement as invalid because employment of a very unimportant character was not covered by its terms.[209]

Further, in *R v Associated Trade Suppliers Ltd & another*,[210] appellant employer attacked the validity of a clause in an agreement[211] on the ground of uncertainty, and urged that it failed both to define two terms used in its heading and to indicate precisely which employees should receive the highest wages. Greenberg, JA[212] dismissed these contentions and stated that the clause was clear and unambiguous. Even though it seemed that the employer had a discretion as to whom he should pay the highest wage, he held that it was probable that the recipient would be the most experienced worker.[213] Both these

[203] 1949 (2) SA 455 (AD) *per* Greenberg, JA (460–6) with Tindall and Schreiner, JJA concurring.
[204] Act 36 of 1937, section 13.
[205] 8 of 1947, section 1.
[206] 1941 AD 316.
[207] Relating to the Iron and Steel Manufacturing and Engineering Industry (Transvaal) Part 4 clause 2.
[208] See 316–20 concurred in by De Wet, CJ; Watermeyer, Tindall, and Feetham, JJA.
[209] At 318. [210] 1945 AD 611.
[211] Relating to the Printing and Newspaper Industry clause 4(3).
[212] See 613–18, concurred in by Watermeyer, CJ; Tindall, JA, and Davis, AJA.
[213] At 616.

findings demonstrate a desire on the part of the court not to strike down an agreement because of minor semantic difficulties, and thus to support the efficacy of the industrial conciliation system.

Determinations under the WA were more frequently and successfully struck down in an endeavour by employers to upset their convictions for non-compliance with their terms. For example, in *R v Lewin*,[214] the accused appealed on the grounds that publication of a determination in the *Social and Industrial Review*, a monthly magazine of the Department of Labour, did not comply with the WA requirement of publication in a "newspaper circulating within the district",[215] and that the Wage Board had misdirected itself in deciding that its recommendation could not discriminate between the races.[216] Stratford, JA[217] upheld the appeal on the first ground, but not on the second, so that the determination lost its force.

Again, in *Ex parte Minister of Justice: In re R v Barone*,[218] the appeal court[219] confirmed the setting aside of Barone's conviction for contravention of a minimum-wage determination on the ground that the Minister had acted *ultra vires* in dating his determination incorrectly. On the other hand, *R v Hoffman*[220] established that a wage determination remained valid even though the Minister had subsequently acted in pursuance of the Apprenticeship Act[221] and had withdrawn certain apprentices from the effect of the wage determination.[222] Here, Wessels, CJ[223] averred that the two Acts had to be seen as supplementary to one another, and that they should be interpreted so as to give effect to each. In his opinion, the alteration of part of the WA determination by the Apprenticeship Act designation would not lead to invalidation of the whole.[224]

This issue of partial or total invalidity cropped up four more times when employers sought to upset their convictions under the WA. The leading decision in this field was handed down in a case stated by the Minister,[225] *Ex parte Minister of Justice: In re R v Gerstnera*,[226] which established the rule that the whole of a determination would become *ultra vires* if the part of it which had been declared invalid was vital to its meaning. In this instance, Stratford, JA[227] found that the

[214] 1930 AD 344.
[215] As required by section 7(2).
[216] As laid down in section 3(3).
[217] See 345–51 with the concurrence of J A J de Villiers, CJ; Curlewis, JA, and Wessels, JA (who gave a short opinion at 351–2).
[218] 1930 AD 412.
[219] *Per* Stratford, JA (414–18) with whom J A J de Villiers, CJ; Roos, JA, and Curlewis, JA (418–20) concurred.
[220] 1936 AD 316.
[221] 26 of 1922.
[222] Number 40 relating to the hairdressing trade.
[223] See 318–21 with the concurrence of Curlewis, Stratford, and J E R de Villiers, JJA.
[224] At 321.
[225] Under the Criminal Procedure Act 31 of 1917, section 388, the Minister of Justice had the power to refer conflicting decisions of provincial divisions for final interpretation by the AD.
[226] 1930 AD 420.
[227] See 421–5 concurred in by J A J de Villiers, CJ; Curlewis and Roos, JJA.

principle underlying the WA was to secure to an employee a proper minimum wage commensurate with his qualifications and services,[228] and that, where a wage determination[229] classified employees unintelligibly, it was invalid as regards those employees, and consequently rendered meaningless and invalid *in toto*.[230]

The appeal court[231] in *Ex parte Minister of Justice: In re R v Cohen*[232] then proceeded to declare a particular clause in a determination[233] invalid, without affecting the rest of it, where the clause in question had attempted, contrary to the WA, to lay down a weekly wage for a piece-worker, irrespective of how many pieces he had completed. This approach was confirmed and regularised in *R v Stoller*,[234] in which the AD decided that the principles, applied in determining whether the invalidity of part of an ordinance, regulation, or by-law, passed by a subordinate legislature, invalidated the whole enactment,[235] would be of equal force in regard to wage determinations.[236]

In this case, Stoller's conviction was confirmed by De Wet, CJ[237] on the basis that the determination which he had contravened in three respects remained valid, even though one of its clauses[238] might have been invalid, because the latter was severable from the rest. In doing so, he adopted the reasoning of Wessels, CJ in *Hoffman*, to the effect that the question of validity of a determination, part of which was invalid, depended on all the circumstances of the case.[239] The Chief Justice did not take into account[240] *Gerstnera* or *Cohen* above, as the question of severability had not been argued there.

A final example of a situation in which the principle of severability was applied, with fatal effects for the whole enactment,[241] was provided by the case of *Kneen v Minister of Labour & another*.[242] In his judgment, Greenberg, JA[243] outlined the test to be applied as follows:[244] "If after deleting that portion of a subordinate legislative enactment held to be invalid, we can reasonably presume the remainder would have been passed by that body had it correctly

228 At 424.
229 Number 17, relating to the Baking and Confectionery Industries (Pretoria).
230 At 425.
231 *Per* Wessels, CJ (522–4), with the concurrence of Curlewis, Beyers, and J E R de Villiers, JJA.
232 1934 AD 521.
233 Number 42, relating to the Clothing Industry, clause 3(2).
234 1939 AD 599.
235 As laid out in *Arderne, Scott, Thesen Ltd v Cape Provincial Administration* 1937 AD 429.
236 In this case number 56, relating to the Motor Transport Delivery occupation.
237 See 611–17 with the concurrence of Watermeyer, Tindall, Centlivres, and Feetham, JJA.
238 Clause 11.
239 At 617.
240 At 616.
241 Determination number 97 relating to the Dairy Trade.
242 1945 AD 400.
243 See 401–9 with the concurrence of Watermeyer, CJ; Tindall and Feetham, JJA; and Davis, AJA.
244 At 407, a direct adoption of Lord Haldane in *A-G of Manitoba v A-G of Canada* [1925] AC 561.

appreciated its powers, then . . . we should declare the purified remainder a valid enactment."

These judgments indicate a passive acceptance of this new system of regulating industrial relations which was the creature of the ICA and the WA, and do not disclose a concerted effort to resist such statutory machinery and its interference with the common law. Whether this is an accurate proposition can be tested further by a consideration of those cases which revolved around judicial interpretation of valid agreements and determinations.

Judicial Interpretations of Industrial Council Agreements and Wage Determinations

A second method used by employers, accused of non-compliance with agreements and determinations, to evade conviction was to claim that, on a correct interpretation of the agreement or determination in question, they were not covered by its terms. The appeal court was confronted with a certain freedom to choose whether to obstruct the effective operation of the Acts by applying strict standards of construction to the agreements (which were often inexpertly drawn up) so that convictions would be difficult to sustain, or to read the agreements in the spirit in which they were arrived at, and in that way to ensure a living wage and safe working conditions for all workers. The path which they elected to walk may indicate their feelings about statutory intervention in the "freedom" of the employment contract, and, therefore, an examination of the judgments in these cases seems warranted.

Gravenor v Dunswart Iron Works[245] provided an appropriately ambiguous industrial conciliation agreement[246] for the AD's perusal. Clause 1 provided that the agreement should apply to all employees in the engineering industry in the Transvaal; Clause 2 laid down wage rates for over 20 kinds of artisans; Clause 3 prescribed the maximum weekly working hours; while Clause 4 laid down the rates for overtime pay. Appellant, an employee in the engineering industry but not one of the artisans defined in Clause 2, claimed overtime pay in accordance with Clauses 3 and 4, but the court dismissed his argument. Stratford, JA[247] maintained that the judges should adopt the meaning intended by the parties, and not the ordinary and natural meaning, which would lead to absurdity.[248] He said that Clause 2 was vital, that the agreement was only intended to protect skilled artisans, and that it was impossible to calculate overtime pay if no basic rate had been provided for.[249]

[245] 1929 AD 299.
[246] That relating to the engineering industry in the Transvaal.
[247] See 300–4, with the concurrence of J A J de Villiers, ACJ; J E R de Villiers, AJA; and Wessels, JA (304–5).
[248] At 303.
[249] At 302–3.

Now, on the facts as reported, an interpretation of this agreement such that Clauses 3 and 4 applied to all employees, while Clause 2 offered extra protection to those employees who possessed special skills would have been equally logical. It would, in fact, have been quite possible to have calculated Gravenor's overtime pay, because all that Clause 4 stipulated was payment of the ordinary wage plus one half. Besides, Clause 2 merely laid down certain minimum wages: could it then be said that a skilled artisan should receive a multiple of the *minimum* wage rate for overtime pay (as the judgment would seem to imply), rather than a multiple of his *actual* wage? This can hardly have been the practice in the industry, and the AD's attitude in this case appears to be unrealistic and restrictive of the intended effects of the agreement.

A similar approach was evident some years later in *R v Becker*,[250] which saw an employer appealing against his conviction for underpayment of certain employees in the building industry, whose function had been to fit grooved and tongued concrete plates into position in the construction of walls of a house. The agreement[251] which Becker was alleged to have contravened had defined brick-laying, masonry, and plastering, in basic terms, as working with concrete blocks, precast or artificial stone. The NPD[252] had held that the employees were engaged in masonry, and so should have been paid the minimum wage prescribed in the agreement.

De Wet, CJ[253] thought otherwise. He argued that the concrete plates were neither blocks nor artificial stone, and that Becker should be given the benefit of any reasonable doubt in this matter.[254] As a result, the conviction was set aside. This could perhaps be regarded as an example of the court's application of a strict construction to statutes which were penal in nature.

But it would be misleading to give the impression that such decisions were typical of judicial attitudes throughout the period, as three decisions of the late 1940's indicate. *R v Lipschitz*[255] arose from the employment by accused of a native in a job which was subject to a closed-shop agreement with a trade union which the native could not have joined, because he was not an "employee" as defined in the ICA. Lipschitz had been paying this employee less than the minimum wage rate laid down by the agreement,[256] but he asserted, on the Attorney-General's appeal against the accused's acquittal in the TPD,[257] that he could not be guilty on a charge of underpayment

[250] 1940 AD 19.
[251] That relating to the Building Industry.
[252] Feetham, JP and Jarvis, AJ.
[253] See 19–26, with the concurrence of Watermeyer, Tindall, and Centlivres, JJA.
[254] At 24–5.
[255] 1948 (1) SA 781 (AD).
[256] Between the SA Motor Industry Employers' Association and the Motor Industry Employees' Union of SA.
[257] Barry, JP and De Villiers, J.

because the employment of the native was illegal under the closed-shop clause.[258] The matter was further complicated by the fact that the Minister had declared that the agreement should be applicable to all employees, irrespective of statutory definition, except for certain clauses, one of which was that which related to the closed shop.

Centlivres, JA[259] saw a way out of this welter of imprecision by reasoning that it was not inconsistent with the context of the closed shop clause to apply the ICA definition of "employee" to it, which meant that the native employee was excluded from its scope, and was legally employed.[260] At the same time, the Minister's declaration that the agreement should apply to all employees signified that Lipschitz should have paid the native worker the minimum wage,[261] and so the judge referred the matter back to the magistrate's court for a re-hearing.

The same issues were raised in another appeal by the Attorney-General from the TPD,[262] *R v Green*,[263] and here Centlivres, JA[264] responded to the detailed and clear arguments of the employer by setting out the court's view of the extent of Ministerial powers, and the scope and objective of the ICA. In doing so, he displayed a healthy realism in regard to the concept and purpose of the closed shop, and argued that an employer was more likely to respect such a provision if he would face prosecution for paying less than the minimum wage to non-union employees.[265]

Further, in *KWV van Zuid-Afrika Beperk v Industrial Council for the Building Industry & others*,[266] appellant employer, a co-operative society which marketed wine on behalf of its farmer-members, contended that, in employing building-workers to construct wine-receiving tanks, it was not engaged in the building industry, so that it was not subject to the ICA. The appeal court[267] dismissed this argument, and held that an employer could be involved in more than one industry, a fact which depended upon the comparative amounts of money spent and staff employed.[268] Here, Centlivres, JA[269] found that the KWV had a relatively large number of permanent employees who were concerned with the "building industry", and that quite a large sum of money was devoted each year to this aspect of its operation. Therefore, he held that the Society could not claim that it did not fall within the jurisdiction of the ICA.

[258] Clause 22.
[259] See 784–8 concurred in by Watermeyer, CJ; Tindall, Greenberg, and Schreiner, JJA.
[260] At 787.
[261] *Loc cit.*
[262] Barry, JP and De Villiers, J.
[263] 1948 (2) SA 476 (AD).
[264] See 482–8 concurred in by Tindall, ACJ; Greenberg and Schreiner, JJA.
[265] At 487–8.
[266] 1949 (2) SA 600 (AD).
[267] Tindall, Centlivres, Greenberg, and Schreiner, JJA; Hoexter, AJA.
[268] At 610.
[269] See 605–14.

The AD likewise insisted on the strict observance of the terms of an industrial council agreement by employers and employees who claimed that they were not subject to it. *R v Reichlin*[270] was an appeal by a convicted employer, who asserted that his trade did not fall within the printing and newspaper industry as defined in an agreement; that he was not bound by the agreement as he had not been a party to it nor represented by the employers' organisation; and that the Minister could not legally have made him subject to the agreement, as he was not eligible to join the employers' organisation. Centlivres, JA[271] rejected all these arguments, and his judgment is an example of his determination to carry out the intention of the legislature, as manifest in the ICA, to the full, although he was perhaps a little too trusting of the good faith with which Ministerial power was exercised.[272]

On the other hand, *Broughton v Durban Municipality*[273] provided a forum for the court to establish the binding nature of an agreement, which emanated from a Conciliation Board, on all those purported to be subject to its terms. Appellant in this instance was a municipal employee whose entitlement to service benefits had *prima facie* been altered by the terms of a Conciliation Board agreement, in spite of a specific award of service benefits in the previous year. Schreiner, JA[274] reasoned that the clear language of the agreement and the statutory backing of the ICA could not be departed from, and he saw the employees' protection as being lodged in the requirement that the Minister had to be "satisfied" as to the "representativity" of the parties to the agreement before promulgation thereof.[275]

Judicial acceptance of the philosophy behind the industrial laws had not always been fully understanding or co-operative, though, as two cases from the mid-1930's vividly demonstrate. *Manoim v Veneered Furniture Manufacturers*[276] took the form of an appeal by a cabinet maker against the dismissal of his claim for the amount by which his employer, respondent here, had underpaid him in terms of the ICA and WA. The employer had been criminally convicted and sentenced for this conduct, but the court had made no order for payment of the shortfall in wages to the aggrieved employees, which the Acts empowered it to do. Two provincial divisions had been faced with the question of whether a civil action could lie against the employers under these conditions, and each had taken one side of the dispute.[277]

[270] 1939 AD 271.
[271] See 273–7, with whom Stratford, CJ; De Wet, Watermeyer, and Tindall, JJA concurred.
[272] At 276.
[273] 1946 AD 892.
[274] See 894–902 with whom Greenberg, JA; and Davis, AJA concurred.
[275] At 902 under the ICA 36 of 1937, section 48(2).
[276] 1934 AD 237.
[277] *Donner v Yzelle* 1932 TPD 253 had decided that no civil action was available to the employee while *Gebela v Banks* 1931 NPD 346 had held that such an action could be maintained.

Wessels, CJ[278] handed down the leading judgment for the AD. He based his opinion of the matter on the construction of section 8 of the WA, which stipulated that a contract to pay less than the minimum wage was void, and the parties to it were guilty of an offence. In considering the question, he took the policy of the Act, which he saw as the "prevention of sweated labour", into account,[279] as well as the plain words of the Act.[280] He held[281] that, by making it an offence to enter into an agreement for less than the minimum wage,

> ". . . the Legislature showed clearly that it had no intention of placing the honest and meritorious workman on the same plane and in the same position as the dishonest and fraudulent workman. It would indeed be lamentable and subversive of the morality of employees if they were freely encouraged by the Legislature to enter into agreements for lower wages than the statutory minimum, and when they had secured such contracts to the detriment of their fellow workers and of rival employers to turn round and claim by civil action the full wage."

Thus he adopted the obvious meaning of the statute, and invoked the "in pari delicto potior est conditio defendentis" maxim against the "dishonest" workman to deprive him of a civil remedy. Beyers, JA[282] added a short concurring judgment, and declared himself unaffected by the possible anomalies which might result from the decision, for "[d]ie werknemer handel onwettig met ope oë".[283]

Much the same sentiments formed the basis of the judicial approach in *Martin v D'Almeida*,[284] in which the court refused the privilege of litigation *in forma pauperis* to a "dishonest and fraudulent workman"[285] who found himself in the same position as had *Manoim*. Curlewis, JA[286] relied largely on the *ratio* of that case, and the judgment of Centlivres, J in the court *a quo*.

The AD was taken severely to task for these decisions by a future judge of appeal, Van den Heever, in the SALJ some years later.[287] He described the *Manoim* judgment as being decided on "truly remarkable grounds", and likened the statements of the Chief Justice and Beyers, JA to ". . . the French Queen's question as to why her starving subjects, who cried for bread, did not eat cake". He realised that these expressions were not due to cynicism but to ". . . judicial seclusion which rendered it difficult to appreciate the economic stresses to which the labouring classes are frequently subjected, often compelling them to feed their children in wages earned in illicit contracts or to let them starve 'honestly and meritoriously'". He

[278] See 241–9, with whom Stratford and J E R de Villiers, JJA concurred.
[279] At 244.
[280] At 245.
[281] At 246.
[282] See 249–51.
[283] At 251: ". . . the employee acts illegally with open eyes" (my translation).
[284] 1936 AD 129.
[285] At 132.
[286] See 131–2 with the concurrence of Stratford, Beyers, and J E R de Villiers, JJA.
[287] He wrote under the name *Aquilius*. See "Immorality and Illegality in Contract" (1942) 59 *SALJ* 16.

submitted that section 8 of the WA conferred a precarious right on workmen to claim the shortfall in wages, which was dependent on judicial discretion, rather than any question of morality.[288] Such criticism of judicial performance seems fully justified here.

As far as the interpretation of WA determinations was concerned, the AD showed in the few cases which came before it that it had become accustomed to dealing with the type of questions raised by the obscure or complicated formulae which typified such declarations. For example, in *Ex parte Minister of Justice: In re R v Schlohs,*[289] De Wet, CJ[290] insisted on a strict construction of section 20(2) of the WA, which required a penalty to be imposed on a convicted employer every time it was proved that he had underpaid his workers. Again, in *R v Woodstock Sweets Co Ltd,*[291] Feetham, JA[292] mastered some detailed evidence as to what constituted a "qualified assistant sweetmaker" in sustaining the accused employer's conviction on a charge of paying less than the minimum wages laid down in a WA determination.[293]

Strong resolve to ensure the full application of the law to wily employers was apparent in two cases which arose, not from WA determinations, but from like regulations issued under various War Measures in force during the Second World War. *R v Giesken and Giesken*[294] raised similar issues to those dealt with in the *KWV* case above, in that the accused were dairy farmers who produced their own milk, but also ran a dairy business which purchased milk from other farmers, mixed it with their own, and then distributed it for sale. Greenberg, JA[295] decided that it was possible for one employer to carry on two or more enterprises, and that the accused had, in addition to their farming operations, been engaged in the "dairy trade" as defined in the award[296] which had prescribed the cost-of-living allowances payable to employees. As the Gieskens had not paid the allowance to those employees who worked in the dairy section of the business, their appeal was dismissed.

In addition, in *African Caterers Ltd v Willie,*[297] the appeal court was not prepared to accept that an employer was exempted from paying the cost-of-living allowance to an employee who was supplied with a free meal during his working hours. The appellant claimed that this constituted "board" as defined in a regulation issued under a War Measure,[298] but Centlivres, JA[299] rejected such an argument on the

[288] At 24. [289] 1943 AD 80.
[290] See 81–5 concurred in by Watermeyer, Tindall, Centlivres, and Feetham, JJA.
[291] 1944 AD 1.
[292] See 2–7, concurred in by Watermeyer, CJ; Tindall, Centlivres, and Greenberg, JJA.
[293] Number 71, relating to the Sweet Manufacturing Industry.
[294] 1947 (4) SA 561 (AD).
[295] See 563–8 concurred in by Watermeyer, CJ; Tindall, Centlivres, and Schreiner, JJA.
[296] Relating to the Dairy Trade, Witwatersrand and Pretoria.
[297] 1949 (3) SA 475 (AD).
[298] Regulation 2(1)*(a)* of War Measure 43 of 1942.
[299] See 478–84 concurred in by Schreiner, Van den Heever, and Hoexter, JJA; and Fagan, AJA.

evidence before the Court, even though, as in *Misnum*, the amount involved was very small—one shilling per week. This last fact is important, as it shows a recognition by the judges of the value of small amounts of money to low-paid workers.

An almost comic element was revealed in *R v Ngcobo*,[300] in which a licensed native medicine man and herbalist appealed against his conviction for underpayment under the WA. Centlivres, JA[301] confirmed the conviction, despite the fact that Ngcobo could not possibly have satisfied the law, even if he had wished to.[302]

Nevertheless, not all convictions were upheld, as *Teikamdas Bros Transvaal Ltd v Wishman*[303] indicated. In this case, a commercial traveller attempted to exploit what he regarded as an ambiguity in a wage determination in order to claim a large sum of money by way of an expenses and subsistence allowance. The AD[304] was not willing to sustain this claim, on the ground that Wishman's lump sum remuneration, after deduction of expenses, exceeded the statutory minimum, and his employer's appeal against conviction was allowed.

Certain other matters pertaining to the WA came before the court, such as the extent of the Ministerial powers of reference to a Wage Board.[305] Of more importance was the AD's decision on the law in the stated case of *Ex parte Minister of Justice: In re R v Bolon*,[306] in which Tindall, JA[307] decided that, where the WA cast the onus of proving that there had been no underpayment of minimum wages on the employer, he had to discharge such on a preponderance of probability: it was not sufficient to raise a doubt in the court's mind. Further, *Attorney-General of Natal v Johnstone & Co Ltd*[308] established that an employer, who was in doubt as to the validity or true meaning of a wage determination, could apply to court for a declaratory order, despite the fact that he might already have contravened the law and that criminal summons had been issued against him. Schreiner, JA[309] did lay down two conditions which had to be satisfied before proceedings could begin in such a case, being a set of undisputed facts, and the withdrawal or suspension of charges by the Crown.[310] In the event, he found that respondent had not contravened the determination, as the prosecution had claimed.

With the completion of this review of the disputes which concerned the ICA and WA, it remains only to consider two instances in which there was a clash between industrial statutes. *R. v*

[300] 1943 AD 118.
[301] See 120–3 with the concurrence of De Wet, CJ; Watermeyer, Tindall, and Feetham, JJA.
[302] At 122.
[303] 1946 AD 52.
[304] *Per* Davis, AJA (53–7) with the concurrence of Watermeyer, CJ and Greenberg, JA.
[305] See *Ex parte the Minister of Justice: In re R v Weinrich* 1930 AD 184.
[306] 1941 AD 345.
[307] See 348–61 concurred in by De Wet, CJ; Watermeyer, Centlivres, and Feetham, JJA.
[308] 1946 AD 256.
[309] See 259–72 concurred in by Watermeyer, CJ; Tindall and Greenberg, JJA; and Davis, AJA.
[310] At 260–2.

Sexby[311] turned on the effect of section 2(3)*(a)* of the WA, which stipulated that a wage determination should not apply to those employees governed by an industrial council agreement. Feetham, JA[312] decided that where employer–employee relations could rightly be regarded as falling under both an agreement and a determination, or partly under each, the agreement should take precedence over the determination.[313] On this occasion, he interpreted the character of the employees' work in such a manner that it could fall under the definition of the "building industry" as defined in an industrial agreement, with the result that the employers were released from abiding by the terms of a wage determination which had, in fact, provided for higher wages and annual holidays.[314] Thus the employees here suffered materially as the result of the judgment.

Lastly, the court was faced in *R v Beerman*[315] with the interrelationship between the Shops and Offices Act[316] and the WA with regard to hours of work. The former statute provided that its sections[317] relating to working hours should not apply to those workers whose conditions of service were regulated by a wage determination.[318] In fact, the employee store-manager, whose hours were in dispute here, earned too much to be subject to the terms of the determination, which governed the hours of most of those who worked under him. This factor did not weigh with Schreiner, JA,[319] who was not prepared to stretch the plain meaning of the Act, and Beerman's convictions stood.

Summary and Conclusions

On the basis of the seventy-eight employment cases referred to in the preceding discussion the task of assessment of judicial performance arises. All twenty-three judges of appeal sat in at least one of these disputes, so that the cases comprise a reasonable sample for the drawing of firmer conclusions in this field than has been possible before.

The cases themselves are spread throughout the period 1910 to 50, though, naturally, their incidence is irregular, owing to their direct relation to the enactment of legislation by Parliament. Certain judges (Innes, Solomon, J A J de Villiers, Watermeyer, Tindall, Centlivres, Feetham, Greenberg, and Schreiner) sat in a substantial number of cases, and several judges seem to have been regularly selected as

[311] 1943 AD 222.
[312] See 224–31 with the concurrence of Watermeyer, ACJ; Tindall and Centlivres, JJA; and Fischer, AJA.
[313] At 227–8.
[314] At 224 and 230.
[315] 1948 (1) SA 954 (AD).
[316] 41 of 1939.
[317] 4 and 6.
[318] Number 70 of December 1939, relating to the Commercial Distributive Trade.
[319] See 956–8 concurred in by Watermeyer, CJ; Tindall, Centlivres, and Greenberg, JJA.

"labour experts" to give the opinion of the court (Innes, Solomon, Wessels, Stratford, De Wet, Centlivres, and Greenberg). In only fourteen of the seventy-eight cases was more than one judgment handed down; twenty-one appeals were successful; and only three dissenting judgments were recorded (J A J de Villiers in *Van Breda* and *UG v Schierhout*, and Wessels in the latter).

The general impression gained from the decisions is one of a judiciary which was quick to adapt itself in most respects to the changing regime of industrial relations in the country. It is true that there were several stumbles along the way (in *Boyd*; *Scales*; *Van Breda*; *Manoim*; and *Gravenor*, for example), but, by the end of the period, the court was displaying a familiarity with the complex nature of the issues which shows that they had fully appreciated the legislative formulations, and accepted the objectives of the statutes.

Judicial incomprehension of the pressures and forces at work in the employer–employee relationship was apparent on a few occasions (in *Matthews v Johannesburg Municipal Pension Fund*; and *Manoim*, for example), but there is evidence, too, of an earnest attempt to carry out the spirit of the laws and not to be confined by their letter (in *Sanders*; *Vermeulen*; *KWV*; and *Reichlin*, for instance). *Sillo v Naude* and *De Jager v Sisana* expose a blank spot in judicial understanding of the plight of the people with whom it was dealing.

Taking each group of cases in turn, the judges seem to have been generally sympathetic to the employees in the field of conditions of employment; to have displayed a slight leaning against the activities of strikers; to have accepted the existence and status of trade unions with a critical but open mind; to have been lenient on the facts but rigid on compliance with the procedure of the workmen's compensation legislation; and to have tried to implement the industrial conciliation and wage statutes as fairly and fully as possible.

These attitudes could be assumed to be in line with the accepted judicial role of support for the legislature in its attempt to remedy and resolve social conflict where it was often most obvious, on the shop floor. In this way, the judges were allowing the courts to be used as a safety-valve for the controlled release of pressure which could otherwise have exploded, with unpleasant consequences for all concerned. The fact that the judges did not object to the legislative regulation of industrial relations, when their judicial mentors in Britain had done so,[320] is, perhaps, an indication of a closer identification with the mood and wishes of the government of the day for a stable unity among at least the white labouring group, as well as their awareness of their own potential part in aiding such a desirable development. In other words, although the statutory regulation of employment relations was something new, which

[320] See Abel-Smith and Stevens *Lawyers and the Courts* 114–16; and Wedderburn *The Worker and the Law* 18–25.

THE HON MR JUSTICE N J DE WET
The eighth Chief Justice of South Africa 1939–43

THE HON MR JUSTICE E F WATERMEYER
The ninth Chief Justice of South Africa 1943–50

slightly redressed the balance between employer and employee, there was no substantial movement in the *status quo*, as had been the case in Britain. On the contrary, the incorporation of white workers in the ruling group was more a confirmation of, than a departure from, the existing social order.

Although it is very difficult to identify the racial group of the litigants in the above cases, it seems that, at a rough estimate, only about ten were not of the white section of the population, and the question accordingly arises whether easy judicial reconciliation with changes in this area may possibly have been affected by this factor, even though such an influence is not overt. A consideration of those cases in which race was the dominant factor should serve to indicate whether judicial willingness to acquiesce in legislative, executive, and electoral demand (as in the field of labour relations) was carried over into the sphere of race relations.

So attention now shifts to judicial performance in those cases in which the major feature was the membership, by one or both of the parties, of a racial group other than the white one, in order to determine whether the judges of appeal allowed their opinions to be unduly swayed by the race prejudice and discrimination which figured so largely in the South African social formation. This task is attempted in the following three chapters by a survey of litigation which challenged discriminatory legislation in general, immigration policy, and the physical separation of the races.

CHAPTER SIX

RACE RELATIONS

It is probably correct to say that the overriding factor in the problems of Southern Africa, in most people's minds, is that of race, upon which the authorities have based their discriminatory practices. The issue of race discrimination is, doubtless, the major pre-occupation of all those who live in the sub-continent, whether they suffer under racist laws, or see such laws as their only safeguard against destruction. How the judiciary, as a branch of government, and composed of men drawn from the hegemonic faction in society, reacted to the difficulties raised by the pursuit of white supremacy as a national policy forms an important part of any assessment of its role in the South Africa of the period 1910 to 1950. While the world has grown accustomed to the more brutal aspects of racism in modern South Africa, in the form of apartheid in most aspects of life from birth to death, there is a tendency to assume its permanence as a social institution, and to ignore or subsume under its head other forms of exploitation. On these points, and particularly in respect of the phase in national development with which this study deals, several factors should be borne in mind throughout the following case-discussion and analysis.

First, and of major importance, is the fact that race discrimination, purely for ideological purposes, has seldom been government policy in South Africa, and certainly was not evident to a marked degree until 1950. On the other hand, race discrimination as an aspect of economic exploitation has always been of major significance, and this was without doubt its chief relevance from 1910 to 1948. In other words, skin colour was used as the foundation stone of an economic strategy which was designed to maintain European control of wealth. This strategy connoted a firm grip upon political power, as well as the systematic destruction of any likely *foci* of black resistance in the rural areas, which simultaneously produced a dispirited and disorganised pool of cheap labour to ensure financial viability of European industrial enterprise.

A second variable to be considered is the difference in treatment by the government of what were regarded as the three components of the non-European group *viz* the coloured people, the Asians (mainly Indians), and the Africans (or "natives"). In general, it can be said that coloured people were more favourably dealt with than Asians, who, at least economically, were treated better than Africans. But, within each group, there was a small faction who found it possible to qualify for the political franchise (except for the Asians), which gave them a little influence in affairs of state.

Thirdly, allied to this distinction and providing much of its "justification" in the eyes of those in power, was the concept of "civilisation" adopted by the British as a gauge to determine which of the subject groups would be acceptable to them. Standards of "civilisation" depended largely on the extent to which various black factions collaborated with, or sought the protection of, the colonial authorities in the series of battles which raged throughout much of the nineteenth century, or were prepared to be "Christianised" by the missionaries who generally preceded the conquering imperial armies. Proof of the "civilisation" of a native led to his exemption from the disabilities imposed by colonial laws on natives in Natal. In the "liberal" Cape Colony, the Parliamentary franchise was the result of the earning of a wage in excess of a certain amount, or the ownership of property of a particular value. But even this last qualification was rigidly regulated by the refusal to recognise communal land tenure as "ownership" sufficient to achieve the voting power.

These attitudes, prevalent in the former British colonies, must be distinguished from the harsher but perhaps less equivocal outlook of the Boer governments in the OFS and ZAR. They admitted no possibility of non-European participation in government, while displaying a paternalistic concern mixed with cruel punishment of the native inhabitants of their territories, born of their belief in their role as Christian guardians of the "heathen hordes", as well as their fear of, and inability to subdue, the power of various black tribes within their boundaries.

These different ways of approaching the issue of treatment of "non-European" South Africans comprised one of the predominant "problems" at the National Convention which led to the Union. In the end, the Cape Colony failed to extend its comparatively liberal franchise system to the other provinces, though it preserved it within its own borders. The Cape delegates endeavoured to guarantee it by giving a measure of procedural protection to those clauses in the South Africa Act which laid down the franchise qualifications.[1] Nevertheless, it was obvious that the view of the other provinces had not been altered by this arrangement, and the first few decades of Union would be crucial in determining which approach to the race question would triumph. Although the primary locus of struggle was to be found in the legislature and its electorate, the courts were used to some extent as a forum for the resolution of this dispute, so that judicial origins and attitudes were also of great importance.

Fourthly, in any evaluation of judicial role in this conflict the observer must try, as far as is possible, to see the problems through the eyes of those who sat on the appellate Bench. All the judges were white men, who, without exception, had had little real contact with

[1] See the section "The Franchise and Race" below.

the country's black citizens. In addition, the all-pervading British influence in university education and at the Bar in South Africa would, for most judges, have been a major determinant of their outlook on racial affairs, and would have led to a self-evident adoption of imperial mentality as regards subject nations. Calling attention to this factor is not an attempt to provide an excuse for any prejudiced remarks which may be alluded to in the following pages, nor is it a plea for a watered-down concept of justice by which to assess judicial actions. It is, rather, a reminder of the history which, to a lesser or greater degree, must have played a large part in the formation of social opinion among the élite, of which the judiciary was an important section.

Although it is impossible to give even a brief account of Southern African history in this period, two developments ought not to be passed by. Firstly, the confusion and rapidity of change wrought by wars and depressions must have startled even those used to the "frontier" life to be found in parts of the sub-continent. This could have led to two possible reactions in judicial terms: an attempt to accommodate or even to pre-empt this change in order to contain it, or an effort to retain the values and stability of past times. Secondly, with particular reference to South Africa, the period under review witnessed the gradual but inexorable transfer of the balance of political power to the white lower-middle and working classes, predominantly Afrikaans-speaking, and most threatened by any economic advances on the part of black South Africans. This shift must inevitably have influenced legislative policy, for all whites had the vote after 1930,[2] and its growing influence must have been noticed by the judiciary, whose reaction will have to be gathered from what follows below.[3]

Finally, although the dominant feature of many of the cases which are considered below is the race of the parties, other matters are raised, such as the extent of executive power, constitutional conflicts, and questions of private law, which could be approached separately from the race aspect. These other questions no doubt concerned the judges and helped them to their decisions, but the racial factor remains the central aspect of all the cases.

Two sets of disputes, which accounted for a substantial proportion of appeals to the AD, were those surrounding the rights of Asians to immigrate into the Union, and to have interests in land in the Transvaal. These are reviewed in the two chapters which follow. The rest of the cases which revolved around issues of race are outlined in

[2] When the franchise was extended to white women. See the Women's Enfranchisement Act 18 of 1930.

[3] In this brief review of South African race history, various sources have been relied on, among them: Wilson and Thompson *Oxford History of South Africa*; Walker *A History of Southern Africa*; Bundy *The Rise and Fall of the South African Peasantry*; Roux *Time Longer than Rope*; Moodie *The Rise of Afrikanerdom*.

this chapter, and discussion starts with those which served to expose judicial attitudes to customs peculiar to black groups.

FROM POLYGAMY TO SEDUCTION

The decision in *Seedat's Executor v The Master (Natal)*[4] affords an example of the application of "civilised" values to the contract of marriage. Here, the appellants maintained that Seedat's two wives were both "surviving spouses" as defined in the Natal Succession Duty Act,[5] which laid down different rates of succession duty for different classes of legatees. Seedat had married both wives in India, under whose law the ceremonies were recognised as valid, but Innes, CJ said[6] that a polygamous union was ". . . reprobated by the majority of civilised people, on grounds of morality and religion",[7] so that Seedat's first wife could not be regarded as a "surviving spouse". With regard to the deceased's ten children, on the other hand, the Chief Justice was prepared to compromise, and to hold that, as they were regarded as legitimate in India, they should have the same status in Natal.

This approach is a clear indication of a judicial intention to impose "Christian" principles on the wider South African population, for there can be no disputing the fact that the vast majority of the Union's citizens[8] both recognised and practised polygamy at that time. But Innes, CJ was not prepared to tolerate even the prospect of polygamy: he extended the definition of a polygamous union to embrace a monogamous union which contemplated the possibility of a further marriage without dissolution of the original bond.[9] He recognised that the result would be hard for many, but he refused to allow the court to change the law on the ground of international comity, as he saw that as a task for the Legislature.[10]

A further aspect of the exercise of rights under customary authority which confronted the court in the mid-1920's concerned the power of a chief of an African tribe to control and dispose of communal land on his own initiative and responsibility. The government, which had done so much to destroy the power of the tribal chiefs in order to defeat their subjects in war, now wished to use them as an instrument of control and implementation of policy. They did so by putting them on the state payroll and giving them limited administrative authority in the small areas set aside as reserves.

The court was forced to consider the whole question of dismissal and appointment of chiefs in the case of *Mathibe v Union Government*

[4] 1917 AD 302.
[5] 35 of 1905.
[6] See 306–15 concurred in by Solomon and C G Maasdorp, JJA, and J A J de Villiers and Juta, AJJA.
[7] At 307.
[8] Primarily in its "non-European" section.
[9] At 308.
[10] At 309.

& another,[11] in which appellant claimed that he was the lawful chief of his people by virtue of native law, custom, and usage. Unfortunately for him, although such factors had been referred to as relevant in the pre-Union legislation of the ZAR,[12] another law had granted the State President unlimited powers of appointment and dismissal of chiefs,[13] so that J A J de Villiers, JA[14] felt unable to uphold the appeal.

This case had a sequel soon afterwards in *Mathibe v Tsoke,*[15] when the chief appointed by the government succeeded in obtaining the sanction of the court[16] for the enforcement of a levy on his whole tribe in order to complete the purchase of a farm. In dealing with this case, and others like it, the court was faced with legal questions upon which there were no fixed rules in textbooks, nor written authorities, with the result that they depended heavily upon the evidence of "expert" witnesses, and tended to lean towards maximum fulfilment of legislative policy. For example, in *Rathibe v Reid & another,*[17] a member of one section of a tribe appealed against the dismissal of his action for nullification of a deed of sale of a farm entered into between Reid and the paramount chief of the tribe. Rathibe alleged that the approval of an assembly of every section of the tribe was necessary before alienation of land could take place, while respondents claimed full power and absolute discretion for the chief to enter and bind his tribe into a contract without a general meeting. The TPD[18] had found, on the evidence before it, that the chief was still supreme, a sort of legislature, executive, and judiciary in one person, and the AD sustained this view of the matter.

J A J de Villiers, JA[19] acknowledged that there was a strong conflict of opinion on the question,[20] but he preferred the "unlimited" view of the chiefly power, advocated by various (white) government officials and a paramount chief, over the "democratisation" stance adopted by various other "experts", both black and white.[21] An additional factor which weighed with the judge was the consultation by the paramount chief of his council (*legothle*) before he sold the land to Reid. De Villiers, JA used the fact that tribal land was communally owned as support for his finding that the rest of the tribe was bound by the chief's action, rather than as an argument for wider consultation by the chief with the components of his tribe.[22]

[11] 1925 AD 81.
[12] Law 4 of 1885 and Law 3 of 1876.
[13] Law 11 of 1881.
[14] See 83–9 concurred in by Kotzé, JA (89–90), and Innes, CJ; Solomon and Wessels, JJA.
[15] 1925 AD 105.
[16] Judgment of Solomon, JA (108–17) with the concurrence of Innes, CJ; J A J de Villiers, Kotzé, and Wessels, JJA.
[17] 1927 AD 74.
[18] De Waal and Krause, JJ.
[19] See 75–88 with the concurrence of Innes, CJ; Hutton, McGregor, and Stratford, AJJA.
[20] At 77.
[21] At 78–83.
[22] At 86–8.

The tendency of the court to grant dictatorial powers to chiefs over "their own people" had become evident in the previous year in the case *Mokhatle & others v Union Government (Minister of Native Affairs).*[23] Appellants in this instance were members of a tribe who, because of consistent defiance, insult, and abuse of their chief, which had promoted dissension in the tribe, had been ordered by the Governor-General, as Supreme Chief of all natives,[24] to leave a certain location and not to return without his permission. Appellants claimed that this order was null and void, and they sought damages as a result of the government action against them, a claim which the TPD[25] had disallowed.

The main question before the AD was, therefore, the extent of, and control over, the power of a paramount chief to remove a recalcitrant subject from his tribal property. After full consideration of the voluminous evidence in regard to this matter which had been laid before the provincial division, much of which had come from Africans of chiefly stock and missionaries, Kotzé, JA[26] decided that there was no reasonable ground for disturbing the finding of the court *a quo* that the power of expulsion could be exercised without investigation or hearing.[27] In addition, appellants had contended that they had been banished, which involved criminal jurisdiction not possessed by the Supreme Chief under ZAR law. The learned judge of appeal again dismissed this argument, likening Mokhatle's expulsion to that of a member of a club, religious, or social body, which involved no exercise of criminal jurisdiction.[28]

However, for present purposes the most important point advanced by appellants was that their removal had been contrary to statute,[29] which had prescribed that the native laws and customs should continue in force so long as they were not in conflict with the general principles of civilisation recognised by the civilised world. This formulation might be thought to have provided an ideal opportunity for the court once more to have taken a stand against autocracy, but Kotzé, JA refused to grasp the nettle. While he assumed that the "civilised world" denoted the European or western civilisation, and took civilisation to mean an "advanced stage of social development", he averred that civilised states could be autocratic or democratic in nature. The judge maintained that the power of removal was "certainly" in keeping with the practice of civilised countries, because the object of the Transvaal law had been to enable the supreme chief to deal with the management of native affairs in a simple, direct, and

[23] 1926 AD 71.
[24] By virtue of Law 4 of 1885 (Transvaal).
[25] *Per* Curlewis, JP and Tindall, J.
[26] See 74–82 concurred in by Innes, CJ; Solomon, J A J de Villiers, and Wessels, JJA.
[27] At 77.
[28] At 78.
[29] Law 4 of 1885 (Transvaal), section 2.

expeditious manner, which was the method "best understood by the native mind".[30]

Kotzé, JA backed up his conclusion by comparing pre-Union legislation in Natal,[31] which had given the colonial Governor similar powers of removal, and, he said, "[t]he Colony of Natal, since it became a part of the British Dominions, has always been regarded as a civilised country . . .". Moreover, "[w]hen the Governor-General acts in native matters in Natal and in the Transvaal as Supreme Chief he does so in both instances as the official head of State, and so representing the Sovereign of our highly civilised British Commonwealth of Nations".[32] In one sense, then, it was part of the notion of "civilisation" held by the judiciary that "backward" people could be ordered around without redress.

This arrogant way of approaching the dispute before the court can be attributed partly to the judge's age and past experiences, but Innes, CJ and three future Chief Justices agreed with this judgment without comment. The AD thus handed unrestricted licence to control the place of residence of dissident blacks to the executive. This may have seemed a trivial issue at the time, but the principle established by this case can be regarded as one of those which fostered the idea that blacks in South Africa were mute units to be moved and manipulated at the whim of the state, at worst, or were to be treated differently from non-Africans in matters of personal liberty, at best.

That the court was capable of an insistence that chiefs should conform with "civilised" methods of dealing with disputes is manifest in *Montsioa v Matlaba & others*,[33] which arose as the result of an armed raid by appellant chief on respondents, who, he claimed, were subject to his jurisdiction. Montsioa based his claim on the contention that respondents were members of the same tribe as his own, or that they had come under his sway by virtue of express agreement or native custom. The court[34] rejected all these arguments after examination of the facts before it, a conclusion which is neither surprising nor unmerited on the evidence as reported. This decision served to affirm the supremacy of the legal process over self-help.[35]

The vexed question of which legal system (customary or civil) to apply to disputes between Africans arose once again towards the end of the period under review in *Ex parte Minister of Native Affairs: In re Yako v Beyi*.[36] This was a case stated for the AD's decision by the Minister of Native Affairs in order to clarify the capacity in law of a

[30] At 79.
[31] Law 1 of 1891, section 37.
[32] At 81.
[33] 1919 AD 241.
[34] In the judgments of C G Maasdorp, JA (244–55); J A J de Villiers, AJA (255–68); with the concurrence of Wessels, Actg AJA.
[35] On this point, see also *Shahmahomed v Hendriks & others* 1920 AD 151, *per* Innes, CJ at 153–61.
[36] 1948 (1) SA 388 (AD).

native woman to sue for damages on account of her seduction. Schreiner, JA[37] concluded that a native woman was not debarred, as such, from succeeding in such an action, and that, if successful, her damages would not necessarily be limited to the amount which her guardian would have been entitled to claim under native law. Therefore, he asserted the applicability of Roman-Dutch law to the issue, although the President of the Native Appeal Court had seemed to resort to Roman-Dutch principles only when native law could supply no answer.

In doing so, Schreiner, JA stated his view of the duality of systems as follows:[38]

> "No doubt when colonisation takes place among a people having their own customary law, and when the law of the colonists becomes the law of the land, difficult questions of policy are likely to arise as to the proper extent of recognition and use, at any particular period, of the customary law of the native inhabitants; and presumably South Africa has not been exceptional in this respect."

In his opinion, when faced with a choice of systems, the judicial officer should choose that which would produce the fairest result in the circumstances. He also expressed his disapproval of various remarks, derogatory of natives, uttered by the President of the Native Appeal Court, and disagreed with the latter's denial of the relevance of class distinctions in choosing a system of law to be applied.[39]

Although the AD's position was not welcomed by one academic commentator,[40] who said that it had lost sight of the rights of the native defendant and had misconstrued legislative intent,[41] its decision deserves commendation on at least one ground, in that it stressed the aim of a single system of law applicable, in time, to all South Africans. Implicit in such an attitude is a commitment to minimise the differences which exist among those who constitute the country's citizenry, and to emphasise the eventual attainment of a legal equality among all inhabitants. Now this may seem inconsistent when compared with the implicit criticism of the attempt in *Seedat* to impose "Christian" principles on black customs. However, this apparent contradiction is explained when the outcome of the judicial action is taken into account: here, insistence on uniform standards of law contributed to the achievement of equity and justice, whereas in *Seedat* such an approach was based on cultural bigotry and worked hardship for the litigants. An important qualification, which must be mentioned in this regard, is the fact that *Yako v Beyi* concerned a civil action in private law, whereas issues of public order and constitutional rights were involved in *Mokhatle,* which may go some way towards explaining the different judicial approaches.

[37] See 391–403 concurred in by Watermeyer, CJ; Tindall, Centlivres, and Greenberg, JJA.
[38] At 396–7.
[39] At 398–9.
[40] H L Swanepoel, in (1950) 13 *THR-HR* 106.
[41] At 133.

Despite the small number of cases dealt with so far, a possible trend in judicial attitudes can be discerned *viz* an insistence on rigid standards in individual private law issues, which are departed from when government power and control could be threatened as a result of the decision, in which case the court is willing to grant a wider exercise of discretion to the executive than it might otherwise have been prepared to do. The foundation of such an approach is the dual conception of "civilisation" in the judicial mind, which regards unequal treatment of the "uncivilised" as regular and legitimate in terms of "civilised standards". The accuracy of this tentative proposition can be tested by the outcome of the cases which follow below.

Civil Rights and Race

This section contains the comparatively few legal challenges to laws which deprived certain South Africans of their expected rights as citizens of the country, and which reached the AD. Some cases which might have fallen within this description have been allotted to other categories within this study because of peculiar features which fit them more comfortably into those categories:[42] the disputes here have as their chief characteristic a difference in treatment of the situation under review because of the race of the participants.

To set the scene, it is worthwhile to note some isolated remarks which occurred in three judgments handed down in the mid-1930's and late 1940's, and which point to a particular facet of judicial temperament that may help to explain some of the decisions which will be noted below.

In 1933, Wessels, CJ stated,[43] in regard to fixing sentences for Africans, that:

> ". . . in punishing them we must remember that they are not civilised Europeans but kaffirs living more or less in a state of nature and when they act according to their natural and inherited impulses they do not deserve to be punished too severely as if they were civilised Europeans dwelling in a city or village. On the other hand they must learn to restrain their natural impulses and not treat life too cheaply."

This is a prime example of the children–guardian type of relationship which so many white South Africans saw as a fundamental aspect of their dealings with Africans, and which was to the latter's benefit here, as sentence was reduced accordingly.

Stratford, JA's approach[44] to the value of the evidence given by African witnesses is in the same vein:

[42] For instance, *R v Christian* 1924 AD 101; *R v Vezi* 1947 (4) SA 551 (AD), and the cases on Asian and black rights to land below.

[43] In *R v Xulu* 1933 AD 197 at 200 concurred in by Curlewis, Stratford, and J E R de Villiers, JJA.

[44] In *R v Tshelembe & others* 1933 AD 323 at 323 concurred in by Wessels, CJ; Curlewis and J E R de Villiers, JJA.

"The circumstances surrounding the death of the deceased, of course, include a kaffir-beer drinking party or carousal. That is an attendant circumstance one finds unfortunately in the majority of these cases, and it is one that, equally of course, tends to prevent the collection of reliable testimony about the occurrence. As in the present case, a fight very often is the outcome of these beerdrinking parties; often too resulting from the slightest of provocations, someone gets hurt or killed and at the subsequent trial the Court has only the testimony of natives who were at the time of the occurrence befuddled with drink and very greatly excited."

Again, in this case, this rather indulgent attitude helped the accused to escape a conviction on a charge of murder.

These quotations must be contrasted with the statement of Hoexter, AJA in 1949,[45] to the effect that the amount of damages awarded by a court for pain and suffering should not vary according to the injured plaintiff's standing. He elaborated thus:

"A highly cultured man may be less sensitive to pain than his uneducated neighbour, and a robust society leader may be less sensitive to pain than a frail social nonentity. It is the physical and mental make-up of the person injured which must be considered in assessing his pain and suffering, and that make-up cannot be determined by reference to his social or cultural or financial status. Most decidedly it cannot be determined by reference to his race."

Again, he gave a concrete illustration of what he meant by saying that: "A millionaire is not entitled to a higher award of damages for pain and suffering because money means very little to him, and conversely a pauper is not to be prejudiced by the fact that money means a great deal to him."[46] The fact that the plaintiff was a lowly African workman suing a white person, and that the AD increased the amount of damages awarded more than twelvefold, added weight to the judge's remarks, which can rightly be regarded as a beacon of impartiality as between race and class in South African jurisprudence. These statements perhaps indicate the outer limits of the spectrum of judicial views as regards race, between which the judgments in the following concrete instances of race discrimination fall.

The Cape Chinese Exclusion Act[47] had provided that its effect should not extend to those who held exemption certificates under the Act, but also that "any Chinaman, not being a British subject, born or naturalised in this colony, who shall be twice convicted, after the passing of this Act, of . . . gambling . . ., shall be deported to . . . China, after the expiration of the sentence passed upon him".[48] In *Ah Yet & others v Union Government (Minister of the Interior),*[49] appellants were exempted Chinamen who had been convicted twice on charges of gambling, but had paid fines instead of serving the alternative

[45] In *Radebe v Hough* 1949 (1) SA 380 (AD) at 385 concurred in by Greenberg and Schreiner, JJA. This should be contrasted with a recent example of judicial comment about the "apparent desire-to-stab" [my translation] of blacks and coloureds in South Africa. See *S v Augustine* 1980 (1) SA 503 (AD) *per* Rumpff, CJ at 506A.

[46] At 386.

[47] 37 of 1904, section 2*(e)*.

[48] Section 34.

[49] 1921 AD 97.

terms of imprisonment, and who now appealed against an order of deportation served against them by the government. Their claim rested on two grounds: that the Act did not apply to them as exempted persons, and that, if it did, they did not fall within its terms, as they had not served the prison sentences imposed on them.

Innes, CJ,[50] in confirming their liability to deportation, rejected both these arguments. While he acknowledged that ". . . it would be difficult to imagine a more confused and slovenly statute", and that to give full effect to the exemption clause would have brought relief to appellants, he decided that this would also have made nonsense of most of the rest of the Act's provisions, which applied solely to holders of exemption certificates.[51] To avoid this result, he concluded that exemption applied only to the general prohibition on entry into and residence in the colony; that the deportation clause could be applied to the appellants; and that they had qualified for deportation, as the formula "after expiration of sentence", though clumsy, could apply equally to the payment of fines.[52] In this way, the Chief Justice extracted the maximum of sense from a statute which drastically affected human liberty, by an extensive interpretation of the law, an approach which was contrary to professed judicial policy.[53]

A further case which bears traces of *Ah Yet* and *Mokhatle* occurred some years afterwards in *R v Mpanza*.[54] The Governor-General, in the exercise of his powers under the Native Administration Act,[55] had ordered a native holder of a certificate, which exempted him from the operation of native law,[56] to move from a Johannesburg township to a Natal village. Mpanza, the person concerned, disobeyed the order, was convicted for this offence, and then appealed against his conviction on the basis that he was excluded from the operation of the Act by virtue of a letter of exemption issued to him in 1908 in Natal, which meant that he was subject to the ordinary laws of the colony.

The question faced by the AD, according to Watermeyer, CJ[57] was whether the Native Administration Act fell within the ambit of "native law" from the effects of which Mpanza was relieved. The Chief Justice concluded that the power of removal was part of native law, to which Mpanza was not subject, because

[50] See 101–3 concurred in by C G Maasdorp, JA (104–6), Solomon and Juta, JJA, and J E R de Villiers, AJA.
[51] At 100–1.
[52] At 103.
[53] As evident in *Dadoo v Krugersdorp Municipal Council* 1920 AD 530; *Moller v Keimoes School Committee* 1911 AD 635; and *Principal Immigration Officer v Bhula* 1931 AD 323 among many.
[54] 1946 AD 763.
[55] 38 of 1927, section 5(1)*(b)*.
[56] By virtue of Law 28 of 1865 (Natal), deemed to have been issued under the Native Administration Act 38 of 1927, section 31(3).
[57] See 768–72, with the concurrence of Tindall, Greenberg, Schreiner, JJA; and Feetham, AJA.

"[o]ne of the fundamental principles of our South African law is that, except possibly in times of national emergency, the individual citizen, provided he obeys the law of the land, is not liable to have his personal freedom restrained by executive action, and the idea of a Supreme Chief, at his discretion and without trial, directing an individual to move his place of residence from one part of the country to another is foreign to that system",

and because *Mokhatle* had recognised the existence of such a power in a paramount chief.[58] As a result, he allowed the appeal.

The apparent difference in treatment of *Ah Yet* and *Mpanza* can be sought in the circumstances, both statutory and factual, in the passage of time, or in the change in judicial personnel. However, it can also be seen as consistent, in that Mpanza was regarded as "civilised" and so not subject to the arbitrary treatment meted out to "uncivilised" people.

A milestone in judicial attitudes to Africans' civil rights and to statutory interpretation was reached in *R v Detody*.[59] A pre-union Transvaal Ordinance[60] had required every native to carry a pass at night, and had defined "native"[61] to mean a person belonging to the aboriginal races of Africa south of the equator. Accused was an African woman, who appealed against her conviction for not carrying a pass, on the ground that successive Transvaal statutes had not been applied to women, despite similar definitions, and that custom had overridden the effects of statute in this case. A majority of the AD reversed the decision of the TPD[62] and decided that women should not have to carry passes, and each of the judges of appeal gave his reasons for his conclusion.

Innes, CJ[63] rejected the argument that the statute had become obsolete by disuse,[64] because it was a comparatively recently enacted law, and because the South Africa Act[65] had specifically provided for the continuation in force of all laws in the several colonies at the time of Union. However, on the claim that the Legislature had never intended the law to apply to women, he took a different line. He admitted that the language was general and that words importing the masculine gender were taken to include females, but stated that these guides could be negatived by a contrary legislative intent. He cited *Wookey's* case[66] in support, and said that the court should look at the mischief aimed at by the law, and the manner in which it had been applied by successive administrations in the Transvaal, for "[c]ustom . . . cannot prevail over the plain and unambiguous meaning of a statute, but where language is open to two constructions, then the fact that it has been uniformly read in one sense by those entrusted with the administration of the measure cannot be ignored".[67]

[58] At 771.
[59] 1926 AD 198.
[60] 43 of 1902, section 3.
[61] In section 2.
[62] Curlewis, JP is the only person mentioned in the report.
[63] See 199–211.
[64] At 201.
[65] Of 1909, section 135.
[66] Ch III, "Civil Liberties" above.
[67] At 202.

After a close analysis of previous rules and regulations governing the application of passes,[68] he expressed himself satisfied that the main mischief aimed at was stock stealing, which was not a female activity.[69] The idea of the ordinance under review, he maintained, was to prevent crime and disorder; it could hardly have been aimed at immorality among women, for it left them free to wander in their own locations; and there was also no warrant for the idea that in 1902 relations between white men and coloured women were in a state which called for the latter's exclusion from town streets at night.[70] For all these reasons, and because the legislature had failed specifically to include women within the scope of the law, he allowed the appeal and set Detody's conviction aside.

Solomon, JA[71] covered much the same ground in agreeing with the Chief Justice, although he seemed to be more concerned with the possibility of a change of legislative intent with the advent of a new administration in the Transvaal after the Anglo-Boer War in 1902.[72] On this aspect of the matter, he decided that the creation of night passes by the ordinance, and the fact that another proclamation of similar vintage had been expressly limited to males, could not be taken to indicate such a significant shift in intention: viewed in context, their provisions should be limited to males.[73] J A J de Villiers, JA[74] joined the majority opinion, despite an initial feeling that the Crown's case was strong. His mind was changed by the *Wookey* principle and the history of the application of pass laws to men alone.[75] The three senior members of the court thus constituted the majority which allowed the appeal.

Kotzé, JA[76] was the chief spokesman for the minority, and he preferred to dispose of the "abrogation by disuse" argument on the basis of British canons of construction, rather than the terms of the South Africa Act.[77] Kotzé, JA was certainly the member of the court most qualified to speak on the application of the pass laws in the ZAR, as he had been Chief Justice there for most of the period, but he chose to ignore republican practice in the interpretation of the British ordinance in point. He relied on the golden rule of interpretation, that ordinary words should receive their ordinary meaning, unless there was a clear and cogent reason to the contrary,[78] to reach the conclusion that females were intended to carry passes. He could find nothing in the circumstances or the balance of the legislation to indicate that the words should be limited to men; on the contrary, he argued that ". . . it was of utmost importance in the interests of morality and good order that native women should be protected . . ." (presumably from the attentions of war-weary British soldiers).[79] He reiterated, though, that surrounding circumstances could

[68] At 203–8. [69] At 209. [70] At 211. [71] See 211–21.
[72] At 218. [73] At 220. [74] See 221–3. [75] At 222.
[76] See 223–38. [77] At 225. [78] At 230. [79] At 233–4.

only be considered when statutory language was uncertain or obscure, and he warned against undue speculation as to legislative policy,[80] in dismissing the appeal.

For Wessels, JA,[81] the second dissident judge, the question was the extent to which the history of the legislation should be taken into account, and he, like Kotzé, JA, attached great significance to the break in continuity of administration caused by the Anglo-Boer War. He looked to subsequent rather than prior legislation, and asserted that it was extremely dangerous to ignore the plain legislative meaning here, on account of enforcement policy and necessity, which would have varied with time.[82] He, too, would have disallowed the appeal.

What can be said about this decision and its attendant judicial division? In the light of *Wookey*, the finding of the majority here is not technically surprising, but *Detody* would have had a far wider effect in the country, in emphasising the freedom of movement which should be accorded to African women in urban areas. Judicial attitudes to women and their position in the community may have contributed greatly to the majority finding here. As regards the judges themselves, it is interesting to note that all, except Kotzé, had been resident in the Transvaal at the time of the enactment of the ordinance and at least the eight years following.[83] It might seem characteristic for Innes to have adopted such an attitude a year before his retirement in which he devoted so much time to furthering the cause of Africans; but was it the force of his personality which swung Solomon and De Villiers to his side, and did an eccentric stubbornness prevent the minority from joining him? These questions are incapable of a firm answer, but there can be no doubt that the facts of the case allowed both interpretations, and that the decision of the majority dealt a blow for the civil freedom of Africans in the towns.

The next topic in the racial category to occupy the Bench's mind was the supply of intoxicating liquor to coloured people. The Liquor Act[84] allowed a Liquor Licensing Board to impose conditions upon the sale of liquor to persons of a particular class, so long as the conditions were "exclusive of total prohibition". In *Maske v The Aberdeen Licensing Court*; *Gilbert v The Aberdeen Licensing Court*,[85] two licensees challenged a condition imposed on them by respondent to the effect that no coloured person could be supplied with liquor except on a written permit signed by a magistrate or senior policeman, and that a restricted amount could be supplied per week. Maske and Gilbert asserted that this could have the effect of total prohibition, and that the condition was *ultra vires* on that account.

[80] At 234. [81] See 238–42.
[82] At 242.
[83] See Ch II "Structure and Judicial Personnel of the AD 1910–1950" above.
[84] 30 of 1928, section 81.
[85] 1930 AD 30.

Curlewis, JA[86] decided that the practical difficulties of such a system could indeed lead to total prohibition, especially as there was no duty on anyone to issue a permit. Moreover, he said, ". . . we must not lose sight of the fact that if the conditions in question can be imposed by a licensing board in respect of coloured persons they can equally be imposed in respect of Europeans, or at any rate, in respect of a class of Europeans",[87] and so he allowed the appeal.

However, within a year the court was faced with another challenge to a licensing condition on a similar argument. In *Van der Merwe v Wellington Licensing Board,*[88] respondent had stipulated that "all coloured females be restricted from entering bottle stores or off-sales depots", which appears *prima facie* to amount to the possibility of total prohibition. Not so, said Curlewis, JA:[89] this merely made it more difficult to obtain liquor, but it did not leave the question subject to the sole arbitrament of a third person. A coloured female would be able to ask someone else to buy liquor for her, and if she was not successful in this matter, it would be due to her own fault and misfortune, "that is to her lack of education and lack of helpful acquaintance". For this reason, he contended, the condition was *intra vires* the Board.[90]

This about-face on the part of the same judge seems difficult to explain: in *Maske* and *Gilbert* it might just as well have been said that any coloured person could have obtained liquor by asking a white person to buy it for him, so that no one was totally prohibited from obtaining liquor. Curlewis, JA distinguished *Maske* and *Gilbert* in *Van der Merwe*[91] as "entirely different" because three or four persons could have brought about a situation of total prohibition in the former case, whereas the present condition merely made it more difficult for liquor to be obtained. But the difference between the cases as reported remains minimal, and the likely explanation for the divergence in judgments appears to be a change of mind by the court.

After this brief example of racially discriminatory conditions applied to private business, three vital cases in the sphere of segregation of public amenities must be considered, the best-known of which is *Minister of Posts & Telegraphs v Rasool.*[92] The Post Office Administration and Shipping Combinations Discouragement Act[93] empowered the Postmaster-General to issue such instructions as he might deem necessary for the conduct and guidance of officers in carrying out the provisions of the Act, and for the supervision and control of services. In December 1931, he exercised this power and

[86] See 34–46 concurred in by J A J de Villiers, CJ; Wessels and Stratford, JJA.
[87] At 42.
[88] 1931 AD 33.
[89] See 35–9 with the concurrence of J A J de Villiers, CJ; Wessels and Roos, JJA.
[90] At 38.
[91] At 37.
[92] 1934 AD 167.
[93] 10 of 1911, sections 3(2) and 4.

divided Pietersburg post office into two sections, one for Europeans and the other for non-Europeans, whereas before there had been a separate service for natives alone. Rasool, an Indian, had applied successfully to a judge in chambers[94] for a *mandamus* compelling the withdrawal of the instruction on the ground that it was *ultra vires* the Postmaster-General, and a full bench of the TPD[95] had confirmed this ruling. The Minister then appealed to the AD, and, for the purposes of the appeal, equality of service in each section of the segregated post office was assumed. The AD upheld the appeal, and lent judicial sanction to administrative race discrimination, with only one dissenting voice.

Before the AD, Roberts, counsel for the appellant Minister, stressed[96] the sovereign nature of subordinate legislation, within the bounds of the grant of power, and argued that mere separation was not unlawful (it occurred in hospitals, buses, and cemeteries) so long as the principle of equality was observed. Ivan Curlewis[97] (son of the judge of appeal) replied for Rasool that discrimination on grounds of race or colour within South Africa was in itself unequal: the fact of equality of service was immaterial and irrelevant, he said, and the power to discriminate had to be granted expressly by the empowering legislation.

Stratford, ACJ[98] reviewed the judgments of the courts below, and stated the question for decision as being whether the instruction to segregate the post office effected a discrimination between classes partial or unequal in its operation. This would seem to be answered by the admission of equality of service, he said, but he had to dispense with earlier TPD decisions[99] which seemed to suggest that segregation was *per se* unequal, as well as putting the Postmaster's instruction to the test outlined for subordinate legislation by Lord Russell in *Kruse v Johnson*.[100] He countered these difficulties[101] by asserting that

> ". . . if [it] decided that a bye-law is invalid on the sole ground that it divides the community for the purpose of its operation into White and Coloured, I cannot agree with it, for such conclusion runs counter to accepted principle and good sense. A classification by a bye-law, if it presumably is to serve a useful purpose, is not invalid on that ground alone whether the line of division be race, colour, religion, or any other".

He saw the only qualifications to this as being absurdity or the serving of no useful purpose, while the present separation seemed to him to be convenient and sensible.[102] He considered section 147 of the South Africa Act, which provided that the control and adminis-

[94] Barry, J.
[95] De Waal, JP, Tindall and De Wet, JJ.
[96] At 168–70. [97] At 170–1. [98] See 171–6.
[99] *Williams and Adendorff v Johannesburg Municipality* 1915 TPD 106; *Moses v Boksburg Municipality* 1912 TPD 659; *Swarts v Pretoria Municipality* 1920 TPD 187.
[100] [1898] 2 QB 91.
[101] At 175.
[102] *Ibid.*

tration of matters specially or differentially affecting Asiatics throughout the Union should vest in the Governor-General in Council. Although the matter had not been raised, he maintained that the present case did not fall within its scope, as the section was an empowering, rather than a prohibitory one, which concerned only executive power, not legislative action.[103] For all these reasons, he would have upheld the appeal and thereby the validity of the segregation.

Beyers, JA[104] agreed with the final order of the Acting Chief Justice, but he sought justification for his decision in the history of the Transvaal, in which non-Europeans had never been equal with Europeans. Ominously, he declared[105] that: "Die verklaring dat in die oë van die wet almal gelyk is, kannie onvoorwaardelik aanvaar word nie,"[106] and accepted counsel's point that segregation in hospitals, cemeteries, public beaches and facilities existed throughout the Union. Rasool had not discharged the burden of proof of discrimination which rested upon him, Beyers, JA said,[107] and he could not have recourse to section 147 of the South Africa Act, on the grounds outlined by Stratford, ACJ.

The last member of the majority, J E R de Villiers, JA[108] traversed much the same ground as had Stratford, ACJ, and pointed out the "vital" distinction between discrimination coupled with equality as opposed to inequality.[109] For him, ". . . discrimination which [was] not accompanied by inequality of rights, duties, privileges or treatment, [was] not *per se* unreasonable merely because it was made on grounds of race or colour . . .", for it must be shown to involve "oppressive or gratuitous interference" with rights.[110] As this was not the case here, he concurred in allowing the appeal.

The lone dissentient was Gardiner, AJA,[111] who set the tone of his judgment at the outset when he reaffirmed the "fundamental principle of our law—that in the eyes of the law all men are equal".[112] After outlining the terms of section 147 of the South Africa Act, he stated that they intended "to refer to the Governor-General in Council all matters of administration whereby express provision was made for Asiatics, quite irrespective of whether such administration affected them prejudicially or not". On this interpretation, any differential treatment by regulation, whether worse, better, or equal (but not the same), had to receive the approval of the Governor-General.[113]

[103] At 176.
[104] See 176–8.
[105] At 177.
[106] "The statement that everyone is equal in the eyes of the law cannot be accepted without qualification." (My translation.)
[107] At 177.
[108] See 178–83.
[109] At 181.
[110] At 182.
[111] See 183–93.
[112] At 185.
[113] At 186–7.

But Gardiner, AJA went further in this regard, and contended that an Act of Parliament alone could authorise the kind of differential treatment which had occurred in this case, which derogated from the principle of equality before the law to which the courts had to give effect. He acknowledged that the South African legislature had made inroads into the principle, and had created one status for Europeans, an inferior status for Asiatics, and a further and more inferior status for Africans.[114] Yet he maintained that any fresh classification along colour lines could only be humiliating treatment, an impairment to a person's *dignitas* which the legislature alone could cause.[115] He gained support from a number of provincial division decisions,[116] and recommended the dismissal of the appeal, with the satisfaction of knowing that his "view [was] in accordance with what hitherto ha[d] been the trend of judicial opinion in South Africa".[117]

Whether this last statement is accurate or not, there can be no doubting the strength of feeling with which Gardiner, AJA delivered judgment in this case. It is impossible to say whether the composition of the appellate Bench here, with the two senior judges absent,[118] made any difference to the outcome, but it is worthy of note that altogether five judges[119] supported Rasool's view, whereas only three upheld the validity of the "separate but equal" doctrine. This decision is similar in effect to that in the American case of *Plessy v Ferguson,*[120] of 1896. It serves as a classic example of the AD giving judicial sanction to the race prejudices of the whites, and marks a retreat from the principle of the equality of all citizens before the law.

Within three years the Railway Administration attempted to impose a similar type of segregation in respect of benches at railway stations. Under the Railways and Harbours Regulation, Control and Management Act,[121] the administration was given the capacity to frame regulations "in regard to the reservation of railway premises (including conveniences) for the exclusive use of males or females, persons of particular races, or different classes of persons or natives". *R v Herman*[122] was an appeal by a coloured man who had been convicted for contravening a railway regulation[123] which had reserved certain benches on Kimberley station for "Europeans" and others for "non-Europeans". Herman had been sitting on a "Euro-

[114] At 187–9.
[115] At 190–1.
[116] *Williams and Adendorff v Johannesburg Municipality supra; R v Plaatjes* 1910 EDL 63; and *Ebrahim v Licensing Officer, Pietermaritzburg* 1925 NPD 222.
[117] At 193.
[118] Wessels, CJ was on leave; Curlewis, JA was Acting Governor-General. On consideration of other opinions of these two judges, it is doubtful whether the outcome would have been different: in addition, if either had been present, Gardiner, AJA would not have been on the Bench.
[119] All the Transvaal judges, and Gardiner, AJA.
[120] 163 US 537 (1896).
[121] Act 22 of 1916, section 4.
[122] 1937 AD 168.
[123] General Railway Regulations, number 19*(d)*.

pean" bench and had refused to move when asked to do so, because he belonged to an association of coloured people which wished to test the legality of such segregation. On appeal, he challenged the reservation on the basis that the public was divided into groups of a particular colour, not race.

J E R de Villiers, JA[124] rejected this argument *ab initio,* and held that a reservation for non-Europeans was a valid reservation for persons of a particular race. While he admitted that it was true that the AD in *Moller v Keimoes School Committee*[125] had laid down that European meant "white" in South Africa, this obviously meant that European was equal to "white" from a racial point of view, not from skin coloration, for otherwise how would an "albino kafir" be regarded. He went on:[126]

> " it follows that a European is a person who is white as a racial quality, and from a racial point of view, that is, who belongs to a white race; and that a non-European, on the other hand, is a person who is not white from a racial point of view and as a racial quality; that is, he does not belong to a white race. In other words a non-European is a person belonging to a race which is not white as such."

On the basis of this circular and empty series of statements he dismissed the appeal.

Feetham, AJA joined De Villiers, JA with a short judgment, and made substantially the same point: "The division of persons into 'Europeans' and 'non-Europeans' is, therefore, a division which is based fundamentally on distinctions of race, and is only based on distinctions of colour in so far as such distinctions have a racial significance."[127] Stratford, ACJ concurred without comment in this garbled attempt to lend legal order and sanction to the hole which successive South African governments had dug for themselves in the field of racial definition and discrimination.

By 1950 the whole question of enforced segregation had taken a significant turn with the apartheid policy of the newly-elected government. Once more the focus of attention moved to the railways.

Under the same power to regulate the reservation of railway premises or coaches which it had used in 1937, the Railway Administration enacted regulation 20*(c)* to the following effect: "Where one or more coaches forming part of a train bear notices indicating in express terms that the exclusive use thereof has been reserved for persons of a particular race, the other coaches forming part of that train, . . ., shall not be deemed to be reserved for the exclusive use of persons of any particular race and the provisions of sub-regulation *(a)*(ii) [which in effect restricted members of one race to those carriages reserved for them] shall not apply in the case of a

[124] See 171–2 concurred in by Feetham, AJA (172–4), and Stratford, ACJ.
[125] *Supra.*
[126] At 171–2.
[127] At 173.

reservation effected in the manner contemplated by this sub-regulation." By virtue of this sub-regulation, certain first class coaches on the Cape Town suburban line had been reserved for Europeans only. A Train Apartheid Resistance Committee had been formed to combat these measures, meetings had been held and speeches made, and certain coloured people deliberately entered those coaches reserved for Europeans.

R v Abdurahman[128] came to Bloemfontein as a result of this situation. The accused had been convicted of inciting coloureds to commit the offence of entering coaches reserved for Europeans in a speech he had made on Cape Town's Grand Parade in September, 1948. He raised a number of legal issues on appeal to the AD, but his main argument was that regulation 20*(c)* was *ultra vires*, as partial or unequal treatment had resulted from it. The Crown countered by invoking its general power to control, manage, and superintend the railways as the basis for coach reservation without the necessity for a regulation.

Centlivres, JA was the court's lone spokesman here.[129] He assumed the Crown's point to be correct, provided that reservation resulted in substantial equality of treatment, but noted that, to make the disregarding of reservation notices a criminal offence, regulations were necessary. He said that the question for the court was, therefore, whether regulation 20*(c)*, or its application, was partial or unequal as between different classes, and, if so, whether the Act authorised such treatment.[130] While he recognised that it could be applied impartially, Centlivres, JA decided that, to apply it on all trains as an invariable practice, would result in substantially unequal treatment, because only Europeans could use the whole train, and only non-Europeans were subject to criminal sanction.[131]

As a reaction to the Crown's claim that the discrimination must have been manifestly unjust or oppressive, he stated that, "[b]earing in mind that it is the duty of the Courts to hold the scales evenly between the different classes of the community and to declare invalid any practice which, in the absence of the authority of an Act of Parliament, results in partial or unequal treatment to a substantial degree between different sections of the community . . .", he thought that this test was put too highly, and rejected previous judicial *dicta* which seemed to indicate such a test.[132] Here, in fact, substantial inequality of treatment had resulted from an application of the regulation,[133] and, as the Act did not authorise such inequality,

[128] 1950 (3) SA 136 (AD).
[129] See 141–50. He was joined by Watermeyer, CJ; Greenberg and Schreiner, JJA; and Murray, AJA.
[130] At 143.
[131] At 144.
[132] At 145–6.
[133] At 147.

either expressly or by necessary implication, he held that the application of the regulation had been *ultra vires,* and allowed the appeal. By so doing, he affirmed the court's attitude that the provision of separate but equal facilities could not lead to a complaint in law,[134] so that the *ratio* of *Rasool* remained unchanged.

In the field of non-statutory race discrimination, few cases can have called for judicial comment and inventiveness more than *Jockie v Meyer,*[135] and in few cases can the judges have displayed less sensitivity to the harmful effects of race prejudice. This was a war-time case, which arose from the docking of a British merchant ship in Port Elizabeth for reconstruction work. As could be expected, the ship's owners booked hotel accommodation near the dockyard for the ship's officers for the duration of their stay, but did not disclose that the acting first officer was Chinese. Jockie checked into the hotel, dressed in the uniform of the mercantile marine, but was asked to return his room key a quarter of an hour later, and was informed that the hotel was full. He then went to stay in a boarding house, but instituted a claim for damages against the hotel owner (Meyer) on three grounds: for disbursements, for inconvenience, and for humiliation and loss of prestige. A magistrate awarded him £50, but the EDLD[136] reduced this to £10 on appeal by Meyer, so Jockie appealed to the AD. He claimed £200, comprising £1 disbursements, and £199 general damages, arising out of alleged breach of the contract of accommodation. Meyer had by this time admitted in evidence that Jockie had been turned out of the hotel because he was Chinese.

Tindall, JA[137] approached the matter entirely on the basis of the hotelkeeper's duty to give a traveller accommodation in the absence of a good ground of refusal (which he assumed to have been present),[138] but stated that this could not be seen as licence for an unlimited stay, so that damages for inconvenience had been correctly fixed at £10.[139] On the most important question, that of damages for humiliation, he refused, after a consideration of South African and English authority on the point, to admit the possibility of success for such a claim based on a breach of contract:[140] it should rather have been founded on the *actio injuriarum*. Therefore, the magistrate had not been entitled to award damages for injured feelings, and Jockie's appeal was dismissed, though the judge "sympathised" with him.

The technical correctness of Tindall, JA's legal reasoning can be accepted here, but the timidity which led him merely to express

[134] At 149.
[135] 1945 AD 354.
[136] Pittman, JP, and Gardner, J; Gane, J dissenting.
[137] See 356–68 with the concurrence of Watermeyer, CJ; Feetham and Greenberg, JJA; and Davis, AJA.
[138] At 361.
[139] At 362.
[140] At 363–7.

sympathy with the victim of racial discrimination is worthy of deprecation. This was surely a case in which forceful comment on the equities of the situation was called for, as the judges were wont to do under different circumstances.[141] The effect on public opinion and education might have been salutary, and judicial silence here represents not only a lost opportunity to indicate what they probably felt, but also a "hands-off" attitude which signalled that any subsequent interference by them would be unlikely.

The final group of cases within this section concerns judicial attitudes to appeals which reached Bloemfontein as the result of convictions under various laws in South Africa which prohibited sexual contact between the races before 1948. The general effect of the laws was that whites and natives could not legally have sexual intercourse, while pre-Union statutes in the former republics widened the definition of natives to include coloured and Asian people. On the whole, the judges of appeal accepted the necessity, both moral and material, for such laws, and did their best to ensure that convictions were not upset on grounds of technicalities.

For instance, *R v Hassam*[142] concerned the voluntary submission of a white woman to intercourse with a "coloured Asiatic", who was subsequently convicted[143] primarily on the woman's evidence. On a question of law reserved by the Crown, Innes, CJ[144] held that, though the complainant woman was an accomplice, the conviction should stand, as her evidence had been sufficiently corroborated. Again, in *R v Schonken,*[145] where the Crown had not been able to prove that the accused (a Member of the Transvaal Provincial Council) had had sexual intercourse with a native female servant, the AD[146] confirmed his conviction on an alternative charge[147] of entering another's dwelling during the night with an intent to commit a crime therein.

Further, in *R v H,*[148] Centlivres, JA,[149] while confirming that *mens rea* was an essential element of the offence of illicit carnal intercourse between a European and a native,[150] refused to accept that the accused had discharged the onus of proof of absence of *mens rea,* which he had claimed on the basis that he had thought his partner in crime was coloured, and not African. In doing so, Centlivres, JA

[141] See, for example, the judgments of Innes and Laurence, JJ in *Moller v Keimoes School Committee supra; Whittaker* and *Morant v Roos and Bateman* 1912 AD 92; and *R v Roux & another* 1936 AD 271.

[142] 1925 AD 91.

[143] Under Ordinance 46 of 1903 (Transvaal), section 19(2).

[144] See 91–3 concurred in by Solomon, J A J de Villiers, Kotzé, and Wessels, JJA.

[145] 1929 AD 36.

[146] Judgment of J A J de Villiers, ACJ (40–6); Curlewis and Stratford, JJA; and Hutton, AJA.

[147] Under Ordinance 26 of 1904 (Transvaal), section 6.

[148] 1944 AD 121. This case is of further importance in establishing the necessity of proof of *mens rea* in statutory offences, and the status of the "*versari in re illicita*" doctrine in criminal law.

[149] See 123–31 concurred in by Watermeyer, CJ; Tindall, Feetham and Greenberg, JJA.

[150] At 127 under the Immorality Act 5 of 1927, section 1.

remarked that H must have known that he was committing an act which was morally wrong, in that ". . . he, being a married man, had carnal intercourse with a female to whom he was not married . . .",[151] an interesting but not surprising insight into the moral principles of at least one of the judges of appeal.

On the other hand, the AD showed itself prepared to accept the accused's version of a sexual tryst in *R v L*,[152] in which Davis, AJA[153] overturned a conviction on a charge of illicit intercourse[154] on the basis of medical evidence of L's impotence, but altered it to a conviction for attempt to contravene the Act, and left the sentence undisturbed.

These cases bring to an end the discussion on issues of race discrimination as such. Race prejudice on the national level, as it affected the right of South Africa's inhabitants to participate in national government through the vote, is the next topic for consideration.

The Franchise and Race

As mentioned above, the South Africa Act had preserved the voting rights of coloured and African voters in the Cape Colony after Union,[155] and had prescribed that any change in this situation could only be brought about by the affirmative vote of a two-thirds majority of both Houses of Parliament sitting together.[156] The franchise as it related to coloured men was not tampered with during the period under review, but the right of qualified Africans to vote was varied, and two important cases dealing with this matter were brought on appeal to Bloemfontein.

The qualification which male Africans had to satisfy before they could vote depended upon their earning wages of a certain minimum amount per annum, or their ownership of fixed property of a certain minimum value. As regards the latter, title to land in the Cape was not uniform for blacks, there being certain forms which were not sufficient to qualify the holder for the franchise.[157] With the object of standardising land-titles, an additional Native Commissioner had been appointed for Kingwilliamstown, to investigate and determine rights of occupation and ownership by natives. Evidently, suspicions were aroused that this might be the precursor of an attempt by the government to disturb native voting rights, and Ndobe, an African clergyman and landholder, refused to give evidence or produce the title deeds to his land, after answering a subpoena from the

[151] At 129.
[152] 1946 AD 190.
[153] See 191–7 concurred in by Watermeyer, CJ; Tindall, Greenberg, and Schreiner, JJA.
[154] Under the Immorality Act 5 of 1927, section 1.
[155] Section 35(2).
[156] Section 35(1).
[157] An example of this is the "Glen Grey" title, devised by C J Rhodes when Cape Prime Minister in 1894.

Commissioner. He was convicted for this refusal, and, in his appeal to the AD,[158] he argued that the whole of the Native Administration Act,[159] under which the investigating commissioner had been appointed, was *ultra vires,* because four of its sections[160] fell within the provisions of section 35 of the South Africa Act and the special procedure laid down had not been followed.

The court, therefore, had to consider the question of the legislative powers and procedure of Parliament, and, more particularly, which type of Act fell within the description of section 35, and so required the assent of a two-thirds majority of a unicameral assembly in Parliament. Section 35 provided as follows:

> "(1) Parliament may by law prescribe the qualifications which shall be necessary to entitle persons to vote at the election of members of the House of Assembly, but no such law shall disqualify any person in the Cape of Good Hope who, under the laws existing in the Colony . . . at the establishment of Union, is or may become capable of being registered as a voter from being so registered in the Province of the Cape . . . by reason of his race or colour only, unless the bill be passed by both Houses of Parliament sitting together. . . .
> (2) No person who at the passing of any such law is registered as a voter in any province shall be removed from the register by reason only of any disqualification based on race or colour."

In the event, the sections complained of by the appellant were adjudged to fall outside the scope of this formulation, but, in reaching this conclusion, J A J de Villiers, CJ,[161] who spoke for the court, made several important statements about the competence of the court to interfere with the legislature's exercise of power.

He agreed with the court *a quo* that only laws which directly prescribed the qualifications of voters would be hit by the prohibition (against enactment by ordinary Parliamentary procedure) contained in section 35, because to hold otherwise would gravely hamper and fetter "the rights of Parliament". But, he maintained, this did not make it necessary for the law to appear to deal with voters' qualifications: if it did so in fact, the circumstance that it appeared in a law which also dealt with other matters would not save it from compliance with the special procedure.[162] In addition, he held that section 35(1) safeguarded incipient rights, while section 35(2) preserved existing rights.[163] These comments affirmed the validity and clarified the operation of the section in a way which fulfilled legislative intent without narrowing its effect.

Further, in reaction to Ndobe's claim that any future title deed, devised by the government and issued by proclamation, might lead to disqualification of voters, the Chief Justice warned that any new deed of grant would have to respect the provisions of section 35. He

[158] *R v Ndobe* 1930 AD 484.
[159] 38 of 1927.
[160] Sections 5(1)*(b)*, 7, 23(2), and 25(1).
[161] See 488–97 with the concurrence of Wessels, Curlewis, and Roos, JJA.
[162] At 491.
[163] At 492.

said: "It is trite law that Parliament cannot delegate larger powers than what it possesses. If the Governor-General, therefore, at any time were to proclaim legislation in conflict with the powers possessed by Parliament under section 35 the proclamation would be *ultra vires.*"[164] Finally, he could not agree with the contention of counsel for the Crown that a court could not enquire whether Parliament had acted unicamerally or not when passing an Act. He agreed that Parliament could make its own rules and procedures, but the court retained the right to enquire whether an Act had been validly passed, though it would assume this until the contrary appeared.[165]

Similar issues were presented for decision in *Ndlwana v Hofmeyr, NO, & others*[166] several years later, a period which had seen the passage of the Statute of Westminster by the British Parliament which had curtailed the operation of the Colonial Laws Validity Act as regards the dominions of the commonwealth, *inter alia.* The situation here was almost the converse of that in *Ndobe,* as Ndlwana challenged the action of the House of Assembly and Senate in sitting as one when passing the Representation of Natives Act,[167] which transferred all African voters on to a separate roll. Ndlwana argued[168] that this did not disqualify him from voting, but merely put his name on a different list, and thus that the Act did not fall within the scope of section 35, and should have been passed in the normal bicameral way. Secondly, he contended that a large portion of the Act had nothing to do with voter qualifications, and so should not have been passed unicamerally, and, as it had been, was invalid for that reason. Thirdly, he averred that, prior to the passing of the Statute of Westminster, the Union Parliament had had no authority to repeal or alter section 35, no matter how it acted, and that it followed from this fact that, now that the Union Parliament was sovereign, it could only act bicamerally in altering or repealing section 35.

All these points had been rejected by Van Zyl, JP in the CPD.[169] Before the AD, the court first asked Buchanan, KC, to deal with the preliminary question of whether it had any power to pronounce on the validity of an Act of Parliament, since the Union Parliament had attained supremacy as the sovereign law-making body in South Africa after the enactment of the Statute of Westminster, according to Stratford, ACJ.[170] Ndlwana's counsel rehearsed his arguments outlined above, but the court would not accept them. The Acting Chief Justice stated that an Act of Parliament proved itself by mere

[164] At 495.
[165] At 496–7.
[166] 1937 AD 229.
[167] 12 of 1936.
[168] Through his counsel, Douglas Buchanan, KC and D Molteno. Details of arguments appear in the judgment of Van Zyl, JP in the CPD.
[169] See 229–35 of AD report, concurred in by Sutton and Centlivres, JJ.
[170] See 236–8 concurred in by J E R de Villiers and De Wet, JJA, and Watermeyer, AJA.

production of its printed form published by proper authority, and that Parliament's will could not be questioned by a court of law, whose function it was to enforce that will.

He went on to say that "[i]t is obviously senseless to speak of an Act of a Sovereign law making body as *ultra vires*. There can be no exceeding of power when that power is limitless."[171] He maintained that Parliament was free to adopt whatever procedure it wished, so long as each of its constituent parts functioned. He dismissed *Ndobe,* upon which Ndlwana had rested much of his attack, with virtually a judicial shrug of the shoulders, by noting that it had been decided before the Statute of Westminster.[172]

This unwillingness of the court to become peripherally involved in what was a sensitive political test case was welcomed by at least one contemporary commentator.[173] Coertze wrote in the first issue of the *Tydskrif* that the AD had given a

> ". . . prysenswaardige beslissing, want die toetsingsreg het sy fundering in 'n verouderde staatsfilosofiese begrip, en daarby 'n filosofie wat op sy eie tyd nie rekening met die werklikheid gehou het nie, die begrip nl van skerpe skeiding tussen die drie staatsmagte. Waar die Hof 'n toetsingsreg het, moet dit vroeër of later . . . notisie neem van die politieke winde van die dag—'n uiters ongewenste toestand."[174]

But even this supporter of the judicial view warned that the appeal court had gone too far in refusing completely to go into the merits of the case. Parliament was a creation of the Constitution, he claimed, and the Court, by refusing to give effect to the procedural protection clauses of the South Africa Act, was abdicating part of its essential duty.[175]

Coertze's warning foretold all too real a crisis within fifteen years, with the raging argument over the meaning of *Ndobe* and *Ndlwana* during the constitutional dispute over the removal of coloured voters from the common roll. Government legal advisers and representatives relied heavily on *Ndlwana* in their claim that the special procedure was no longer mandatory, while proponents of the opposite view doubted the correctness of Stratford, ACJ's judgment in the case, and preferred many of the points made by De Villiers, CJ in *Ndobe*. The latter approach triumphed in *Harris v Minister of the Interior,*[176] but the *Ndlwana* decision, which had fuelled the flames by lending judicial support to the government case, had seriously harmed the cause of those who advocated a guardian-like role for the courts in the face of uninhibited legislative action.

[171] At 237. [172] At 238.

[173] L I Coertze in (1937) 1 *THR-HR* 114.

[174] ". . . praiseworthy decision, because the testing-right has its foundation in an outdated concept of constitutional philosophy, and moreover a philosophy which in its own time did not keep account of reality, namely the idea of clear separation of the three state authorities. Where the Court has a testing-right, it must sooner or later take note of the political winds of the day—an exceptionally undesirable condition." (My translation, at 115–16.)

[175] At 116–17.

[176] 1952 (2) SA 428 (AD).

The Definition of Race Groups

In a society in which the regulation of one's life from cradle to grave depends directly upon one's "race", it is obviously of vital importance to know what group one "belongs" to, and, if there is any doubt, to claim membership of the group which is accorded fewer disadvantages. Thus, those who suffered the effects of laws which applied only to one "race" attempted to remove themselves from the operation of such laws by alleging that they actually belonged to another "race". Cases of this type appeared before the AD throughout the period 1910 to 1950, and were concerned with all the racial categories recognised in South Africa. Although the Population Registration Act provided the first general definition of each group only in 1950,[177] most Acts which dealt with race before that time defined the groups in their definition sections, and four divisions were generally described *viz* white or European; Asiatic or Indian; coloured (including the Malay subgroup); and natives or Africans.

Shortly after Union, the AD had to face an example of this type of case, and the approach it adopted in this instance was to bind and constrain it for the rest of the period. The Cape School Board Act of 1905[178] promoted the establishment of separate public non-denominational schools for children of "European parentage or extraction", and there was one such school in the isolated district of Keimoes in the north-western Cape. Moller, who lived in the district, sent his two children to this school, where they were initially accepted, and their fees paid. But because Moller was married to a coloured woman, the parents of other children at the school brought pressure to bear on the School Committee, with the result that it barred Moller's children from further attendance and tendered back the fees, which Moller refused. As there was compulsory education for children of "European parentage or extraction", and as the only other schools where his children could have been accepted were mission schools, Moller was aggrieved, and he applied to C G Maasdorp, JP in the CPD for an order compelling the Keimoes School Committee to receive his children as pupils. This action was unsuccessful, as was his appeal to a full bench of the CPD,[179] and so *Moller v Keimoes School Committee & another*[180] came before the appeal court.

Moller's case was argued by W P Schreiner, KC, former Prime Minister of the Cape Colony.[181] He pressed the point that Moller's children did indeed satisfy the statutory formula, as their father was a pure European, and their maternal grandfather a "pure bred Englishman", which left only their maternal grandmother as the

[177] Act 30 of that year.
[178] Act 35 of that year, section 60.
[179] Buchanan, Hopley, and Searle, JJ.
[180] 1911 AD 635.
[181] With him J A Greer, at 636–8.

source of any non-European blood. As there was no question of colour raised in the Act, he contended that the children were of "European parentage and extraction", and should have been admitted by the school committee as a result.

The AD rejected this view of the case, and unanimously confirmed the decisions of the lower courts not to grant Moller the order he sought, because his children were not of "European parentage or extraction". In arriving at this conclusion, the various judgments delivered by each member of the court display differences in emphasis which provide insights into judicial temperament and motivation.

Lord De Villiers, CJ[182] set out the facts, and followed by stating that the court was unable to ignore the "universal" meaning attached to the term "European" throughout South Africa:[183] when once it had been established that one of a man's nearer ancestors was black or yellow, he was regarded as being of other than European descent. In construing the statute, he proferred remarks which have often been cited as an instance of the judges' bowing to white prejudice. He said:[184]

> "[T]he Court should endeavour to ascertain its popular sense and place itself as far as possible in the position of the authors of the enactment. As a matter of public history we know that the first civilised legislators in South Africa came from Holland and regarded the aboriginal natives of the country as belonging to an inferior race, whom the Dutch, as Europeans, were entitled to rule over, and whom they refused to admit to social or political equality. We know also that, while slavery existed, the slaves were blacks and that their descendants, who form a large portion of the coloured races of South Africa, were never admitted to social equality with the so-called whites. Believing, as these whites did, that intimacy with the black or yellow races would lower the whites without raising the supposed inferior races in the scale of civilisation, they condemned intermarriage or illicit intercourse between persons of the two races. Unfortunately the practice of many white men has often been inconsistent with that belief, but the vast majority of Europeans have always condemned such unions, and have regarded the offspring of such unions as being in the same racial condition as their black parents. These prepossessions, or, as many might term them, these prejudices, have never died out, and are not less deeply rooted at the present day among the Europeans of South Africa, whether of Dutch or English or French descent. We may not from a philosophical or humanitarian point of view be able to approve this prevalent sentiment, but we cannot, as judges, who are called upon to construe an Act of Parliament, ignore the reasons which must have induced the legislature to adopt the policy of separate education for European and non-European children."

Here, compulsory mixing at schools could not have been intended, he argued, and he threw a sop to those of more liberal spirit by remarking that it was ". . . regrettable that there should be this social chasm between the races, but it undoubtedly exists, and it has had its effect on legislation throughout South Africa". He avoided the complex question of how far back "in a person's pedigree it would be

[182] See 639–44.
[183] At 642.
[184] At 643–4.

allowable to go in order to decide whether his European extraction [was] unmixed" by saying that it was "fortunately unnecessary".[185]

Innes, J appeared to approach the issue with great circumspection,[186] and even some reluctance. He recognised the important social and political consequences of the decision, but refused to be swayed thereby, for "[w]hen the intention of the Legislature can be clearly gathered from the language which it employs [as here], then our only duty is to give full effect to that intention".[187] He admitted that "extraction" could be interpreted as "wholly" or "in part", but he preferred the former meaning, as more natural, and backed by the evidence of legislative intent. As soon as the latter was enquired into the "central issue" of colour had to be confronted,[188] as "[t]he most radical and distinctive difference between one section of our population and another is that between the white and the black".[189] Commenting on educational segregation, he said.

> "Whether the policy embodied in such a provision is wise or unwise, whether it can be effectually carried out or not, these are points upon which it is not desirable to express any opinion. But that it is a policy which may inflict hardship on deserving members of the community is plain. And I should like to express my individual view that the machinery of the Act for the education of children of other than European extraction seems inadequate."[190]

Innes, J's last remark[191] was echoed by Laurence, J,[192] who deplored the inadequate educational system for non-Europeans, but admitted that the remedy was a matter for the legislature.[193] He, too, seemed to rest uneasy with the outcome of the appeal, for he was ". . . strongly of opinion that restrictive or disabling provisions, such as are incidentally introduced in the present Act . . ., should be construed in a liberal spirit, and that no further or wider effect should be given to them than the language of the legislature clearly demands".[194] However, he felt constrained to agree with the Chief Justice that to bring pupils of all shades together would disrupt "the whole system".[195]

No such protestations of regret emanated from J A J de Villiers, JP[196] who was content to adopt the "common use" of "European" in South Africa as indicative of colour, with no reference to geography. "Pure" extraction was meant by the Act, and the court could not fail

[185] At 644. There is irony in this phrase, since there was a school of suspicion in the Cape that there was coloured blood in the De Villiers family. See Trapido *White Conflict and non-White Participation in the politics of the Cape of Good Hope 1853–1910* 402–3.

[186] See 645–50.

[187] At 645.

[188] At 647.

[189] At 648.

[190] At 649.

[191] Which is almost a forerunner of the *Rasool* decision, in that it implies that separate but substantially equal education would be acceptable.

[192] See 650–2.

[193] At 652.

[194] At 651.

[195] At 651–2.

[196] See 652–4.

to give effect to this intention.[197] So, too, Kotzé, JP[198] refused to be perturbed by any possible difficulties in drawing the colour line, as the present case was clear. He acknowledged that prejudice of a section of the community should not be adopted as persuasive in determining the law, but offered what appears in retrospect to be a disturbing view of the affair:

> "a certain amount of sympathy must naturally be felt for the innocent children, but the appellant has no one but himself to blame in this matter. It is true he married his wife before the Act was passed, yet he could hardly have been ignorant of the conditions of life and race existing in a country like South Africa."[199]

For Kotzé, JP, therefore, it was part of the court's duty to enforce the existing order of white–black relations.

Judicial utterances here have been described in some detail, both for their own effect, and for the seminal influence of *Moller's* case on future litigation concerning racial definition and prejudice. There are many reasons why the court took the view of the matter which it did: for most of the judges, the unquestioning acceptance of years of political and social experience in South Africa would have negated any thoughts of an alternative attitude, and possibly it was too soon after Union to stir the racial pot and so exacerbate the inherent divisions in the ruling group. Notwithstanding these factors, this decision marks a low point in the court's record of adherence to standards of justice, free from racial considerations.

No excuse can lessen the harmful effects of this case, both in terms of the weight of precedent in future disputes involving race, and in the wider community, as an encouragement to just such racial prejudice as several judges purported to denounce. The outcome of *Moller* encouraged the campaign of those who advocated race discrimination and segregation, and compromised those who were seeking a more just dispensation.

Two other cases dealt with the definition of "coloured" in this period. *R v Sellong*[200] was an application for leave to appeal by an "aboriginal native" against her conviction for a contravention of a provincial ordinance[201] which prevented any "coloured person" from residing for more than 48 hours in a township unless certain conditions had been satisfied. Appellant claimed that she was not hit by the prohibition as she was not a "coloured person", but Lord De Villiers, CJ[202] dismissed this argument on the ground of clear legislative intent, and the "absurdity" that would otherwise result in European separation from coloureds, but not from Africans.

The circumstances surrounding *Moller* were almost duplicated some years later in *Seneque v Natal Provincial Administration*.[203] Here a

[197] At 653.
[198] See 654–7.
[199] At 656.
[200] 1914 AD 192.
[201] 6 of 1904 (ORC), section 105.
[202] See 193–4 concurred in by Innes, JA and C G Maasdorp, AJA.
[203] 1940 AD 149.

new headmaster had refused the appellant's children re-admission to the school which they had attended for some years, on the ground that proof of their pure European descent had not been given. He had requested proof of three generations' "purity" on each side of the family, and his barring of the children on lack of such proof had been supported by the Provincial Council, which controlled education. In court, Seneque maintained that he and his late wife were of pure European descent, but chose rather to press home the point that the Administration was obliged to abide by the former headmaster's decision, and sought a *mandamus* to this effect. The AD was, therefore, spared the difficult problem of determining the purity of Seneque's racial roots, but their decision could not have remained unaffected by this factor, which may have contributed greatly to a split in judicial attitudes here.

For the majority, Watermeyer, JA[204] began by paying respects to the "I'm sorry, but . . ." syndrome in the following fashion:[205]

> "I have a great deal of sympathy for the appellant whose children have been brought up as Europeans and were apparently regarded as Europeans until a new head teacher called for proof . . . But however one's natural sympathies may incline one to regret that the question was ever raised in the case of the appellant's children, the matter must be decided according to ordinary legal principles."

After this formula of exculpation, he went on to dismiss the appeal on "ordinary legal principles". These related to the legal status of the regulation which made education compulsory for European children, and of the original headmaster's act of admitting the children in the first place, and to where the *onus* of proof lay in respect of any legal right to further education that might have been established. Tindall and Centlivres, JJA joined him in this view of the issues.

De Wet, CJ[206] was not prepared to do the same. The fact that education was compulsory for European children[207] meant that they could not be refused admission except on good cause shown, support for which submission he gained from parts of the judgments in *Moller*. The Chief Justice averred that the facts in this instance were stronger, and that, once a head teacher had decided to admit pupils as Europeans, the Administration was not entitled to exclude them except on good cause shown to the satisfaction of a court.[208] In other words, the Administration, having delegated a discretion to the head teacher to admit children or require proof as to their descent, was bound by this decision unless and until it showed that it was erroneous either in fact or in law, otherwise each succeeding head teacher could demand fresh proof of racial purity.[209] De Wet, CJ would have allowed the appeal.

[204] See 157–63.
[205] At 157–8.
[206] See 151–7.
[207] By virtue of Act 6 of 1910 (Natal).
[208] At 154. [209] At 157.

Unlike *Moller,* the race definition aspect of *Seneque* was submerged beneath other legal arguments, but the fact of the Chief Justice's dissent shows that two judicial opinions were feasible. There is little doubt that the "equities" of the situation pushed De Wet, CJ into dissent, and it is interesting to note that the three judges in the majority were all "lawyers' lawyers", lacking that formal connection with political life which had been such a feature of the Chief Justice's career.[210]

From disputes revolving around the "coloured" axis, attention shifts to several cases, the central feature of which was the meaning to be given to the word "native", as defined in certain statutes. In *R v Kogan,*[211] the appellant had been convicted of selling liquor to a Mozambican, George Ferreira, whose father was from Zanzibar. Kogan claimed that Ferreira was not a member of "any aboriginal tribe or race of Africa", the definition of "native" in the Act[212] which prohibited the sale of liquor to the same. Innes, CJ,[213] a well-known advocate of prohibition of the supply of liquor to natives,[214] would not swallow this legal nicety, and held that the ". . . intention of the Legislature . . . was to prohibit the supply of liquor to those classes of the community who, from a want of training in civilisation, were unable to refrain from excess in the use of liquor".[215] Although he was prepared to countenance the possibility, at some time in the future, of cutting down the field of those prohibited from obtaining liquor[216] (presumably when they became more "civilised"), he was, for the present, content to dismiss the appeal.

In *Ngcobo v Natal Native Trust,*[217] the question was whether appellant, an "exempted" native, could be ejected from a mission reserve, in terms of a pre-Union law[218] which had defined a "native" to be a native other than an exempted native. Wessels, JA[219] decided that "[t]he higher the civilisation of a native and the more Christianised he [was], the more likely would he be able to obtain a letter of exemption", and that it would thus be anomalous to exclude such a person from an area set aside for Christianised natives.[220] In upholding the appeal, the court showed that realistic considerations would, on occasion, be allowed to prevail over legal formalism.

[210] This might have contributed to their tendency to see the problem in "legal", rather than "human", terms, leading to a more cautious approach, and preventing them from adopting De Wet, CJ's more controversial view.
[211] 1918 AD 521.
[212] Cape Liquor Law Amendment Act 28 of 1898, section 5 as amended by Act 1 of 1916, section 1.
[213] See 524–6 concurred in by Solomon and C G Maasdorp, JJA; J A J de Villiers and Juta, AJJA.
[214] While in the Cape Parliament, he had been responsible for passing the Act which prohibited the sale of liquor to natives, known as the "Innes Liquor Act".
[215] At 526. [216] *Loc cit.*
[217] 1929 AD 245.
[218] Law 49 of 1903 (Natal).
[219] See 246–9 concurred in by Curlewis and Stratford, JJA; and J E R de Villiers, AJA.
[220] At 248.

R v Timol[221] added a further dimension to the definition of native in the Liquor Act,[222] as in *Kogan,* when J A J de Villiers, CJ[223] said that "native" did not mean someone "born in" Africa, otherwise most of the persons in court would have been natives.[224] Rather, he maintained, its "ordinary meaning" in South Africa *viz* a member of an "aboriginal tribe", should be adopted. This was not sufficient, though, as *R v Fakiri*[225] amply demonstrated. Here, the accused had failed to pay the tax demanded of those who were members of "an aboriginal race or tribe of Africa",[226] on the ground that both his parents had been children of Zanzibaris, and that he still lived among a group of people similar to himself who did not regard themselves as natives. They were prepared to pay the tax which related to non-natives.

The court side-stepped the issue of whether Zanzibar was a part of Africa in dismissing Fakiri's appeal. Tindall, JA[227] skilfully argued that, because the evidence for the Crown was sufficient to raise a reasonable doubt that Fakiri was a native as defined, the statute demanded that he discharge the burden of proof that he was not a native.[228] Tindall, JA assumed that Africa did not include Zanzibar, and accepted that Fakiri's place of origin was Zanzibar. But that was insufficient to discharge the onus of proof, he said, because Zanzibar's long and close connection with the mainland made it highly probable that African natives were living in Zanzibar, and Fakiri might have been descended from them.[229]

The arguments and confusion over who was a "native" came to a head in 1945 in *R v Radebe & others,*[230] an application for leave to appeal from the Natal Native High Court. A pre-Union Natal law[231] had defined a "native" in the customary way to include "all members of the aboriginal races or tribes of Africa South of the Equator". Radebe claimed that one of his co-accused did not fall within such a description, as he was the illegitimate son of an Indian father and an African mother, and so was not subject to the jurisdiction of the Native High Court, which had convicted him and his co-accused of faction fighting. The AD upheld this argument, and the trial and convictions were set aside, as the Act had defined a "native case" as one in which all the accused were "natives".

In his judgment, Schreiner, JA[232] considered the various tests

[221] 1930 AD 303. [222] 30 of 1928, section 175.
[223] See 304–5 with the concurrence of Wessels, Curlewis, Stratford, and Roos, JJA.
[224] At 304.
[225] 1938 AD 237.
[226] By the Natives Taxation and Development Act 41 of 1925, section 19.
[227] See 239–43 with the concurrence of Stratford, CJ; J E R de Villiers and De Wet, JJA; and Feetham, AJA.
[228] At 239.
[229] At 242–3. [230] 1945 AD 590.
[231] Act 49 of 1898 (Natal), section 5.
[232] See 594–611 concurred in by Watermeyer, CJ; Tindall and Greenberg, JJA; and Davis, AJA.

which had been used for allotting people to racial groups *viz* blood or descent; appearance; and habits or mode of life.[233] Here, as the latter two tests pointed to the accused in question as being a "native", the crucial question for the court was whether descent alone should be determinative of membership of a particular group, or whether other factors should also be included. Schreiner, JA looked at past South African legislative attempts at definition, and said that:

> "In order to guard against confusion I would like to point out here that the word 'native' has a popular meaning which may correspond more or less with the meaning contained in a statutory definition, but many statutory definitions by making use of the word 'native' in the definition succeed in defining the word 'native' in terms of the word 'native' and thereby introduce confusion."[234]

After reviewing the effect of various cases, he was confronted with the following general formulation:[235]

> "Whenever a group or class of persons in a community is subject to special laws not applicable to members of the community generally as such the condition of the group or class constitutes a status and the question whether a particular person falls within the group or class must be decided by following the lines usually followed in ascertaining a person's status. It is a general rule that legitimate children take the status of their father, illegitimate children that of their mother."

This statement of the law, if applied to the case under review, would have resulted in the co-accused being a "native", but Schreiner, JA surmounted this problem thus:

> "It is not permissible to hold that whatever the language of the legislation the test to be applied is that of civil status because all such legislation relates to status. Racial descent and civil status are distinct and if civil status is by any legislation made to depend on racial descent such descent cannot itself be ascertained from the law of status."[236]

He returned to the question of which test should be decisive of racial group, and decided to adopt the "natural meaning" of membership of a race or tribe as being membership by blood or descent. Factors such as appearance and habits would be considered only as evidence of descent.[237] Here, as Radebe's co-accused did not have a preponderance of native blood, he failed the sole test of descent and was not a native as defined, so that the Native High Court had had no jurisdiction in the case.[238]

The "descent" test was confirmed as the correct one three years later in *R v Abel,*[239] another appeal against conviction for a contravention of the prohibition against the supply of liquor to "natives". Centlivres, JA[240] expanded slightly on Schreiner, JA's formulation by stating that, when the *only* evidence was that of repute or appearance, such evidence, while not the best, was

[233] At 597.
[234] At 603–4.
[235] At 606.
[236] At 606–7.
[237] At 609.
[238] At 610.
[239] 1948 (1) SA 654 (AD).
[240] See 656–64 concurred in by Watermeyer, CJ; Tindall, Greenberg, and Schreiner, JJA.

sufficient to justify an inference that the person in question was a native.[241] Here, the magistrate had stated that the recipient of the liquor, who had initially acknowledged that he was an African, looked like a native, and he had not been willing to change his mind, even after a subsequent claim by the "native" that he had discovered that his real mother was a coloured person.

The appeal turned more on the weight of the evidence given, and on the magistrate's apparent view that the onus of proof, that the recipient of the liquor was not a "native", rested on the accused.[242] Centlivres, JA used a presumption of statutory interpretation, that against the alteration of the common law or that in favour of a strict interpretation of statutory provisions which interfered with elementary rights, to support his view that the Liquor Act did not cast the onus on the accused.[243] After some discussion of the role of an appellate body as regards credibility and demeanour of witnesses who had appeared before a court of first instance, he decided that he could not say that Abel had had a fair trial, and so he allowed the appeal.[244]

In this way, after years of uncertainty, a firm method of determining legally who satisfied the statutory formula used to describe a "native" was devised. Two years later, the new National Party government put the matter, as far as is legally possible, beyond doubt in its Population Registration Act.[245] This confirmed the supremacy of the "descent" test where both natural parents were known and classified, but otherwise gave equal prominence to the criteria of appearance and social acceptance.

This study would not be complete without a discussion of two cases which turned on the definition of "Asian" contained in two statutes dealing with the right of such persons to own land in the Transvaal, of which more in a later chapter. Transvaal Law 3 of 1885[246] prohibited persons "belonging to one of the native races of Asia, including the so-called Coolies, Arabs, Malays, and Mahommedan subjects of the Turkish Empire" from owning fixed property in the Transvaal. The Rand Townships Registrar acted according to the letter of the law and refused to register the transfer of some property to Gandur, a "Christian white Syrian". Ward, J in the WLD supported the Registrar's action, and so *Gandur v Rand Townships Registrar*[247] came before the AD.

Counsel for Gandur, Esselen KC[248] relied on *Moller's* case to support his contention that the legislature intended "native" in its definition to have its commonly accepted South African meaning of

[241] At 663.
[242] At 660.
[243] At 662.
[244] At 659–60, and 664.
[245] Above, sections 1 and 5(5).
[246] In article 1, a translation of which appears here.
[247] 1913 AD 250.
[248] See 251–2.

"coloured", and alleged that the reference to "Mahommedan" subjects evinced an intention to exclude Christians from the prohibition. Stratford, KC,[249] for the Registrar, pleaded for a literal interpretation of the words in the statute.

Lord De Villiers, CJ[250] answered these arguments with an acknowledgement that the primary meaning of "native" bore no reference to colour, but he maintained, as in *Moller,* that it had attained a secondary meaning in South Africa by virtue of which it was confined to coloured races. The court should attempt to ascertain the popular sense of the words and place itself in the legislature's position, he said. If the Transvaal government had intended whites to be covered by the law, it would have indicated to them the locations where they were to reside, and they had never done so, for, "[l]ooking at the whole tenour of the laws relating to locations, I am quite satisfied that [they . . .] would have been horrified at the idea of confining white men, even if they came from Asia Minor, in locations, like those set aside for Coolies, Arabs, and other Asiatics".[251] On the basis of this startling admission of his own prejudicial outlook on race matters, he allowed the appeal, and ordered the registration of Gandur's property. For the Chief Justice, it seems, it was acceptable to subject black South Africans to degrading residential conditions, purely because of their race.

Innes, J[252] pursued a different line in justifying his allowing the appeal. He averred that the word "races" normally signified the primary idea of "native", so that the use of the expression "native races" here was explained by its South African connotation of "coloured".[253] He took it as a matter of such general knowledge that the court was entitled to recognise it, and referred to *Moller* for further backing.[254] Solomon, J[255] adopted a similar approach, and gained much support from contemporaneous laws of the ZAR; he, too, had "never heard of a location for white persons", which would have been the outcome had the legislature intended the law to be applied in the way argued by respondent.[256]

This judgment, while no doubt a happy event in the life of the Christian white Syrian, Gandur, confirmed the disadvantaged position of coloured Asians, who then resorted to strategies such as nominee-holdings and formation of limited-liability companies in order to escape the provisions of the law. The Union government attempted to close the latter loophole in the law with the Asiatics (Land and Trading) Amendment Act (Transvaal),[257] which, after

249 At 252.
250 See 252–4.
251 At 253.
252 See 254–7.
253 At 254.
254 At 255.
255 See 257–9.
256 At 259.
257 37 of 1919, section 11, inserted by Act 35 of 1932, section 7.

some amendments, defined "Asiatic" as ". . . any Turk and any member of a race or tribe whose national home is in Asia, but shall not include any member of the Jewish or the Syrian race or a person belonging to the race or class known as the Cape Malays".

Mall v Registrar of Companies[258] was fought on the basis of this definition. Appellant, who owned shares in a landowning company in the Transvaal, claimed to be a Cape Malay by reason of "blood, status, language, appearance and habits of life", even though her father (and his parents) were Asiatics. The Rand Townships Registrar had refused to transfer certain land to the company because he maintained that Mall was an Asiatic, and so fell within the prohibition contained in the law. Before the AD, Mall argued on the basis of *Radebe* that descent, aided by appearance and habits, was the decisive test, while respondent relied on precedent in alleging that she was in fact an "Asiatic" as defined.

Feetham, AJA,[259] after an extensive review of the facts and the law,[260] upheld the appeal on the ground that the words "or class" in the statutory definition indicated that habits and social environment, as well as descent, could be taken into account in determining racial group.[261] In view of Mall's uncontradicted evidence, she had satisfied the court that she was a Cape Malay and so was excluded from the definition of Asiatic in the Act. Although this would lead to anomalous situations with regard to landholding, Feetham, AJA refrained from expressing an opinion on how the laws might be altered to deal with such situations.[262] He also refused to lay down any rigid test as to the racial purity of Cape Malays, in consideration of their mixed racial heritage.[263]

Although many other cases in this period were concerned, in part, with racial categorisation, this case brings to an end this survey of those appeals in which racial definition was the major component of appellants' cases. The stage has now been reached where judicial attitudes to general aspects of race, as outlined in this chapter, can be assessed.

Summary and Conclusions

All the judges of appeal who served in this period sat in at least one of the cases discussed above, except for Van den Heever and Fagan; and J A J de Villiers, Stratford, Watermeyer, Tindall, and Greenberg each sat in at least ten of the cases. The trend noticed previously, whereby certain judges seemed to have given the greater number of judgments, continued here, with Innes, J A J de Villiers, Lord De

[258] 1946 AD 727.
[259] See 730–43 concurred in by Watermeyer, CJ; Tindall, Greenberg, and Schreiner, JJA.
[260] At 730–8.
[261] At 740.
[262] At 742–3.
[263] At 741.

Villiers, Kotzé, and Centlivres speaking out in most of the cases in which they sat, while Greenberg remained a "silent concurrer" on every occasion on which he was on the Bench. Four judges delivered dissenting opinions—Kotzé, Wessels, De Wet, and Gardiner—in three cases in which there were split decisions *viz Detody, Rasool,* and *Seneque.*

A feature of the thirty-seven cases discussed is that fifteen of them resulted in success for the appellant concerned, an indication both of the ambivalence of the issues before the court and a willingness by the AD to reverse findings and conclusions of the provincial divisions. Another aspect of the court's operation that has been noted before continued here, with the judges tending to agree in a single judgment after about 1925, and not to give separate concurring opinions, except where there was a division in their ranks (*Detody, Rassool*).

Considering each group of cases as outlined above, the disputes concerning traditions and customs peculiar to non-Europeans occurred early in the life of the court. As a result, they display the paternalistic outlook typical of the colonial period in endeavouring to "civilise" individual black litigants, while contentedly condoning "unfettered" government action in continuing the myth of the Governor-General as Supreme Chief of "uncivilised" natives (*Mokhatle* is a good example).

As regards race discrimination in general, the impression generated by the cases is one of a judiciary willing to carry out legislative and electoral opinion in matters of race to the full. Except for *Detody* and, to a lesser extent, *Abdurahman* and *Abel,* there is no apparent attempt by the court to mitigate the harsh effects of oppressive laws, or to criticise their substance and application. Whether it be in respect of segregation of public amenities, the exercise of discriminatory liquor or sex laws, or crass prejudice, nowhere is there a sign of an endeavour to adhere scrupulously to the doctrine of equality of all people before the law, or even to remind the law-giver, ever so gently, of this principle.[264]

This tendency to fail fully to consider the implications of a decision and simultaneously to adopt a positivistic approach can be seen most vividly in the complete abdication of social responsibility by the judges in *Ndlwana v Hofmeyr.* A further facet of this judicial outlook is the frequency with which the judges resorted to the "I'm sorry, but . . ." formulation in disposing of the cases of appellants who had suffered as a result of discrimination. This was most marked in *Moller,* which, with most of the "race group definition" cases, provides further substantiation of the picture of a judiciary concerned to preserve legally the racial categories traditionally accepted in South

[264] Perhaps the remarks of Innes and Laurence in *Moller, supra,* can be seen as exceptions to this rule. In addition, there are one or two statements in the following chapters which counter the general trend observed here.

Africa, and even to reinforce the race barriers through sharpening the distinctions between the groups.

Some interesting observations can be made about the composition of the Bench in a number of outstanding cases: Watermeyer, Tindall, Feetham, Greenberg, and Schreiner formed a group which sat in cases such as *Mpanza, Abdurahman, Radebe,* and *Mall,* which were all comparatively liberal in effect, yet the first four were all on the Bench in *Jockie.* Again, it would seem logical that Lord De Villiers and Innes should form the core in both *Moller* and *Gandur,* along with Solomon in *Gandur* and J A J de Villiers in *Moller,* yet Innes, Solomon, and J A J de Villiers made up the majority in *Detody* fifteen years later.

This dimension of the appellate judicial character, then, does not seem to lend support to the arguments of the majority of commentators who sing the praises of a judiciary seeking to protect the interests of all those who appeared before it, regardless of racial origin. On the contrary, the court seems to have identified itself with contemporary social conventions, as embodied in legislation, as far as matters of race were concerned. The accuracy of this assertion will become apparent in the discussion of judicial attitudes to Asian immigration, and to non-European land tenure, in the chapters which follow.

CHAPTER SEVEN

IMMIGRATION BY ASIANS

One of the most pressing issues faced by the infant Union administration in 1910 was that of the movement between the provinces of the Asian section of the national population, and the desire of many other Asians to enter the country as immigrants, usually to join members of their families already resident there. The problem, as it was regarded by the government, was centred on the Indian group, which constituted the vast majority of "Asians" in South Africa, and whose members had been imported as indentured labour for the cane fields of Natal from 1860 onwards. When they had completed their stipulated years of service, those labourers who wished to were allowed to remain in the colony, and they gradually spread to the Cape and ZAR. Many of them prospered commercially, but they were not allowed to participate in government in any of the areas which subsequently united to form the South African state.[1]

Repatriation was one suggested solution of the problem, but this was not an easy matter, as many Indians were South African-born by this time, and were indispensable to the economy. Besides, the Imperial Government also had to consider another of its possessions, India, and the feelings of her people and administration, in any such scheme. In addition, M K Gandhi[2] had helped to form the Natal Indian Congress in 1894, which served as a focus of resistance to race discrimination. For these reasons, full repatriation was unlikely to be politically feasible, with the result that the authorities fell back on an attempt to limit immigration into, and movement within, South Africa by Indians.

Until 1913, certain statutes in force in the colonies which made up the Union[3] regulated the legal position, but in that year Parliament enacted the Immigration Regulation Act[4] to apply to the whole country. This provided that "any person or class of persons deemed by the Minister on economic grounds or on account of standard or habits of life to be unsuited to the requirements of the Union or any particular Province thereof" should be a prohibited immigrant,[5] and the Minister of the Interior declared "every Asiatic person" to be in such a category. This determination was eventually challenged in the

[1] For a useful outline of the situation and struggles of South African Indians, see Pachai *The South African Indian Question 1860–1971* Ch II–IV and Roux *Time Longer than Rope* Ch X.

[2] Who led India to independence from Britain, after leaving South Africa in July, 1914 (Pachai *op cit* 23).

[3] Such as the Cape Immigration Act 30 of 1906; Natal Immigration Act 30 of 1903 and several Transvaal Acts, 2 of 1907, 15 of 1907 and 36 of 1908.

[4] 22 of 1913.

[5] Section 4(1)*(a)*.

AD in 1923 in *R v Padsha*,[6] when it was upheld by a narrow majority, but this did not mean the end of litigation in immigration matters, as will be seen.

Whether because of the influence of Gandhi as an advocate or the fact that the legal process was the only possible avenue of relief, much time was spent by the AD from 1911 to 1913, and again after *Padsha*, on matters which turned on Indian immigration. The cases which reached Bloemfontein provided an opportunity for the appeal judges to express their feelings on the wider issues of race relations, organised resistance to laws, and the exercise of administrative discretion. Thus they provide valuable material for the isolation of judicial attitudes and role.

As the statutory regime changed in 1913, and as few cases on Indian immigration were reported from that date until 1923, it is convenient to describe and discuss the cases in two phases *viz* from 1911 to 1913, and then from 1923 onwards.

Lord De Villiers's Court

Although there had been organised opposition to the various colonial immigration laws before Union, the level of resistance was remarkable, even by South African standards, in the early years of the life of the AD, and the issue of Indian rights stimulated much political controversy and emotion. Gandhi and his followers waged many campaigns of passive resistance. They marched between the provinces, refused to register with the authorities, and submitted themselves to mass arrest. There was widespread disruption of "law and order", of which the judges were acutely aware.[7] It is against this background that the actions of Lord De Villiers and his colleagues must be seen in the cases which were decided at this time.

Mahomed, NO v Union Government (Minister of the Interior)[8] set the trend for most decisions of this period. Here the President of the British Indian League appealed as representative of five Indians who had been domiciled in the Transvaal, deported to India, and refused passage through the Cape in an attempt to re-enter the Transvaal. By the Cape Immigration Act of 1902,[9] the five fell within the definition of "prohibited immigrant", but that Act had specifically exempted from its terms those who were domiciled in South Africa at the time.[10] A further Immigration Act four years later[11] had narrowed this exemption to domiciliaries of "European descent", but it did safeguard "any rights, privileges, or protections" acquired at its commencement.[12] Appellants contended that, as they had been

[6] *Infra.*
[7] For a detailed account of Indian resistance in this period, see Pachai *op cit* Ch II.
[8] 1911 AD 1.
[9] Act 47 of that year.
[10] See sections 2 and 3*(f)*, respectively.
[11] Act 30 of 1906.
[12] See sections 4*(f)* and 1, respectively.

resident (and domiciled) in the Transvaal in 1902 and 1906, their right of entry into the Cape had been recognised by the first Act, and protected by the second, as a result of which the authorities had wrongly denied them transit.

The AD[13] did not accept this argument, on the ground that the rights and privileges mentioned by the later Act were rights acquired under the earlier Act, not rights previously enjoyed under the common law. They held that appellants had acquired no such statutory rights. Innes, J, who spoke for the court,[14] said that a privilege had been held out to the five by the 1902 Act, of which they had not availed themselves. This Act had created no rights or privileges, he went on, it had merely imposed disabilities on certain persons not domiciled within South Africa: it had not improved the appellants' position, it had just not made it worse. He gained support for his view by a consideration of the Act as a whole, and ended with the oftspoken formula of exculpation:[15] "The result is, no doubt, hard . . .; but where the meaning of the Legislature as expressed in a Statute is clear, the Court is bound to give effect to it."

This was to retreat behind the screen of legislative intent, and can be taken as evidence of the court's desire to implement government strategy to the full. The judgment in *Ooka v Union Government (Minister of the Interior)*[16] strengthens this impression. The only variation from *Mahomed* was that Ooka had been resident in the Cape Colony from 1900 to 1905, when he had gone to India. Before departure, he had obtained a certificate from a Resident Magistrate, to the effect that he was domiciled in the Cape, and that the restrictions of the 1902 Act did not apply to him. Notwithstanding this document, the appellant was refused entry to the Cape on his return in 1912, a course of action which the AD held to be in accordance with the law.

In a brief judgment,[17] Innes, ACJ[18] relied on *Mahomed* to support his decision that the issue of the certificate to Ooka gave the latter no rights other than those he could have claimed under ordinary rights of domicile. He maintained that appellant had acquired no rights under the earlier Act which could have been protected by the 1906 Act, with the result that he had been correctly denied entry to South Africa. It is perhaps strange that the court did not regard the obtaining of the certificate as the type of action, which they had referred to in *Mahomed* the previous year, which was necessary to establish rights of residence in the colony. It seems as if the only

[13] Consisting of Lord De Villiers, CJ; Innes and Solomon, JJ; J A J de Villiers, JP; and A F S Maasdorp, CJ (AJA).

[14] See 6–13.

[15] At 13.

[16] 1912 AD 784.

[17] See 788–9.

[18] With whom Solomon and Laurence, JJ; J A J de Villiers, JP; and Mason, J concurred.

action which would have satisfied the court in this situation, would have been for an Indian, domiciled in South Africa, to have entered the Cape during the period 1902 to 1906, as this would presumably have established a right which would have been preserved by the repealing Act. The effect of *Ooka* was to confine all Cape Indians, who had not been born in South Africa, within the borders of the Cape Province, for fear of being excluded on attempted re-entry.

Two cases at this time are of interest in that both appellants found themselves on the wrong side of the authorities because of their acts of passive resistance. In *R v Sodha,*[19] the wife of an Indian who was entitled to a certificate of registration under the Transvaal statute[20] but who was in jail for refusal to comply with the law, appealed against her conviction on a charge of being a prohibited immigrant found within the province.[21] She had been unable to pass the test for admission to the Transvaal,[22] but claimed that as her husband's removal, as a prohibited immigrant, had not yet been ordered, she was entitled to be in the Transvaal, as the wife of a person who was not a prohibited immigrant. Lord De Villiers, CJ rejected this contention curtly.[23] He decided that appellant's husband's act of passive resistance rendered him liable to be removed from the province, and so he was in fact a prohibited immigrant, with similar consequences for his wife.

This judicial frame of mind was again apparent in *Ismail v Union Government and Registrar of Asiatics,*[24] in which appellant asked the court to prohibit his deportation from the Transvaal. The most recent Act[25] laid down that Asiatic minor residents were entitled to registration, but it prescribed no time limit for applicants to register. The previous statute,[26] and a regulation issued under the later Act,[27] however, both required application for registration within a month of a minor's sixteenth birthday. Ismail, who was 17 years old, had failed to apply to register within this time limit because he had participated in a passive resistance campaign. When he eventually did so, the authorities refused him a certificate, and ordered his deportation.

The AD declined to intervene in this matter, though the judgments are of some interest. Innes, ACJ[28] held that, as no time limit had been fixed by the 1908 Act, the previous rule should continue in force, and

[19] 1911 AD 264.
[20] Act 36 of 1908.
[21] Under Asiatic Law Amendment Act 2 of 1907, section 5.
[22] Which consisted of the ability "to write out . . . and sign, in the characters of a European language, an application for permission to enter the Province", section 2(1).
[23] See 268–9, with which Innes, J; Laurence, Actg JA; C G Maasdorp and J A J de Villiers, JJP agreed.
[24] 1912 AD 605.
[25] 36 of 1908 (Transvaal), section 3*(c)*.
[26] 2 of 1907 (Transvaal), sections 4 and 6.
[27] Section 17.
[28] See 609–13 with whom Solomon, J and C G Maasdorp, JP concurred.

that Ismail had to abide by the consequences of his deliberate election to become a passive resister. Laurence, J,[29] in deciding that the time limit was sixteen years and a month, preferred to rely more upon the regulation issued under the 1908 Act, but he added some remarks of a general nature. He noted that the modern tendency was for the courts to spend a great deal of time in the tangled task of unravelling the obscurities of recent legislation, a matter which affected the rights, liberties, and disabilities of an important section of Crown subjects. He hoped that the Union Parliament would deal with the issue in a coherent, systematic, and statesmanlike manner,[30] and he warned of the dangerous latitude afforded by the passing of skeleton statutes which left the operative machinery to be supplied by regulations.[31] This also gave the widest discretion to administrative officials, and supplanted the proper functions of both the legislature and judiciary by substituting executive action.[32]

The exercise of administrative discretion was in issue in another immigration case in the early years. In *Chotabhai v Union Government (Minister of Justice) and Registrar of Asiatics*,[33] the authorities refused to register the minor son of an Asiatic, who held a valid certificate of registration in the Transvaal, on his reaching the age of sixteen. They ordered his removal from the province, and his appeals to a single judge[34] and a full Bench of the TPD[35] proved fruitless. Appellant's difficulty lay in the fact that he did not belong to any category of persons mentioned in the 1907 Immigration statute,[36] but the Registrar could exercise a discretion in "hard cases" such as his.

All five judges of appeal held that the Registrar had failed to exercise his discretion in this instance, and they made it clear that he ought to have allowed Chotabhai to register. Lord De Villiers, CJ[37] and the Maasdorp brothers[38] went further, and decided that, though not included in the terms of the 1907 Act, appellant had been lawfully resident in the Transvaal at the time of application, so that he was entitled to a certificate of registration. Innes[39] and Solomon,[40] JJ were rather more cautious in stating that Chotabhai was entitled to claim the exercise of the Registrar's discretion, rather than a registration certificate, as they regarded the list of persons in the 1907 Act as exhaustive.

In justifying their conclusions in this case, the appeal judges made

[29] See 613–19, with whom J A J de Villiers, JP agreed.
[30] At 614–15.
[31] At 617.
[32] At 618.
[33] 1911 AD 13.
[34] Wessels, J in chambers.
[35] De Villiers, JP and Bristowe, J; Mason, J in dissent.
[36] Act 2, section 3(2).
[37] See 21–31.
[38] C G Maasdorp, JP, see 51–6; and A F S Maasdorp, CJ (AAJA), see 56–61.
[39] See 31–41.
[40] See 41–51.

some remarks which reveal their attitudes to "law" and their own function. Lord De Villiers, CJ said:[41]

> "It is not part of the duty of the courts of law to criticise the policy pursued by the Legislature in its enactments, nor do I now wish to offer any criticism of the policy of the Acts relating to Indian immigration. I must, however, make this remark, that, however desirable it may be to restrict Indian immigration, this Court must apply the same rules of construction, which it would apply to acts with less desirable objects. The maintenance of the liberty of the subject is of more importance than even the prevention of undesirable immigration, and, if the Legislature desires to place restrictions upon the liberty of any class of subjects, whether they be Europeans or Asiatics or natives, it should do so in language which admits of no doubt as to its intention."

Innes, J[42] acknowledged that the policy of the statutes was a drastic one which discriminated unfavourably against one section of the community, and so it called for the strictest interpretation. A F S Maasdorp, CJ echoed these feelings when he stated[43] that

> ". . . it is a principle of our law that any Act of Parliament or other statute, which is intended to deprive any individual of any rights, shall be clear, definite and distinct, and that, if there be any doubt as to meaning, it is to be interpreted in the sense least prejudicial to those rights and in favour of the individual . . .".

Solomon, J and C G Maasdorp, JP failed to mention this aspect of the case in their judgments.

The attitude of suspicion towards administrative action which was evident in *Chotabhai* came again to the fore in *Shidiack v Union Government (Minister of the Interior)*,[44] a case which also showed the limits beyond which the court was not prepared to hamper the Executive. The Cape Immigration Act[45] provided that the term "prohibited immigrant" should include any person who was unable through deficient education "to write out and sign in the characters of any European language an application to the satisfaction of the Minister". In this case, two young sons of appellant, a Syrian who had come to the Cape in 1900, had failed on three occasions to satisfy the educational test, whereupon the Chief Immigration Officer decided that they should not be allowed into the country. The CPD[46] refused to intervene to prohibit Government plans to return the children to their port of embarkation.

In his argument before the AD, Shidiack relied on a number of statutory provisions; chief among which was the requirement of the "Minister's satisfaction" set out above. This, he claimed, stipulated a personal exercise of Ministerial discretion. Innes, ACJ[47] approved of this interpretation, and declared that regulations which purported to allow a subordinate officer to evaluate the educational test were *ultra vires*. He agreed that a public officer could properly act through a

[41] At 25.
[42] At 31–2.
[43] At 60.
[44] 1912 AD 642.
[45] 30 of 1906, section 3.
[46] McGregor, AJ.
[47] See 647–59 in which judgment Solomon, J and C G Maasdorp, JP concurred silently.

deputy for ordinary Ministerial purposes, but decided that, where the nature of the statutory section and its subject-matter showed that the discretion could only be properly exercised in a judicial spirit, the responsibility for its exercise could not be vicariously discharged.[48] Accordingly, the appeal court ordered that a new test should be administered to appellant's sons, but, after the expression of Ministerial dissatisfaction with the results thereof, it refused to intervene to prohibit the government from excluding the children.

In this regard, Innes, ACJ affirmed[49] that the court would not interfere with the *bona fide* exercise of discretion by a public officer. Nevertheless, he felt it necessary to warn[50] against ". . . a growing tendency in modern legislation to clothe with finality the decisions of public officials in matters which seriously affect the rights of the public". The effect of this movement was to exclude the jurisdiction of the courts, he said,[51] which might lead to a "serious menace to the liberty of the subject", to which the courts did well to draw attention.

A similar sentiment was expressed by the court in *Kharwa v Union Government (Minister of the Interior)*,[52] which also concerned the exercise of Ministerial discretion. Here, the Natal Immigration Act[53] provided that someone who appeared to be a prohibited immigrant could enter the province after depositing £100, after which the person had one week to prove that he was not prohibited. Failure to secure this proof could result in forfeiture of the deposit, at the discretion of the Minister. Kharwa had put up the deposit for another Indian, who had failed in his attempt to prove that he was not prohibited, and had departed of his own accord. Kharwa then brought a legal action for the return of his deposit, on the ground that the order of a competent tribunal was necessary for forfeiture.

Solomon, J[54] admitted that much difficulty was caused by inadequacies in the wording of the statute,[55] but concluded reluctantly that the Legislature had intended the Minister to have a completely free hand in ordering forfeiture. He regretted this situation,[56] and felt bound to express his opinion[57] that the provisions of the section which authorised forfeiture were "unnecessarily stringent"; he thought that forfeiture should only apply if the prohibited immigrant failed to leave the country.

In addition to these cases which had to be decided on their merits, the AD in this period had to decide at least five applications by would-be immigrants for leave to appeal against decisions which

[48] At 648. [49] At 651.
[50] At 653.
[51] *Loc cit.*
[52] 1913 AD 260.
[53] 30 of 1903, section 10(1)*(a)*.
[54] See 261–6 with the concurrence of Lord De Villiers, CJ and Innes, J.
[55] At 262–4.
[56] At 265.
[57] At 266.

excluded them from the country,[58] as well as an attempted appeal on a question of law, reserved for the NPD, which had acted incorrectly in giving its opinion.[59] All five applications were unsuccessful, and the facts of three[60] seem to disclose particularly harsh actions by immigration officers, who in many instances had an absolute discretion. Indeed, Innes, J was moved to say[61] that legislation which granted such discretion was ". . . very extraordinary . . . but the terms of the statute are clear and the Court cannot refuse to give effect to it".

Finally, *Govindasamy v Indian Immigration Trust Board, Natal*[62] falls outside the period of Lord De Villiers's Chief Justiceship, but provides a good example of the court's attitude to the conditions under which Indian immigrants lived, and is worth considering here. A pre-Union Natal statute[63] levied a medical fee on certain employers, which depended on the number of Indian immigrant male employees whom they employed. This group was defined[64] to include all Indians introduced from India, and "those descendants of such Indians as may be resident in Natal". Appellant employed some colonial-born descendants of indentured Indians, together with "free" Indians, who had served their period of indenture, but had remained. He appealed against the ruling of the NPD[65] that he was liable for medical fees in respect of all these employees.

Solomon, JA[66] upheld the appeal in part. He used the canon of construction[67] that, where it appears from the context that the legislature did not intend an extended meaning of a phrase, the ordinary sense should be adopted. This led him to exclude the colonial-born employees from the effect of the definition clause, as far as medical fees were concerned. He was not prepared to extend this reading of the Act to "free" Indians, however, and Govindasamy was held liable to pay medical fees on their behalf. C G Maasdorp, JA[68] could not agree with the majority opinion here, as, "[w]ith all the restrictions placed upon Indians it may well be . . . thought right to exercise a little paternal care over them".[69] For this reason, he was not willing to exclude colonial-born Indians from the wide statutory definition of "Indian immigrant", and thought that the appeal should be dismissed altogether.

[58] See: *R v Pillay* 1912 AD 2; *Hassan v Union Government (Minister of Justice) and Registrar of Asiatics* 1912 AD 20; *Nathalia v Principal Immigration Restriction Officer* 1912 AD 23; *R v Choma* 1913 AD 153; and *Bibi v Immigration Officer for Natal* 1913 AD 495.

[59] *Immigration Officer for Natal v Ratanjee* 1913 AD 498.

[60] *Hassan, Nathalia*, and *Bibi, supra*.

[61] See *Nathalia, supra*, at 27.

[62] 1918 AD 633.

[63] The Indian Immigration Law 25 of 1891, section 50.

[64] In section 118.

[65] Dove Wilson, JP and Tatham, J; Hathorn, J dissenting in part.

[66] See 636–43, with whom Juta, AJA (643–5), Innes, CJ and J A J de Villiers, AJA concurred.

[67] At 637.

[68] See 645–9.

[69] At 647. The Trust Board appealed to the Privy Council, where Lord Dunedin adopted Maasdorp, JA's view of the issue. See (1921) 38 *SALJ* 302.

Some of the personalities connected with the early life of the Appellate Division
(l to r) J A J de Villiers, Charlie Neethling, J B M Hertzog, C L Botha, F E T Krause
Amsterdam, *circa* 1890

(VA 721, Cape Archives)

To sum up this period briefly, it can be said that the court adopted a generally strict approach to immigration control, in full sympathy with legislative intent. None the less, the judges were not prepared to tolerate administrative excess or misdirection, even in furtherance of legislative policy. Indeed, they went out of their way, on several occasions, to express their concern at the way in which the policy was being implemented.

Second Phase: 1923 to 1947

Ten years after the coming into force of the Union statute, the Immigration Regulation Act,[70] *R v Padsha*[71] presented the court with its first test of the legality of Ministerial action under its terms. The Minister of the Interior, General Smuts, had declared that he deemed "every Asiatic person to be unsuited on economic grounds" to the requirements of the Union and every Province. The CPD had held this notice to be *ultra vires*,[72] while the NPD had come to the opposite conclusion.[73]

Padsha had been convicted under the Act[74] for aiding certain prohibited immigrants to enter the Transvaal, and he appealed unsuccessfully to the TPD,[75] which preferred to follow the Natal court. On appeal in Bloemfontein, his counsel[76] argued that Asiatics did not comprise a class, for they had nothing in common economically or as a class: the Ministerial order was wide enough to exclude a Japanese admiral and a coolie. He maintained further that the Act did not purport to exclude a race or allow a race to be excluded. For the Crown, Lansdown[77] relied on the necessity to prevent interference by Asian agitators with the country's native races; the responsibility of Parliament, not the courts, to restrain an errant Minister; and the state's right to keep foreigners from its shores, as support for his case.

Solomon, JAJ de Villiers and Juta, JJA made up the majority of the AD which was prepared to accept that the Minister's action was *intra vires*. In general, their justification followed the line that the notice was only meant to apply to "coloured" Asiatics, who formed a class as defined, and that this action was not so unreasonable that the court could question it. Innes, CJ and Kotzé, JA delivered strong dissenting opinions, and, as all five judges spoke at some length of their reasons for their decisions, this case deserves a detailed discussion.

Solomon, JA[78] started by setting out the gist of the provincial division decisions which were in conflict with each other, and then

[70] The relevant details of which are described at notes 4 and 5, above.
[71] 1923 AD 281.
[72] *Mahomed v Immigrants' Appeal Board* 1917 CPD 171.
[73] *In re Seedat* 1914 NPD 198.
[74] Section 20*(a)*.
[75] Wessels, JP; Mason and De Waal, JJ.
[76] P Millin, see 282–4.
[77] See 284.
[78] See 285–9.

addressed the question of the meaning of "Asiatic". He referred to the secondary sense of "coloured" which the court had adopted in *Gandur v Rand Townships Registrar*,[79] and asked whether there could be any reasonable doubt that the Minister had intended this sense when he used the word in connection with immigration. This meaning would be shared by the "ordinary man" in conversation, the learned judge said.[80] On the matter of coloured Asiatics forming a class, he stated that the number of persons which could fall into that group was immaterial, and that unsuitability on economic grounds could coincide with racial grounds.

He developed this point by contending that, if "economy" meant the "well-being of the state", the introduction of further coloured people into South Africa with its "vast coloured population and acute coloured problem" would not be economically beneficial. Even if the narrower concept of "material" well-being had been intended by the legislature, he maintained that most coloured Asians (being traders or labourers) were economically unsuited.[81] Solomon, JA went further by claiming that every Asiatic who was a professional was also a potential trader or labourer: if this seemed unlikely, it was no more unlikely that such a person should desire to come to South Africa. He provided political justification for his view by noting[82] that such a professional Asiatic would exercise influence over others, and so might become a "disturbing factor in the industrial processes of the country, as actually happened in the now historic case of Gandhi".

Juta, JA echoed many of these statements in adopting a similar view of the issues raised in the case.[83] He spoke[84] of the "material" well-being of South Africa and remarked that ". . . some of the greatest economic problems which have to be solved . . . arise from the fact that we have a large number, far outnumbering the Europeans, of natives and coloured people". He noted the disproportionately large numbers of poor whites, and he, too, regarded the introducion of highly educated and civilised Asians as a threat to peaceful industrial relations, as had already proved to be the case.[85] His words show how closely he indentified national economic well-being with that of the white group. He also relied on legislative efforts to exclude coloured Asians from the pre-Union colonies to back up his judgment.

J A J de Villers, JA made up the majority,[86] and he appeared to be less certain of his stand, as he agreed with a "great deal" of what the

[79] Ch VI "Race Relations", above.
[80] At 287.
[81] At 288.
[82] At 289.
[83] See 294–7.
[84] At 296.
[85] At 297.
[86] See 290–4.

minority adhered to, which he proceeded to set out.[87] But he differed absolutely[88] from all the other members of the AD when they said that the Minister was confined to economic grounds or the standards and habits of life as a basis of classification of prohibited immigrants. For De Villiers, JA, the Minister was free to fix on any common attribute (whether race or colour of skin or any other) which appeared to him best calculated to further South African economic interests. He thought that the Minister was not asked to base his opinions on any economic attributes possessed by members of the prohibited class, and he sought support in pre-Union legislation on immigration, which had excluded Asians on economic grounds.[89] Finally, he viewed it as undesirable that Parliament had delegated such extensive powers to a single individual. In his own words:[90] "Whatever motive may have induced Parliament to forsake the traditional habit of calling things by their names, one views with misgiving and alarm the rapid and progressive abdication of its chief function by the Legislature in favour of the Executive."

Innes, CJ worked methodically through the facts of the case and the history of the legislation in declaring the Ministerial action to be *ultra vires*.[91] On the basis of *Shidiack*, he asserted that the Minister had to abide by the statutory limitations, which here demanded that the common quality, which was the basis of the "class" indicated, must be an economic factor.[92] The Chief Justice disagreed with the Natal court in *Seedat*, which had given the widest possible meaning of the word "economic", as this almost eliminated the restrictions which the statute purported to impose. He claimed[93] that the basis of classification in the notice was "racial", in that the economic attributes of members of the same race might vary infinitely, while the economic attributes of men of different races might be identical.

Innes, CJ went on to point out that the Ministerial notice drew no colour distinction (even though it might have been so applied administratively), and he would not accept that legal precedent confined its operation to coloured people. He admitted[94] that certain sections of South Africa's population needed economic protection, but used the examples[95] of an Indian rajah, cricketer, priest or scholar, and a Japanese prince or scientist to show that not all Asians were unskilled labourers. Sir James ended his judgment[96] by drawing attention to the tendency of modern legislation to limit or remove the jurisdiction of the courts, which, he thought, should only be done in the clearest language. "Courts of law", he said, "should not be astute to construe doubtful words in a sense which will prevent them from doing what *prima facie* is their duty, namely, from investigating cases of alleged injustice or illegality." If the words of the law did not

[87] At 290. [88] At 292. [89] At 293–4. [90] At 294.
[91] See 297–304. [92] At 299–300. [93] At 301.
[94] At 302. [95] At 303. [96] At 304.

convey the real intention of the legislature, then Parliament, not the courts, should remedy the defect.

Kotzé, JA joined the Chief Justice in dissent, and repeated many of the reasons given by Innes, CJ, though at greater length.[97] He laid great stress[98] on the ability of the Courts ". . . to test the exercise of [a Minister's statutory] power by the terms in which the Legislature has chosen to confer it": here, the meaning of the words "class" and "economic" had to be ascertained in order to determine whether the Minister had acted *intra vires*. As regards "class", Sir John adopted[99] the "common attribute" test referred to by the Chief Justice, but he found himself in a slighly awkward position when faced by "economic", for he had assumed the wide scope of "well-being of the State" in his earlier judgment in the CPD in *Mahomed*.[100] This would have tended to align him with the majority in *Padsha*,[101] but he overcame this difficulty by stating that his previous interpretation had been too broad, and he decided[102] that the Minister had used race as the factor for classification here.

Kotzé, JA was also not prepared[103] to confine "Asiatic" to mean Asians with dark skins, and he found support for this view in pre-Union legislation and the absence of racial categories in the Union Act. For him, "every Asiatic" admitted of no ambiguity or qualification, and, if literally applied, could lead to the startling result that whites could be excluded. After he had spent much time[104] in establishing that all Asiatics would be hit by the Ministerial prohibition, he maintained[105] that even an exclusion of coloured Asians would have exceeded the Ministerial mandate, as it was based on racial, and not economic, grounds. He would have allowed the appeal.

The outcome of the majority decision, however, was to uphold the validity of the Minister's classification, which gave judicial sanction to the conclusions of the more racially aware and prejudiced courts of Natal and the Transvaal, while discarding the more liberal approach of the CPD. It is interesting to note that, although four of the judges of appeal came from the Cape, they displayed quite different attitudes to the question of Asian immigration. Only Solomon and Juta, JJA appear to hold views endorsing discrimination which could be said to be close to those of the other. J A J de Villiers, JA takes up a position which gives complete freedom to the Minister, while the opinions of the minority seem to stem from different concerns: Innes, CJ

[97] See 305–17.
[98] At 308.
[99] At 309.
[100] Above, note 71, and see 310.
[101] See judgment of Solomon, JA, at 288.
[102] At 311.
[103] At 313–14.
[104] See 314–16.
[105] At 316.

disapproves of the harmful effect on the educated section of the Asiatic population, whereas Kotzé, JA appears to be aware of the possible damage to the interests of white Asians. These last three judges also showed their alarm at the changing nature of the relationship between the branches of government, which was leading to the increased power of administrative discretion and exclusion of the courts' jurisdiction.[106]

The decision in *Padsha* ended most attempts by Indians to immigrate to South Africa, but the issue of the rights of Asian immigrants within the country continued to come before the AD. It is useful to consider the cases which occurred subsequently to 1923, as the composition of the Bench changed substantially over time, with the result that a new group of judges faced the question and pronounced upon its equities.

Section 20*(a)* of the Union Act, under which Padsha had been convicted, provided that: "Any person who aids and abets any person in entering and remaining within . . . any Province in contravention of this Act, knowing that person to be prohibited from so entering or remaining, shall be guilty of an offence." In *R v Rasool*,[107] the court of appeal was confronted by a situation in which an Indian father, who had a right, frequently exercised, to enter Natal from the Transvaal, had been convicted for a contravention of this section as the result of taking his three-year old son with him on one such visit. The AD, as in *Padsha*, was not unanimous in this case, but a narrow majority overruled a full Bench of the NPD[108] and upheld the appeal.

Solomon, JA delivered the leading judgment,[109] for the purpose of which he accepted that the infant son had been a prohibited immigrant, a fact which Rasool had known. But he maintained[110] that there could be no aiding or abetting by the father, unless the son had contravened the Act, which required the exercise of volition and a conscious action on his part. As a child of three was incapable of such behaviour, he could not have been guilty of contravention of the Act, although his physical presence in Natal could have led to his removal by the authorities. Sir William thought[111] that Parliament could not have contemplated the conviction under section 20*(a)* of those who assisted infants or lunatics, and so Rasool's appeal was sustained. Kotzé, JA, as was often the case, gave a concurring judgment,[112] though he added little to what had gone before. Innes, CJ was content to concur without comment in the majority opinion.

J A J de Villiers, JA could not agree with this view of the

[106] This factor was taken up in an article "Administrative Law in South Africa" by Arthur Lourie in (1927) 44 *SALJ* 10–23.

[107] 1924 AD 44.

[108] Dove Wilson, JP; Carter and Hathorn, JJ.

[109] See 46–9.

[110] At 47.

[111] At 49.

[112] See 49–51.

situation.[113] After spending some time in outlining carefully why he regarded the son as a prohibited immigrant,[114] he examined the three requirements for the commission of a section 20*(a)* offence, and concluded that they had been met. He differed from Solomon, JA in that he saw the son's mere physical presence in Natal as a contravention of the Act, and in that he felt that the process of aiding and abetting just required two persons, and not the active co-operation of each in the commission of an offence.[115] He was joined in his opinion, that the appeal should have been dismissed, by Wessels, JA,[116] who set great store by legislative intent, which he saw as the punishment of those who encouraged certain people to enter the Union. He claimed that the age or intention of the prohibited immigrant was irrelevant,[117] with the result that Rasool had been correctly convicted, although he did admit that curious results might follow from such a conviction.

The court also took a stance sympathetic to the interests of an Indian immigrant in *Principal Immigration Officer v Medh.*[118] Section 25(1)[119] empowered the Minister, in his discretion, to grant any person exemption from certain prohibitions contained in the Act, or to issue a temporary permit to any prohibited immigrant to enter into and reside in the Union under certain conditions. Medh, who had been involved in the passive resistance movement from 1908 to 1911, had first been given such a temporary permit to enter the Transvaal in 1911, followed by a letter of exemption in 1914, which was made conditional upon his retention of a domicile in the Transvaal. He ignored this by living in India from 1918 to 1927, and, on his return, the Immigration Appeal Board refused him entry because it considered that he had broken the condition. The question of law was referred to a full Bench of the TPD,[120] which found that the letter of exemption was valid authority for Medh's entry.

The judges of appeal agreed with the court *a quo's* interpretation of the section. J A J de Villiers, JA referred[121] to the anomalous position that a person or class of persons could be declared as prohibited from immigrations, and then taken out of that category by exemption. Nevertheless, on the ordinary grammatical meaning of the words of the section, he held that a person was either exempt from the prohibitions, or not—there could be no intermediate position.[122] The section did not empower the Minister to make exemption condition-

[113] See 51–7.
[114] At 51–5.
[115] At 56–7.
[116] See 57–9.
[117] At 58.
[118] 1928 AD 451.
[119] Immigration Regulation Act 22 of 1913.
[120] Krause, Van Pittius, and Barry, JJ.
[121] See 454–9 concurred in by Curlewis and Stratford, JJA; and J E R de Villiers, AJA.
[122] At 457.

al, and so the appeal was dismissed. In a similar case some years later, it became clear that the authorities countered the effect of *Medh* by issuing all subsequent immigrants with a document in the form of a temporary permit, so that entry and residence could be conditional. The appeal court in *Mithal v Principal Immigration Officer*[123] confirmed the principle of *Medh*,[124] but it decided that the new document was, in fact, not an exemption, so that conditions which it contained had been lawfully imposed.

Bhyat v Commissioner for Immigration[125] provides a further instance of the judges' interpreting an immigration statute in favour of the rights of an individual Indian. In this case, the TPD[126] had interpreted the words "exempted person" in an Act[127] which had amended the Immigration Regulation Act to have the narrow meaning of "British Indian". Greenberg, J had referred to the title and other sections of the Act, in reaching this conclusion, and the result was to confirm that appellant was a prohibited immigrant. The court of appeal[128] disagreed with this construction, and held that the words should have their plain meaning of "any person exempted under the amended Act". Stratford, JA relied[129] for support upon the cardinal rule of construction *viz* "the intention of the law-giver from the language employed in the enactment", which, he asserted,[130] should not be departed from where there was no "absurdity, inconsistency, hardship, or anomaly".

This reading of the statute allowed Bhyat to remain in South Africa as the child of an exempted person, and it amply demonstrates the selective use of rules of construction by the judges to achieve the result which they felt to be appropriate. In the words of Stratford, JA himself:[131] "Sometimes perhaps one finds one of these rules over emphasized and sometimes another, but, all must yield in the last resort to the intention of the Act to be gathered from a consideration of its provisions in their entirety." Certainly, the poor drafting of some early Union statutes allowed the judiciary a comparatively free hand to interpose a large measure of their personal preferences into their approach to the legislation before them.

A pair of cases which offers further illustration of the selective use of the presumptions of construction by the judges occurred in this period, and was concerned with the same legal issues. Section 10 of the Union Immigration Regulation Act had provided that no

[123] 1947 (1) SA 811 (AD).
[124] At 815, *per* Davis, AJA, in whose judgment Watermeyer, CJ; Tindall, Greenberg, and Schreiner, JJA concurred.
[125] 1932 AD 125.
[126] Greenberg and Barry, JJ.
[127] Indians Relief Act 22 of 1914, section 3(2).
[128] Wessels, Curlewis, Stratford, and Roos, JJA.
[129] See 127–31.
[130] At 129.
[131] *Loc cit.* There are echoes of *R v Abel* 1948 (1) SA 654 (AD) in this decision.

prohibited immigrant should be exempt from its provisions if that person had been allowed to enter through oversight, misrepresentation, or suchlike means. Fourteen years later a subsection was added to section 10,[132] to the effect that, if a prohibited immigrant was in possession of a registration certificate, an Immigration Board to which he appealed might set aside that certificate, if it had been obtained by his own fraudulent misrepresentation (or that of someone on his behalf). The question which this amendment raised was: did it apply to all registration certificates, whenever obtained, or only to those procured subsequent to 1927?

This matter worried the Immigration Appeal Board, which stated a case for the decision of the TPD,[133] which held that the amendment could only be prospective in operation. The immigration authorities were not satisfied with this outcome, and so the case of *Principal Immigration Officer v Purshotam*[134] came to Bloemfontein. Respondent admitted that he had obtained his registration certificate by his own fraud in 1915, but he claimed to be lawfully domiciled, and denied that he fell under the provisions of section 10. The appeal court rejected this version, and decided that the amending section was retrospective in operation.

J A J de Villiers, JA delivered the majority judgment[135] in which he emphasised that the court had to consider the general scope and purview of the statute, the remedy, the former state of the law, and the legislative contemplation, in coming to its decision.[136] He set out the details in each of these categories, and remarked[137] that it was difficult to escape the conclusion that Parliament had intended to cover all cases, past or future. For this reason, Purshotam's argument could not be sustained, and the amendment was held to be retrospective. Stratford JA, however, could not agree with this conclusion,[138] as he regarded the amending section as having materially altered the law and the rights of certificate holders. For him, the amending language was not clear enough to override the rule of interpretation against retrospectivity, and, as he was in doubt, he thought it right to adopt a meaning which worked least hardship and was "more equitable".[139] He would have dismissed the appeal.

The possible anomalies which could arise from the majority attitude were brought home to the court three years later in *Principal Immigration Officer v Bhula*.[140] Here, the TPD[141] had answered

[132] By the Immigration and Indian Relief Act 37 of 1927, section 5.
[133] Krause, Van Pittius, and Barry, JJ.
[134] 1928 AD 435.
[135] See 439–46, with which Curlewis, JA and J E R de Villiers, AJA agreed.
[136] At 440.
[137] At 443.
[138] See 446–51.
[139] At 450.
[140] 1931 AD 323.
[141] De Waal, JP; Greenberg and Krause, JJ.

questions of law submitted by the Immigration Appeal Board to the following effect: that the amended section was not retrospective so as to apply to Asiatics in the Transvaal who had obtained certificates prior to 1913 (the date of the original Immigration Regulation Act). As respondent in this case fell into the latter category, he was entitled to retain his certificate, even though it had been obtained by fraud. The immigration authorities were again unhappy and took the matter on appeal.

Wessels, JA[142] set out the history of the legislation and previous litigation, and distinguished *Purshotam*[143] on the grounds that Bhula had obtained his certificate before 1913, and that he himself had been innocent of the fraud through which it had been procured. He clarified the present state of the law, whose policy, he said,[144] was not to go behind a certificate once granted, except for the fraud of the holder, or his agent. He met the appellant's argument that the amended section 10 applied to all certificates, whenever issued, by citing a provision in the 1913 Act which safeguarded rights granted under a prior Transvaal statute, as well as falling back on principles of interpretation.[145]

These were to the following effect: that statutes regulated future conduct and were construed as operating only on cases or facts which came into existence after they had been passed; that, if there were two sections in an Act which seemed to clash but which could be interpreted so as to give full force and effect to each, then such an intepretation was to be adopted rather than one which would partly destroy the effect of one of them; and that, where a statute was clear, the Court had to give effect to the intention of the Legislature, however harsh its operation might be to individuals affected thereby, but where two meanings might be given to a section, one of which led to harshness while the other did not, the court would hold that the Legislature had rather intended the milder than the harsher meaning. In the present instance, as the amending section was silent as to the rights of pre-1913 certificate holders, and as the distinction between those who had obtained certificates before and after 1913 allowed two apparently conflicting sections to be effective, Wessels, JA invoked these rules[146] and dismissed the appeal. Stratford, JA added a few remarks[147] to drive home the correctness of some of his earlier comments in this matter, and amplified his contention that all "lawful" certificate holders were protected.

The AD was called upon, on at least three other occasions before World War II, to decide questions concerned with Asian immigra-

[142] See 326–38. J A J de Villiers, CJ; Curlewis and Roos, JJA concurred silently.
[143] At 328.
[144] At 330.
[145] At 333.
[146] At 334–6.
[147] See 338–9.

tion, two of which[148] showed that the court was willing fully to implement legislative intent when, in their eyes, the circumstances warranted such action. The third case, *Principal Immigration Officer v Hawabu*,[149] provides a further example of the choice of principles of construction of statutes in order to achieve the result which the judges thought best. The words in dispute occurred in the Indians Relief Act,[150] which laid down that no woman, deemed to be the wife of a person exempt from the operation of the immigration laws, could be admitted to the Union if the exempted person had ". . . in any province offspring by any other woman . . ." who was still alive.

Hawabu, respondent in this case, was excluded under this section of the Act, because her husband, D, had previously married another Indian woman, A, by whom he had had two children. The latter three were all in India at the time of Hawabu's application to enter South Africa, but the children were only there temporarily and were the holders of certificates of identity in Natal. The Immigration Appeal Board decided that these two children satisfied the condition that D had offspring "in any province", and they barred Hawabu's entry on this basis. However, the Board sought the NPD's[151] opinion on this matter, and were informed that they had misconstrued the law, in that the test of whether D's children were "in any province" was one of physical presence.

The court of appeal reversed this reading of the law. J E R de Villiers, JA[152] admitted[153] that the ordinary meaning of the words ". . . ha[d] in any province offspring . . ." was that of physical presence as adopted by the Natal court, but they were capable of a secondary meaning here. The important factors to be taken into account when considering which meaning was to be assigned to words were to be found in their context; the scope, policy, and object of the Act; and the consequences which might follow from the adoption of one or other meaning.[154] In the light of these matters, and the possible hardship that might befall a first wife and family whose husband introduced a second wife into a province in their absence for an hour, De Villiers, JA preferred the "ordinary residence" test,[155] which, he said, would lead to greater stability.

This case again illustrates the agility of the court in interpreting legislation which was slightly ambiguously framed, and underlines the importance of the judges' own attitudes to sensitive political

[148] See *Mahomed v Principal Immigration Officer* 1929 AD 190; and *Essop v Commissioner for Immigration* 1932 AD 223.
[149] 1936 AD 26.
[150] 22 of 1914, section 3(2)*(b)*.
[151] Hathorn and Lansdown, JJ.
[152] See 28–36, joined by Curlewis, ACJ; Stratford and Beyers, JJA; and De Wet, AJA.
[153] At 30.
[154] At 32.
[155] At 35–6.

issues, such as immigration. An interesting statement by De Villiers, JA here,[156] albeit *obiter*, was that, even where words were capable of only one meaning, there was an "exceptional class of extreme cases" in which courts had felt themselves compelled to "modify" or "cut down" words used by the Legislature. The admission that this process (which the learned judge called "amputation" rather than interpretation)[157] was recognised, stands in healthy contrast to the manifold expressions of obedience to legislative intent which adorn so many other judgments of this period.

Summary and Conclusions

In considering judicial attitudes to Asian immigration in the twenty-four cases mentioned above, it is useful to draw tentative conclusions for each of the two periods outlined, and then to attempt some general remarks.

As has been pointed out above, Lord De Villiers's Chief Justiceship is marked by a judicial approach which leaves little doubt about the five original appeal judges' sympathy for legislative policy to curb Indian immigration.[158] Only two appeals were wholly successful,[159] and state authorities triumphed in all but one of the fourteen cases in these three years.[160] Nevertheless, there were signs of dissatisfaction with the manner in which the legislation was implemented. These surfaced in the form of comments about, and sometimes warnings against, the tendency to grant too great a discretion to the executive and its administration.[161]

The ten cases which occurred from 1923 onwards, on the other hand, are spread more widely in time (and judicial personnel, for that reason), though eight of them were heard before 1932. There appears to be a more withdrawn, even-handed attitude on the part of the court, with four appeals succeeding,[162] and only six resulting in an endorsement of state action.[163] It seems that the AD, having made it clear in *Padsha* that the general principle of exclusion of Indians from South Africa was acceptable, was quite prepared to grant relief to the odd individual litigant[164] who was able to bring his case to Bloemfontein.

General patterns of judicial performance in this area evince one or two unusual features. In a third of the cases, more than one judgment was delivered, which is a higher proportion than usual, and six

[156] At 31.

[157] *Loc cit.*

[158] Lord De Villiers's remarks in *Chotabhai*, quoted above at note 41, form one example.

[159] *Chotabhai* and *Ratanjee*.

[160] *Chotabhai* was the lone exception.

[161] See the remarks of Laurence, Innes, Solomon, J A J de Villiers, and Kotzé quoted above, particularly in *Ismail, Shidiack, Kharwa, Nathalia*, and *Padsha* (from the later period).

[162] *Rasool, Bhyat, Purshotam*, and *Hawabu*.

[163] The exceptions being *Rasool, Medh, Bhyat*, and *Bhula*.

[164] For example, *Rasool* and *Bhyat*.

dissenting opinions were contained in four of the cases.[165] There was a high level of activity by the thirteen judges who were on the Bench before *Hawabu*. Nine of them delivered judgments in forty per cent (or more) of the cases in which they sat. Curlewis was noticeably silent in all seven cases which he heard, while Kotzé expressed his opinion in both cases which came before him. Innes, Solomon, and Stratford appear to have been the leading judges in this field, as they often spoke for the court even when they were not the senior judge on the Bench.

The overall impression gained is one of a judiciary which supported the general doctrine of a racially discriminatory immigration policy, but which was prepared to manipulate the canons of construction to secure isolated relief for individual Indians. Anxiety about Executive power seems to diminish after *Padsha*, and the judges were not averse to using the rules of interpretation to uphold certain actions of the immigration authorities.[166]

Padsha remains the dominant decision in this collection. It is a prime example of a case in which the court could have upheld the principle of equality, but chose not to do so. There were conflicting provincial decisions on the point;[167] four of the appeal judges were Cape men;[168] and ten years had passed since the enactment of the statute, so that agitation and debate on the immigration issue had somewhat subsided. Yet the AD was prepared to allow white race prejudice and statutory discrimination to gain the upper hand. The effect of *Padsha* overshadows some defiant remarks in a number of cases,[169] and its outcome might have been a further spur in Innes's retirement from the Bench four years later.

But the problems of Indian immigrants did not end at the ports of the Union, and it is appropriate now to examine the issue of Asian land tenure in the Transvaal.

[165] Innes, C G Maasdorp, J A J de Villiers, Kotzé, Wessels, and Stratford each dissented once.
[166] *Purshotam* and *Hawabu*, for instance.
[167] Above, notes 71 and 72.
[168] All except J A J de Villiers.
[169] For example: *Ismail*, *Chotabhai*, *Shidiack*, *Kharwa*, *Nathalia*, and the minority in *Padsha* itself.

CHAPTER EIGHT

LAND OWNERSHIP AND OCCUPATION IN THE TRANSVAAL

One of the foundation stones of the apartheid policy in South Africa over the last three decades or so has been the residential separation of the races in cities and towns throughout the country. This division into white, coloured, and black areas rests on the Group Areas Act,[1] which is based upon various statutes of the ZAR. The latter were introduced primarily to prevent Asians from gaining control over land in the Boer republic.[2] Although President Kruger and his Volksraad passed a law in 1885[3] which severely curtailed the right of Asian ownership and occupation of land, its measures were not fully implemented, because of threats of intervention by British colonial authorities in Southern Africa.[4] Ironically, this situation was remedied when the British took over the administration of the Transvaal in 1902, and Lord Milner's team proceeded to expedite the enforcement of the law.[5]

As will be seen in what follows, the pre-Union Transvaal government, and the Union goverment itself, passed many laws to contain the growth of coloured interests in land, most of which were reactions to ingenious schemes designed by Asians to outflank the law. As well as statutory arrangements which demanded racial segregation, mainly of Asians, several private township developers inserted clauses in their contracts of sale or lease, which forbade transfer of rights in land to coloured people. Naturally, there was a great deal of litigation on this matter in the Transvaal courts, and a number of cases reached the AD.

Two important points should be noted here. Firstly, the laws were aimed at Asian people (or sometimes "coloured" people), and were not used to govern the living conditions of black people in the urban areas.[6] Secondly, all but one case originated in the Transvaal: the Cape and Natal had no similar laws enforcing urban segregation at

[1] 41 of 1950, consolidated in Act 36 of 1966. For a recent example of the havoc wrought by this Act, see *S v Adams* 1981 (1) SA 187 (AD).

[2] For a detailed account of the build-up to the Group Areas Act, see Van Reenen *Land—its ownership and occupation in South Africa* 1–112.

[3] Law 3.

[4] Acting under the London Convention of 1885, article 14 of which guaranteed freedom of movement, property ownership, and commercial activities for British subjects within the ZAR. See Pachai *The South African Indian Question 1860–1971* 13–18.

[5] See Van Reenen *op cit* 11–16.

[6] Who were subject to different laws, chiefly the various pass laws which curtailed movement, and the Native Land Act 27 of 1913.

that time,[7] while the OFS authorities had long since prohibited Indians from owning or occupying land.[8] The triumph of illiberal attitudes towards Asians in urban areas, to which the Group Areas Act testifies, is an indication of the outcome of the struggle between the race ideology generally associated with the Cape and those of the other three provinces, which was referred to in the first chapter. Judicial attitudes in this field, therefore, are of great importance, in that the sanction of the courts for a particular view could have contributed significantly to its acceptability to the public and its elected representatives.

The statutory framework in the Transvaal (under which legal action against Asians was instituted) consisted of a series of complicated laws, the earliest of which was Law 3 of 1885. Article 2*(b)* of this law outlawed the ownership of fixed property by a defined group of people, mainly of Asian origin. From 1875 onwards, various Gold and Mining laws of the Republic established the principle that coloureds could not hold any mining rights. This policy was adopted by the Gold Law of 1908, which also prohibited the residence on, or occupation of, a certain class of land by coloured people.[9] These were the most important laws governing Asian interests in land before Union. The cases described below give a more detailed picture of the statutes, and the judges' attitudes to their application in practice.

THE LAWS IN OPERATION 1910 to 1925

The first example of a legal challenge to the conditions imposed by statute on the use of land came to Bloemfontein two years after Union in *Ritch & Bhyat v Union Government (Minister of Justice)*.[10] First appellant, a European, owned certain plots of land in the town of Boksburg, which were subject to restrictions on their use. These had been imposed under the republican *Voorkeurrecht*, (akin to a 99-year lease), and repeated in the Gold Law of 1908,[11] to the effect that no right could be gained by a coloured person, nor should any holder of title permit a coloured person to reside on the land. In 1911, the title had been converted to freehold under similar conditions.[12] Sometime after Ritch had accepted transfer of the land, he had allowed second appellant, an Indian, to occupy it. As the result of this alleged breach of the conditions of use, the State had sued Ritch successfully in the TPD[13] for forfeiture of the property.

[7] Van Reenen *op cit* 78–84; Pachai *op cit* 24–6.
[8] Wetboek (1891) Ch XXXIII, section 7.
[9] For a review of these laws, see Van Reenen *op cit* 85–105.
[10] 1912 AD 719.
[11] Section 130.
[12] By virtue of the powers vested in the Governor by the Transvaal Townships Act 34 of 1908, section 62.
[13] Smith, Mason, and Bristowe, JJ.

On appeal, Ritch and Bhyat attacked the conditions on two grounds: that they produced differential treatment between Europeans and non-Europeans by the imposition of special disabilities on the latter; and that they enabled the government to cancel the grant of title and resume possession without compensation for improvement.[14] Innes, ACJ[15] had to consider these arguments in terms of a confused Transvaal statute,[16] the effect of which, he concluded, was that the Governor could not attach conditions to the freehold title which were substantially at variance with those which affected the leasehold stands.[17] He held[18] that the Governor had, in fact, imposed materially different conditions here, as coloured occupation was now restricted to domestic servants (whereas *bona fide* servants had been permitted before), and as European landholders were now subject to forfeiture for allowing breach of a condition (as opposed to the fine levied previously).

The Acting Chief Justice decided that the provisions of the 1908 Act were imperative, because the conditions which they laid down were in the public interest, so that the Governor could not stray outside the statute in laying down conditions of occupation. Finally, he maintained that Ritch's acceptance of title which contained the prohibited conditions had not conferred validity on those conditions where they exceeded statutory limits. Appellants could rely on the illegality of the condition which the Government sought to enforce, and, for this reason, their action was successful.[19] Sir James acknowledged that prohibitions against coloured occupancy were "not uncommon" and had been given effect to by the courts.[20] In his short concurring judgment,[21] Solomon, J relied on the "general presumption in the construction of statutes against the taking away of rights or the imposition of burdens", unless clearly indicated by legislative language.[22]

This case would appear to indicate a court aware of the problems involved, and reluctant to allow the unlimited extension of such racially discriminatory conditions on land use. The next dispute, *Gandur v Rand Townships Registrar*,[23] revolved around the meaning to be given to the other main instrument of residential segregation, Law 3 of 1885. The issues and outcome of this case have been canvassed above,[24] but the judgments bear brief repetition in this context, as

[14] At 728.
[15] See 725–38.
[16] The Townships Act above.
[17] At 731.
[18] At 732–3.
[19] At 737.
[20] At 734.
[21] See 738–43. C G Maasdorp, JP and Laurence, J concurred silently, while J A J de Villiers, JP concurred with a brief comment (at 743–4).
[22] At 740.
[23] 1913 AD 250.
[24] See Ch VI "Race Relations", above.

they shed further light on judicial outlook. All three judges admitted that the primary meaning of the statutory formulation[25] would have included appellant within its terms, but they preferred to adopt the secondary meaning current in South Africa and confine the prohibition to "coloured Asians".

For Lord De Villiers, CJ[26] and Solomon, J[27] the chief motivation for this interpretation seemed to be their horror at the thought of white men being confined to locations "like those set aside for Coolies, Arabs, and other Asiatics".[28] Innes, J attempted a more conventional "legal" process of reasoning,[29] but he, too, eventually relied upon the fact that the favoured meaning was a matter of such general knowledge that the court could take cognizance of it. The immediate effect of this judgment was to remove all white Asians (including Palestinian Jews and Siberian Cossacks) from the prohibited class, which improved their position. Yet, at the same time, it confirmed the parlous condition of coloured Asians in this respect, and it indicated the court's preparedness to interpret the legislation in the interest of the race prejudice of white South Africans.

It had long been the practice for Indians to use whites as their nominees to hold land for them in their efforts to evade the prohibition.[30] A second method, that of forming a private company with Indian shareholders, which would lease fixed property and employ Indians, gained enormous popularity[31] after a decision by the WLD in 1916,[32] which sanctioned such arrangements. However, there were other ways of hitting at such circumventions of the law, and *Madrassa Anjuman Islamia v Johannesburg Municipality*[33] provides an illustration of that used by respondent local authority.

Under the Transvaal Vrededorp Stands Act,[34] freehold title in certain land obtained from the Johannesburg Municipal Council was subject to conditions prohibiting its acquisition or occupation. The statute provided[35] for a breach of one of these conditions to be visited with notice by the Council to the title holder, requiring him to put a stop to the breach. On his failure to do so, the land would be forfeit to the Council. In addition, the Council could bring an action for the ejectment of the offending Asian.

The Anjuman, a limited liability company with Asian shareholders, owned a "stand" which fell under these prohibitions, and it

[25] Law 3, article 1.
[26] See 252–4.
[27] See 257–9.
[28] Lord De Villiers, CJ at 253.
[29] See 254–7.
[30] See Van Reenen *op cit* 24–7.
[31] See Pachai *op cit* 122, note 26. A total of 308 companies, all the shareholders of which were Indians, was registered in the years 1916–1918.
[32] *Reynolds v Oosthuizen* 1916 WLD 103.
[33] 1917 AD 718, hereafter *Madrassa I.*
[34] 27 of 1907.
[35] Sections 4*(d)* and 13, respectively.

The Bench, 1925: *(l to r)* Sir John Kotzé, Sir William Solomon, Sir James Rose Innes, Jacob de Villiers, Sir John Wessels

permitted D, its Asian employee, to reside on the stand. The respondent municipality had applied to the WLD for an interdict[36] restraining the Anjuman from such conduct. Ward, J refused to grant this because he held that the Act itself provided a remedy, which prevented the Council from petitioning the court to seek different relief. The TPD[37] reversed this decision on appeal and granted the interdict, whereupon the Anjuman sought relief from the AD.

Solomon, JA[38] reviewed the situation, and agreed with counsel for the appellant that the general canon of construction, that remedies mentioned in a statute should be exclusive, had been established in South African law.[39] On the other hand, he asserted that there were exceptions to this rule, one of which was the granting of an interdict to protect a right,[40] a remedy "particularly appropriate" in this instance.[41] On the question of the Municipality's *locus standi* to seek an interdict, Solomon, JA thought that its reversionary rights in the land (in case of forfeiture) gave it sufficient interest to approach a court in such matters.[42] Finally, he stated that the effectiveness of an interdict in ensuring compliance with the conditions, when compared with those remedies provided by the Act, had justified the decision of the court *a quo*, and he would have dismissed the appeal.[43]

Kotzé, AAJA was moved to state his particular reasons for agreeing with the rest of the court.[44] He scrutinised the Act concerned here, and decided that Transvaal policy had been the creation of separate wards for Asians on the ground of protection of public health,[45] the responsibility for which empowered the Municipality to take action against those who ignored the condition.[46] As the legislature could never have intended the Council to apply for ejectment again and again, he said, the granting of an interdict presented no new principle, so that the appeal could not succeed.[47] The agility with which the judges of appeal acted to infer the most suitable solution for the containment of Asian land occupancy demonstrates a mood sympathetic to legislative wishes, for their avowed approach to the construction of laws which removed citizens' rights was a restrictive one, to protect such rights.[48]

However, the court had not reckoned with the resourceful tenacity of Asians to insist upon their right to hold land, for the same parties

[36] Similar to the injunction in English law.
[37] J A J de Villiers, JP, Wessels and Curlewis, JJ.
[38] See 720–7.
[39] At 722.
[40] At 723. [41] At 725.
[42] At 726.
[43] At 727.
[44] See 727–30.
[45] Sir John, having been Chief Justice of the ZAR at that time, would have been well versed in the events surrounding the acceptance by the British colonial authorities that segregation was justifiable on sanitary grounds.
[46] At 730.
[47] *Ibid.* Innes, CJ; C G Maasdorp and Juta, JJA concurred.
[48] See Solomon, J at 740 of *Ritch & Bhyat*, for example.

appeared in Bloemfontein two years later, in *Madrassa Anjuman Islamia v Johannesburg Municipal Council.*[49] The Anjuman had attempted to avoid the effect of the previous judgment by leasing its property to a company, D Ltd, which had been formed by its servant, D, who had been the "occupier" in the last case. D was the sole director and manager of D Ltd, which also employed only coloured and Asian people, none of whom was present on the stand outside normal business hours. The Municipality once again sought the aid of the TPD, for which J A J de Villiers, JP concluded that the conversion to D Ltd had been a "transparent device for circumventing the law", and a contempt of court. He said that the court had to look at the essence, rather than the form, of events, and that occupation of the stand by D and other employees was *in fraudem legis*, as distinct from *contra legem.*[50]

Solomon, ACJ was again the chief spokesman for the court of appeal.[51] In a brief judgment, he maintained that it was obvious in the context of the Act that "occupy" meant "habitual physical presence" of Asians on the stand. As a company was incapable of being physically present at any place, the occupants in this instance were its employees who were Asians.[52] He held that the race of the shareholders of D Ltd (they were all Asians or coloureds) made not the slightest difference, so that it was unnecessary to pronounce on the *in fraudem legis* issue. As the Anjuman had permitted D and the others to occupy their property, the Acting Chief Justice dismissed their appeal.[53]

Kotzé, AAJA relied on the "context and motive" of the Act in agreeing that "actual physical" rather than "fictitious legal" occupation was the mischief sought to be combated.[54] Mason, AAJA referred to the policy of "limited segregation for sanitary reasons" embraced by the Act, and averred that, where some personal prohibition had been imposed by legislation, the personal element could not be eliminated by the substitution of a company for the individual normally contemplated.[55] The Anjuman took this issue to the Privy Council in London, but the latter's advice to the King was substantially the same as the opinion of Solomon, ACJ, and the appeal failed.[56]

None the less, the issue did not die with this dispute, for a year later *Dadoo Ltd v Krugersdorp Municipal Council*[57] arose for decision. Dadoo, an Asian, had registered appellant company in 1915, whose

[49] 1919 AD 439, hereafter *Madrassa II.*
[50] His judgment is set out at 439–45 of the AD report.
[51] See 447–50.
[52] At 449.
[53] At 450.
[54] See 450–2.
[55] See 452–7. C G Maasdorp, JA and Wessels, AAJA concurred without comment.
[56] Reported in [1922] 1 AC 500, *per* Viscount Cave, at 502–6.
[57] 1920 AD 530.

objects were the acquisition of, and traffic in, landed property, and whose shares were held by Dadoo and another Asian. Dadoo Ltd then proceeded to purchase and receive transfer of two plots within respondent municipality, one of which was leased to Dadoo for business purposes, while the other was used by Dadoo (or his Asiatic manager) as a place of residence. On application from the Krugersdorp Municipality, the TPD[58] ordered the transfer of the titles to be set aside, on the basis that they had been registered *in fraudem legis*, and thus contrary to law. In reaching this conclusion, Wessels, J[59] embarked on a far-reaching inquiry into the social origins of the legislature's "real intention", so that nothing direct or indirect should be done to flout this, and he relied heavily on the judgment of J A J de Villiers, JP in *Madrassa II.*

On appeal, Greenberg, for Dadoo Ltd,[60] challenged the Town Council's *locus standi*, and argued that, if it had standing, there had been no breach of the law, as the land had been transferred to a company. He also appealed for a strict construction of the Acts, as they constituted class legislation, and he warned against a confusion of what was actually or virtually prohibited, with what was really beyond the purview though within the policy of a statute. Tindall, counsel for the Municipal Council, relied[61] on the analogy provided by *Madrassa II.* It is important to note that *Dadoo* was concerned with ownership of fixed property, whereas *Madrassa* turned on the question of Asian occupation, because ownership does not imply physical presence of the owner on the property, which seems to have been the crux of the discrimination.

Innes, CJ handed down the leading judgment for the AD,[62] in which he differed from the provincial division and allowed the appeal. He did not need to deal with the question of the Council's *locus standi*, as he based his opinion on the alleged illegality of Dadoo's flotation of the company. To determine whether this action had evaded the spirit of the law, the Chief Justice examined the limits and extent of the *in fraudem legis* doctrine in much detail. On the question of giving effect to legislative policy, Sir James said:[63]

> "A Judge has authority to interpret, but not to legislate, and he cannot do violence to the language of the lawgiver by placing on it a meaning of which it is not reasonably capable, in order to give effect to what he may think to be the policy or object of the particular measure."

He asked what was meant by the infringement of the spirit, rather than the letter, of a law: did this mean that there were two, equally valid enactments?[64]

[58] Wessels and Curlewis, JJ.
[59] His judgment is set out at 531–7 of the AD report.
[60] See 537–8.
[61] At 539.
[62] See 539–53.
[63] At 543.
[64] At 543–4.

Innes, CJ went on to consider the Roman and Roman-Dutch views of the *in fraudem legis* rule, and he concluded that a transaction would fall within this description when it was "designedly disguised so as to escape the provisions of the law, but [fell] in truth within these provisions".[65] As a result, he said, the words of the law-giver should be read in the light of its intention to be gathered from the enactment as a whole, and from a consideration of the mischief with which it dealt.[66] Notwithstanding this statement, the Chief Justice held that it was perfectly legitimate for parties genuinely to arrange their transactions so as to "remain outside" the operation of the law.[67] Applying these guidelines to *Dadoo*, there was nothing to indicate that the legislature had had companies in mind when it had passed the laws: if it had done so, he argued, difficulties would have arisen when the racial composition of a landholding company's shareholders changed from white to Asian.[68]

In addition, the Chief Justice observed that the Union Parliament had recently specifically acted to extend the prohibition on ownership of fixed property by Asians, which had originally been contained in Law 3, to all companies in which Asians had a controlling interest.[69] The failure by the 1885 Volksraad to enact such a provision indicated that companies had not been within their brief, and he reminded the Council that a company was a legal *persona* distinct from its members.[70] In contrast with earlier attitudes, Innes, CJ cited the "wholesome rule of law" which required a strict construction of statutory provisions which interfered with elementary rights,[71] in support of his decision here.

Solomon, JA also expressed his opinion at some length[72] and he followed the Chief Justice in most respects. He advocated great caution in speculation by a Court as to legislative intent, and paid his respects to the rule that a statute which encroached on rights should be strictly rather than liberally interpreted.[73] He took the *in fraudem legis* doctrine to mean that the law looked at the substance, rather than the form, of a transaction,[74] and, like Innes, CJ, he was perturbed by the possible problems consequent upon a change in the race of shareholders of a company.[75] Unlike the Chief Justice, though, Solomon, JA clearly expressed his regret at feeling compelled to arrive at a "far from satisfactory" result.[76]

[65] At 547.
[66] *Loc cit.*
[67] At 548.
[68] At 549.
[69] See Asiatic Land and Trading (Transvaal) Amendment Act 37 of 1919.
[70] At 550.
[71] At 552.
[72] See 553–62.
[73] At 555.
[74] At 558.
[75] At 561.
[76] At 562.

It could not have come as a great surprise to the court[77] that J A J de Villiers, JA dissented from the majority judgment in this matter,[78] in the light of his views expressed in the provincial division in *Madrassa II*.[79] In seeking the *mens legis*, he maintained that the object of the laws in question had been to prevent coloured persons obtaining powers over the control and disposal of land, which would be contravened as much by the transfer of land to a company of Asiatics as to individual Asians.[80] He relied on precedent, which laid down that an Asian could not buy property through the interposition of a European,[81] for support for his contention that an Asian was similarly barred from acting through a juristic person, such as a company,[82] and he remarked that principles should not be overridden by rules of construction.[83]

For these reasons, *inter alia*, he held that the transactions of Dadoo Ltd had been *in fraudem legis*, and were null and void, though he said that he had come to such a conclusion with great diffidence, because the question was complicated, and he was in disagreement with his colleagues.[84] He complained that his duties in the TPD had not allowed him enough time to prepare his reasons fully.[85] He ended with a categorical rejection of the argument that respondent had no *locus standi*, a capacity which, he said, was founded in its ownership of land in the same area as Dadoo Ltd, and its responsiblity as a health authority.[86]

It is difficult to determine why the AD should have been moved to allow this appeal, in the light of *Madrassa II* and the recent enactment by the Union Parliament, which clearly showed that the judges, despite their disclaimers, were moving against broad legislative intent in 1920. The composition of the Bench cannot be regarded as of major significance, for each of the judges had formed part of the majority in one, or both, of the *Madrassa* decisions.[87]

It is likely that legal principles such as the sanctity of ownership of property, when divorced from questions of occupation, and the status of a company in commercial law were significant forces which moved the majority in *Dadoo*. An additional spur to the court was the knowledge that the Legislature had already put paid to any widespread future use of the loophole in the existing law, so that their

[77] C G Maasdorp and Juta, JJA concurred in the majority judgment without further comment.
[78] See 562–74.
[79] *Supra*, at note 50.
[80] At 565–6.
[81] *Lucas' Trustee v Ismail and Amod* 1905 TS 239.
[82] At 569.
[83] At 571.
[84] At 573.
[85] At 573–4.
[86] At 574.
[87] Solomon and C G Maasdorp, JJA had sat in both *Madrassa* cases on appeal, while J A J de Villiers, JP had heard both cases in the TPD; Innes, CJ and Juta, JA had been on the Bench in the first *Madrassa* appeal.

decision would have had a limited effect in practice. Perhaps, though, the majority attitude is an example of the liberal side of the judicial character, moving against the general drift of ruling opinion in the country.

Any hopes about a more lenient dispensation in this area were dashed emphatically by the next two cases in this category which came before the AD. Both of these involved an interpretation of the Asiatic Land and Trading Amendment Act (Transvaal) of 1919. As has been seen, this Act applied the property-ownership prohibitions to companies in which members of the "non-white" races had a controlling interest, with the proviso that the terms of Law 3 should be applied to property "acquired" before 1 May 1919, as if the 1919 Act did not exist.

The Transvaal Investment Co Ltd, a private company with two Asian shareholders, purchased certain land within Springs Municipality in February 1919, but it only gained transfer of title on 30 June of that year, which was four days before Act 37 came into force. Springs Municipality had obtained an order from the TPD[88] directing the company to sell the land, but the latter took the dispute to the court of appeal,[89] where its counsel[90] argued that it had gained a right to acquire the property by 1 May, which should be preserved.

The judges of appeal unanimously rejected this argument, but four of them were moved to give their reasons for this decision, a possible indication of the difficulty of the problem. Innes, CJ[91] recognised the retrospective character of the Act, which the court would normally try to avoid, he said, unless legislative intent was clear in this regard, as here.[92] He had given much thought to appellant's contention that the proviso (in respect of property acquired before 1 May 1919) would have been unnecessary if "acquired" was to be interpreted as the acquisition of full *dominium* in the property, because land ownership had not been prohibited before 1919.[93] Nevertheless, it seemed to the Chief Justice that a more reasonable explanation for the insertion was Parliament's reluctance to influence the hearing of several court cases in progress at the time (such as *Dadoo*).[94] He agreed that the policy of the Act was harsh; but that was no consideration for a court of law if there had been a clear expression of legislative intent, he said.[95]

Solomon, JA[96] thought that appellant's claim was "perfectly legitimate", and he reminded the court that it was a "well-established

[88] Stratford, J.
[89] *Transvaal Investment Co Ltd v Springs Municipality* 1922 AD 337.
[90] J P R van Hoytema, KC, at 338–9.
[91] See 340–5.
[92] At 341.
[93] At 342.
[94] At 344.
[95] At 345.
[96] See 345–51.

rule of construction" that, where two statutory interpretations were possible, that one which did not take away existing rights should be preferred.[97] But, after a consideration of the circumstances which gave rise to Act 37 of 1919,[98] he decided that the protection of the right to ownership would be contrary to its whole object. J A J de Villiers, JA added little which was new in his judgment,[99] although he laid stress[100] on the provision in the Act which allowed land to be sold within two years, if it had been transferred between 1 May and 3 July 1919. Mason, AJA proceeded along the same lines,[101] and concluded that the "direct and unqualified enactment" that fixed property acquired after 1 May should be sold within two years could not fairly be restricted to properties the rights of acquisition to which were obtained subsequent to that date.[102]

In this way, the AD showed that it would not countenance even a limited evasion of the stringency of Act 37. This approach was borne out in *Transvaal Arcade Ltd v Rand Townships Registrar*,[103] in which Innes, CJ held that the provisions of the Act applied to companies in which Cape Malays had a controlling interest.[104] He did so, despite the fact that the Deeds Registrar in Pretoria was allowing the transfer of land registered in the name of Cape Malays, and that the effect of this case was to place Cape Malays in a worse position than that of blacks as regards ownership of land.[105] Even though this was patently at odds with South African social custom, Innes, CJ yet again maintained that only Parliament could supply relief.[106]

Application of Statutes after 1925

The 1919 Act seemed to put a stop to the use of companies by Asians to own land, but *Mahomed & Son Ltd v Estate Horvitch*[107] illustrates a further method by which a company owned by Asians tried to gain control over fixed property, albeit unsuccessfully. The Act had outlawed any registration of a mortgage bond over fixed property in favour of an Asian, otherwise than as security for a *bona fide* loan or investment in the ordinary course of business.[108] Appellant company had entered into a detailed agreement with Horvitch, the effect of which had been to "lend" the latter a sum of money, secured by a mortgage bond, in return for the supreme rights of control and disposal of land belonging to Horvitch, but with no

[97] At 347.
[98] At 348–9.
[99] See 351–4.
[100] At 354.
[101] See 354–60.
[102] At 360. Juta, JA concurred silently.
[103] 1923 AD 442.
[104] See 444–9 with the concurrence of Solomon, J A J de Villiers, Kotzé, and Wessels, JJA.
[105] Which he acknowledged at 448.
[106] At 449.
[107] 1928 AD 1.
[108] Act 37 of 1919, section 2.

mention of a date of repayment of the "loan", though a date had been fixed in the "bond".

Unfortunately for appellant, Horvitch became insolvent, and when the company attempted to file a preferent claim in his estate, it was rebuffed by a ruling from the TPD to the effect that the bond was invalid under the Act.[109] Stratford, JA dismissed the appeal on behalf of the AD,[110] on the basis that, apart from the history of the transaction, the agreement did not constitute a loan, since the money had never to be repaid and had obviously passed as consideration for control of the property.[111] This being the case, he regarded the insertion of a repayment clause in the bond as an attempt to give it the appearance of one passed to secure a loan, with the result that the bond was invalid.[112]

Notwithstanding the general impression of judicial support for legislative moves to stamp out Asian land interests in the Transvaal, there were a few instances in which the AD stood firmly against the extension of such prohibitions. The 1908 Gold Law[113] provided that "no coloured person shall be permitted to reside on proclaimed land in districts comprised in class A, except in bazaars, locations, mining compounds . . .". "Proclaimed land" was defined as land proclaimed a public digging, and the town of Springs was situated on such land in a mining district comprised in class A, with no bazaars, locations, or mining compounds within its bounds. Moosa, an Indian, lived in the town, and the Town Council sought an interdict from the WLD[114] to prohibit his further residence and eject him from his plot. This action was dismissed on the ground that restricted effect should be given to an unjust enactment, and that the Council lacked *locus standi.*[115]

In *Town Council of Springs v Moosa & another,*[116] the AD rejected an appeal against this decision. J A J de Villiers, ACJ spoke for the court[117] when he stated that the Gold Law prohibition did not apply to Springs because the town was on "improved land" on which no prospecting or digging had been allowed before 1908.[118] Admittedly, the Gold Law of that year had vested in the Crown the right to mine metals underneath such "improved land", but the Act as a whole clearly showed that the Legislature had not intended that people should be disturbed except for mineral exploitation.[119] He also observed that the extensive powers granted to the Mining Commis-

[109] See the judgments of De Waal, JP and Greenberg, J at 2–9 of the AD report.
[110] See 10–15 concurred in by Solomon, CJ; Wessels and Curlewis, JJA.
[111] At 13.
[112] At 14–15.
[113] Act 35 of 1908 (Transvaal), section 131(1).
[114] Krause, J.
[115] See 401–9 of AD report.
[116] 1929 AD 401.
[117] See 411–17.
[118] At 412.
[119] At 413.

sioner were in no way consonant with the needs of town life, and represented a marked departure from previous policy in this matter.[120]

For De Villiers, ACJ, Parliament had not intended "improved land" which fell under the 1908 Gold Law to be hit by all its provisions which governed "proclaimed land", including those which banned black and coloured residence.[121] As he said:[122] "An interpretation clause has its uses, but it also has its dangers, as it is obvious from the present case. To adhere to the definition regardless of subject matter and context might work the gravest injustice by including cases which were not intended to be included." Thus was Moosa's right to occupation of his land upheld,[123] and the effect of the Gold Law prohibition on coloured residence territorially curtailed.

A second case in which the AD acted resolutely to quash an action by local government in excess of its authority was *Wing Lee Ltd v Johannesburg City Council.*[124] Here, respondent refused to renew appellant's trading licence on the ground that the business would be under the control of a Chinese person, whereas the business premises were under a prohibition as to coloured occupancy.[125] The validity of this condition was, however, in dispute, because of alleged waiver and acquiescence. Curlewis, JA[126] decided that the Council had exceeded its jurisdiction in refusing to grant the renewal, and that it should be directed to re-hear appellant's application.

The AD ultimately confronted and resolved the issue of the existence of *locus standi in judicio* on the part of the local authority to act to enforce conditions prohibitive of Asian land interests, which it had side-stepped on a number of occasions,[127] in *Roodepoort-Maraisburg Town Council v Eastern Properties (Prop) Ltd.*[128] In this instance, appellant local authority had applied to the WLD for an order directing respondent company, which owned six plots in its area, to eject coloured people from certain of these plots, and interdicting such use of the land in the future. Greenberg, J granted the order requested, but this had been overturned on appeal to the TPD,[129] on the ground that the Council, although the owner of 35 stands in the township, had no *locus standi* to bring the action.

In Bloemfontein, two points of law were considered by the court of appeal: the existence of *locus standi*, and the application of the

[120] At 414.
[121] At 416.
[122] At 417.
[123] Wessels and Curlewis, JJA concurred.
[124] 1931 AD 45.
[125] By the General Dealers (Control) Ordinance 12 of 1926 (Transvaal), section 6(2).
[126] See 49–60. J A J de Villiers, CJ and Wessels, JA concurred in this judgment.
[127] See *Madrassa II, Dadoo*, and *Moosa, supra*.
[128] 1933 AD 87.
[129] Barry, Solomon, and Grindley-Ferris, JJ.

prohibition against coloured occupancy, imposed by the Gold Law of 1908,[130] on the plots owned by respondent company. The title deeds of these plots did not contain such a prohibition, and two of them were not marked on the original township plan, but had been granted under different statutes.[131] The issue of *locus standi* dominated the proceedings, the Town Council claiming it as the owner of plots, and, as the local authority, as the supervisor of health and sanitation, and the repesentative and guardian of the interests of the township's inhabitants.[132]

Stratford, JA[133] relied on precedent[134] to adopt as settled law the proposition that, where the Legislature had prohibited the doing of an act in the interests of a person or class, the latter could obtain the intervention of the court to enforce the prohibition without proof of special damage.[135] As the judge held that it was manifestly in the interests of other stand-holders to prevent coloured occupancy, he agreed with Greenberg, J that the appellant, on the basis of ownership of land, had sufficient interest to seek compliance with the law.[136] On the question of the two plots which were not on the original township plan, Stratford, JA was moved by the clear words and context of the statute to decide that they, too, were hit by the prohibition because they fell within the boundaries of the township.[137]

Wessels, CJ added his opinion[138] on the *locus standi* question with these words: "[A]ny person can bring an action to vindicate a right which he possesses . . . whatever that right may be and whether he suffers special damage or not, provided he can show that he has a direct interest in the matter and not merely the interest which all citizens have." Beyers, JA[139] set great store by ZAR state policy of distinction between white and coloured. He sought support in Roman-Dutch rather than English law in pointing out that his concurrence in the judgment did not mean that *locus standi* could be based only on ownership of stands. In this way the AD[140] showed itself willing to implement a segregation policy which gave full expression to the race prejudice of whites, both historic and current.

Yet, it seems as if, in matters not entirely dissimilar, the judges were prepared to adjust their attitudes to changing circumstances, as the next two cases show. Both disputes concerned the regulations

[130] Section 130.
[131] Law 15 of 1898 (ZAR), section 92, dealt with by the Townships Act 34 of 1908 (Transvaal), section 13(2).
[132] See 93–4.
[133] See 92–101.
[134] *Patz v Greene and Co* 1907 TS 427, and *Madrassa I, supra.*
[135] At 95–6.
[136] At 98.
[137] At 100.
[138] At 101–2.
[139] See 102–4.
[140] Curlewis and J E R de Villiers, JJA concurred here.

passed by the Executive Council of the ZAR in 1895 to govern the Malay location in Johannesburg. Regulation 8 prohibited the sub-lease of any stand, while regulation 22 provided a penalty for a contravention of any of the "foregoing regulations".

In *Hatch v Koopoomal*,[141] appellant was a European businessman who had taken a lease on a stand in the Malay location which had itself been hired from the Municipality by respondent, an Asian. Koopoomal had originally failed in an action for rent due from Hatch in the magistrate's court, on the ground of the illegality of the lease, but the TPD reversed this decision.[142] In his appeal, Hatch relied on the illegality of the agreement of lease in terms of the regulations, among other arguments. Koopoomal's chief reply was that, on a true construction of the regulations, sub-letting was not prohibited where the local authority had consented to or acquiesced in such a practice, which, she claimed, was the case here.

Curlewis, JA[143] dealt with this contention by saying that there was insuffcent evidence to justify a conclusion that the lease between the litigants had the approval or consent of the Municipality, even though the latter acquiesced in leases between Asians.[144] He would willingly have applied the principle of interpretation (that legislative intent should be effected, rather than its plain language which led to absurdity) because of the hardships consequent upon an adverse judgment for Koopoomal, but he regretted that the clear language here led to no such illogicality.[145] On the basis of the regulations alone, the appeal had to succeed, and the "lease" was declared null and void, as it was contrary to the spirit of the law, regulations, and public policy.

Beyers[146] and J E R de Villiers,[147] JJA added short passages indicating their agreement with Curlewis, JA but Stratford, JA dissented.[148] He differed from the majority in a crucial respect, he said, because he regarded the making of a criminal out of every licensee who attempted to sub-let his stand (the natural outcome of the application of regulation 22 to regulation 8) as repugnant and absurd.[149] For Stratford, JA there was all the difference in the world between restricting a man's legal right to do something, and forbidding him to do the same,[150] and he would have dismissed the appeal.

This difference of opinion was to prove important three years later, in *Jajbhay v Cassim*,[151] when four new colleagues had joined Stratford

[141] 1936 AD 190.
[142] Tindall and Maritz, JJ.
[143] See 194–206.
[144] At 203.
[145] At 204–5.
[146] See 210–12.
[147] See 212.
[148] See 206–10.
[149] At 208.
[150] At 209.
[151] 1939 AD 537.

on the AD.[152] Jajbhay, the registered holder of a stand licence in the Johannesburg Malay location, had sub-let his stand to Cassim, which was illegal (as had been established in *Hatch*). All had gone smoothly until Jajbhay attempted to obtain an order from the TPD[153] for the ejection of Cassim from occupation of the stand, on the basis that the illegality of the sub-lease entitled Jajbhay to reclaim possession of the property.

Stratford, CJ[154] used the opportunity to give expression to his ideas on the whole topic of illegal or immoral contracts, a problem which, he felt, was dealt with satisfactorily nowhere in the world. He discussed the Roman roots of the two maxims "*ex turpi causa non oritur actio*" and "*in pari delicto potior est conditio defendentis*"; deplored the state of English law in this respect;[155] and then said:[156]

> "Now the Roman-Dutch Law, which we must apply, is a living system capable of growth and development to allow adaptation to the increasing complexities and activities of modern civilised life. The instruments of that development are our own courts of law. In saying that, of course I do not mean that it is permissible for a court of law to alter the law; its function is to elucidate, expound and apply the law. But it would be idle to deny that in the process of the exercise of those functions rules of law are slowly and beneficially evolved. That evolution, to be proper, must come from, and be in harmony with, sound first principles which are binding upon us."

Chief Justice Stratford followed this remarkably frank exposition of his attitude to the law and judicial role by divining the moral principle behind the two Roman maxims as the will to "discourage illegality and immòrality and advance public policy".[157] Here the court was concerned with the *in pari delicto* rule, and he reviewed the use of the maxim, and exceptions thereto, in English, American, French, and South African law.[158] He emphasised the equitable side of the judge's function,[159] and concluded that ". . . in cases where public policy is not foreseeably affected by a grant or a refusal of the relief claimed, . . . a Court . . . might well decide in favour of doing justice between the individuals concerned, and so prevent unjust enrichment".[160] For this reason, he was for dismissing Jajbhay's appeal.

Watermeyer, JA also went into some detail in his judgment,[161] in which he asserted that the courts would discourage illegal transactions, ". . . but the exceptions show that where it is necessary to prevent injustice or to promote public policy, it will not rigidly

[152] One of whom, Tindall, had been on the Bench in the TPD in *Hatch*.
[153] Murray, J rejected this claim.
[154] See 540–5.
[155] At 540–1.
[156] At 542.
[157] *Loc cit.*
[158] At 543.
[159] *Loc cit.*
[160] At 545.
[161] See 545–57.

enforce the general rule".[162] Tindall[163] and Centlivres,[164] JJA added brief concurrences in support of the Chief Justice, while De Wet, JA agreed without comment.

This case is important for other reasons,[165] but it adds to the present discussion, as it shows that the AD was prepared to give sensible recognition to the actual situation concerning sub-letting in the Malay location, albeit between two coloured people. But, on a wider front, the statements of the judges, and particularly those of the Chief Justice, on the adaptability of Roman-Dutch law and the importance of equity and public policy in judicial decision-making, provide proof of their awareness of, and willingness to act in accordance with, such factors. The absence of such a response under different conditions gives a clue, perhaps, to their institutional and personal priorities.

The restrictions on Asian rights to own land gave rise to two further cases before 1950. In both of these, one of the parties tried to withdraw from an agreement of sale and purchase of fixed property on the ground of the other party's status as an Indian. In *Collin v Toffie*,[166] no final result could be achieved because of the non-joinder of the State in the action, where its proprietary interests were concerned.[167] And in *Corondimas & another v Badat*,[168] the narrow meaning given to the word "acquire" in *Transvaal Investment Co Ltd v Springs Municipality* was widened, in order to uphold the validity of an agreement of sale of land subject to a suspensive condition.[169] This decision once more displays the AD's expertise in moulding the meaning of words so as to arrive at an equitable outcome in private law, which here meant that a European was prevented from relying on an Indian's inferior legal status to escape from his contractual obligations.

Restrictive Conditions in Contracts

The litigation discussed thus far has turned upon statutory prohibitions against Asian interest in land, but these did not comprise the only barrier to Asians acquiring such interests, formidable though they were. The developers of many private townships in the Transvaal inserted a clause into the contracts of sale of their plots, which stipulated that there could be no transfer to, nor lease of, such freehold property to any Asian person. Inevitably, legal disputes

[162] At 550.
[163] See 558.
[164] See 558–9.
[165] See, for example, the comments of L B Behrmann in (1946) 63 *SALJ* 40, and Coote "Another Look at *Bowmakers v Barnet Instruments*" (1972) 35 *Modern Law Review* 38.
[166] 1944 AD 456.
[167] Judgment of Tindall, JA, see 460–9, with whom Watermeyer, CJ; Centlivres and Feetham, JJA; and Davis, AJA concurred.
[168] 1946 AD 548.
[169] Judgments of Watermeyer, CJ, see 550–2, and Feetham, AJA, see 552–62. Tindall, Greenberg, and Schreiner, JJA concurred.

arose from the attempted evasion of these conditions, and three cases which reached Bloemfontein will be set out briefly, in order to isolate any divergence from the judicial approach which has become apparent above.

The first time that the Asian land question ever confronted the AD was in *Alexander v Johns*.[170] Here, Johns owned a stand under freehold title, on condition that he should not "suffer or allow" the lease of the proprty to any "Arab, Malay, Chinaman, Coolie, Indian, or other coloured person". What he had done, was to let the property to another European, L, without notification of this condition; whereupon L had sub-let to an Indian, M, on exactly the same day. Alexander, a European who owned a plot in the same township, applied to the WLD[171] for an interdict against M's continued occupation of the stand, and against Johns's toleration of this course of events. The former was granted, but the court held that Johns had not been guilty of collusion in the matter.

On appeal against this decision, the issue of Alexander's *locus standi* to bring the action was raised by Johns. Innes, ACJ[172] asserted that each contract with an owner of land in the township was made for the benefit of the holders of other plots, so that Alexander was entitled to enforce the condition. In addition, he found on the evidence that Johns had connived at the transactions, so that an interdict against such practices should be granted against him, too.

The stipulation in the lease which is of interest in *Witwatersrand Township Estate and Finance Corporation Ltd v Ritch*[173] was of a slightly different complexion. Here, it was provided that the lessee should not allow "coloured persons, other than domestic servants, to live or dwell on the stand", for the violation of which the lease could be forfeited. Ritch had, since 1904, leased a stand to C, an Indian, who traded from it, and who required one of his (Indian) assistants to sleep on the premises, in the aftermath of two robberies (or so he claimed). Appellant had sued Ritch unsuccessfully in the WLD[174] for a declaration that the lease be declared null and void, and that he be ejected.

On appeal, there was evidence of dancing and entertaining on the premises, and of three Indians sleeping above the shop, while C maintained that his assistants took their meals and kept their clothes at his own house. Lord De Villiers, CJ[175] thought that the Indians' sleeping on the premises raised a very strong presumption that they also resided there, which, he felt, was strengthened by the evidence of

[170] 1912 AD 431.
[171] Bristowe, J. See 433–8 of the AD report.
[172] See 441–6. Solomon, J concurred silently, while C G Maasdorp, JP added some thoughts on the subject at 446–8.
[173] 1913 AD 423.
[174] Ward, J.
[175] See 426–7.

entertainment and treatment for illness at the shop, and so he was for upholding the appeal. Solomon, J[176] stated that the ordinary meaning of "live or dwell" was where a person habitually slept, and he expressed interest in the contents of the employee's wardrobe. For, he remarked,[177] "[i]f he had consulted his convenience, he certainly would have kept his clothes at the same place where he slept, unless of course, his change of clothing was such a very rare act that it made little difference to him where they were kept"—a rare touch of sardonic comment from a normally impassive judge. After a methodical review of the evidence, Solomon, J decided that the employee had in fact "dwelt" above the shop, and J A J de Villiers, JP joined in this opinion.[178]

This reading of the facts does not seem altogether surprising in the context of the rest of the cases in this field, but it is placed in a different light when another aspect of this case is taken into account. For Ritch was also accused of allowing breach of a prohibition against opening or allowing on his plot "any store or place containing explosives". Notwithstanding the apparent ambiguity in this phrase, all three judges held that the keeping of explosives was the mischief aimed at, rather than the opening of trading activity, so that Ritch was not in breach of the condition.[179] Thus, the court was prepared to tolerate commercial activity, even if carried on by an Indian, but not the sleeping overnight of an Indian employee of that business. This gives some idea of judicial priorities.

The final case in this category ties in with *Wing Lee Ltd*, in that the same contractual prohibition *viz* "no coloured person other than servants will be allowed to occupy the lot", was at the root of the dispute in each. In *Norwood Land and Investment Co Ltd & another v North Eastern Districts Association (Propy) Ltd*,[180] the appellant was a company composed entirely of Asians, which had leased a lot, subject to the above conditions, upon which it carried on business as a general dealer. The company's managing director and sales manager, both coloured, resided on the premises with their families. This practice induced respondent to seek, and obtain, a court order[181] restraining the company from allowing such occupation to continue. The company appealed against this decision on the ground that its employees were "servants" within the meaning of the condition, and so were permitted to reside on the stand.

Stratford, JA[182] stated the question for decision as being a choice between a wide meaning (anyone subject to the orders of another) or

[176] See 428–30.
[177] At 429.
[178] See 430–2.
[179] See Lord De Villiers, CJ at 426, and agreement by Solomon, J and De Villiers, JP, both at 430.
[180] 1929 AD 32.
[181] From the WLD, *per* Greenberg, J.
[182] See 34–6.

the ordinary meaning (menial and domestic) of the word "servant", which had to be made with an eye on the objects of those who drew up the prohibition.[183] He then presented a vivid picture of the realities of South African life, as he saw them, as follows:[184]

> "Anyone having experience of life in South Africa will readily realise that the total exclusion of the coloured domestic servant from residence on or occupation of the lots would have made the lots unsaleable. For it is notorious that domestic and menial service is generally performed in this country by coloured persons and only very rarely by white persons. . . . Broadly speaking . . . coloured persons do not render services of a higher order to the white. They are not employed by the white as directors of companies, or managers of businesses, and in my judgment the remote probability of such employment was not present to the minds of the makers of these leases."

For these reasons, Stratford, JA "unhesitatingly" adopted the restricted meaning of "servants", and dismissed the appeal.[185] There are few statements in this area which show more clearly how the judges shared the contemporary attitudes of the average white South African to those regarded as coloured.

Summary and Conclusions

A review of the eighteen cases noted above produces a pattern similar to that seen in the group concerned with Indian immigration. Most of the land disputes occurred in the first half of the period under discussion, though the issue continued to be raised at intervals almost to 1950. A remarkable aspect of the reported litigation is that more than one judgment was delivered in two-thirds of the cases, of which only two were dissenting opinions.[186] This is a very high proportion, which points, perhaps, to the intricacy of the problems faced by the judges, as well as the existence of different reasons for arriving at the same result, which they wished to place on record.

Another noticeable feature of the appeals in this field is the extent to which the AD was prepared to disagree with the conclusions reached by the courts *a quo*, and to overrule them. Almost half the appellants were successful, which indicates the fluidity and ambiguity of the legal framework in this area. It seems, too, as though the court was more reluctant to preserve the social *status quo* than it had been on questions of immigration,[187] although it did so in all three cases in which private contractual rights were at stake.

As for the judges themselves, nineteen were involved in at least one of the cases dealt with, though naturally the earlier judges heard the bulk of the disputes.[188] There was no apparent break from the

[183] At 34.
[184] At 35–6. [185] At 36.
[186] J A J de Villiers, JA in *Dadoo*, and Stratford, JA in *Hatch supra*.
[187] This conclusion is reached by determining whether the outcome of an appeal tended to conform with or oppose the interests of the ruling authorities. According to this measuring device, the *status quo* was disturbed by 44 per cent of appeals on Asian land questions, compared with the figure of 25 per cent of immigration cases.
[188] Roos, Van den Heever, Hoexter, and Fagan were the exceptions.

previously-noted tendency for the senior judge on the Bench to deliver the decision of the court, with the result that Innes, Solomon, and J A J de Villiers were prominent in most of the cases in which they were on the Bench. However, the level of participation of Stratford, and, to a lesser extent, Beyers is worthy of interest.[189]

Despite the partial reluctance to support the existing order which has been referred to above, there can be little doubt that the overall approach of the AD was largely in sympathy with the legislative objectives of residential segregation and disqualification from land-ownership by Indians. Only four cases give evidence of a limited rejection of this policy,[190] and one or two comments show open support for it.[191] When it was necessary to justify a particular result, the judges resorted to the use of appropriate canons of construction, especially that which decrees a strict interpretation of a statute which removes rights.[192]

The shift in judicial attitudes which took place in the three years between *Hatch* and *Jajbhay* pays ample tribute to the judicial capacity to recognise the need to adapt the law to changed social practices.[193] But it likewise highlights the court's reluctance to act similarly when other interests were at stake. The part played by Stratford in the above change in the AD's opinion is significant, as his dissenting treatment in *Hatch* became substantially the unanimous verdict in *Jajbhay*. His involvement as counsel in *Gandur* and *Madrassa I* may have given him a particular knowledge of, and interest in, the issues.

In order to situate the consideration of Asian interests in land in the Transvaal in its proper context, it is useful to have a brief look at the legal disputes which turned on the presence of another disadvantaged group, black South Africans, in urban areas. A review of the relatively small number of cases in this field which reached the AD provides a glimpse of the type of problems and conditions encountered by blacks, and the way in which the judges of appeal handled them.

Blacks in Urban Areas

The status of blacks[194] in urban areas was initially governed by several pre-Union pass laws,[195] which were brought together in a

[189] Both Stratford and Beyers handed down judgments in every case which they heard in this category.

[190] See *Ritch & Bhyat, Dadoo, Moosa* and *Wing Lee supra.*

[191] See remarks of Lord De Villiers and Solomon in *Gandur*; Kotzé in *Madrassa I*; Solomon in *Dadoo*; and Beyers in *Roodepoort–Maraisburg Town Council supra.*

[192] See Solomon in *Ritch & Bhyat, Dadoo*, and *Transvaal Investment Company*; and Innes in *Dadoo supra.*

[193] As does *Corondimas supra.*

[194] More commonly called "natives" in the period of this study. The terms will be used in accordance with their context here.

[195] For example, The Native Passes Proclamation 37 of 1901 (Transvaal); Coloured People in Towns and Villages Law 8 of 1893 (OFS); Cape and Natal statutes concerning local government, public health, and vagrancy.

Union statute, the Natives (Urban Areas) Act of 1923.[196] This Act laid down general guidelines for the supervision and control of blacks in towns and cities, but it lodged much responsibility for its implementation with the local authorities involved.[197]

One of the first questions which the AD had to face arose out of the fact that coloureds, Asians, and natives had often been grouped together for residential purposes in the past. Now the Urban Areas Act provided for the setting up of "locations"[198] for natives, but it permitted the continued presence of coloureds within the bounds of such townships.[199] In *Molife v Superintendent of Locations & another*,[200] appellant native had bought the rights under a site permit in a native location from a coloured person. Unfortunately for Molife, the land in respect of which the site permit had been issued was in the part of the location which the Pretoria Town Council had set aside for coloured occupation. As a result, when he sought respondent's permission for the transfer of the site permit to his name, his application was refused on the basis of this policy. Barry, J in chambers granted an order directing registration of the site permit in his name, but the TPD[201] overruled this decision, and Molife came to Bloemfontein on appeal.

Roos, JA did not tarry long in dismissing this appeal,[202] after he had considered a preliminary point.[203] He held that the superintendent had a very wide discretion in terms of the regulations, and that he had acted reasonably and in accordance with policy in this instance.[204] This matter-of-fact acceptance of the setting up of separate locations for natives was evident in three later cases[205] which involved people found residing in areas set aside for other races under the Act. Different groups of appeal judges implemented legislative policy without question on these occasions.

A natural outcome of the policy that all natives should live in a solely native location was that those natives who were resident outside should be required to move within the location's limits. The Act[206] empowered the local authority to remove a native from his dilapidated or insanitary dwelling, but such an action had to be

[196] 21 of that year.

[197] Although a location superintendent was appointed by the local authority concerned, his issuing of site permits in accordance with municipal regulations was held by the AD to be the performance of a statutory duty and not subject to local control. See *Tshandu v Swan & another* 1946 AD 10, *per* Tindall, JA, 14–28.

[198] A "location" was the word commonly used to describe an area set aside for the residence of natives, and will be so used here.

[199] Section 4(3)*(a)*.

[200] 1931 AD 19.

[201] Tindall, Greenberg, and Solomon, JJ.

[202] See 23–7 concurred in by J A J de Villiers, CJ; Wessels and Curlewis, JJA.

[203] The origin of the Pretoria location, at 24.

[204] At 26–7.

[205] *R v Kostas* 1932 AD 138; *Ex parte Minister of Justice: In re R v Anderjas* 1938 AD 411; and *R v Singh* 1945 AD 108.

[206] Natives (Urban Areas) Amendment Act 25 of 1930, section 18(1)(*a*).

accompanied by an offer of "other adequate housing accommodation at the rent and on the conditions prescribed in respect thereof. . ." in the same or another location. The AD had to decide the meaning of this provision in *R v Manchengeza*,[207] because the accused had failed to move in accordance with the order of the local Medical Officer of Health.

On appeal, Manchengeza argued that the phrase "in respect thereof" in the section referred to his old house, and that he was not obliged to move because the new rent he would be required to pay was almost twice that of his former dwelling. Roos, JA[208] had no doubt that the phrase in fact referred to the new accommodation, and that the local authority was entitled to act on grounds of public health, even if this resulted in the closure of an entire township, as here.[209] On this basis, he confirmed Manchengeza's conviction and sentence of a fine.

A slightly different set of circumstances was presented to the court some years later in *R v Nkonyane*,[210] where the appellant had been convicted and fined for a refusal to move into the Piet Retief native location. However, in this case Nkonyane contended that the Crown had failed to prove that "reasonably adequate" accommodation existed for him in the location. The facts showed[211] that his former residence had been a fertile plot in the town, with a spring of water, and a lavatory attached to a four-roomed dwelling; whereas his location plot was one-eighth the area of the former, with no lavatory or water. The nearest water point was 144 yards away, while there were ten communal sanitary conveniences (each for five persons) for the 1 600 inhabitants.

Watermeyer, CJ agreed[212] that the location arrangement was not so comfortable or convenient, which might be a hardship; but, he claimed,[213] ". . . we are not concerned with the general policy of the Act; the only question which we have to consider is whether in the circumstances of this case the appellant was legally justified in failing to take up his residence in the location". As Nkonyane had not produced evidence that the accommodation was inadequate, his appeal failed, despite the long title of the Act, which mentioned that "improved conditions" for natives were contemplated.[214] This remarkable decision gives a clear illustration of the court's view of the needs and living standards of blacks.

A further aspect of this process of compelling blacks to move to a location came to the AD's attention in *Makubira v Benoni Municipal-*

[207] 1932 AD 67.
[208] See 67–70 with which Wessels, ACJ; Stratford, JA; and Hutton, AJA concurred.
[209] At 69.
[210] 1944 AD 489.
[211] See 491–2.
[212] See 490–3 with the concurrence of Tindall, Centlivres, and Feetham, JJA; and Davis, AJA.
[213] At 492.
[214] *Loc cit.*

ity.[215] Respondent local authority had a native location under its control, in respect of which it had issued regulations which forbade site occupation without a permit, as well as residence in a location dwelling by any person not in possession of a permit.[216] Makubira had been convicted for disobeying both these rules, but he argued on appeal that he had an absolute right to live in the location without a permit, after the issue of the proclamation[217] which had compelled his residence in the location. He claimed further that the requirement of a permit was inconsistent with the Act, as it had given an additional power to exclude a native from the location, and as it entailed a new procedure for the expulsion of natives from an urban area.

These contentions did not sway the court of appeal. Curlewis, ACJ[218] said that the clear object of the statute was segregation, but that the making of regulations necessarily implied some limitations on a native's right to live in a location, in accordance with which a permit system seemed a reasonable means of control.[219] He held that the regulations were, therefore, valid, and he dismissed the appeal.

However, on two other occasions the court did not regard regulations which governed location life so complacently. In *R v Majoro*,[220] appellant had been convicted of the offence of brewing, manufacturing, using or possessing "kaffir beer" without a permit in a location.[221] He attacked this finding on the basis that the regulations in terms of which he had been convicted were *ultra vires*, in that the Act merely empowered the Minister for Native Affairs to deal with the conditions under which householders might keep "kaffir beer".

Watermeyer, JA agreed with the argument,[222] and held that the regulation which had imposed penalties and prohibitions on persons other than householders was invalid. Thus he allowed Majoro's appeal, but Tindall, JA went further in his concurring judgment.[223] He would also have declared *ultra vires* another regulation,[224] which demanded that householders who sought a "beer permit" should pass a personal fitness test. Tindall, JA could not support such a regulation, he said, inasmuch as the Act had contemplated that all householders should be entitled to brew and possess "kaffir beer". It should be noted here that blacks were not entitled to possess other forms of liquor at that time.[225]

[215] 1935 AD 313. [216] Regulations 22*(d)* and 24*(d)*.

[217] In terms of Act 21 of 1923, section 5(1).

[218] See 314–18 with the concurrence of Stratford, Beyers, and J E R de Villiers, JJA; and De Wet, AJA.

[219] At 316.

[220] 1938 AD 523.

[221] Regulation 5 of those issued by the Minister for Native Affairs under Act 21 of 1923, section 23(2)*(d)ter*.

[222] See 525–8 with which Stratford, CJ and De Wet, JA concurred.

[223] See 528–31.

[224] Regulation 2.

[225] Liquor Act 30 of 1928, section 94; and Natives (Urban Areas) Act 21 of 1923, section 19.

The second example of the invalidation of a location regulation occurred in *Johannesburg City Council v Makaya*,[226] and concerned the exercise of a slightly more serious power than the control of the use of beer. In this instance, appellant local authority had made a regulation[227] which empowered a magistrate, in the exercise of his criminal jurisdiction, to order the ejectment from a native location of a person whom he had found guilty of a failure to comply with an order of the superintendent to remove from the location. The City Council acted against Makaya under this regulation, whereupon he sought relief from the TPD,[228] which decided that the regulation was *ultra vires*, and set aside the ejectment order.

The court of appeal dismissed the City Council's attempt to upset this ruling. Greenberg, JA[229] looked at several possible sources to find the authority for a magisterial order of ejectment, but was bound by precedent, to the effect that a municipal council had no power "to confer jurisdiction or impose duties of any kind upon courts of law" unless Parliament had granted such a power.[230] The Council maintained that its power to make regulations for the management and control of locations, and for the entry into, and sojourn in, locations of persons not resident therein, was sufficient indication that it had the power to obtain ejectment. Greenberg, JA rejected this claim[231] on the grounds that similar provisions had granted the authority to eject specifically; that power to make regulations for summary ejectment had been dealt with elsewhere; and that the Legislature had provided for effectively high penalties already.

This case shows that the judges were not prepared to sanction the exercise of executive power which they regarded as in excess of statutory limits. One or two appeals, however, turned not on the validity of a regulation, but on the propriety of action taken in terms of a regulation. In a second case involving the Johannesburg City Council and Makaya,[232] the AD had to interpret the regulation which demanded that every person desirous of living in a location had to apply to the superintendent for a permit so to do, which the official was obliged to issue if satisfied that the applicant was a "fit and proper person".[233] Greenberg, JA[234] held that the questions to be taken into account in determining such a quality related solely to the applicant's personality, and that the availability of other suitable accommodation for the applicant was not a relevant factor here.[235]

[226] 1945 AD 252, hereafter *Makaya I*.
[227] Section 5*(b)*, Ch I of Native Location Regulations for the District of Johannesburg.
[228] Barry, JP and Ramsbottom, J.
[229] See 254–61 concurred in by Watermeyer, CJ; Tindall and Feetham, JJA; and Davis, AJA.
[230] At 256.
[231] At 257–9.
[232] *Johannesburg City Council v Makaya* 1948 (3) SA 468 (AD), hereafter *Makaya II*.
[233] Regulation 5*(a)* of the Johannesburg Native Location Regulations.
[234] See 474–80 concurred in by Tindall, ACJ; Centlivres and Schreiner, JJA; and Davis, AJA.
[235] At 478.

Yet, in more pressing circumstances, the court was more reluctant to find in favour of a homeless native. The requirements of industry and a shortage of workers during World War II attracted a large number of blacks to the industrial centres of South Africa, as a result of which the government passed a War Measure which empowered local authorities to establish emergency camps for the accommodation of the homeless.[236] The Johannesburg City Council set up such a camp, and issued rules for its control, one of which demanded a fee to cover rent of a site and provision of services in the camp.[237] Hleka, a site-permit holder in the camp, refused to pay this charge until he was provided with a house, for which behaviour he was convicted,[238] and sentenced to imprisonment with hard labour. His appeal to the TPD[239] had been turned down, and so he took his case to Bloemfontein.[240]

Hleka argued before the AD[241] that the rules were invalid on the ground that the provision of accommodation in the camp was a condition precedent to the issue of rules by the Council. Van den Heever, JA could not agree,[242] because the Governor-General, who had approved the rules, had practically unlimited powers under the War Measures Act.[243] In addition, he said,[244] the word "accommodation" was capable of a very wide range of meaning which depended on the context and circumstances: for it to mean "housing" here, the very objects of the regulation would be defeated. Van den Heever, JA rejected suggestions that the fee charged was too high, on the basis that the whole emergency camp enterprise was already running at a loss, and he showed more concern at the thought that civil obligations were being enforced by criminal sanctions.[245] Nevertheless, the possibility of the frustration of the scheme in the absence of criminal punishments was sufficient to convince him of their necessity in this situation.[246] In this way, the appeal was dismissed.

If these cases are compared with those discussed above in the sphere of Asian land tenure, several preliminary distinctions must be observed. All the cases concerned with blacks were heard in the second half of the period of this study, whereas the Indian cases tended to be concentrated in the first half. Therefore, it should not be a surprise to learn that only one judgment was given in each case, in accordance with trends noticed previously. Further, the difference in

[236] 18 of 1947, regulation 3(i).
[237] Rule 32.
[238] Under rule 31.
[239] Maritz, JP and De Wet, AJ.
[240] See *Hleka v Johannesburg City Council* 1949 (1) SA 842 (AD).
[241] Through his counsel, G Lowen, at 843–5.
[242] See 846–56 concurred in by Watermeyer, CJ; Centlivres, Greenberg, and Schreiner, JJA.
[243] 13 of 1940.
[244] At 850–3.
[245] At 854.
[246] At 855.

the character of issues which were raised on appeal is apparent,[247] and can be ascribed to the more humble socio-economic position occupied by blacks at that time.

Notwithstanding this divergence in certain respects, the cases in each category do display a few similar features. Most important of all must be the willing way in which the court implemented a harsh legislative policy without showing much concern for, or understanding of, the human consequences of the statutes. Secondly, the judges accepted, almost without question, the control of the lives of a substantial part of the population by way of administrative regulation. Thirdly, most of the cases once more came from the Transvaal,[248] which is probably due to vigorous application of the policy, and the greater urbanisation of blacks in that province. Fourthly, in a few cases the black litigant was successful in the AD,[249] as in the field of Indian land interests. Finally, two judges[250] were again prominent in terms of the frequency with which they spoke for the court when they were on the Bench.

So it seems that, despite some superficial dissimilarities, the treatment of Asians and blacks was very much the same when regard is had to judicial approach. The predominant aspects of this were an acceptance of legislative will, provided that the legal procedures had been observed, and a close identification with the race policy of the social élite.

[247] There being no disputes on actual ownership of land, nor on the conduct of commercial enterprises.

[248] The exceptions being *Anderjas* and *Manchengeza*.

[249] See *Majoro*, and *Makaya I* and *II*.

[250] Roos and Greenberg.

CHAPTER NINE

…ARY AND ASSESSMENT …DICIAL PERFORMANCE

The cases set out and discussed in the preceding chapters form the core of the broadly "political" issues which came before the AD from 1910 to 1950. As such, they comprise a solid foundation upon which to base a process of assessment and criticism. The purpose of such an exercise is to attempt to establish whether the South African appellate judiciary pursued a course in line with the sentiments and policies of the ruling group, or whether it strove to enhance the cause of justice and equality by modifying the effects of socially discriminatory facets of the law. As has been argued above,[1] such a course was an (admittedly narrow) option for the judiciary in 1910 and subsequently, the chief reasons for which were the generally liberal backgrounds of the judges, combined with the common-law emphasis on the equal treatment of all legal subjects. This being the case, it is important to reiterate the limitations which inhibit a study of this nature. Firstly, the somewhat artificial selection of cases which come on appeal, and the slightly rarefied air of appellate proceedings, can act to produce a picture not typical of wider judicial performance.[2] Thus, conclusions arrived at in respect of the AD cannot necessarily be extended to the provincial divisions, though the fact that most judges of appeal had considerable experience at provincial level partially counterbalances this trend to judicial isolation.

Secondly, the method of selection of the cases discussed raises the issue of subjectivity in research method. To this must be added the fact that those cases actually analysed, and on which evaluation is to be made, comprise only about one-eighth of all those reported between 1910 to 1950.[3] On the other hand, this is not an insignificant fraction, especially when it is remembered that the bulk of the disputes reported had a remote connection, if any, with wider questions of public importance. As a result, they provide scant insight into judicial approach to political affairs, and would not be usefully included here. Further, the dictates of space and coherence meant that an additional hundred or so cases which were concerned with "politics" have not been included, even though they were investigated in some detail.[4] It must be said, however, that this

[1] Ch I.

[2] Especially when it is realised that the vast majority of legal disputes are heard by magistrates.

[3] See Table VII below.

[4] These include cases concerning judicial attitudes to legislative and executive power, and the liability of state corporations.

additional body of material does not significantly alter the pattern established by those cases actually included.

Thirdly, the way in which the cases have been allotted to categories is, in a certain sense, a matter for debate. Some disputes could have been classified differently. But, as has been explained above, these groups arose, not from any preconceived framework, but as a result of the frequency of occurrence of certain types of dispute. It is unlikely that the allocation of a case to a class other than that to which it has in fact been assigned would cause any marked change in the general impression generated by the present arrangement.

With these cautionary remarks in mind, judicial performance can now be assessed.

The actions of individual judges during their tenure of the appellate Bench will be considered first. Then the conclusions about judicial activity and approach in the various sections will be combined and compared. Finally, an attempt will be made to establish a general evaluation of the court's role in society as a whole, in the light of social conditions, and the opinions of those who have spoken of such matters in the past.

Judges as Individuals

In looking at the record of the twenty-three men who acted as permanent members of the appellate Bench in the period 1910 to 1950, the fact that each sat in every case as just one participant in a corporate decision-making process is a consideration not to be ignored. The subtle pressures induced by the need for arriving at a decision acceptable to a majority of those hearing the case, as well as the influence exerted by the more senior and authoritative judges, would undeniably have led to a certain degree of compromise and bargaining on the Bench. The internal workings of the court in that period are beyond investigation and accurate speculation, but it is as well to keep this kind of intra-group relationship within focus when judicial careers are evaluated.

Nevertheless, something of value can be gained by examining in detail the participation of the appeal judges in the cases discussed above. A summary of their judicial activities is set out below in Tables V and VI, which need some elucidation and interpretation.

The purpose of Table V is to provide a barometer of each judge's actions within the sample of cases which he heard, and to indicate the categories into which his cases fell. Thus, to take Wessels as an example: he sat in 49 of the cases discussed, made up of five from the civil liberties field, one from resistance and rebellion, fifteen from industrial relations, and so on. He gave judgment on 22 occasions, on five of which he handed down the leading judgment; on ten of which he gave the only judgment for the court; on four of which he gave judgment which was in concurrence with at least one

TABLE V
Summary of Judicial Activity

Judge and Year of Appointment	*Number of Judgments*				*Total of:*		*Opinions as percentage of Cases*	*Cases by Category*					
	Leading	*Sole*	*Concurring*	*Dissenting*	*Opinions*	*Cases*		*Civil Liberties*	*Resistance*	*Industrial Relations*	*Race Relations*	*Immigration*	*Land Tenure*
LORD DE VILLIERS, 1910	7	8	1	0	16	21	76	2	1	4	3	10	1
ROSE INNES, 1910	21	18	7	1	47	72	65	9	10	18	13	16	6
SOLOMON, 1910	7	8	15	2	32	67	47	8	10	16	9	15	9
C G MAASDORP, 1910	1	0	6	2	9	32	28	6	4	6	6	5	5
J A J DE VILLIERS, 1910	2	8	15	4	29	76	38	7	10	24	16	10	9
JUTA, 1914	0	0	5	0	5	21	24	1	6	5	4	2	3
KOTZÉ, 1922	0	0	11	2	13	20	65	0	4	5	6	2	3
WESSELS, 1923	5	10	4	3	22	49	45	5	1	15	14	5	9
CURLEWIS, 1927	2	6	3	0	11	42	27	5	0	13	8	7	9
STRATFORD, 1927	5	9	2	2	18	46	39	3	0	15	11	7	10
ROOS, 1929	0	3	0	0	3	13	23	0	0	4	3	3	3
BEYERS, 1932	0	0	8	0	8	13	62	4	0	4	1	1	3

De Wet, 1937	0	14	0	1	15	32	47	4	5	15	3	1	4
Watermeyer, 1937	2	11	2	0	15	73	21	9	12	31	11	1	9
Tindall, 1938	1	9	2	2	14	74	19	9	12	32	10	1	10
Centlivres, 1939	1	18	1	0	20	58	34	6	12	30	5	0	5
Feetham, 1939	0	5	2	1	8	42	19	5	8	16	7	0	6
Greenberg, 1943	1	10	2	0	13	52	25	6	7	22	10	1	6
Schreiner, 1945	0	9	1	0	10	40	25	6	4	18	7	1	4
Van den Heever, 1948	0	1	0	0	1	7	14	0	0	6	0	0	1
Hoexter, 1949	0	1	0	0	1	7	14	0	0	6	1	0	0
Fagan, 1950	0	0	0	0	0	1	0	0	0	1	0	0	0
Sub-Totals	57	149	92	20	318	—	34% average	—	—	—	—	—	—
Acting Judge Davis, 1944–8	0	4	0	0	4	18	22	1	0	7	3	1	6
Other Acting Judges (12)	0	1	6	1	8	30	27	0	2	12	6	6	4
Totals	57	154	98	21	330	[216]	33% average	[25]	[22]	[78]	[37]	[24]	[30]

other spoken judgment; and on three of which he spoke out in dissent from the majority on the Bench. In this way, he was reported as having handed down a judgment in 22 of the cases which he heard, which implies that he was a silent concurrer in the other 27 disputes. Where useful, figures have been converted to percentages, and have been totalled. In addition, the participation of R P B Davis, who acted most frequently as a judge of appeal, and that of twelve acting judges, have been summarised and included at the foot of the table.

Certain features which appear from a study of Table V confirm trends noted in the sectional conclusions. For instance, the move to the practice of a single judgment for the whole court (instead of a leading judgment and at least one reported concurrence) is borne out by the fact that more than half of the opinions handed down by every judge from De Wet onwards constituted the only judgment in the case.[5] Among the earlier judges, this is true of only Curlewis and Roos. Naturally, the converse situation applies as far as the frequency of concurring judgments is concerned: of the judges before De Wet, only Wessels, Curlewis, Stratford, and Roos gave separate concurrences on fewer than half the occasions upon which they were moved to speak.

The importance attached to a dissent from the majority view is attested by the fact that no judge concurred in another's dissenting opinion: each felt bound to state his reasons. Dissenting opinions were few and far between,[6] which indicates either a remarkable degree of agreement on the way to approach legal questions before the court, or a strong but unexpressed need for unanimity. When the frequency of a judge's dissent from the majority of the court is put in percentage terms, only C G Maasdorp, J A J de Villiers, Kotzé, and Wessels are seen to have dissented in five percent or more of the cases in which they sat.

Some judges were noticeably inclined to speak only when they gave judgment for the whole court (such as Roos, De Wet, Centlivres, and Schreiner), while some preferred only to concur (such as Maasdorp, Juta, Kotzé, Beyers and J E R de Villiers). Yet others seem to have divided their opinions fairly evenly between leading judgment, sole judgment, concurrence, and dissent *viz* Wessels and Stratford. Again, levels of judicial willingness to give reasons, even if another judge had already handed down the leading opinion, were high in the first half of the period, but declined relatively rapidly from 1935 onwards. The fact that most of the earlier judges saw themselves as public figures, and felt bound to have their say, is the most likely explanation of this trend, but pressure of

[5] By 1978, 95 per cent of AD cases contained unanimous decisions. See Cameron "Mute Concurrence in the Appellate Division: Is Silence Golden?" (1979) 42 *THR-HR* 419 at 420.

[6] Cameron, *loc cit*.

the case-load and a rational distribution of the work probably hastened the process.

Table VI offers a different aspect of the judicial function, and one which must be approached with much care. The information presented attempts to gauge the extent to which each judge participated in cases which resulted in a perpetuation of the *status quo*. This concept is a debatable one, influenced, to some extent, by the values of the assessor. The guiding principle here is that the outcome of a case is deemed to have preserved the *status quo* if it did not disturb state authority, or the interests of the ruling group. Where legislation itself represented a departure from accepted ways, and the judiciary did nothing to dilute the effect of such an initiative, such behaviour is taken to be supportive of a change in the *status quo*. In other words, this summary of judicial activity tries to assess how conservative each judge was in his attitudes to social change. Thus, to take two well-known examples, *R v Padsha* would fall into the "Yes" column because white group interests and prejudices triumphed, while *R v Detody* would be classified as "No" because the decision signalled a step back from a more rigorous application of race discrimination.

Now it is clear that legislative wishes, legal doctrine, and the facts of the cases will have determined the course of judicial decision-making on many occasions, and might have excluded all but a conservative ruling by the court. But it is also possible that these same factors will have dictated a result which went counter to the accepted order, examples of which are furnished by the employment statutes enacted in the 1920's and 1930's. What is important in this treatment of judicial activity is not the absolute level of conservatism, but the performance of individual judges, relative to their colleagues on the Bench, and the subject-matter of their decisions.

Many cases are difficult to classify. In the area of industrial relations, a ruling was held to be against the current order if it promoted the needs of the less-privileged members of society, such as workers or the voteless, even if in accord with statute. Some cases were excluded from the count since it was too difficult to determine their effect on the social order. The tentative character of the figures in Table VI is thus obvious.

Despite this uncertainty, there is some benefit to be gained from a study, both of the totals (as expressed in percentages) and the detailed breakdown into categories for each judge. The latter provides much of the explanation for the former, because of the erratic distribution of cases and different levels of conservatism in each category over the period.[7] In this way, a judge with a large proportion of resistance and rebellion cases among those which he heard can be expected to have a high score in the "Yes" percentage column, because in those cases the

[7] See Table VII, below.

TABLE VI
Judicial "Conservatism"

Judge	*Percentage*		*Totals*		*Civil Liberties*		*Resistance*		*Industrial Relations*		*Race Relations*		*Immigration*		*Land Tenure*	
	No	*Yes*	*No*	*Yes*	*No*	*Yes*	*No*	*Yes*	*No*	*Yes*	*No*	*Yes*	*No*	*Yes*	*No*	*Yes*
LORD DE VILLIERS	14	86	3	18	2	0	0	1	0	4	0	3	1	9	0	1
ROSE INNES	32	68	21	49	6	3	2	8	7	9	1	13	3	12	2	4
SOLOMON	27	73	17	48	4	4	2	8	6	9	1	8	2	12	2	7
C G MAASDORP	31	69	10	21	4	2	1	3	2	4	0	6	1	3	2	3
J A J DE VILLIERS	25	75	18	55	4	3	2	8	5	17	2	14	2	7	3	6
JUTA	20	80	4	16	1	0	1	5	1	4	0	4	0	1	1	2
KOTZÉ	21	79	4	15	—	—	0	4	2	2	0	6	2	0	0	3
WESSELS	25	75	12	37	4	1	0	1	3	12	1	13	2	3	2	7
CURLEWIS	33	67	14	28	4	1	—	—	3	10	2	6	3	4	2	7
STRATFORD	33	67	15	31	3	0	—	—	3	12	2	9	4	3	3	7

Beyers	30	70	4	9	3	1	—	—	1	3	0	1	0	1	0	3
J E R de Villiers	31	69	9	20	4	2	—	—	3	4	1	7	1	3	0	4
De Wet	43	57	13	17	2	2	2	3	6	7	1	2	0	1	2	2
Watermeyer	55	45	38	32	5	4	2	9	19	10	6	5	0	1	6	3
Tindall	51	49	36	35	4	5	2	9	18	12	5	5	0	1	7	3
Centlivres	55	45	31	25	3	3	2	9	20	9	3	2	—	—	3	2
Feetham	42	58	17	23	1	4	2	5	9	6	2	5	—	—	3	3
Greenberg	55	45	27	21	3	3	0	6	13	6	7	3	0	1	4	2
Schreiner	70	30	26	11	4	2	0	4	12	3	7	0	0	1	3	1
[Van den Heever]	84	16	5	1	—	—	—	—	5	0	—	—	—	—	0	1
[Hoexter]	100	0	6	0	—	—	—	—	5	0	1	0	—	—	—	—
[Fagan]	100	0	1	0	—	—	—	—	1	0	—	—	—	—	—	—
Average Percentages					64	36	18	82	46	54	26	74	31	69	36	64

court displayed a strong tendency to uphold state authority. By contrast, the presence of a large proportion of civil liberties cases is likely to produce the opposite result. Naturally, if a judge dissents from the majority in a case which upholds the *status quo*, his participation is seen as being in favour of change, and *vice versa*.

A study of the totals in percentage terms produces a discernible and interesting pattern. Apart from the last three judges, who heard too few cases to make their inclusion worthwhile, the remaining twenty judges fall into three groups as regards their propensity to decide in favour of the *status quo*. The first group, from Lord De Villiers to Wessels, found for the preservation of the existing order in an average of 75 per cent of the cases which came before them. In the next group, from Curlewis to De Wet, this average falls to 69 per cent, while in the final group of six, from Watermeyer to Schreiner, there is a dramatic drop to 45 per cent. In other words, as time passes in the period, there appears to be a constantly accelerating willingness on the part of the appeal judges to hand down decisions which diverge from the customary social order.

There may have been many reasons for this development. Increasing stability in national life, changes in the political priorities of government, and differences in the type of case coming before the court may all have contributed to this movement. In particular, a large number of disputes concerning labour legislation appeared on the roll in the last fifteen years. In these, the judges showed their adaptability to legislative efforts partially to alter the *status quo*, by improvements in white workers' rights against their employers. Such cases undoubtedly contributed greatly to this change. But there were also a good few appeals on questions of resistance and land tenure by blacks at that time, which would have dampened this effect. Similarly, the shift from the first group to the second could be ascribed partly to the fact that no resistance and rebellion appeals were heard by any of the latter group, except De Wet.

A further conclusion which can be drawn from Table VI is that there is scant evidence to support a contention that Afrikaans-speaking judges were more conservative than their English-speaking counterparts. Any shift to an apparently less conservative corporate stance by the appellate judiciary should not be seen as the consequence of the appointment of five obviously English-speaking men (Tindall, Centlivres, Feetham, Greenberg, and Schreiner). English-speaking judges had proved themselves bastions of conservatism in the past (Solomon and Juta, for example), while Afrikaners such as De Wet had displayed adaptability to change. The impression conveyed strongly is that factors other than language played a greater part in determining levels of conservatism.

Since interpretation of the figures is contestable it is perhaps wisest merely to point to the main trends, and to see if there is supporting or contradictory evidence elsewhere in the material. To this end, it is a useful exercise to examine the records of particular judges in both tables, and to indicate peculiar features.

As can be expected, most of the earlier judges actually gave judgment in a high proportion of cases which they heard, and of these Lord De Villiers was the most prolific, with his separate opinion recorded on three-quarters of the occasions on which he was on the Bench. He heard a large number of immigration cases, which goes some way towards explaining why his percentage of "conservative" opinions is unusually high. By contrast, Rose Innes and C G Maasdorp participated in a larger-than-average share, for their time, of disputes, the outcome of which threatened the existing order.

J A J de Villiers appears to have been more willing than most Chief Justices or senior judges to remain silent on the Bench. Conversely, the level of activity of Kotzé and Beyers belies their brief tenure and junior status on the appellate Bench. Roos and Juta seldom expressed their views in reported judgments, and almost always found themselves taking a conservative position in regard to disputes before them. It is interesting to note that Curlewis and Stratford, who had relatively similar backgrounds and careers before elevation to the AD, seem to have approached the type of issues covered by this study in the same way, with the exception of a higher level of handing down of judgments on the part of Stratford.

It is wise to treat the records of the later judges with some caution, in view of the fact that most of their careers as judges of appeal were incomplete in October 1950, as well as the predominance of labour relations cases among those which they heard. Nevertheless, the judicial styles of Watermeyer and Tindall show some remarkable similarities in the fields under discussion. Feetham appears to have been more conservative than his contemporaries, with Schreiner at the opposite end of the spectrum.

It is difficult to pronounce categorically upon the performance of the judges who made up the AD in the period 1910 to 1950, even within the relatively narrow selection of cases outlined in this work. For one thing, the changing nature of Southern African society and the type of conflict which culminated in an appeal to Bloemfontein militates against the establishment of a firm base line for a comparison of judges' records as individuals. However, it seems certain that, from about 1937, with the arrival of De Wet, there occurred a shift in judicial emphasis.

From this time onwards, the appellate judiciary adopted a more self-confident and detached attitude to its work, as if the society to which it belonged was no longer under siege. This coincided with the appointment to the court of a new group of professional lawyers, who had no close connections with party politics.[8] These men had

[8] See Ch II above. De Wet is the sole exception.

not been caught up in the trauma and confusion of the Anglo-Boer War and the creation of the Union. It was almost as if there was a conscious withdrawal by the judges into a middle-of-the-road professionalism, a safe haven in which the court could embrace more flexible views on sensitive subjects without fear of seeming partisan. This feeling of strength and security emerges in the decisions of the time, in industrial and race relations, resistance, and land tenure. Many of these show that the court was prepared to adapt its attitudes to changing social circumstances, and to assume a stance less conservative than its predecessors.

Now this apparent willingness to change signifies the extent of judicial security, rather than the later judges' involvement with, and recognition of, the need for social progress. Indeed, it could justifiably be claimed that the approach of the judges before 1937 was far more directly fashioned by the problems of Southern Africa, as they perceived them, than was that of those who followed. The earlier judges were, almost without exception, acutely aware of the major political forces which opposed each other, both in the sub-continent and the world. They faced the unenviable task of making the court one which would inspire the confidence of the rival groups in South Africa, chief among which were, for them, English- and Afrikaans-speaking whites. As a result, it is not altogether surprising that the earlier judges were not prepared to be legal or social innovators in the type of case covered by this study, for fear of antagonising the white-dominated Legislature and Executive. The party-political past of most of these men, whose ideas had been fashioned in the late nineteenth century, taught them that a watchful conservatism would earn respect for the judiciary from those in power.

The judicial careers summarised above bear ample testimony to this trait in the court's character. It is precisely because the AD had pursued this cautious policy before 1937 that the later judges felt sufficiently established, and removed from the cut-and-thrust of contentious public debate to pursue a less conservative line in fulfilment of their role in the government of South Africa. This is not to imply that the judges after 1937 played an active part in the liberal cause. It is, rather, to point to the assumption of a more conventional judicial position as the seemingly passive administrators of justice.

A General View of the Cases

After this discussion of the judicial personnel and their actions in this period, it is important to consider the cases canvassed in the body of this work as a whole. Comparisons of different approaches by the AD over time and according to subject-matter of the disputes provide clear indications of judicial loyalties and interests. Table VII offers a very basic picture of the court's activities in the fields designated above, and various features require comment.

TABLE VII

Summary of Cases

Category	*Number of Cases*	*Judgments*				*Successful Appeals*		*Status Quo Preserved?*				*Trend to Single Judgments*
		Dissenting		*Multiple*								
		Number	*%*	*Number*	*%*	*Number*	*%*	*No*	*%*	*Yes*	*%*	
Civil Liberties	25	5 in 4 cases	16	12	47	16	64	16	64	9	36	5 multiple judgments after 1925
Resistance and Rebellion	22	1	5	8	36	3	14	5	18	17	82	All single after 1923
Industrial Relations	78	3 in 2 cases	3	14	18	21	27	34[a]	46	39[a]	54	5 multiple judgments after 1930
Race Relations	37	4 in 3 cases	8	8	20	15	40	10	26	27	74	2 multiple judgments after 1930
Immigration	24	6 in 4 cases	17	8	33	7	27	5	31	19	69	1 multiple judgment after 1930
Land Tenure	30	2 in 2 cases	7	12	40	10	33	11	36	19	64	4 multiple judgments after 1925
Totals (Averages)	216[b]	16 cases	8	62	29	72	33	81	38	130	62	17 multiple judgments after 1930

NOTES: *(a)* Five industrial relations cases proved impossible to classify in this respect.
(b) Approximately 1 850 cases were reported from the AD in this period: the number discussed comprises about 12%. A further 104 cases which were noted in research have not been included here.

Firstly, as mentioned earlier, the size of the sample is about one-eighth of the total group of cases reported from 1910 to 1950. However, within the limits of "public interest" as defined in the Introduction, the proportion of decisions perused rises to the order of at least nine-tenths. Within the confines of the court's participation in "political" matters, as a result, the cases selected comprise the overwhelming majority.

Secondly, moving to the right in the table, the level of dissenting judgments indicates the complexity and emotive quality of the problems raised in each category. It would seem that the high level of division of opinion which is found in questions of civil liberty and immigration demonstrates considerably different personal attitudes to questions of individual freedom raised in the cases. By contrast, the rarity with which the judges disagreed in the area of resistance and rebellion represents a desire to preserve unity in the face of subversion against the government; while the unanimity evident in the sphere of industrial relations is likely to have been determined by the simplicity of the facts of most cases, together with a lower level of judicial concern at the outcome of appeals.

The extent to which judicial controversy was stirred by the different classes of cases appears from the third set of figures in the table. If it is assumed (as it probably can be with some justification) that a judge would have been moved to express his opinion on the topic before him, either in concurrence or dissent, if it raised issues of great interest to him, then an order of judicial priorities can be drawn up according to the frequency with which more than one judgment was reported. So it would seem that civil liberties were of most concern to the AD over the years, followed by land tenure, resistance and rebellion, immigration, race relations, and industrial relations.

This list implies a relative lack of interest in the result of appeals involving working people and non-white South Africans, or a failure to comprehend the grievances of members of those groups. On the other hand, a great deal of interest in individual liberty and property rights is apparent.

Fourthly, when appellants' success in winning over the court is considered, a slightly different picture presents itself. Civil liberties again head the list in terms of the highest rate of appeals allowed, followed by race relations, land tenure, industrial relations, immigration, and rebellion and resistance. This order holds, with the exception of a straight exchange between industrial relations and immigration, even when the success of the State as appellant is removed from the statistics. What these figures show is a reluctance to upset the decisions of the provincial divisions in two-thirds of the appeals discussed, roughly on a par with levels of judicial concern with the subject-matter of the appeal. The exceptions to this trend are found in race relations, in which a high proportion of appeals succeeded, and rebellion and resistance, in which few appellants won their cases.

Part of the explanation for this last factor is to be found in the analysis of the propensity for the state or *status quo* to triumph in each sector. Here, resistance and rebellion heads the list, with a conservative result in four of every five appeals, followed by race relations, immigration, land, industrial relations, and civil liberties. This pattern bears out the court's unwillingness to tolerate subversion, or to support any alteration of the existing racial divisions and class relationships in South Africa.

As far as the actual functioning of the court was concerned, it can be confirmed that, in the second half of the period 1910 to 1950, it became the habit of the AD to entrust the formulation of its view to only one member in each case. Indeed, only seventeen appeals reported after 1930 contained more than one judgment, whereas the figure had been forty-five out of the hundred cases before that date. The tendency for the Chief Justice to give judgment in important matters has been noted above, as has that of one or two judges to become "experts" in certain fields.

Table VIII shows the distribution of the cases discussed through the period 1910 to 1950. A fairly even spread over the years emerges, with one hundred cases heard before 1931. Within the classified areas, however, several periods of quietude occur. For example, between the years 1925 and 1940, only five civil liberties and no resistance and rebellion cases were heard by the AD. Similarly, there were only two immigration appeals from 1933 to the end of the period, while only three such appeals and five disputes concerning land tenure reached Bloemfontein from 1914 to 1927. Industrial and race relations cases were reported fairly regularly over the forty years.

This fluctuating preponderance of cases in different fields can have important consequences when judicial attitudes to particular subjects are evaluated. Thus, the relatively high level of conservatism which characterises the immigration decisions becomes less significant when it is realised that almost all the appeals were heard before 1933, because it has been established that the judiciary was generally more conservative earlier in the period. On the other hand, the higher level of conservatism found in the race relations field is emphasised when it is noted that half the cases came to the AD after 1930, and so fell within a period in which the judges appear to have grown less conservative.

If all the cases are viewed together, the following picture of the court emerges. The main feature of the AD's record in the areas discussed is manifest in the form of a strong commitment to legislative policy and the ideology of the ruling group. This trait in the judicial character is especially clear in the fields of race relations, immigration, and land tenure, although somewhat tempered in the last by respect for the sanctity of private property.

TABLE VIII

Distribution of Cases Discussed over Time

Year	Number of Cases in Category						Total
	Civil Liberties	*Resistance*	*Industrial Relations*	*Race Relations*	*Immigration*	*Land Tenure*	
1910			2				2
1911				1	3		4
1912	3	1	3		6	2	15
1913			2	1	4	2	9
1914		1	1	1			3
1915	1	1					2
1916			1				1
1917	1	2	1	1		1	6
1918		1		1	1		3
1919				1		1	2
1920	2		2	1		1	6
1921				1			1
1922	1		1			1	3
1923		3	3		1	1	8
1924	1	1	1		1		4
1925			1	3			4
1926			1	2			3
1927			1	1			2
1928			1		2	1	4
1929	1		2	2	1	2	8
1930			7	3			10
1931			1	1	1	2	5
1932					2	2	4
1933	1			2		1	4
1934	1		2	1			4
1935	1					1	2
1936	1		2		1	1	5
1937				2			2
1938			1	1		2	4
1939			3			1	4
1940			1	1			2
1941		4	3				7
1942	2		2				4
1943	2	2	5				9
1944		2	3	1		2	8
1945	1		2	2		2	7
1946	3		6	3		2	14
1947		1	2		1		4
1948	2	3	7	2		1	15
1949	1		5	1		1	8
1950			3	1			4
Totals	25	22	78	37	24	30	216

A different side of this judicial alacrity in implementing legislative intent is evident in the sphere of industrial relations. In this instance, the possibly disastrous outcome of tardiness in carrying out the legislative reforms intended to allay worker discontent may have contributed largely to the judicial response of rapid adaptation. The legislature made this course easier for the judges to adopt as it involved no radical changes to the *racial* structure of the South African social formation. On the contrary, it further consolidated the position of dominance to which the white artisan had grown accustomed, and served to begin to bridge the gap between English- and Afrikaans-speaking whites.

Further evidence of the very conventional approach of the appellate judiciary is afforded by the resistance and rebellion category. Here the predominant sentiment is one of resolute support for the government of the day, but with a significantly more lenient treatment of rebels in the Afrikaner cause than whites in the worker cause, and blacks. Again, therefore, chief among judicial goals was unity among the "white races", but on the terms of those who held the reins of power.

This appears to hold true, even in the rather different examples included in the civil liberties section. In an atmosphere of considerable tolerance for the protection of free speech, the AD[9] seems to have been less alarmed by the extreme language of a communist addressing blacks than the utterances of those who represented a threat to unity among whites. The conservative side of the collective judicial personality is evident here in the treatment of women as social minors.

A recurrent facet of judicial attitudes over the years was isolated support for relief in individual cases of hardship. There are examples of this in every area and at all times, and this characteristic goes some way towards explaining the unusually firm support given by the court to civil liberties. As long as the effect of the decision was not likely to range so widely as to cause a fundamental change in the South African order, the court was willing to uphold a single appeal which went against that order. The judges often achieved the desired result by manipulating the canons of construction of statutes.

General Assessment of the Role of the Court 1910 to 1950

In attempting to sum up the impressions of the AD which the cases included above have generated, it is useful to pay attention to the conclusions reached by other writers who have addressed themselves to an evaluation of the role of the South African judiciary. As was adverted to in the introduction, there are various schools of opinion on this issue.

Firstly, the conventional and by far the larger and longer-standing body of opinion holds that the judiciary has fulfilled its task with

[9] See the conclusions in Ch III above.

absolute independence and impartiality. Members of this group further maintain that any apparent inequality in the administration of justice can be ascribed solely to discriminatory legislation, the objects of which the courts are bound to apply, without questioning its equity.[10] The most extreme expression of the sentiments of this group is to be found in the comment of H J May, for a time one of South Africa's leading constitutional lawyers. At a time when South African judges were being attacked by Afrikaner Nationalist politicians for alleged interference with legislation, he wrote[11] that:

> ". . . when men appear before them on trial they know that only the law will influence them—not social status, nor political views, nor race nor creed nor colour; nor even forgotten incidents which have no bearing on their trial; nor anything save the law and the relevant facts of the case. . . . [E]ven the possibility of a thought of corruptiblity is unthinkable; and in that word is included any deviation even of conscience in doing their duty."

This sort of adulation has led to a position in which, among South African élites, judges rank second only to Cabinet Ministers in terms of prestige.[12] But it has also produced a climate in which debate about the judicial role has been stifled.[13] Kahn, in his review[14] of a book[15] generally laudatory of the courage and correctness of the South African judiciary, spoke[16] of the unpleasantness, for a South African lawyer, of a discussion therein which implied that the judges wished to resist apartheid. He went on[17] to say that there was no reason to regard the judgments referred to as more than the "dispassionate application of the generally accepted rules in favour of reasonableness and natural justice . . .".

It is precisely this idealisation of the judiciary, and its separation, and thus exculpation, from the injustice perceived in the legal system and wider society, which other writers have challenged. The general picture presented by this loose alliance of observers is one critical of judicial actions, especially over the last thirty years.[18] In effect, they allege that the courts have consistently, but increasingly, failed to fulfil their task as guardians of justice, which course of conduct is often attributed to the dominance of positivism in the legal system. As these writers differ in their particular view of the judicial function and performance, and as they have reached their conclusions after mature reflection and some research, it is worthwhile to look more closely at the work of four of them, in the order in which they wrote.

[10] Reference can be made to Hahlo and Maisels "The Rule of Law in South Africa" (1966) 52 *Virginia Law Review* 1 at 10, 12, and 14; Broome *Not the Whole Truth* at 266; and Van der Vyver *Seven Lectures on Human Rights* 12–16.

[11] *The South African Constitution* at 247.

[12] Van der Merwe *et al* (Eds) *White South African Elites* 95–7.

[13] See Dugard *Human Rights and the South African Legal Order* Ch 9, and 378–9.

[14] (1958) 75 *SALJ* 112.

[15] McWhinney *Judicial Review in the English-speaking World.*

[16] At 114.

[17] *Loc cit.*

[18] For example, see International Commission of Jurists *Erosion of the Rule of Law in South Africa* (1968) iv; Mathews and Albino "The Permanence of the Temporary" (1966) 83 *SALJ* 16.

Millner was one of the first to investigate judicial backgrounds and to relate these to the wider society in which the judges operated.[19] He classified South Africa as a "caste" society in which equality before the law existed only within the separate castes, and not between them.[20] He identified the judiciary's inarticulate major premise as being a deeply embedded conviction of human inequality,[21] a product of history. He puts it thus:[22]

> "Incorruptible though it is, and dispassionate though it may strive to be, the judiciary cannot finally escape the web of feeling, the wordless sentiments which shape its innermost thoughts; and where the issues touch these springs of thought, only the most resolute independence of mind, the most singular capacity for objectivity and detachment can hope to rise above it. . . . Judicial thinking takes place in this matrix of incompatible elements, ever swayed by the striving of the law towards normative or formal equality, yet unable to challenge the fundamental inequality of the caste society itself."

He examined the "separate-but-equal" doctrine and the "*audi alteram partem*" rule as applied by the judiciary in order to point out the limits of judicial departure from the ideology of the dominant caste.[23] In addition, he indicated[24] an "incurable positivism" on the part of the judiciary as the basis for their refusal to interfere with legislative action and to declare unjust laws as "non-laws". He concluded:[25]

> "The judge in South Africa who cannot reconcile himself morally to apartheid laws becomes, in spite of himself, a vehicle of those laws. For the enforcement of the laws enacted in any social order is a necessity of that social order and so long as those in power remain so, they must in one way or another maintain or create a judiciary which will uphold their laws. . . . And the judge, dedicated to uphold the principle of justice, becomes its executioner."

His attitude to judges before 1948 was slightly different. In an article[26] in which he deplored the trend of judicial appointments under the present regime, he wrote[27] that the earlier judges

> ". . . strove valiantly, and not entirely ineffectually, to realise the concept of political freedom and equality upheld in English courts and adopted as part of South African law. That they should fail in this enterprise was inevitable, for reasons embedded in the constitutional and legislative structure of [South Africa], and to some extent in the premises governing, however obscurely, their own psychological processes. Nevertheless, they tried . . .".

So Millner gives the judges some praise for effort, but stresses that the seeds of their failure are contained within their own personalities, and should not be sought solely in other spheres. He also emphasises the existence of a limit beyond which a judiciary departs from the principles of justice if it upholds "unjust" law. He maintains that such a situation had come to pass in South Africa by 1960.

[19] "Apartheid and the South African Courts" (1961) 14 *Current Legal Problems* 280.
[20] *Ibid* at 284. [21] *Ibid* at 285.
[22] *Ibid* at 286. [23] *Ibid* see 287–95.
[24] *Ibid* at 300. [25] *Ibid* at 305–6.
[26] "Eclipse of a Judiciary: The South African Position" (1962) 11 *ICLQ* 886.
[27] At 887.

Kuper provided a different analysis, much closer to that of the uncritical school, in an unpublished dissertation[28] of 1965, in which he investigated judicial attitudes to particular issues of race[29] in all divisions of the Supreme Court. He concluded[30] that the court had decided matters as they arose, "without relating [its] judgments to the general pattern of race relations". This had led to inconsistency and the absence of an attempt to apply English or Roman-Dutch common-law principles to the position of the races in law.[31] He examined the evidence relating to the theory that the judges had become more conservative over time, and decided that a review of the decisions did not support such a view.[32] He looked, too, for any possible differences in approach between the provinces, but thought that the impact of the Cape courts had been "neither significant nor extensive".[33]

Kuper identified the major forum of struggle as that between the court and the Administration,[34] with particular emphasis on judicial reluctance to implement segregation by by-law. He agreed that the court had set itself against rapid social change,[35] but maintained[36] that, in doing so, it had been protecting the spirit of the "more liberal facets of the English Common Law". He claimed[37] that the court had championed "the rights of men against those who championed the rights of race" in its opposition to partial segregation. In his final words:[38] "The judges . . . had given new life and new meaning to the Cape tradition, they had extended that force into the Union, they had attempted to write those values into the law of the land."

Kuper's conclusions seem to be contradictory, in that he remarks on the court's failure to implement common-law principles in matters of race, yet claims that the judges acted in the spirit of the English common law. His writing is, perhaps, an example of the type of commentary which points out the shortcomings of the judiciary in certain fields, but is reluctant to extend these findings to an overall assessment of judicial role. So Kuper, while critical of the court's attitudes in some areas, concludes that the judges had partially succeeded in promoting liberal values in their treatment of the disputes before them.

The next writer who considered these questions, though in a more cursory manner than Kuper as regards the Supreme Court, revived

[28] "The Supreme Court and Race Relations in South Africa", presented for BA (Honours) at the University of the Witwatersrand.

[29] For example, municipal segregation, the separate-but-equal doctrine, defamation with race connotations, and the status of evidence given by non-whites.

[30] *Op cit* at 136.

[31] *Loc cit.*

[32] *Ibid* at 139.

[33] *Ibid* at 140.

[34] *Ibid* at 141.

[35] *Ibid* at 142.

[36] *Ibid* at 143.

[37] *Loc cit.*

[38] *Loc cit.*

and extended Millner's arguments. Sachs, in his *Justice in South Africa*,[39] pursued a detailed study of the administration of justice at all levels and throughout the country from 1652. In Chapter 8, headed "Race Conflict and the Legal System", he reviewed judicial attitudes over time, and pointed out various shifts. In his eyes,[40] the judges could be criticised, not for conscious bias nor open prejudice, but for willing and dignified acquiescence in, and implementation of, unjust laws.

A fourth variation of a critical commentary on the work of the South African judiciary is to be found in the work of the leading scholar in the field. Dugard has been writing on this topic for the last fifteen years,[41] but the product of much of his thought is contained in *Human Rights and the South African Legal Order*, which appeared in 1978. Of particular interest for present purposes is the chapter entitled "Race, Security, and the Judges", in which Dugard reviews a small selection of cases in the areas of race and security in the period 1910 to 1974, in an attempt to identify opinions and philosophies.

On the question of race, he concludes[42] that the record of the AD suggests a fluctuating approach which does not support the theory that the court was more "liberal" in its early days than at present. He finds it easier[43] to identify particular liberal judges (such as Innes, Centlivres, and Schreiner) than to classify any court as such. What the decisions clearly demonstrate, he says,[44] is that the "aloofness of the courts from policy in the field of race relations is therefore but one of the many judicial myths of South Africa". As regards security issues, Dugard comes to few definite conclusions,[45] other than that some courts showed a stronger preference for authority than others, a deference to Government during both World Wars being noted.[46] He expresses disappointment[47] at the failure of recent courts to make a vigorous stand for justice in the hour of need, even if this could not properly be described as a dereliction of duty.

Dugard then proceeds to look critically at the South African judicial process, and complains chiefly[48] that the judiciary "refuses to recognise that it does make law, albeit only 'interstitially', that it does make policy decisions, and that it is part of the South African political process". He sees the tradition of legal positivism as the main culprit

[39] Published in 1973. The provisions of the Internal Security Act 74 of 1982, and its predecessors, have prevented South Africans from having access to Sachs' valuable work. For this reason, too, discussion of his book has to be presented indirectly. Those with access to the original text are advised to consult it.
[40] At 262.
[41] See some of his work mentioned in Ch I, above.
[42] *Op cit* at 322–3.
[43] *Loc cit.*
[44] *Ibid* at 324.
[45] *Ibid* at 360.
[46] *Ibid* at 362.
[47] *Ibid* at 365.
[48] In Ch 11, "The Judicial Process: A Critical Assessment" at 368.

for the establishment and continued existence of such attitudes.[49] He argues,[50] along the lines of the realist school of thought, that the inarticulate premise which pervades judicial approach in South Africa is "loyalty to the status quo", and that it is this factor which explains some of the more controversial decisions on race and security matters. He calls for an open recognition by the judges of their social and political role,[51] and for critical judicial comment on broadly "political" legislation.[52]

Dugard ends his assessment with the quotation of an exchange between Judges Learned Hand and Jerome Frank of the United States, which is relevant to the present critique. It runs thus:[53]

> "'A society so riven that the spirit of moderation is gone, no court *can* save', warned Judge Hand; to which Judge Frank replied 'Judge Hand thinks it folly to believe that the courts can save democracy. Of course, they cannot. But it seems to me that here, most uncharacteristically, Judge Hand indulges in a judgment far too sweeping, one which rests on a too-sharp either-or, all or nothing dichotomy. . . . Obviously, the courts cannot do the whole job. But, just as obviously, they can sometimes help to arrest evil popular trends in their inception.'"

Differences in approach are thus evident among these writers who do not subscribe to the views of conventional admirers of the South African judiciary. In degree of divergence from the accepted wisdom, Kuper is the closest, as he discounts any implicit bias in judicial approach, while he disapproves of isolated decisions. Dugard comes next in the spectrum, advocating overtly interstitial action by the judges, within a modification of the present framework. Millner concentrates on the effect of the judges' backgrounds on their behaviour, and recognises in turn the close relationship between the judicial function and the creation and perpetuation of a particular form of society. Finally, furthest from the traditional approach, Sachs analyses judicial conduct from a Marxist perspective, and sees the judiciary contributing directly to the maintenance of social domination by the ruling bloc, but even he does not decry the efforts of individual judges who are concerned about the effects of their judgments.

It is plain that elements of the conclusions of all these writers are supported by the material contained in the present study, though Millner's approach is probably the closest to it. In saying this, however, the limits of the assessment under review must be clearly defined, even at the cost of some repetition.

The description and discussion above are based on the principle that the judge is faced with a choice when he interprets the law and facts of the case before him.[54] In some instances, the choice is reduced

[49] *Ibid* at 373.
[50] *Ibid* at 380.
[51] *Ibid* at 381.
[52] *Ibid* see 384–6.
[53] *Ibid* at 388.
[54] Dugard proceeds on this basis: *op cit* at 303. See also the "Postscript", below.

by the clarity of the legal formula, and the ease with which the facts fit its stipulations, but the choice remains, nevertheless. The exercise of this choice will necessarily reflect the judge's attitudes, even if he tries to conceal them, from which a fair idea of the judicial character, both individual and corporate, can be gained. It is the manner of the exercise of the choice, and its effect on wider South African society, which are vital here. The legal correctness of the decisions is not itself at issue, although the influence of the "law" as understood by the judges is naturally the major determinant in judicial choice. In most of the cases discussed, either of two decisions could have been defended as legally proper.

Further, the interpretation of judicial performance as set forth in this work is an attempt partly to explain trends in decisions, in terms of judicial upbringing and contemporary social conditions,[55] and partly to evaluate such conduct in terms of justice and equality.[56] In addition, the way in which such behaviour has influenced subsequent actions of the Supreme Court, and its implications for the wider social formation, will be referred to.

In the final analysis, the overall picture which emerges is one of a group of men who saw their dominant role as the protectors of stability in the social formation of which they formed an integral part. This conception of their task was, doubtless, influenced by their racial and class backgrounds, education, and training. The judges expressed it in terms of a positivistic acceptance of the concept of legislative sovereignty, despite a patently racist political structure, and of a desire to preserve the existing order of legal relations, notwithstanding its basis in manifest societal inequalities. In doing so, they endorsed the type of inter-group relations found outside the Cape before Union, and discarded the slightly more relaxed racial code which had existed in the Cape.[57]

A further aspect of this judicial anxiety to reinforce racial divisions based on skin colour is to be found in the clear efforts by the AD to create a common bond between English- and Afrikaans-speaking whites in the face of the perceived threat from black South Africans. This policy is most marked in the rebellion and industrial relations cases, but its negative side can seen in the treatment of black efforts to upset the preferred distribution of power.

Secondly, allied with this support for the *status quo* went a failure to comprehend the plight of South Africans who fell outside the ruling group. Those affected by this judicial insensitivity were chiefly black or members of the working class. Prime examples of such an approach are to be found in the fields of race relations, immigration, and land tenure, though the disputes on industrial relations and

[55] Along the lines of Millner's discussion.
[56] An exercise similar to those carried out by Dugard and Kuper.
[57] This finding goes against the conclusion reached by Kuper *op cit* at 143.

rebellion contain their own instances. It is perhaps true to say that only the white skins of most of the litigants in the latter categories saved them from the unfeeling treatment meted out to black South Africans.

It is not suggested that there was any deliberate and conscious curial approach in this matter. The judges' outlook is, rather, the product of their backgrounds as privileged members of an élite group. The court of appeal, especially in the days soon after Union, displayed an unquestioning acceptance of the metropolitan power's ideology of race, suitably modified in accordance with South African conditions. This is, surely, a classic illustration of the "innate, indelible" feeling of superiority of whites over blacks with which history had saturated the judicial mind.[58]

To a lesser degree, a similar trait is evident in the judicial treatment of white workers. Here, though, the assumption is that a faction whose aspirations threaten the fabric of society can be contained by incorporation into the ruling white group. In a sense, the appellate judiciary was party to the buying-off of the white labour aristocracy by concrete improvements in their pay and working conditions,[59] the price of which was accelerated economic exploitation of black workers.

Thirdly, throughout the cases discussed, there is support for appellants who had suffered instances of individual injustice, whether at the hands of the administration or another citizen. In a certain measure, this aspect of the judicial character arises from the upbringing of those appointed to the appellate Bench, and the nature of the "law" and legal process as they understood them. It manifests itself most vividly in the field of civil liberties. There are further isolated examples in the areas of race relations, immigration, and land tenure. But what is equally clear is that the court was very seldom prepared to extend such relief to an individual when the consequences of such action would connote like treatment for a much larger number of people in the same position as appellant.[60]

Fourthly, if a journey through time is undertaken, it will be noticed that the actively authoritarian tone of the early years of the court's life faded into a paternalistic blandness by the late 1930's. This movement[61] has, no doubt, much to do with the increased security felt by the judges, as well as their acceptance of the functional limits set for the AD by the decisions of the first appeal judges. It seems that this progression in time and experience may have produced a less conservative outlook on the topics discussed, though this may also have been a direct function of changing attitudes and needs in the

[58] See Millner "Apartheid and the South African Courts" at 285.

[59] See the concluding section of Ch V above.

[60] *R v Detody* 1926 AD 198 is a rare exception.

[61] Which substantiates the conclusions of Dugard and Kuper on this point. See also Dean "The Judiciary" in De Crespigny and Schrire *The Government and Politics of South Africa* at 49.

social élite from which the judges were drawn. What is certain, though, is that the court became far less outspoken on sensitive political matters, far less willing to criticise legislative action on issues of public importance. This seems contradictory at first sight, until it is remembered that judicial conservatism is a measure of the judges' political response to the issues before them, rather than their willingness to state their opinions. In other words, the apparent retreat into bland indifference after 1937 necessarily connotes a less activist judicial position. In this way, any chance of the court taking a leading role, albeit an educational one, in the formation of social opinion disappeared.

McWhinney[62] has written that: "[A] court may become the prisoner of its own particular thought-ways—the special processes of reasoning, research, and argument developed in its ordinary day-by-day work." The extent to which the attitudes of the AD to non-constitutional, but "political", issues before 1950 influenced the stand taken by that court in the crisis over the "coloured vote" cases in the 1950's is a matter for speculative debate.

It could be argued that the acquiescent implementation of unjust and discriminatory legislation before 1950 made the credible assumption of a more dominant stance in favour of justice and liberty in the 1950's an impossible option. For the politically conservative attitudes of the more outspoken judges of appeal before 1937 had combined with the functionally more timid approach of those who followed, to produce a climate of legal and political opinion which made a successful stand impossible. Evidence exists that there was considerable anxiety within National Party circles at the prospect of a direct confrontation between Parliament and the courts.[63] How much greater might this have been if the court had succeeded in establishing a more singular devotion to social, rather than procedural, justice in the preceding decades?

Notwithstanding this argument, it is probable that a more plausible explanation for the AD's stance in the 1950's is to be found in the legal and political context of the particular events of those years, as well as a judicial mind which was able to separate "constitutional" issues from the rest of the disputes before it. This apparent dichotomy would have enabled the judges to see their stand on the entrenched sections as distinct from, and unaffected by, their predecessors' attitudes and approach, for the latter had faced no direct constitutional challenges. It is likely, too, that Centlivres and his fellow judges of appeal referred for guidance to the dispute between Kotzé and Kruger in the ZAR of the 1890's.

With this episode in mind, it is important to draw attention to the view of the judiciary held by a certain element of the majority in

[62] *Judicial Review* Chapter X at 198, with particular reference to the South African judiciary.
[63] See Schoeman *Van Malan tot Verwoerd* 58–62, 73–4, 121 and 123.

Parliament in the 1950's. The conservative judicial tone of the first forty years had not been extreme enough for part of the ruling National Party, a situation which had been exacerbated by the AD's support for the government and the war effort in World War II. The influence exerted on Afrikaner Nationalist policy by this faction produced a legislature determined to thrust the judiciary into a subordinate seat. The fact that the Supreme Court had managed to alienate a body of right-wing politicians is significant, but must be countered by its failure to provide a generally sympathetic forum for those who had no other formal access to political power, however remote, and for whom the judicial process was thus almost irrelevant.

Besides the constitutional issue, it seems likely that the approach of the earlier appellate judiciary to broadly "political" issues has deeply influenced the reaction of modern South African courts to legislative iniquity. Almost all the judges of appeal, to this day, completed the formative period of their professional life in the years before 1950, and subsequent social changes are unlikely entirely to have erased the habits engendered by that experience. The cases analysed in this study provide ample demonstration of the fact that the South African appellate judiciary, in the period 1910 to 1950, did little to undermine those values on which the post-1900 policies of segregation and apartheid have been constructed. Whether their approach to the litigation on issues of public importance actually contributed to the entrenchment of those values, by implicit judicial approval and the peaceful containment of opposition,[64] is beyond the scope of this work, though the suspicion is present that it did.

But there can be little argument that the picture of the appellate judiciary, as a body of fearless fighters for the less-privileged and unrepresented majority, is a myth whose perpetuation serves the cause of inequity. In truth, the members of the AD, while formally independent from political influence, manifestly incorrupt, and consciously impartial, were integral parts of the very structure which had created and now maintained injustice, from which they made little effort to extricate themselves. As Millner has pointed out, judicial backgrounds and character go a long way towards determining such a situation, and, therefore, this conclusion should not come as a surprise. Indeed, the question should rather be why the contrary impression has been nurtured, sustained, and accepted by so many over so long a period.

In the end, then, judicial performance can be summed up as having been situated within the main current of ruling opinion in South Africa over the four decades, a course of conduct quite in accordance with curial history and contemporary events. In this process,

[64] As argued by Sachs *op cit.*

standards of justice suffered, and it has been shown that the judiciary failed to recognise the symptoms of its erosion. If criticism is to be made, it must be that the AD failed to display a positive commitment to justice on those occasions when the legislative will was advancing injustice in the social formation. In this way, the judges unwittingly aided the development of the socio-legal system which ignores many of the basic principles of justice in South Africa today.

POSTSCRIPT: THE JUDICIARY IN GOVERNMENT

There are one or two aspects of the conclusions reached in this study which bear clear reiteration, in the light of current debate about the South African judiciary.[1] For many of the contributions to this discussion imply, firstly, that the judiciary before 1950 managed somehow to curb injustice in a substantial way, and, secondly, that the judges since then have disappointed in not living up to the traditions established by their predecessors. As a result, several commentators have called upon the Bench to challenge the political values of the present regime.[2] It is believed that the outcome of the analysis of cases conducted above is relevant to these issues.

In the first place, it is hoped that the assumption that the South African appellate judiciary before 1950 performed some kind of "guardian of justice" role in government has been shown to have been misconceived. For the dominant conclusion reached here is that the AD approached broadly political issues in the mainstream of the political *status quo*, and at no time challenged the exercise of power by the legislature, no matter how unjust. In other words, a call for a return to "former" court traditions does not presuppose a challenge to Parliamentary action by the court.

But there is a further lesson in this book for those who propound for the South African judiciary some sort of function as a protagonist of democratic values, rights and freedoms in the face of legislative and executive injustice. As was pointed out at the outset, there were several factors which *might* have prompted the judiciary's approach to broadly political matters to diverge from that of those in control of Parliament and the Cabinet. But subsequent judicial practice, outlined above, has indicated that this was not a real option in any serious sense.

The reasons for this behaviour are, it is suggested, not too difficult to discover and can be very briefly categorized as follows. Firstly, the

[1] See Forsyth and Schiller "The Judicial Process, Positivism, and Civil Liberty II" (1981) 98 *SALJ* 218; Dugard "Some Realism about the Judicial Process and Positivism—a Reply" (1981) 98 *SALJ* 372; Cameron "Legal chauvinism, executive-mindedness and justice—L C Steyn's impact on South African Law" (1982) 99 *SALJ* 38; Van Blerk "The Irony of Labels" (1982) 99 *SALJ* 365; Dyzenhaus "L C Steyn in Perspective" (1982) 99 *SALJ* 380 and "Judging the Judges and Ourselves" (1983) 100 *SALJ* 496; Kentridge "Pathology of a Legal System" (1980) 128 *Univ of Pennsylvania Law Review* 603; Rabie "Regbank en akademie" (1983) 16 *De Jure* 21; Wacks "Justice and Injustice" (inaugural lecture, University of Natal, 1983).

[2] Through open criticism of, or refusal to enforce unjust legislation, or resignation, for example. See Dugard, Dyzenhaus, and Wacks *op cit*.

constitutional model which was applied to the three branches of government in the Union of South Africa allotted the weakest position to the judiciary. For the execution of court orders depended upon the willing co-operation of the state administration, which could have been withheld, both officially and informally.[3] What is more, Parliament had the competence to negate the effect of particular judgments of the court through legislation, as well as to remove various classes of disputes from the jurisdiction of the court, if dissatisfied with judicial action. The growth of administrative tribunals and legislative blocking of the loophole in the law which allowed ownership of land by "Asian" companies form good examples of the limits of judicial power. But even the threat of such action must have played a large part in curtailing judicial capabilities.

Secondly, the system whereby judges were appointed to the AD ensured the forging of a close alliance of character between the members of the Bench and Parliament. It should not be a surprise that a male judge, comparatively advanced in years, an adherent of the dominant religion and a product of the élite educational institutions, should identify with similar men in the legislature.

Thirdly, even further inhibitions on judicial innovation appear if the focus shifts to the level of individual judicial decision-making. Here, the way that the appeal judges interpreted legal standards was substantially fashioned by their own past experiences and their perception of contemporary social circumstances and needs, all of which were viewed through spectacles coloured by their ideological frames of reference. Additional strictures arose from the dictates of the facts of the case before the court, the weight of precedent and relations with counsel and fellow-judges.

Finally, but of the most importance, is the ideological role performed by the law and the legal process in the ordered government of society. This is a vast and intricate area of knowledge, to which it is impossible to do justice here, but which urgently needs investigation in the South African context. Suffice it to say that the court system can be seen as the means whereby the legislature and executive enforce their policies, as well as the safety-valve through which recalcitrant elements in society can let off steam in a controlled and containable manner. In the fluid and at times revolutionary atmosphere in South Africa before 1950, it would have been vital for the courts to fulfil this function. That the AD did so has been shown above,[4] particularly in the industrial relations cases. This would simultaneously have induced a cautious and conservative judicial approach.

[3] For a recent example of such action, see the aftermath of *Komani NO v Bantu Affairs Administration Board, Peninsula Area* 1980 (4) SA 448 (AD); *Oos-Randse Administrasieraad en 'n ander v Rikhoto* 1983 (3) SA 595 (AD).

[4] See *R v Roux & another*, ch III above, for example.

Therefore, it is submitted that for constitutional, functional and ideological reasons, and because of various traits which were prominent in the judicial character, active campaigns to protect, let alone establish, democracy in the face of legislative and executive injustice were outside the brief and beyond the scope of the South African AD before 1950. The judges were locked into a role supportive of the political *status quo*—this book indicates that they did not object vociferously to the assumption of such a position.

This amplification of the conclusions reached above has important consequences for the arguments concerning the South African judiciary today. This is because all the reasons set out above are of equal, if not greater, force at present, which means that the court is similarly confined to a role in favour of the political *status quo*. In acting in this way, the Bench is continuing the judicial practice followed by the AD before 1950. The South African courts cannot unilaterally change their position in government, however comfortable it might be for those of a liberal spirit to believe that the judiciary can effectively act as a mediating force in favour of democratic values.

This is, indeed, a bleak description of judicial capability,[5] but one which flows directly from the preceding analysis. Whether it is of universal validity is too wide an issue to be canvassed here, though it should be pointed out that the reasons for the restriction of judicial powers outlined above apply not only to South Africa. Similarly, the value of judicial action in alleviating individual cases of injustice, and the effect of such decisions on the political process, are separate questions which require further research and analysis. What is clear, however, is that plaintive pleas to the judiciary to challenge the ruling political ideology will not be answered in the affirmative.

[5] Which accords more closely with the view of Judge Hand in the exchange with Judge Frank, quoted in ch 9 above.

INDEX